WITH STONES IN OUR HANDS

Muslim International

Sohail Daulatzai and Junaid Rana *Series Editors*

WITH STONES IN OUR HANDS

Writings on Muslims, Racism, and Empire

Sohail Daulatzai and Junaid Rana

Editors

Muslim International

UNIVERSITY OF MINNESOTA PRESS

MINNEAPOLIS • LONDON

Published by the University of Minnesota Press
111 Third Avenue South, Suite 290
Minneapolis, MN 55401-2520
http://www.upress.umn.edu

ISBN 978-0-8166-9611-6 (hc)
ISBN 978-0-8166-9612-3 (pb)
A Cataloging-in-Publication record for this book is available from the Library of Congress.

Printed in the United States of America on acid-free paper

The University of Minnesota is an equal-opportunity educator and employer.

25 24 23 22 21 20 19 18   10 9 8 7 6 5 4 3 2 1

CONTENTS

Writing the Muslim Left

An Introduction to Throwing Stones

Sohail Daulatzai and Junaid Rana

It would be easy to say that this is a volume born out of a response to the decade and a half since 9/11. But that would be too easy. In fact, the past continues to haunt unfolding events, making it increasingly difficult to write in present tense. As we write, there is too much to comment on, too much taking place, too much of a moving target to yield an instant conclusion. The inspiration for this edited volume is not singular, much less unified, but there is a resolve that is unequivocally critical. It is not just a critical response to how knowledge of the world is produced but a crucial and, we hope, timely invigoration of solidarity politics. In the language of the settler logic that renders anticolonialism illegal, this is stone throwing. It is the heave against the walls of settler colonial devastation and accumulation. It is the stone that goes against the leviathan of extreme and ordinary state violence: targeted killing, assassination, collateral damage, drone strikes, detention, detainment, surveillance, infiltration, policing, torture, military capitalism, necropolitical calculation, death making, war machines, and on and on. It is a stone thrown at the temptation of the devil. Like Edward Said in Lebanon tossing a rock into the abyss, this is a volume that follows in this metaphorical imaginary. This is no simple task, nor is it all of one kind.

In this volume's multiplicity, we offer an opening of a political position that we call the Muslim Left. In tandem with this perspective, we elaborate on a social and cultural movement that serves as a destabilizing force that we have referred to as the Muslim International.[1] The Muslim Left and the Muslim International are not meant to be the final word on a debate but rather part of an ongoing conversation that we see as generative, productive, and at times provocative.[2] In the least, it is an acknowledgment that a critical stance is necessary, and it derives from a hope of critical knowledge becoming insurgent, evoking the legacy of Third World studies.[3]

While not all of those in this volume would necessarily agree with what we call the Muslim Left and the Muslim International, there is an undeniable force, a momentum, that is organized in terms of opposition and dissent. The Muslim Left and the Muslim International most immediately reference a radical history of critique and protest that imagines another world in line with struggles for social justice, decolonial liberation, and global solidarity. Yet, for many readers, these terms will seem incommensurable, perhaps unjustifiable, and, even further, an anachronism of a bygone era. Some will ask, What is the Left? Who does the Left serve? What remains of the Global Left? Isn't the Muslim Left really just the Third World Left? The Muslim Left and the Muslim International are not in themselves new. We name them as such to provide coherence to what has gone unthinkable, contradictory, and forgotten. Drawing on the genealogies of the Third World Left, these terms recall histories that are actively ignored and that, we argue, are a central component of the revitalization of collective struggle. What is more, they point to a willful neglect that we diagnose as a failure of the Global White Left that leads to our conclusion: for decolonial struggle to succeed, the Muslim Left and Muslim International, among other categories of the religious and antiracist Left, must be accounted for and politically developed through active engagement. In making such a claim, we do not merely rely on crass identitarianism but look to the social movement tools of coalition and alliance. In broad terms, we frame this approach by evoking the binaries secular and religious, sacred and profane, as oppositions, a defiance against predetermined and foregone conclusions. As a set of politics, this is a dissent against the normalization of our anti-Muslim present, not only as political opposition—as our collective of scholars and activists chronicle throughout this volume—but as intellectual opposition crafted through careful study, thorough analysis and scholarly debate. With this task at hand, we have brought together a range of scholars, activists, and organizers who capture the pulse of a moment and are working through the difficult task of imagining another future different from our current predicament in which stones are compared to bullets, assassinations, and targeted killings.

As an intellectual and political project, this is a call for those drawn to the necessity of decolonization and a return to internationalist politics for their radical possibilities. In this desperate time, to be a Muslim as a faith category and a racial figure entails a dangerous existence amid a vocal and public turn that vilifies Islam as antimodern and antihuman. To follow such a construction is to understand the dictates of white supremacy in which there are those worth saving and those worth killing. Such a calculation is not uniform to a category called "Muslim," although it is a preeminent way we understand this racialization as defined through white supremacist logics of domination—think of how quickly popular consent is gained for the state-organized killings of "Islamic militants," "radical extremists," "terrorists," "jihadis," and any other number of conjurings of the Muslim in the racialized imagination. We must carefully parse such crafting of monstrosity and the meaning of this death-making so routinely now part of modern life and the values of so-called enlightened democratic countries. In response, what we propose is based in questions of political and activist work that is life-affirming and demands another vision of how we are to be collectively organized, something other than death and destruction. Antioppressive, anticolonial, and anticapitalist is our position. Pursuing the Fanonian dialectic with the force of Sylvia Wynter's scholarship, we ask, "Can the Muslim be human?"[4]

THE MUSLIM FIGURE, COLONIALISM, AND PERMANENT WAR

Alongside the vitriol spewed by Donald Trump and his administration, with his Muslim bans, his anti-immigrant diatribes, and his revanchist militarism, there is a widespread anti-Muslim posture rampant across the political spectrum from liberals and conservatives, Democrats and Republicans, to Marxists and feminists. White supremacy did not begin with the election of Donald Trump, nor will it end with his presidency. Instead, the Trump administration is symptomatic of a broader shift to the Right over the last fifty years and a deeper malaise that sits at the heart of a purportedly democratic West. Witness the rise and gains in Europe of right-wing parties and candidates espousing overtly racist and xenophobic rhetoric in England, Hungary, Switzerland, the Netherlands, France, and throughout the continent, including German chancellor Angela Merkel, who declared multiculturalism a failed project because of the threat of Muslim migrants and refugees.[5] And though the Right is steeped in demonizing Muslims, so too are liberal and leftist formations vocalizing platforms that are refracted through and grounded in deep civilizational discourses about the "Muslim problem" and the threats that mosque building, migrants, refugees, the veil, and other signs of "Islam" will pose to a white Christian Europe. Trump's rise cannot be dismissed, but nor can it be seen as an exception. Instead, he must be seen as an extension of brutality in an already racist architecture of control that continues to define the white world, for which the figure of the Muslim has been an avatar.

While September 11, 2001, is often represented as a watershed moment in the production of anti-Muslim racism, the emergence of the racial figure of the Muslim has older historical roots in the encounters, conflicts, and wars of imperial expansion that have defined liberal modernity. The historical legacy of U.S. colonialism and empire building—a political economy that draws on European colonial and imperial histories—is a foundation for the devastation of racial capitalism wielded through slavery, genocide, and conquest in the Americas.[6] Both as jingoistic foreign policy and all-out war, the geographies named "Middle East" and "Muslim world" are yielded in relationship to U.S. empire and fundamental to the making of U.S. nationalism within the global order.[7] In this formulation of national consciousness, the idea of "American" is made in relationship to the specter of the category "Muslim" (and its various guises: immigrant, fundamentalist, "terrorist," suicide bomber, etc.) that is rendered other, foreign, undemocratic, and, finally, anti-American. Despite the work of activists and academics to claim the liberal sense of belonging by pairing Muslim with American, this strategy is nothing more than the dream of a democratic future that disregards the structures and legacies of white supremacy.

To take seriously the settler colonial system of white supremacy that uses the racial state to dominate, oppress, and kill, the meaning of the adjective and noun *American* must be made clear. And while there are those who would claim the necessity of a rights-based approach to politics, we would proffer that such a position is filled with contradiction and defined by the limits of the project of liberal modernity. Here the caution is not that a politics of possibility can be found in a number of locations; rather, it is a question of what is deemed acceptable politics of dissent, protest, and, indeed, radicalism. Rights claimed from the liberal state are premised on a notion of politics, which, while still a possibility, relies on a reformist position at the cost of ceding space for insurgent politics. Moreover, the liberal state is only one formation of politics that must be rethought in relationship to a global politics of solidarity that we broadly are referring to as internationalism but can also find itself in specific iterations like the Muslim Left and Muslim International. In this context of U.S. exceptionalism, one can predict the remark that despite the crimes of U.S. colonialism, life within the empire is far better than anywhere else—a serious collapsing of a number of registers of value, life, and violence that refuses to unravel the military brutality unleashed every day around the world. There is a safety in snuffing out the fires of rebellion against U.S. empire. It is far easier to claim no culpability when not facing direct harm. Counter to the liberal notions of individual responsibility, crafting a response requires an analysis of biopolitical structures that operate at the level of groups and populations. The work of collective solidarity is a starting point to the difficult task of imagining another world.

The workings of U.S. empire, racism, and white supremacy, while constantly invoked as bounded to the domestic racial politics of the United States, is in the figure of the Muslim always global. With this tension between domestic and global racial formation, there is much to unravel in terms of how the racial figure of the Muslim is an object deployed in the system of global white supremacy. The National Defense Authorization Act of 2012 declared that "the world is a battlefield," and the 9/11 Commission Report referred to the "American homeland as the planet,"[8] a conceptual framework that marks the threat of "terror" as permeating both the domestic and global realms of U.S. power. In creating the need for a securitizing logic that is rooted in a history of protecting white life and white property, we have witnessed the global expansion of U.S. and Western military power, from the establishment of the U.S. Africa Command (AFRICOM) to Iraq and Afghanistan, Pakistan and Yemen, Somalia, Libya, and elsewhere, as well as in drone technologies, aerial bombardments, and covert forms of subversion and devastation. But there is a boomerang effect to this death-making architecture under the guise of "antiterrorism" and "counterterror" as domestic police forces are becoming increasingly militarized with weaponry and technologies deployed and practiced abroad in U.S. theaters of war. In addition to the already ruthless nature of policing, one predicated upon the containment and killing of Black and Brown life, a surveillance architecture has expanded that includes informants, wiretapping, and sabotage to those deemed threatening to the state. In these ways, it is important to understand that domestic policing and U.S. military power abroad are flip sides of the same white supremacist coin, a constellation of domination that has at its center a racial logic predicated upon state-sanctioned violence, murder, and terror with impunity.

ANTI-MUSLIM RACISM AND WHITE SUPREMACY

Regardless of the overwhelming imperial relationship that works to submerge the memory and presence of Muslims in the Americas, the history of anti-Muslim racism has seeped into the forefront of the American imagination to foment systematic forms of racism, sexism, xenophobia, and homophobia, to name only a few of the oppressions tied to this violence. The specter of Islam and Muslims is thought to be a recent occurrence brought on by migration policies in North America, despite the history of settler colonialism and native genocide that would precede the enslavement of Muslim Africans in the Atlantic slave trade across the Americas and the Caribbean. These systems of dominance normalized anti-Muslim racism at the core of empire.

The racialization of Muslims has a deep and profound history dating back to the contact with the so-called New World and the systematic expulsion of Muslims from *reconquista* Spain in the late fifteenth and early sixteenth centuries. In these simultaneous histories, the origin of the concept of race and the foundation of white Christian supremacy within the European imagination were made through the figure of the Moor, a multivalent term in Spanish for Arabs, Africans, and Muslims.[9] In this process, Islam shifts from religion as ideological difference to a racialized object with a distinct state of racial being. Our contention is that the figure of the Muslim as a religious and racialized category emerged out of the confrontation between Catholic Spain and the expulsion of the Moor in 1492. Indeed, the history of the idea of race developed out of religious sentiment in which Muslims in the European context and Indigenous people in the so-called New World were racialized in comparison to one another.[10] And while religion is racialized in this moment, the parallel progression toward secularization of religion in Christian Europe is in fact a secularization of race, racism, and, most potently, white supremacy. This historical movement toward a modern conception of race formed the emergent racial capitalism that became the springboard for European expansion, settler colonialism, and New World slavery.

As the project of modernity has unfolded over the last five hundred years, the insertion of the Muslim figure into the concept of race has been rooted in the complex historical legacies of colonialism and slavery. European and U.S. colonial and imperial history with Muslims and other peoples of the Global South continues to fundamentally shape migration patterns and create economic and political refugees. At the core of European and U.S. empire building has been the animating force of white supremacy, which finds its expression in warfare, conquest, and other forms of political, economic, and military devastation. This has led to systemic global inequality such that warfare and domination are inseparable from the histories of migration and its regimes of control. In this way, the notion of a fortress Europe and gated America ties together the logic of anti-Muslim racism, xenophobia, and the production of the national security state.

In the Americas, the establishment of an imperial formation that obscured anti-Muslim racism was always in the context of settler colonialism and the violence of chattel slavery. The legacy of slavery, where roughly 30 to 40 percent of enslaved Africans in the Americas were Muslim, requires an in-depth and extensive recuperation.[11] Furthermore, the presence of Black Muslim thought and praxis—from the Moorish Science Temple to the Nation of Islam, and from Malcolm X to the shift toward "orthodox" Islam through figures such as Jamil Al-Amin and others who emerged out of the Black Power moment—has unfolded into a formidable system of philosophy and Islamic theology that are situated in the Black radical tradition.[12] And as previously mentioned, the immigrant Muslim presence from the nineteenth century to the present is more a direct result of U.S. colonial aggression into the so-called Muslim world and the ongoing shifts and accumulation of capital in the Global North.[13]

In the early part of U.S. settler colonial history, Islam became the twin of anti-Black racism as a foundational part of social hierarchy that encompassed a number of racialized rhetorics. As Denise Spellberg argues, Thomas Jefferson imagined Islam as a foil for tolerance and the ideal of the freedom of religion in which the inclusion of Muslims was the test of the limits of pluralism in the United States.[14] That this was conceived as a radical move of inclusion spoke to the deep-seated antipathy for Islam and Muslims in which Jefferson and the founders conflated religious difference with racial ideas. Into the contemporary moment, anti-Muslim racism evokes a number of intersectional categories, to name a few: Black, Brown, immigrant, indigenous, Latina/o, Arab, Sikh, Hindu, Islam. In this are the moving pieces of an ongoing theorization of how race is deployed not as a fixed entity, as many scholars are still accustomed to think, but indeed as a floating signifier, in the words of Stuart Hall.

It is in this sense that we argue that anti-Muslim racism is able to work without the appearance and armature of a normative form of racism. Religion, specifically Islam in the context of racial modernity, because it is assumed not to be biologically or phenotypically fixed, becomes the ruse for a purely ideological battle that is not based in biological determinism but is instead seemingly a philosophical difference with other religions, philosophies, and political positions. Buried not too deep in this conversation of disparate philosophy is often the idea of biological difference—for example, the arguments that religious people are hardwired to think a certain way, "that their culture is different from ours" or that "they hate our way of life and will destroy us." Embedded in these rationales is a combination of biological and cultural reasoning that is central to racialization and a versatile and flexible process in fixating on a racial object. This is to say that the racialized Muslim is not a fixed racial object but becomes one and is profiled as a racialized threat as potentiality.[15] Anti-Muslim racism, then, is about a kind of racialized becoming that is always in flux and is different from other forms of racism that have become part of a racial common sense. Anti-Muslim racism is the incarnation of a shifting conceptual apparatus that comprises racism as a technique and white supremacy as a systemic end. Such is the power of a racialized notion of the figure of the Muslim that to fail to recognize it as racism is a central tenet of its ongoing power and its generative form of dominance. It is an incitement to violence that is obscured and justified in a state logic of antiterror and the facile claims to a purported secular coexistence in which religious freedom is available to some and racial hierarchy is obscured.

By deessentializing the Muslim as a religious figure, and moving away from belief as the dominant organizing principle, we highlight how the term *Muslim* extends beyond religion and instead is a racialized classification. It is in this way that we refer to the geographic and religious categorization of terms such as *Middle East, Palestine, Arab, Sikh, Copt*, and others that are glossed as Muslim in a racialized framework. To be clear, this is not a generalizable rule in which it is *always* the case, but the power of such a racialized notion of the Muslim is that it *can* be the case. It is thus that we argue for a particularity of the contemporary racial figuration of the Muslim in comparison to what are assumed to be equivalent terms, such as Jew, Christian, or Hindu. While the assumptions of a perennialist approach to the major faith traditions would have it that these religions are equal and similar, this flattened analysis of power disregards the modern history of colonialism and U.S. empire. In doing so, Islam and Muslims are made to have a different relationship than other religions to such categories as violence, migration, war, empire, and genocide. In other words, Islam is made distinct as a racial object of white supremacy.

In the repertoire of white supremacy that draws on imperial wars of conquest and dominance, practices of settler colonialism, the genocidal elimination of populations, and the social hierarchy of heteropatriarchy, anti-Muslim racism has taken on specific characteristics that draw on the historical examples of native genocide and anti-Black racism. Yet, in the contemporary moment, settler colonialism and racial capitalism have shifted and expanded in ways that render the global figure of the racialized Muslim as an impossibility and as nonsensical to modern subjecthood. In the apt phrase of Sherene Razack, the "casting out"[16] of Muslims from modern law and the mythology of normative notions of family and sexuality has become the alibi for a broad range of racial practices of domination, coercion, exclusion, and, fundamentally, death. As this racialized logic of settler colonialism transpires in the heart of U.S. empire, elsewhere imperial ravages of war upend the world. Such devastation can be seen in the recent crisis of Syria—and before this, of Iraq, Afghanistan, Libya, Nigeria, Yemen, Egypt, and the ongoing occupation of Palestine—that creates a nameless population in a ubiquitous process of elimination and extermination. And despite religious and geographic breadth, these are all read as a so-called Muslim problem, in other words, the looming specter of a racial figure. Some might argue that we are proposing a sort of inclusion of the racialized Muslim in the liberal project as a solution to the limitations of modernity. On the contrary, what we are proposing is a complex understanding of how white supremacy has continued to adapt and fold itself into forms of dominance and violent oppression in a *global* sense of race, in line with the articulations of Denise da Silva.[17] In our thinking, anti-Muslim racism does not only draw from anti-Black or settler colonial logics. Instead, the racialized Muslim is a planetary figure that is neither universalized nor uniform, as we have been describing. It is a horizon, a possibility, a potential, that is placed within temporal and spatial contexts as described in the numerous approaches within this volume.

THE MUSLIM LEFT AND THE MUSLIM INTERNATIONAL

We understand the notion of the Muslim International by situating the discourses around the figure of the Muslim within a critical ethnic studies approach that further thinks through how a religious subject is a racial subject.[18] We see the framework of the Muslim International not only as an opportunity to enrich research agendas toward capturing a range of social and political experiences and ways of life but also as a significant formation to contest racism and white supremacy. As the racial figure of the Muslim is part and parcel of other racializations and social formations, it forces us to contend with how such a construction projects race, racism, and racialization as normalized through the global War on Terror.

In addition, this project of claiming the Muslim Left and a broader movement of a Muslim International seeks to differentiate itself from the logics and intellectual formation of Islamophobia and instead name anti-Muslim racism as an operative and generative logic of white supremacy. While it is true that the term *Islamophobia* has gained traction and resonance in mainstream debates around the rhetorical and everyday violence directed at Muslims, the acceptance of this term also has much to do with how the logics of white supremacy are left out of the debate. The problem with Islamophobia is that, rather than contesting racial hierarchy and the status quo, it dovetails with the rhetoric of color-blindness and the post-racial, as it suggests individual fears and anxieties that can be alleviated and overcome if one meets a Muslim, or reads the Qur'an, or comes to know something of Islam. This of course ignores the systematic and institutionalized forms of racial violence that target Muslim bodies—or those deemed as such— and also ignores the broader and longer history of white supremacy that produces and reproduces these logics on a planetary scale. We would also argue that this defies the ways that racism and white supremacy work in intersectional ways and across communities of color.

Considering the current historical moment in which the War on Terror has expanded and intensified, this project seeks to center the United States as the dominant site of racialization around the figure of the Muslim in its current logic of empire and the ongoing War on Terror. And in doing so, we seek to interrogate and challenge the master narrative of exceptionalism that imagines the United States in what Thomas Jefferson named an "empire of liberty," a legitimizing discourse used to construct color-blind multiculturalism. In this vision, the figure of the Muslim is the quintessential Other who seeks to undo the so-called hard-fought gains not only of the post–civil rights consensus but also of the post–Cold War neoconservative revelry in the "end of history" triumphalism. Our anthology seeks to underscore the fact that the emergence of the figure of the Muslim, and the racial and imperial panics that it has mobilized, is not exceptional but rather endemic to racial domination and capitalist exploitation at the heart of U.S. empire.

Without a doubt, Edward Said's monumental influence is a point of departure.[19] Though this project is indebted to his rigorous and principled interventions, we take as our critical point of departure not just the history of European colonialism and its settler colonial projects but also the genocidal logic of U.S. nation building, with its slave-structuring foundations and its imperial logics and frameworks. Troubled by the limiting frames of Black and ethnic studies, area studies, and religious/Islamic studies in making legible the new forms of racecraft and coloniality in effect today, this project brings together essays that reflect a breadth of engagement and respond to a variety of positions around which the Muslim Left emerges as an intellectual and political tradition, forging a range of cultural and social responses that articulate a different sense of aesthetics, ethics, and subjectivities in relationship to broader affiliations and critical struggles.

Islam and Muslims are at the center of the latest form of twenty-first-century racecraft. Though not new, theorists of racialization have increasingly pushed a critical position that forces the consideration of white supremacy in tandem with racism.[20] White supremacy has always been there, as political economy, as mode of dominance, and in relation to settler colonialism, but for long, it has been on the back burner of analysis of race and racism. Although it has been at the margins of theory, it has been a central aspect of modern social life.[21] Similarly, the recent critical turn in ethnic studies has brought to the fore the race-making powers of white supremacy in relationship to settler colonialism, the practices of racial genocide, and the ongoing devastations of imperial wars. These are important racialized processes that tie the figure of the Muslim and Islam through the amalgamation of these systems of dominance.

The history of radical challenges to racial capitalism and the legacies of slavery and colonialism have been central to the Muslim International, a nonnational and transnational space that has historically overlapped with, and informed, a variety of other Third World liberation projects. That there was a revanchist and violent response by the European and U.S. empires to reassert control and undermine the popular struggles around decolonization and Black Power is both tragic and telling: tragic in that the radical possibility of emancipation was forestalled, telling in that client states emerged throughout the Global South that became ventriloquists for white supremacy, spewing the language of the market and freedom and extending new forms of coloniality and racial capitalism that sought to undermine and eviscerate the possibilities of the Muslim International and other projects of radical decolonization.

There are those who will have facile misreadings of the idea of the Muslim International that leave us wondering why it is so inconceivable as a conceptual tool and a political formation. Instead of understanding it as a liberatory project that includes artists, intellectuals, social movements, and, sometimes, state actors, there will be those who misread the Muslim International as reactionary and complicit with violent state building apparatuses that undermine popular struggles and protest. These misconceptions of the Muslim International presume that the only kinds of transnational or internationalist politics involving Muslims are necessarily those aligned with U.S.-backed client states, such as Saudi Arabia, Pakistan, and other

Muslim majority nation-states, as if there were no forms of dissent, protest, and organized opposition movements from within those countries.

But as we suggest, not only does this further conceal the deep histories of the Muslim International that are part of a larger tapestry of anti-imperialist resistance and challenges to racial capitalism; it also reveals the necessity of naming the Muslim International and the urgency for a project like this one. In this way, struggles such as the Boycott, Divestment, and Sanctions Movement is a movement that enacts strategies that are anticolonial and global and make apparent the complexity of grassroots organizing and revolutionary struggle in relationship to Islam and Muslims.

For us, the Muslim International and the Muslim Left are not simply provocations but positions of seeming impossibility made real. That the word Muslim and the presumed secularity of the Left can seem so incommensurable is the purpose. Why would we need to think of a Muslim Left? some might ask. Why is it unthinkable? we would reply. The Muslim Left, we argue, has a genealogy that is larger than the sum of its terms. It is found in works of a range of thinkers, revolutionaries, and poets of the world. We hear its echoes and find its traces in the Lotus Project in Lebanon, which brought together writers and intellectuals across an Afro-Asian imaginary; the Progressive Writers Association in India and Pakistan, which forged independent radical social thought in the early to mid-twentieth century; the radical internationalism of Malcolm X, El Hajj Malik el-Shabazz, who intervened as a philosopher, theologian, and political critic; the poetry of Agha Shahid Ali, Suheir Hammad, Yasiin Bey, Faiz Ahmad Faiz, and June Jordan, which imagines solidarity as social worlds of possibility. We find it in the prognostications of Frantz Fanon in his imaginings of an Arab–Black–Muslim decolonial future. It is the solidarity of Angela Davis with Palestinian liberation and freedom fighters such as Rasmea Odeh. It is the organic intellectuals and organizers, such as Houria Bouteldja of the Party of the Indigenous of the Republic in France, who theorizes a decolonial future. It is James Baldwin wrestling with the Nation of Islam, expressing solidarity with Algeria, and sojourning to Istanbul. The legacy of the Muslim International is to be found in the work and scholarship of Eqbal Ahmed and his advocacy of anticolonial struggles around the world.

Both the notions of the Muslim Left and the Muslim International are drawn from a protest tradition. With an ethical agenda that is anticolonial and anticapitalist, the spirit that embodies these politics is one of abolition and practices of nonhierarchy. And although such lofty aims speak to a future yet unknown, the project of the Muslim Left is a reevaluation and a pushing of the boundaries of the world we inhabit. In the pieces that compose this volume, the contributors collectively gesture toward this point of view that also speaks to the shifting and rapidly changing notions of social practice that imagine a more just world.

THE BOOK: THROWING STONES

We have divided these essays and interviews thematically to address how anti-Muslim racism is brought into cultural wars, U.S. racial projects, and the global expansion of empire and racialization. In bringing together scholars and activists, this anthology combines an eclectic range of voices, analysis, and engagement around issues of race, empire, and the figure of the Muslim.

The essays are divided into four main thematic areas: "Imperial Racism," "Decolonizing Geographies," "Technologies of Surveillance and Control," and "Possible Futures: Dissent and the Protest Tradition." These sections correspond to areas of research and intervention that reflect the contributors' intellectual breadth across a wide array of public debates. The chapters are a mixture of polemic, reflection, meditation, and explanation that draws on scholarly and activist traditions and methodologies. These authors and interlocutors represent the range of thought that addresses the problem of anti-Muslim racism and the foundational logic of white supremacy. The direction we provided the contributors drew on their strengths as scholars and activists, with free rein to address those issues and concerns that are not generally discussed.

Part I, "Imperial Racism," provides the broad contours for thinking about how contemporary forms of imperial power have been undergirded by a particular logic of racecraft around the Muslim. This part offers some broad strokes to many of the threads that are followed in the rest of the book. The main ideas tackle the themes of scholarly dissent, the idea of politics, activism, and the impact of anti-Muslim racism. Part II, "Decolonizing Geographies," offers essays that imagine the racial figure of the Muslim in global, decolonial, and critical terms to think through the complexity in the politics of representation and histories of migration. Following on this, the essays in part III, "Technologies of Surveillance and Control," elaborate a range of relationships and theories of power, including genomic racism, drone warfare, discourses of human rights and imperial racism, youth surveillance, and media representations. These essays offer a sampling of the broad range of techniques at use to control Muslims as a racial object. The final part, "Possible Futures: Dissent and the Protest Tradition," charts a range of responses and activist strategies to the antiracist future. Overall, part IV offers critical analysis and approaches to decolonization and global solidarity that culminate in ideas and debates of present and future action.

NOTES

1. Sohail Daulatzai, *Black Star, Crescent Moon: The Muslim International and Black Freedom beyond America* (Minneapolis: University of Minnesota Press, 2012).

2. An earlier rumination appears in Sohail Daulatzai and Junaid Rana, "Left," *Critical Ethnic Studies* 1, no. 1 (2015): 39–42.

3. It is useful to recall how Gary Okihiro brilliantly describes Third World studies as a unified field of study committed to global solidarity and liberation struggle. As Okihiro demonstrates, post-1968 ethnic studies and Black studies emerged as a domesticated version of the revolutionary call for a Third World studies that called for an alignment with the oppressed and the disempowered. Okihiro, *Third World Studies: Theorizing Liberation* (Durham, N.C.: Duke University Press, 2016), 30.

4. Sylvia Wynter, "Unsettling the Coloniality of Being/Power/Truth/Freedom: Towards the Human, after Man, Its Overrepresentation—an Argument," *CR: The New Centennial Review* 3, no. 3 (2003), 257–337, and the riff of this piece and Wynter's work: Junaid Rana, "No Muslims Involved: Letter to Ethnic Studies Comrades," in *Flashpoints in Asian American Studies,* ed. Cathy Schlund-Vials, 101–14 (New York: Fordham University Press, 2017).

5. Rick Noack, "Angela Merkel: German Chancellor Says Multiculturalism Is a Sham," *The Independent,* December 14, 2015, http://www.independent.co.uk/news/world/europe/angela-merkel-german-chancellor-says-multiculturalism-is-a-sham-a6773111.html.

6. For an example of the global history of liberal modernity in relation to settler colonialism and racial capitalism, see Lisa Lowe, *The Intimacies of Four Continents* (Durham, N.C.: Duke University Press, 2015).

7. We note that the terms *Middle East* and *Muslim world* are contested military and othering terms that are in widespread use in often abstract geographic terms that perform a racial Orientalism. For a provocative argument regarding the making of the Muslim world, see Cemil Aydin, *The Idea of the Muslim World: A Global Intellectual History* (Cambridge, Mass.: Harvard University Press, 2017).

8. 9/11 Commission, *The 9/11 Commission Report* (Washington, D.C., 2004), 362.

9. This point has been made from a number of perspectives. See, e.g., Ramón Grosfoguel and Eric Mielants, "The Long-Duree Entanglement between Islamophobia and Racism in the Modern/Colonial/Patriarchal World System: An Introduction," *Human Architecture* 1 (Fall 2006): 1–12; Leerom Medovoi, "Dogma-Line Racism: Islamophobia and the Second Axis of Race," *Social Text* 30, no. 2 (2012): 43–74; Junaid Rana, "The Story of Islamophobia," *Souls: A Critical Journal of Black Politics, Culture, and Society* 9, no. 2 (2007): 148–61.

10. See Rana, "Story of Islamophobia."

11. Sylviane Diouf, *Servants of Allah, African Muslims Enslaved in the Americas* (New York: New York University Press, 1998).

12. See, e.g., two classics in the field: Edward E. Curtis, *Islam in Black America: Identity, Liberation, and Difference in African-American Islamic Thought* (Albany: State University of New York Press, 2002), and Sherman A. Jackson, *Islam and the Blackamerican: Looking toward the Third Resurrection* (Oxford: Oxford University Press, 2005).

13. Melani McAlister, *Epic Encounters: Culture, Media, and U.S. Interests in the Middle East since 1945*, updated ed. (Berkeley: University of California Press, 2005).

14. Denise A. Spellberg, *Thomas Jefferson's Qur'an: Islam and the Founders* (New York: Alfred A. Knopf, 2013).

15. Junaid Rana, "The Racial Infrastructure of the Terror-Industrial Complex," *Social Text* 34, no. 4 (2016): 111–38.

16. Sherene Razack, *Casting Out: The Eviction of Muslims from Western Law and Politics* (Toronto: University of Toronto Press, 2008).

17. Denise Ferreira da Silva, *Toward a Global Idea of Race* (Minneapolis: University of Minnesota Press, 2007).

18. Junaid Rana, *Terrifying Muslims: Race and Labor in the South Asian Diaspora* (Durham, N.C.: Duke University Press, 2011), and Daulatzai, *Black Star, Crescent Moon*.

19. A few works that must be mentioned are Edward W. Said, *Orientalism*, 1st ed. (New York: Pantheon Books, 1978); Said, *The Question of Palestine* (New York: Vintage Books, 1980); Said, *Covering Islam: How the Media and the Experts Determine How We See the Rest of the World* (New York: Pantheon, 1981); Said, *Culture and Imperialism* (New York: Knopf, 1993); and Said, *The Politics of Dispossession: The Struggle for Palestinian Self-Determination, 1969–1994* (New York: Pantheon Books, 1994).

20. For example, see Moon-Kie Jung, *Beneath the Surface of White Supremacy: Denaturalizing U.S. Racisms Past and Present* (Stanford, Calif.: Stanford University Press, 2015).

21. David Theo Goldberg, *Racist Culture: Philosophy and the Politics of Meaning* (Cambridge: Blackwell, 1993); Charles W. Mills, *The Racial Contract* (Ithaca, N.Y.: Cornell University Press, 1997).

I

IMPERIAL RACISM

A Palestinian Exception to the First Amendment?

The Pain and Pleasure of Palestine in the Public Sphere

STEVEN SALAITA

At a September 7, 2014, press conference in Urbana, Illinois, an attorney for the Center for Constitutional Rights (CCR), Maria LaHood, identified and condemned the existence of "a Palestinian exception to the First Amendment." LaHood's observation referenced my controversial termination from a tenured position at the University of Illinois at Urbana-Champaign based on a series of tweets critical of Israel. LaHood pointed to disparate standards around condemnation of Israel in relation to other matters in the public sphere. There is much more to unpack, however, vis-à-vis the notion of a Palestinian exception to the First Amendment. This essay examines the confluence of issues that attend to discussion of Palestine, especially on campus: constitutional free speech, academic freedom, representations of Islam and Arabs (which might be accommodated under the guise of Orientalism), donor influence on universities, corporate norms on campus, the overreach of governing boards, media narratives, and the Zionist reliance on authority to regulate conversation.

I argue that in a narrow framework, there indeed exists what might be called a Palestinian exception to the First Amendment. We should not limit ourselves to that framework even when discussing Palestine, however. This Palestinian exception informs and is constituted by broader, and older, forms of suppression. LaHood's invocation of the phrase was not meant to be an exhaustive analysis but a rhetorical flourish highlighting the inconsistent standards that attend anti-Zionism (or sometimes forms of critique that do not quite amount to anti-Zionism). The rhetorical flourish evokes the challenges of pro-justice (i.e., pro-Palestine) work, but it renders those challenges exceptional. They are exceptional in important ways but

3

simultaneously derivative of long-standing failures of the ideologies (and discourses) of free speech and academic freedom.

It would be reasonable to say that Palestine is now an avatar of campus suppression, though we do not have an empirical metric to illustrate the claim. In terms of visible sites of pressure, those around the Israel–Palestine conflict are certainly the loudest, if not the most frequent. Its preponderance represents an evolution, not a shift. Suppression of pro-Palestine speech should therefore be in conversation with the major eras of repression on campus, many of them ongoing. Zionism is deeply engrained in the neoliberal attitudes and economies of the corporatized university. Suppression of Palestine, in turn, informs a broad array of troublesome phenomena to which speech rights are merely instrumental. Conflicts around race, class, gender, sexuality, and ethnicity all help sustain the Zionist policing of viewpoints; Zionist policing thus provides sustenance to administrative malfeasance and the regulation of acceptable speech (both formally and informally). The mutual constitution of Zionism and corporate campus culture presents a crucial site of analysis, but we must first render suppression of Palestine unexceptional to fully understand how and why it can be so assiduously suppressed.

EXCEPTIONALISM

Some of the issues Palestine solidarity activists face are unique, but in total, they do not compose an exceptional situation. LaHood's formulation does not make such a claim. Rather, it emphasizes the current location of repressive governance on campus. Palestine is the target of repression, not its progenitor. The formulation "Palestinian exception to the First Amendment" requires no structural change, only more adjectives. Let us have a glance at the conditions that render Palestine the emphasis of LaHood's comment.

"Palestinian exception to the First Amendment" makes sense only with a particular understanding of the meaning of "Palestinian" in this context. In LaHood's usage, "Palestinian" represents ontology. It situates the Palestinian's presence within the act of political speech. The act of speech thus entraps the Palestinian in sites of special surveillance. The conventions of speaking are not universal. The Palestinian may be granted the privilege of articulation, but only if she articulates narratives conducive to the glorification of modernity. Criticism of Zionism—as apart from mere criticism of Israeli policy—enacts administrative (and state) surveillance. Restrictions on Palestinian speech, then, are contingent on content, but we cannot fully separate content from speaker. One contributes to the perception of the other.

This ontological framing of Palestinian speech clarifies what might otherwise be called an *Israeli* exception to the First Amendment. The notion of an Israeli exception provides interesting analytical possibilities. It reinforces the narratives of exceptionalism central to Zionist philosophies. We hear frequently that Israel has the most moral army in the world, that indeed the state is a "light unto the nations." Couple these mythologies with the common complaint that Israel is singled out for special opprobrium and we encounter a systematic belief, often implied but rarely averred, that the so-called Jewish state deserves a special ethical dispensation. The Israeli exception to the First Amendment would highlight the fact that Israel forestalls criticism by virtue of its dogged singularity. Israel becomes the site of immunity.

Yet the Palestinian, in mind and body, is immune from protection. One need not be ethnically Palestinian to suffer the repercussions of professing unauthorized discourse. The problem affects Arabs in general and Muslims of multiple ethnic and national backgrounds. The same is true of ethnic minorities. Angela Davis, for example, who has long faced recrimination for her class, gender, and race analyses, now faces suppression because of her advocacy on behalf of Boycott, Divestment, and Sanctions (BDS). Alice Walker, Cornel West, and Desmond Tutu have experienced similar backlash. Even Jewish critics of Israel are subject to the Palestinian exception to the First Amendment (e.g., Noam Chomsky, William Robinson, Terri Ginsberg, Ilan Pappe). The location of concern in Palestine, as both a real and imagined space, enacts a sort of exceptional surveillance.

To maintain an exception to the First Amendment is to inoculate a broad system of colonization. The First Amendment itself complicates these matters. Beyond its endless interpretive possibilities, it is a crucial foundation of the American state and is therefore implicated in colonial practices. My claim is not that the First Amendment facilitates colonization but that it informs the cultures of modernity that invigorate Manifest Destiny. It is not useful to distinguish free speech from governmental repression; the two have a dialogic relationship that is too inconsistent to parse into stable, knowable formulas. Free speech and the First Amendment may not be the defining features of state power, but they are central to both the ideals and practices of exceptionalism. Neither free speech nor academic freedom, for instance, has ever consistently protected systematic critique of structural racism, capitalism, iniquity, and militarism. Free speech is also shaky in light of the frequent arrest and deportation of Arabs and Muslims who have no access to attorneys, due process, or prosecutorial evidence.

Palestinians in particular have faced recrimination because of speech (usually critical of Israel) and in turn face criminalization—in other words, they are prosecuted for things other than speech, though speech precipitated the criminalization. Community activist Rasmea Odeh of Chicago is one example. Odeh was arrested and prosecuted for supposedly lying on a decades-old immigration application. Authorities relied on evidence presented by Israel in its politically motivated prosecution of Odeh nearly four decades prior. That Odeh was targeted in the first place for a common violation bespeaks the danger of arousing Zionist acrimony in the United States. Another example is that of Sami Al-Arian, who was arrested in 2003 for allegedly providing material aid to terrorists in Palestine and subsequently lost his tenured position in computer engineering at the University of South Florida. Al-Arian beat the seventeen counts with which the government charged him but was constantly harassed before pleading guilty to conspiracy to contribute services to or for the benefit of a terrorist organization, the Palestinian Islamic Jihad. Like Odeh, Al-Arian was the victim of a fishing expedition triggered by his effective activism.

Speech rights likewise become complicated in relation to whistleblowing and investigative journalism. The U.S. government has always maintained a surveillance apparatus, but after 9/11 and the passage of the USA PATRIOT Act, crucial elements of that apparatus became legal and explicit. The state has recently consolidated forms of authority that undermine common notions of free speech—and in the case of Al-Arian, we can include academic freedom. The First Amendment, in turn, is in conflict with the liberal values it supposedly embodies. This conflict has always existed, but these days, the lionization of free speech as a prerequisite of modernity gives way to iterations of messianic violence as the hallmark of democracy. I am thinking specifically of the War on Terror and its grand gestures of civility and altruism, which overwhelm the more benign constitutional hagiographies of the American psyche.

The First Amendment entails consummate inconsistency. Its mythologies presuppose and outlast its legal postures. In relation to Palestine, special circumstances arise. Rather than informing the mythos of modernity, free speech is simply unable to accommodate critique of Zionism. (I distinguish critique of Israel from critique of Zionism. The latter is more fraught with anxiety and controversy.) This is not to say that critique of Zionism will necessarily be punished or prosecuted—much of it is not—but to raise questions about the inability of free speech to consistently perform its own ideals. That is to say, the First Amendment's contributions to American exceptionalism contain exceptions to its own special dispensations.

SPEAKING PALESTINE

The list of people punished or harassed for speaking in support of Palestine, or in condemnation of Israel (or Zionism), is lengthy. In popular culture, it includes Vanessa Redgrave (an actress), Jim Clancy (a CNN anchor), Reggie Bush (a football player), Roger Waters (a musician), and Stephen Hawking (a physicist). The problem is persistent in academe. Among the affected are William Robinson, Nadia Abu El-Haj, Joseph Massad, Rashid Khalidi, Thomas Abowd, Magid Shihade, Sunaina Maira, Norman Finkelstein, and Terri Ginsberg. Finkelstein and Ginsberg were fired from academic positions. In 2014, I became the center of a controversy when I was summarily dismissed from a tenured position in American Indian studies at the University of Illinois at Urbana-Champaign for tweets critical of Israel (and Zionism). Nobody has been fired from an academic position for supporting Israel (at a narrative level, anyway).

Suppression of speech critical of Israel and Zionism on campus exists in a deep and ever-shifting context. The punishment of purported communists, Black radicals, indigenous peoples, queers, and individuals identifying with (or identified with) other marginalized groups created the various norms of repression in which pro-Palestine advocates (along with those same marginalized groups) are ensnared. Repressive gestures by administrators or politicians can be overt, instances that compose the Palestinian exception to the First Amendment, but repression is often enacted through informal channels. Those channels can be both self-regulating and generative. A hegemonic structure influences reward systems (tenure, merit, awards, committee selection, access, grant monies); that structure reifies the palatability or disrepute of political–material commitments. (Neoliberal iterations of gay rights activism, for example, are not only safe but often rewarded.) Palestine is firmly on the disreputable end of this schema, but only in relation to other modes of structural critique—those against, for instance, capitalism, racism, and colonization. This type of suppression coexists with adherence to the First Amendment because the suppression occurs through long-standing and fine-tuned systems of self-regulation.

Where hegemonic regulation fails, the appeal to authority emerges. Although "appeal to authority" has an origin in rhetoric, it aptly summarizes a distinctive Zionist strategy. When the movement to support academic boycott of Israeli universities began generating success in scholarly associations, pro-Israel advocates sought the authority of university presidents and politicians to shut down its momentum. The Israeli government simply made BDS illegal. It is virtually illegal in France. These moves are characteristic. Zionism has long been synchronous with state power. When Zionist activists moved to forestall BDS through punitive strategies, they rehearsed a particular relationship that conceptualizes U.S. interests as primal and unimpeachable. They also mobilized what they imagine to be the most stable site of intervention, based largely on its power (and ability) to shut down grassroots organizing.

It is impossible to speak of a consistent and practicable First Amendment in today's United States. Beyond the ambiguities of free speech as a legal and cultural phenomenon, the state can enact various abdications of the practice in both private and public—and this beyond the role of corporations in regulating speech, all the more invidious in the era of at-will employment. Because management has the right to terminate employment (i.e., livelihood) because of speech or action anathema to managerial interests (or for no reason at all), many Americans are essentially silenced by the act of earning income. Any commitment to Palestine usually marks an individual as radical, terroristic even, so there is little chance of a Palestinian exception to these restrictive environments. The Palestinian, in fact, is quite likely to enact the restrictions. This problem has long permeated academic workplaces.

We should thus dispense with uncritical exaltation of free speech, the First Amendment, and academic freedom. They exist within, and help define, the same institutional structures from which various forms of repression emerge. Free speech and academic freedom are most useful as rhetorical devices. Although she is an attorney with a deep interest in free speech as a legal matter, LaHood's phrase "a Palestinian exception to the First Amendment" can most efficiently be read as an act of rhetoric. (Here I employ a crude notion of "rhetoric," one that describes a linguistic tactic of persuasion.) LaHood's rhetoric highlights a disparity between Palestine and other issues. She implies that authorities unfairly and disproportionately target Palestine. We could run an empirical study to determine the accuracy of this hypothesis, but it would be superfluous to my argument. LaHood's purpose is not to be statistically accurate (though she may well be) but to produce a formulation that validates an anecdotal impression.

She marks the Palestinian as an outlier in norms of speech rights, though she does not invoke the word *rights*. Its presence is implied by the evocation of the First Amendment. The Palestinian is not only an exception to the First Amendment but an impediment to its realization. This language interacts with all sorts of artful rhetoric around the Israel–Palestine conflict, but it hints at an essential and oft-ignored truth: advocates of Israel on campus do not get punished; advocates of Palestine do. It would be myopic to ascribe this punishment merely to limited speech rights, as such punishment is systematic and institutional, particularly in relation to long-standing forms of repression vis-à-vis people of color. The Palestinian is an artifact and encumbrance of free speech.

THE PAIN OF PALESTINE

The formulation "Palestinian exception to the First Amendment," I hope to have shown, intersects and informs numerous discourses of law, rights, violence, colonization, racism, and tradition. The adjective *Palestinian* need not necessarily be adjectival. It can also intimate an investment in bodies. If we render *Palestinian* a noun, LaHood's sentence prioritizes ethnicity in addition to ideology. Discursive phenomena take place on the Palestinian body. The Palestinian body, in turn, enacts distinctive discourses.

We must explore restrictions on Palestinian speech in light of the Israeli colonization of Palestine. It seems apocryphal, but we sometimes lose sight of this connection. The repression of Palestine in the United States arises in part from domestic politics but also from the specificities of the so-called Israel–Palestine conflict. The two phenomena are related. U.S. support for Israel arises from numerous factors—expediency, economy, strategy, habit—but the relationship of the two states is strong at an imaginative level, one in which messianic narratives influence formations of national identity. A long tradition of scholarship, ranging from Perry Miller to Sacvan Bercovitch to Steven Newcomb, explores the Holy Land mythos endemic to American exceptionalism. Palestine challenges the tidy arrangement of that exceptionalism and thus necessarily becomes an exception to the tropes and practices of free speech. Israel articulates the Palestinian exception to the First Amendment.

For Palestinians in and around their ancestral land, life is defined by the strictures of military occupation and juridical iniquity (beyond Israel, as limited citizenship exists in many Arab nations). Even those Palestinians who possess Israeli citizenship are subject to limited rights inscribed in a nation-state determined to restrict belonging to those the government, in consultation with religious authorities, considers Jewish. In the West Bank and Gaza Strip—generally dubbed the "occupied territories," a phrasing that can elide the continued occupation of 1948 Palestine—Palestinians have no meaningful citizenship at all, at least not of the sort that allows them a say in how they are governed. Israel polices Palestinians with vicious consistency, limiting their movement through a network of checkpoints, denial of travel permits, Jewish-only highways, the apartheid wall, and closed borders. Hundreds of Palestinian children pass through Israeli prisons every year, many without charge or legal representation. The nearly two million inhabitants of the Gaza Strip are disallowed movement by air, land, or sea. It is safe to say, based on a surfeit of evidence, that we can identify structural iniquity in Israel—a Palestinian exception to Israeli normativity, if you will.

These oppressions inform the status of Palestinian speech in the United States, Israel's primary moral, military, and economic sponsor. The "special relationship" between the United States and Israel supersedes diplomatic hyperbole; negative reaction in the United States to pro-Palestine speech enacts the relationship and renders it palpable. Repression and recrimination produce material consequences from mythological relationships. Myth therefore embodies materiality. We cannot fully understand the limitations of Palestinian speech in the United States without at least some assessment of Israeli colonization. Suppression of speech rights (and civil and human rights) is a function of Israeli colonial violence. The dispossession of Palestinians is not limited to their ancestral geography. It finds plenty of purchase on the American landscape. The many Zionist organizations that actively shut down Palestinian voices—the David Project, the AMCHA Initiative, the Simon Wiesenthal Center, the Anti-Defamation League, Israel on Campus Coalition, Hillel, the American Jewish Committee, and StandWithUs, among others—are invested in the Israeli state, particularly its military occupation and neoliberal economy. Zionism is not concentrated in landscapes but in centers of power.

The Palestinian body is colonized even in exile. Palestinian words are subject to occupation. That the American legal system cannot fully accommodate speech critical of Zionism illustrates a symbiosis greater than "shared values." It bespeaks deeply interconnected governing apparatuses and transnational ideologies. Here the inability of free speech and academic freedom to protect condemnation of structural iniquities in the United States provides opportunities to better understand repression as a deterritorialized practice, a phenomenon that has adapted quite well to the dictates of globalization. If the United States remains a colonized space, then Israel abets continued American colonization.

Restrictions on Palestinian speech are not fully discernible based solely on a lack of legal accommodation. The law is structured to stifle certain forms of dissent; in some cases, it is designed to allow for ineffectual protection. This argument relies on a skeptic's view of law, one that acknowledges the subjectivity of their ratification and enforcement. The history of critical theory essentially affirms that skepticism. We understand law as a construct emerging from dialectics of elite desire and mass consent. In this framework, it is possible to say that restrictions on speech are not incidental to law but central to it. Even when law allows for dissent, the juridical system in total can mobilize authoritarian strictures, as in the cases of Odeh and Al-Arian (a reality that has produced countless political prisoners throughout American history). The rule of law is not an inducement to insurrection but a guarantee against it. As long as Israel is coterminous with U.S. power, it will be protected with the same vigor used to safeguard the American state.

The pain of Palestine, then, is an American crucible. Palestinians suffer terribly at the hands of Israel, but systemic forces in the United States (and Canada and much of Europe) preserve the normativity of colonial violence. It is painful on both mind and body.

THE PLEASURE OF PALESTINE

Speaking Palestine contains pleasure. Like pain, the pleasure is physical and psychological. Palestine is above all a commitment. That commitment entails the toil of liberation. Decolonization is an enterprise of labor in addition to rearranged worldviews. Its practices exist palpably on, and in, one's body. Israel's batons, tear gas, rubber (and live) bullets, gun butts, and chemical weapons inflict injury on the body, but it is on the same body that the complex process of healing occurs through the resilience of cauterization and scarring. Even when death results from these injuries, we recognize Palestine as the land of resurrection.

The psychology of Palestine supersedes the limits of the physical. Because Palestine has been globalized, it inspires the recrimination of a Zionist body politic. The reach of Palestine is much greater than Israel's, though. This observation is not true vis-à-vis money, access, economy, and influence, but in the imaginary of global liberation politics, Palestine is ubiquitous. It has become an avatar of the international Left, especially in colonized or postcolonial spaces. The "avatar of the international Left" refers to specific phenomena. I use "avatar" to describe a position of symbolic import; Palestine certainly occupies this description. The position of symbolic import need not be visible to be present. "International Left," impossible to comprehensively define, alludes to actual political communities more than to shared ideology. Palestine is critical to the work of social justice. In turn, engagement with Palestine often exists where social justice takes place.

This position enables—or encourages—us to pursue connectivity across borders and histories, to deexceptionalize Palestine, if you will, and examine it in context of its global positionalities. I have proffered this sort of analysis in the past, as have Dana Olwan, Mike Krebbs, Robert Warrior, J. Kēhaulani Kauanui, Robin D. G. Kelley, and Waziyatawin. Here I want to contemplate the influence of transnational dynamics involving Palestine on American legal rituals (free speech in particular).

A basic observation to start: for better or for worse, Palestine has become a litmus test of political credibility in the international Left. We might take this observation even further and note that BDS replaces, or specifies, Palestine in this schema. The metaphor of a litmus test is not without complication. It implies an unmoving ideological framework, but that implication does not usually illuminate the complexity of activist discourses. The idea of a litmus test is always located in material politics. With Palestine, a strong sense of alignment exists around decolonial narratives. (This wording plays on the emergence of Palestine as a concern of the nonaligned movement.) That this conversation even exists denotes the apportionment of Israel into a firm imperialist category and the preponderance of Palestine in networks of antioppression work. While not absolute, this taxonomical distinction predominates to the point that it is difficult for one to proclaim allegiance to both Zionist and leftist principles. Palestine, then, accommodates and influences sites of organizing outside its own historical geography. The litmus test is actually a recognition of disaggregated affinities, which arise in part from the organization of global capital into superpower economies. Israel overtly aligns itself with, and abets, U.S. technocratic and military power. Few people seriously attempt to dislodge it from the imperium—those who try fail abjectly.

The pleasure of Palestine is most visible in its potential to mobilize decolonial thought and praxis. Beyond the connections numerous scholars make between Palestine and North American indigenous nations, the history of apartheid South Africa continues to loom in Palestine solidarity communities, especially as a referent to BDS. Palestine also connects to the many places in the world where Israel has provided police with weapons and tactical training (including many cities in the United States). Israel participates in counterrevolutionary operations throughout the southern hemisphere.

It is implicated in the genocidal activities of Guatemala's Ríos Montt. It has worked with the Mexican security forces in Chiapas. The governing entities of Palestine, Hamas and the Palestinian Authority (PA), are also embroiled in unsavory alliances, though nowhere to the degree of their Israeli counterpart. (Calling Israel the PA's counterpart, rather than its sponsor, is a bit generous.) For this reason, I do not limit Palestine's national movement to state actors, an approach I extend to Israel. Yet the presence of Israeli society as what might be called a settler collective makes this distinction less concrete. The settler collective benefits from the wealth brought into the country by governmental violence.

Palestine can be a gateway into myriad liberation politics. In fact, it serves as such a gateway when its advocates do their best work. The task of the Palestine solidarity worker, then, is to make real the possibilities of transnational and transethnic organizing. If for no other reason, those possibilities make our work exhilarating. To exhilarate is not simply to excite but to produce momentum and purpose, to create the sort of investment in outcomes that supersedes professional or economic obligation. Thus the pleasure of Palestine as a site of devotion.

Restrictions on Palestinian speech occur in part because arbiters of power are aware of Palestine's exhilarating potential. Zionism is integral to the corporate structures of today's campuses, so it is not merely a matter of donations, as is often surmised, that impels upper administrators to doggedly support Israel, often through suppression of Palestine; Zionism offers a politics of respectability and a default affiliation to all types of normativity. Beyond the threat of exhilaration, those invested in Israel are wary of attempts to globalize Palestine because of Israel's affiliations to normativity and the many sites of injustice they inform. Palestine can only be pleasant for those divested of economic, political, emotional, and psychological interests in Israel.

THE PUBLIC SPHERE

We explore and contest these matters in social fora. To limit their range is to impose restrictions on discursive space. What is often called the public sphere, an idealized geography, in fact emerges from the commonsensical filtering of disrespectful ideas. The public sphere is mediated by the coercions of civilized deportment. The public sphere is not open to all ideas. Those that challenge the dominance of colonial ethos are by nature irresponsible. Their exclusion, however, is by design, though such exclusion pretends to be natural.

To draw from my own experience, my termination from a tenured position in American Indian studies at the University of Illinois at Urbana-Champaign inspired wide-ranging analysis of academic freedom, faculty governance, free speech, and the precarious role of Palestine in the public sphere. Because Palestinian exceptions to free speech exist in the context of other colonial projects, many of these analyses highlight the irony of a singular exception that exists only because of multitudinous oppressions. My punishment for criticizing Zionism (and Israel and cherished Zionist narratives) is difficult to separate from my ethnic background (Jordanian and Palestinian), which formalizes relationships of Arabs with other communities of color in the United States. Put more specifically, it further cements Arabs as people of color in the American polity, subject to the exclusions of privilege that attend the assumption of whiteness.

I believe that much work needs to be done untangling these numerous intersections. Here are a few observations to aid that process:

- The Palestinian exception to the First Amendment is real, that is, it affects human beings by damaging their livelihoods and, in some cases, criminalizing their speech.
- This Palestinian exception to the First Amendment is not exceptional. It exists in the context of long-standing restrictions on speech critical of systemic state power, particularly that proffered by people of color.
- The Palestinian exception to the First Amendment can be located in Israeli colonization in addition to American legal traditions.
- The Palestinian exception to the First Amendment can be located in U.S. colonization in addition to American legal traditions.
- Our understanding of Palestine as both a physical and imagined geography is incomplete without concomitant analysis of intersecting strategies of global neoliberalism.
- The word *Palestinian* in this phraseology can act as both noun and adjective, implicating the totality of Palestine in the dangers of upsetting Israel.
- We cannot effectively end the Palestinian exception to the First Amendment if our work is limited to the provincial spaces in which Israeli colonization takes place.
- The distinct but interrelated specters of Arab culture and Islam inform the precarious standing of Palestine and Palestinians in U.S. public cultures. Specifically, the hostility toward Arabs and Muslims often foregrounds notions of Palestinian inferiority.
- The symbolic position of Palestine as a Third World avatar and Israel as an imperialist client of the United States contributes to the elite's embrace of the latter in maintaining a politics of respectability. While the revolutionary–imperialist

binary is too neatly framed to explain the contingencies of real-world geopolitical machinations, it is sufficiently predominant at the level of perception that silencing Palestinian speech becomes an obligation among arbiters of civility.

The cliché tells us that the best way to counter restricted speech is with more speech, but the cliché's logic is mostly a liberal conceit. More speech can mean anything. It implies *radical* or *subversive* speech, but, in keeping with the sentiments of Frantz Fanon, Angela Davis, Glen Coulthard, and other revolutionary thinkers, I remain skeptical that locution directly precedes dissent—or that dissent directly produces upheaval. Speech, like all modes of communication, exists in systems. More speech often reproduces systematic convention.

Vis-à-vis Palestinians, more speech results in more recrimination, so it is difficult to assert with certainty that the increased awareness of Israeli colonization resulting from (among other things) more speech has ameliorated these suppressive conditions. That is to say, if our concern is an easing of suppression, rather than the perception of Palestine in political communities, then it would be apocryphal to argue that gains in Palestine solidarity activism create increased protections on speech. If anything, the opposite is true.

We are thus tasked with thinking about the Palestinian exception to the First Amendment as erratic rather than linear. Its potential to decrease or increase depends on the mood of the state. Other factors exist, but they too are anchored to state authority. Redress is not a trenchant phenomenon. It would be easy to dismiss speech rights as a site of social change were they not so immediate in the ability to organize for structural change. Speech rights are a means to an end, or they should be, anyway. I do not want to downplay the importance of free speech and academic freedom to those who claim no possession of them and risk freedom or livelihood fighting for their adoption (or implementation). Yet free speech and academic freedom serve a purpose greater than avoiding prison. They enable the sort of agitation that hegemony so effectively subdues.

When considering free speech and academic freedom, then, it is necessary to locate our analyses in the ontologies of the suppressed. The Palestinian, in all its grammatical possibilities, constitutes an excellent site of analysis. The Palestinian, however, always transcends immediate locations of suppression. For this reason, when individuals and institutions suppress Palestinian speech, what appears to be an exception to liberty is in reality an exceptional mandate to limit liberation to the platitudes of a dull and dead-ended ideal.

2

The Perils of
American Muslim Politics

ABDULLAH AL-ARIAN AND
HAFSA KANJWAL

Each Ramadan, many American Muslim leaders anxiously await to hear whether they have made the cut for the annual White House Ramadan celebration.[1] An invitation to these Iftars and Eid festivities, as with similar events the State Department and the Pentagon hold, serves to symbolize recognition in the halls of American power and a degree of success for those Muslims who have sought active engagement within the political arena.[2] Rewarded by a chance to meet the president, they have been formally recognized as leaders in a fraught religious community. Representing a variety of civic, political, religious, cultural, and educational institutions and initiatives, these are individuals whose work is deemed to have contributed to the "diverse and collective experience of what it means to be an American," according to a 2014 State Department report.[3] At best, this engagement has been actively negotiated with the established power of the U.S. state and its political and security apparatuses. In this process of negotiation, of offer and approval, the mainstream archetype of "American Muslim identity" is forged. Ultimately, however, the decision of whom the U.S. government accepts into its fold is as unilateral as the invites it sends. In turn, there is a danger that in allowing the state to shape the contours of this engagement, these "moderate Muslims" become implicated in the ideology and practices of a U.S. empire that has increasingly set its sights on the world of Muslims during the past two decades.

In addition to high-profile interactions with state institutions, American Muslim leaders are also actively participating in initiatives led by a variety of private institutions that have their own interests in managing the political boundaries of this community. In a drastic break from long-standing practice, in 2013 a number of prominent American Muslim figures launched a highly publicized initiative to travel to Israel to participate in an interfaith program that a Zionist organization, Shalom Hartman Institute, has led and funded.

These broader shifts across the U.S. political establishment showcase an increasing tendency within American Muslim activism—particularly since 9/11—to reorient its engagement with policy-making circles (including government, think tanks, private institutions, and media) in a way that risks becoming reappropriated and rearticulated for a new political reality. It has occurred largely by rewarding accommodationism and the "good" half of the "good Muslim–bad Muslim" divide in ways that were never as explicit previously.[4] In this chapter, we explore the historical context for this shift, its increasing manifestations, and the repercussions it holds for American Muslims. While the American Muslim community is diverse, with Black American Muslims representing between 20 and 40 percent of the population, given the varied historical experiences and trajectories, we are primarily interested in examining the role that American Muslims of immigrant backgrounds have played in the course of these developments.[5] Although the history of Black American Muslim engagement with state power is instructive for this discussion, it demands to be examined in a separate piece.

THE ROOTS OF AMERICAN MUSLIM ENGAGEMENT

Our use of the term *American Muslim* underscores the ways in which American citizens who self-identify as Muslims seek to negotiate the contours of both their political and religious identities in an increasingly politicized atmosphere. We are, thus, more interested in how "American-ness" is constructed alongside one's religious identity, not in the quality of one's religious beliefs or practices. Although the terms *American Muslim* and *Muslim American* have been used interchangeably, the latter relies upon strategies of assimilation that have long been critiqued with other minority groups in the United States.

The history of Islam as a minority religion with deep roots dating back to the European discovery, colonization, and economic development of the American continent largely through African slave labor has been explored at length elsewhere.[6] What is of particular interest in this chapter is the means through which the expression of Islam as a religious tradition was consolidated through community institutions that gradually took on a political character in the second half of the twentieth century.

While there was considerable Muslim immigration to the United States in the first half of the twentieth century, the majority of American Muslims today are immigrants or the descendants of immigrants who made their way to the United States beginning in the mid-1960s, primarily from North Africa, the Middle East, and South Asia.[7] In addition to fostering a sense of community and fulfilling the basic spiritual and ritual practice needs of this growing population, local mosques, Islamic centers, and chapters of the Muslim Students Association provided space for advocacy on behalf of various political and charitable causes that were viewed as an extension of one's lived faith. Therefore, by the mid-1980s, it was not uncommon, for example, to see sessions devoted to the ongoing crises in Palestine, Lebanon, or Afghanistan at the annual conference of the Islamic Society of North America in what became consistently the largest gathering of American Muslims.

In due course, more immigrant Muslims began to assimilate into U.S. society, acquiring citizenship, establishing families, and abandoning the "myth of return," that is, the notion that their stay in the United States was a temporary and economically driven diversion from life "back home"—to be sure, not an uncommon evolution among many immigrant communities in the United States. Consequently, their advocacy on behalf of issues that fell under the broad spectrum of "Islamic activism" became increasingly specialized though equally broadened to incorporate a wider audience. National organizations dedicated to public advocacy, lobbying, political mobilization, and engagement with other communities were established to expand the work of community leaders operating at the local level. Groups like the Council on American-Islamic Relations, the Muslim Public Affairs Council (MPAC), the American Muslim Alliance, and the American Muslim Council led a veritable alphabet soup of institutions that sought to address the community's growing needs as it stepped into the public square.

Community engagement initiatives included organizing popular protests and demonstrations; founding dedicated charitable institutions, such as the Holy Land Foundation; and building broad-based coalitions, as well as eventual outreach to policy makers on a range of issues of great interest to the community. For instance, the humanitarian crisis in the Balkans during the early 1990s yielded the Bosnia Task Force, an ad hoc grassroots organization that helped spread awareness within the United States about the atrocities committed against Bosnian Muslims; on the national level, it backed interventionist measures that the Clinton administration took in response to the crisis.[8] Similarly, when the Oslo Peace Agreement was signed in September 1993, President Clinton ensured that, despite the deep skepticism surrounding the accord from large segments of the American Muslim community, some of its leaders would be present on the White House lawn to witness a historic development on an issue that was clearly of importance to this constituency.[9]

By the late 1990s, however, increased political engagement coincided with the rise of the first major civil rights crisis to target the immigrant Muslim community directly. The use of "secret evidence" against and arrest of dozens of community leaders and members throughout the United States allowed their protracted imprisonment without charge.[10] Indeed, the securitization of the U.S. government's outlook toward American Muslims has its roots in the era that preceded 9/11, complete with widespread surveillance, intimidation, intense media scrutiny, and indefinite detentions. Violations of the civil rights of American Muslims galvanized a grassroots campaign that took on a national character, yielding judicial challenges in federal courts, legislative correctives in the form of congressional hearings and a bill to end these abuses, a national media campaign, and eventual widespread electoral mobilization. During the second presidential debate of the 2000 election, candidate George W. Bush decried the use of secret evidence before a national television audience of sixty million Americans in a bid to earn the votes of American Muslims in key battleground states such as Florida, home to the most prominent of the secret evidence cases.[11]

The lesson from the short-lived (and admittedly limited) successes of this experience centers on the ability of American Muslim leaders to challenge dominant views seeking to marginalize and stigmatize their constituency and instead assert counternarratives that uplift the experiences of an otherwise voiceless minority community. When it occurred, political engagement took place in a piecemeal fashion and largely on the community's own terms, which necessarily meant that certain doors were closed to groups who carried the unfortunate baggage of representing a community with policy concerns that often conflicted with the accepted line inside the Beltway.

THE POST-9/11 CRISIS AND BEYOND

Irrespective of the successes and failures in translating community mobilization into tangible changes in policy, on the eve of the post-9/11 crisis, American Muslim institutions were poised to play a critical role in galvanizing grassroots opposition to some of the worst excesses of U.S. domestic and foreign policy. The events of 9/11 and its aftermath served as a critical point of self-reflection for American Muslim leaders and institutions as well as the younger generation of college-aged students and new professionals.

Facing an increasingly Islamophobic narrative in the public sphere, an unprecedented civil liberties crisis, and the prospect of wars in Afghanistan, Iraq, and Iran, with a second intifada arising in Palestine, the leadership was forced to make key decisions on how to move forward. This led to critical shifts in the stances of earlier, more established organizations as well as a flourishing of new ones, such as the American Muslim Civic Leadership Institute, the Cordoba Initiative, and the American Islamic Congress. Viewing themselves as having been insular and disengaged from the broader society, these institutions sought to expand their cooperation with the American political establishment, confront the dominant narrative on Islam and Muslims, and build bridges with other communities.

As expected an outcome as this may be, the ways in which this engagement has taken place, and the almost uncritical and unabashed acceptance of the discourses of empire, raise serious concerns. With a posture determined by the global context created after 9/11, American Muslim leaders and institutions increasingly departed from taking critical stances on issues ranging from continued U.S. support for Israel to the ever-expanding War on Terror. Given the linkages between the domestic and the foreign that delineate the imperial project, an American religious community was forced to sync with a highly contested set of foreign policy positions while contending with the rise of a new national security culture at home.

A significant and often overlooked point to note here is that this development also reflected an important turning point in the U.S. political establishment's view of the Muslim community generally and the ways in which the former dictated the terms of engagement. Leading government institutions and think tanks, such as the National Security Council, the Department of Homeland Security (DHS), USAID, the Department of Defense, the White House, the State Department, the Brookings Institution, the Council on Foreign Relations, the Center for Strategic and International Studies, the RAND Corporation, and Freedom House, set up initiatives that sought to broadly address issues of Muslim engagement, sometimes framed as seemingly innocuous pluralistic, interfaith, or public diplomacy efforts and other times as counterterrorism.

For example, the RAND Corporation's National Defense Research Institute, which receives federal funding to conduct research and analysis for the Department of Defense, has been repeatedly tasked with projects that identify the types of Muslims with whom the U.S. government should engage and under what conditions that engagement should take place. In a five-hundred-page 2004 report titled *The Muslim World after 9/11*, RAND constructed a typology of ideological tendencies in Muslim societies and encouraged the exploitation of Sunni, Shiite, Arab, and non-Arab divides in an effort to promote U.S. policy interests. The report also called for harnessing American Muslim communities to promote U.S. interests on the ground.[12]

In a report from 2007 titled *Building Moderate Muslim Networks,* RAND recognized a parallel between the Cold War era and today.[13] The report calls for creating an international database of potential and existing partners, formulating a well-designed plan for supporting these networks, and arranging for "feedback loops" to track the progress. It required the creation of an institutional structure within the U.S. government to guide, oversee, and monitor these networks. In this regard, the researchers

> recommend targeting five groups as potential building blocks for networks: liberal and secular Muslim academics and intellectuals; young moderate religious scholars; community activists; women's groups engaged in gender equality campaigns; and moderate journalists and writers. Functioning again in a foundation-like role, the United States should asset programs that promote democratic education, particularly programs that derive authoritative teachers supportive of democratic and pluralistic values from Islamic texts and traditions, moderate media, gender equality and advocacy for moderate agendas.[14]

It also includes an "Application of Criteria" that lists the qualities of a "moderate Muslim" and declares that secularists, liberals, and moderate Sufis are the best potential allies for American interests.

From these two reports, and countless others like them, we can see a clear correlation between empire and the strategic use of the American Muslim community. These initiatives inevitably included a number of American Muslims who were expected to play the role of "native informants" and to reach out to various Muslim institutions in the United States and beyond. This demonstrates quite clearly that the broader strategy for engagement was already being developed in these circles and that a number of individuals and groups could be situated in these developing frames. It was a mutually beneficial arrangement for all involved.

While many may consider the increasing involvement of Muslims in the corridors of U.S. empire to be a positive development for American Islam, especially in terms of the role they may play in changing U.S. policy toward Muslim communities at home and abroad, the ways in which this is occurring and the long-term implications for such involvement are being largely ignored. Cosmetic appearances of acceptance notwithstanding, one can scarcely point to any substantive policy changes over the past decade in relation to foreign or domestic issues that historically have been of importance to Muslim communities. Although the discursive techniques the establishment uses have become more inclusive of particular segments of the American Muslim leadership, in some ways, this has only served to sow deeper divisions within the community and alienate dissenting voices.

One of the primary consequences of this type of engagement is the creation of an "official Islam" and subsequently the promotion of "moderate Muslims." One legal scholar noted that, in possible violation of the First Amendment clause prohibiting the establishment of religion, "the government (from the national to local levels) makes claims about the nature of Islam, frequently in order to further the goal of counter-radicalization, and thereby sets out its preferred tenets of Official Islam. Those claims are embedded in everything from presidential rhetoric to government-issued handbooks."[15] As has become more apparent in recent years, a moderate Muslim is not simply one who rejects violence and fundamentalism (the underpinnings of both of these assumptions demand their own critique) but one who is also uncritical of empire, liberalism, and neoliberal economic policies. Critics have repeatedly noted how the conceptualization of a moderate Muslim is intended to fit within a set of binary designations, the "good Muslim–bad Muslim" divide that gained traction during the Bush presidency. It is not simply a description of modes of ritual practice but rather of one's residual benefit to the advancement of government policy. As Mahmood Mamdani asserts, "the implication is unmistakable and undisguised: whether in Afghanistan, Palestine or Pakistan, Islam must be quarantined and the devil exorcised from it by a Muslim civil war."[16] As Tariq Ramadan notes, the binary has existed since Western colonial incursion into Muslim lands—good Muslims were those who "collaborated with the colonial enterprise or accepted the values and customs of the dominant power. The rest, the 'bad' Muslims, those who 'resisted' religiously, culturally or politically, were systematically denigrated, dismissed as the 'other' and repressed as a 'danger.'"[17] In the U.S. context, a "good" Muslim overlooks the role that U.S. policies have played in political and socioeconomic developments in Muslim societies and instead situates blame entirely on *other* Muslims' understanding or interpretation of Islam. The role of the establishment in crafting this moderate Muslim subject by determining the lines of what is acceptable and unacceptable is evident through the patronage of particular voices in the Muslim community, as seen by the RAND reports and subsequently in the policies of the Bush and Obama administrations.

Consider, for instance, a 2006 *New York Times* profile of two prominent American Muslim leaders, Hamza Yusuf and Zaid Shakir, whose "history of anti-American rhetoric" is laid bare as part of their rehabilitation and reinvention as mainstream leaders whose religious devotion became an important asset to the Bush administration's ideological battles.[18] The mainstream media's construction of such "born-again moderates" has been inextricably linked with the broader aims of U.S. empire. Similarly, one particular Islamic center just outside of Washington, D.C., noted for its close ties with federal law enforcement agencies and for being at the forefront of the government's counterradicalization strategy, has been dubbed "the model mosque of America."[19]

Unenlightened Moderation

As a result, those critical of U.S. militarism in Iraq and Afghanistan, the unchecked drone wars in Pakistan and Yemen, the interminable detention of prisoners at Guantánamo Bay, the continued colonization of Palestine, and the unrestricted surveillance and targeting of American Muslims risk marginalization by their own leadership. That marginalization, in turn, feeds into narratives promoting the need to combat "extremism" and "self-radicalization" within the American Muslim community, which then actively legitimizes the securitization of large segments of the population and paves the way for widespread civil rights abuses by authorities. The Associated Press's 2011 report on the New York Police Department's abuses and subsequent revelations by journalist Glenn Greenwald on the National Security Agency's illegal spying on prominent American Muslims affirm that there is indeed a concerted effort to enforce conformity to a particular political (and, indeed, religious) orthodoxy, with catastrophic consequences for those who resist.[20] Consequently, American Muslims have increasingly been placed in strategic positions to legitimate and authorize the actions of empire.

On the occasion that substantive issues are discussed, it occurs in a way that is not ever explicitly critical of the most troubling underlying principles of U.S. policy. The MPAC is one of the leading American Muslim organizations that is "working for the civil rights of American Muslims, for the integration of Islam into American pluralism, and for a positive, constructive relationship between American Muslims and their representatives."[21]

A quick glance at MPAC's website reveals the internalization of some of the more troubling discourses of U.S. politics. On matters of foreign policy, MPAC's regular press releases and reports scarcely depart from the safe confines of the binary structure of U.S. partisan politics, whether in its support for U.S. military strikes in Syria or its timid position on the U.S.-sponsored "peace process" in the Israeli–Palestinian conflict.

Still more alarming is the apparent complicity of mainstream American Muslim organizations in the U.S. government's shift toward viewing their communities through the prism of national security policy. Indeed, participation of groups and individuals in government initiatives such as Countering Violent Extremism (CVE) has become a booming economy unto itself, as reflected in the DHS's $10 million grant program devoted to funding community-based CVE programs. Though the Obama administration initially framed CVE as an extension of its foreign policy as it sought to undermine recruitment efforts by militants in Iraq, Afghanistan, and elsewhere, CVE took on a domestic dimension as a means of confronting the potential radicalization of Muslims at home. Proponents of the measures have defended the community's active participation in government-led initiatives by parroting the threat of radicalization within community spaces and citing examples of American Muslims convicted of plotting terror attacks.[22] While they acknowledge that these programs have resulted in civil rights violations, supporters of CVE have dismissed such abuses as exceptional and have enthusiastically promoted the shift from government intervention to community vigilance, never confronting the reality that the overt securitization of an entire community is assured to result in systemic abuses, even if it is done with the complicity of community leaders. Indeed, reframing CVE from being government led to a community-level grassroots intervention is merely an outsourcing of a job that law enforcement has failed to do: the fundamental issues pertaining to the disproportionate targeting of the American Muslim community remain and create further divides within an already embattled group. Furthermore, these interventions fail to address, let alone acknowledge, the role of law enforcement in *creating* radicals. As one news report states, "critics, including many civil rights groups, say law-enforcement operatives or civilians working with them often egg on suspects to commit crimes they would not necessarily have otherwise. In its most egregious instances, it can result in the entrapment of otherwise harmless—or mentally ill—individuals."[23] To be sure, numerous cases of entrapment have occurred in recent years. Grassroots interventions might do what they can to identity and rehabilitate those who might be prone to radicalism, but these efforts are undermined by the broader realities of counterextremism programming.

In a 2016 letter to the DHS, a number of concerned organizations raised objections that the grant program would result in "the censorship of free religious exercise and political expression, the violation of individual privacy rights, and unconstitutional government intrusion."[24] A CVE pilot program in three U.S. cities drew criticism from civil liberties advocates and community members who took issue with its lack of transparency, its tendency to target schoolchildren, and the vilification of community leaders who refused to take part in the program.[25]

While some organizations might not explicitly declare themselves as "doing CVE work," or receiving CVE funding, they operate in a larger CVE framework that views radicalization through the prism of religious ideology instead of rooted in particular geopolitical realities. As such, the "responsibility" for combating extremism falls within faith communities, instead of a redressal that actually addresses the root causes of extremism. Indeed, a number of new initiatives have emerged, ostensibly to work on Muslim youth and entrepreneurship, but with the broader goals of constructing model Muslim youth who can speak back to the narrative of ISIS and other extremist groups. One such example is Affinis Labs. Cofounded by a former senior White House official and a Silicon Valley entrepreneur, Affinis seeks to combine "a focused sense of mission with the entrepreneurial passion of the startup community to tackle global challenges." In a description of one of its events, a "Haqqathon," held in Abu Dhabi in 2015, in partnership with the Forum for Promoting Peace in Muslim Societies, groups of young entrepreneurs were asked to pitch a project idea that could "help Islamic scholars improve their online presence, messaging and approach to digital and social media so that they can more effectively reach Muslim youth."[26] The project notes that "religious guidance frequently does not reach or influence the demographic that is being targeted by extremists for radicalization and recruitment."[27] Once more, a seemingly innocuous project targeting Muslim youth is intrinsically linked to CVE efforts and builds upon the narrative of the War on Terror, which foregrounds religious interpretation as the primary cause of extremism. Will a series of online platforms for Muslims to "ask sensitive questions about intimacy" or "build identities around Muslim male role models" really address the complete political, social, and economic breakdown of a number of Muslim-majority societies in which the United States has intervened in the recent past?

In addition to the surveillance and infiltration of community spaces by law enforcement agencies, these organizations themselves have advanced self-policing. In 2014, MPAC launched the so-called Safe Spaces Initiative, which examines community activism purely through the lens of its propensity toward engaging in violence and feeds into false narratives that depict mosques and community institutions as breeding grounds for radicalization.[28] The initiative promotes a policy of self-policing within the community, coupled with closer cooperation with law enforcement. One advocate of CVE even lamented that some American Muslim institutions have too often focused on civil rights education because such programs "reinforce the narrative that Muslims and the government are opposing forces."[29]

American Muslim leaders and organizations have thus far successfully managed to straddle the line between service to their community and connivance with the excesses of state power in part by attempting to shift the discourse on Islam and Muslims in the United States to one that privileges accommodationism at every turn. Although programs promoting interfaith dialogue, public relations campaigns, and governmental engagement are important, they cannot be separated from the broader political framework in which they operate. Their aim is to reframe the debate around the root causes of religious and political conflict and avoid the uncomfortable truths of power hierarchies among religious and political identities in the global arena. While dialogue is a necessary component of any democratic society, if it seeks to depoliticize Muslim subjectivities and promote religious identities that are detangled from political realities and can be easily accommodated by mainstream discourses, then it will ultimately backfire. In fact, all one has to do is follow the money on the interfaith trail to find donors who are closely linked to the network of Islamophobia projects actively working to engender hostility toward Muslim communities within the United States.[30] It is not surprising, therefore, that some critical participants have pointed to the "asymmetry in the parameters" inherent in many interfaith dialogues.[31] Such initiatives and attempts to understand the other side, as well as apologetic gatherings to explain Islam and Muslims to Islamophobic audiences, ultimately delegitimize actual grievances and normalize oppressive structures in an already unequal power paradigm. Muslims do not need to "understand the other side." They have historically understood them all too well.

The delegations of American Muslim commentators, policy analysts, community activists, and chaplains that participated in interfaith trips to Israel sponsored by the Shalom Hartman Institute serves as the culmination of a number of worrying trends. By recasting the struggle for Palestinian rights as a religious conflict among interfaith partners, this approach ignores the ideological and structural dynamics at work in the repression of Palestinians. Rather, it actively promotes an Israeli narrative that seeks to conflate Zionism with the Jewish faith and legitimize an apartheid system as the fulfillment of Jewish nationalist aspirations. Because their interlocutors are unwilling to acknowledge the historic injustices Palestinians suffered—as this undermines the Zionist narrative—any "understanding" will come from one side only and will serve nothing more than to prolong the status quo. Within this dynamic, the act of understanding the oppressor is far from a sign of empowerment, as its proponents suggest.[32] It signals willful submission to the realities of that oppression. Given the historical power imbalance and legacy of discrimination against racial and religious minorities in the United States, one would expect that American Muslims would be especially troubled at the prospect of endorsing institutions that attempt to whitewash similar inequalities elsewhere.

However, the attempted co-option of those oppressed minorities by inviting them to understand their oppression is a timeworn strategy for neutralizing opposition. As has been explored at greater length in other critiques of these recent actions, the development of programs such as the sponsored trips to Israel reflects a strategy to weaken a perceived stronghold of support for pro-Palestinian activism in the American Muslim community.[33] The strategy seeks in part to exploit ethnic and cultural divisions within the community as seen in the lack of representation by Arab Americans within this initiative. Indeed, the sole Palestinian American participant in the Muslim Leadership Initiative (MLI) eventually disavowed the program, citing the refusal by organizers to offer a more balanced curriculum and reject funding from sources engaged in promoting Islamophobia.[34] Similarly, given the particular vulnerability of American Muslims, whose political activism engenders far greater public scrutiny than most other communities, these efforts have attempted to disconnect prominent American Muslim figures from the broader Palestine solidarity movement in the United States that the Boycott, Divest, and Sanctions (BDS) movement in part represents.[35] While organizations from the Gates Foundation to the Presbyterian Church have recently taken steps to divest from Israel, American Muslim leaders have remained largely silent on the question, or in the case of some figures, have openly defied calls for BDS through participation in programs such as the one sponsored by the Shalom Hartman Institute or the Iftars hosted by the Israeli Embassy in Washington.[36]

Indeed, such initiatives cannot be divorced from the broader project to promote the "moderate Muslim," for whom endorsement of Zionism is a basic prerequisite. To be sure, those who acquiesce are assured of direct personal gain, from greater employment prospects and funding for projects to networking opportunities with political elites and positive exposure in the mainstream media. Such incentivizing of particular modes of American Muslim advocacy adds another powerful dimension to a phenomenon that is already fraught with internal conflicts and contradictions. In the years since its initial launch, MLI has predictably proven to be a divisive issue within the American Muslim community, with heated online debates resulting from a number of critiques and calls for the boycott of MLI.[37] In turn, many of its proponents launched passionate defenses of their participation, arguing that despite the opposition and isolation they face from within their own communities, they believe that such programs hold the key to pulling American Muslims out of their perceived historic irrelevance in U.S. politics.[38] In revealing their domestic political motivations for engaging in such initiatives, MLI organizers have affirmed that their aims lie in promoting a form of political participation veering toward mainstream respectability, even if it comes at the expense of the Palestinian struggle for justice.[39]

A HIGH-STAKES GAME

The long-term implication of these kinds of developments is the eviction of radical politics from the American Muslim narrative. Most American Muslims nowadays cannot be expected to articulate anything beyond the very narrow and acceptable political positions that the partisan divide of Washington dictates. This is unlike other minorities, who exhibit both the mainstream political trends and radical and progressive activist tendencies that exist locally in communities and outside of the halls of power. This has been particularly true since the 2008 election of Barack Obama, upon whom many American Muslims pinned their hopes for a favorable shift in government policies toward their community. Sadly, it has resulted in even greater pressures to forgo their own agency, toe the administration's line, and sanitize their positions in such a way that makes Obama's legacy for American Muslim activism far more destructive than Bush's.

Ultimately, the question of engagement involves stakes that are far higher than most American Muslims have thus far acknowledged. The ethical component of these opportunities raises serious concerns that have never been fully explored as part of an open and inclusive discussion. For years, American Muslim leaders have been in awe of the pro-Israel lobby and amazed at its level of unrestricted access to power and proven ability to influence U.S. policy. That some leaders would voice their admiration for the lobby and view it as a model for emulation, especially as the latter confronts its own critics from within the American Jewish community, is troubling to say the least. It is useful to think critically about what it means to approach the corridors of power without challenging what that power itself stands for. Adoption of a model that privileges access as the key to advocacy is the line of thinking that has perpetuated problems of political, economic, and social injustice in the first place.

In the event that they are welcomed into positions of authority, the actions of American Muslims have consequences that reverberate across the world. Those leaders of immigrant backgrounds are expected to reflexively place their supposed knowledge of their countries or regions of origin at the service of imperial projects. While Muslims in the diaspora might be able to provide some insight into "native" minds, as well as some much-needed linguistic skills and cultural literacy, their extraterritoriality shapes their agendas and their understandings. Situated comfortably in the lap of empire, their positionality determines their perspectives, and they do not necessarily reflect the complex views and aspirations of people on the ground. In addition to the countless consulting opportunities with various government agencies from the Pentagon to the Department of Commerce, this trend has also manifested in the cross-cultural programs the State Department has sponsored, in which an American Islam is packaged and sent abroad for showcasing as a model of moderation and integration for Muslim countries.[40]

This raises further questions about the ways in which the careful selection of American Muslim leadership is intrinsically linked to the politics of contemporary reformation in Islam. Though important advances are occurring separately and at the local level, this particular reformation is not happening organically within the Muslim community. Rather, it is being manufactured in offices in Washington, D.C., New York, and California. Saba Mahmood captures this phenomenon: "the United States has embarked upon an ambitious theological campaign aimed at shaping the sensibilities of ordinary Muslims whom the State Department deems to be too dangerously inclined toward fundamentalist interpretations of Islam. . . . In this understanding, the US strategists have struck a common chord with self-identified secular liberal Muslim reformers who have been trying to fashion Islam along the lines of the Protestant Reformation."[41] Offering a revealing answer to the tired question of "who speaks for Islam?" a 2005 article reported, "From military psychological-operations teams and CIA cover operatives to openly funded media and think tanks, Washington is plowing tens of millions of dollars into a campaign to influence not only Muslim societies but Islam itself."[42]

The point of the critique offered in this chapter is not to suggest the need for a monolithic approach to American Muslim political activism and engagement. The community's diverse backgrounds and experiences require that a multiplicity of views representing the broad spectrum of approaches to these critical questions be represented. Rather, the trajectory of mainstream activism explored here is highlighted for its corrosive effect on alternative forms of advocacy. It did not develop in a vacuum. It is the product of countervailing forces that have sought to diminish the organizational and mobilizational capacity of American Muslim activism. Perhaps no example of this is more instructive than the civil rights crisis afflicting the earlier generation of American Muslim activists. In addition to curtailing the development of oppositional politics, the gross excesses of state policy against those individuals and organizations dating back to the late 1990s and continuing throughout the Bush and Obama administrations were meant to serve as a lesson to the newcomers.

This is evidenced by the general lack of action against both the underlying policies that permit such widespread abuses and particular civil rights cases that have arisen with alarming frequency. The past decade is replete with examples of institutionalized discrimination and targeting of American Muslims by the government, including ubiquitous surveillance, targeting of leaders, intimidation of community members, infiltration of community spaces, entrapment of youth, criminalization of speech and charitable contributions, political prosecutions, unlawful detentions, punitive prison conditions, and so on.[43] Although most American Muslim institutions have at one point or another decried some aspects of these abuses, these issues are mostly being taken up by activists and institutions outside of the American Muslim community. Silence on these issues reinforces the narrative that the state has tried to promote: dissent is unacceptable, and American Muslims should fear its repercussions. Interestingly, in attempting to be more palatable to their American audiences, when leading voices remain silent on these civil rights issues and yet are vocal about others, such as normalization with Israel, they are participating in the silencing of dissenting views and creating a climate of fear and intimidation—they become an extension of empire itself.

Notes

1. Barack Obama, "Remarks by the President at Eid Reception," White House, July 21, 2016, https://www.whitehouse.gov/the-press-office/2016/07/21/remarks -president-eid-reception.

2. John Kerry, "Remarks at the Ramadan Iftar Dinner," U.S. Department of State, July 24, 2013, https://2009-2017.state.gov/secretary/remarks/2013/07/2123 90.htm; Cheryl Pellerin, "At Iftar Dinner, Carter Salutes Muslim-American Service, Sacrifice," U.S. Department of Defense, July 1, 2016, https://www.defense .gov/News/Article/Article/822803/at-iftar-dinner-carter-salutes-muslim-american -service-sacrifice/

3. Bureau of International Information Programs, *American Muslims* (Washington, D.C.: U.S. Department of State, 2014).

4. Mahmood Mamdani, *Good Muslim, Bad Muslim: America, the Cold War, and the Roots of Terror* (New York: Pantheon Books, 2004).

5. Pew Research Center, "Muslim Americans: Middle Class and Mostly Mainstream," May 22, 2007, http://www.pewresearch.org/2007/05/22/muslim-ameri cans-middle-class-and-mostly-mainstream/.

6. See, e.g., Allan D. Austin, *African Muslims in Antebellum America: Transatlantic Stories and Spiritual Struggles,* rev. ed. (New York: Routledge, 1997); see also Sylviane A. Diouf, *Servants of Allah: African Muslims Enslaved in the Americas* (New York: New York University Press, 1998); Edward E. Curtis IV, *Islam in Black America* (New York: State University of New York Press, 2002).

7. See, e.g., Kambiz GhanaeBassiri, *A History of Islam in America: From the New World to the New World Order* (Cambridge: Cambridge University Press, 2010); see also Yvonne Yazbeck Haddad, *The Muslims of America* (New York: Oxford University Press, 1993).

8. Abdul Malik Mujahid, "What American Muslims Did for Bosnia," *Sound Vision,* http://www.soundvision.com/article/what-american-muslims-did-for-bosnia.

9. Edward E. Curtis IV, ed., *Encyclopedia of Muslim-American History* (New York: Infobase, 2010), 53. See also Mohamed Nimer, *The North American Muslim Resource Guide: Muslim Community Life in the United States and Canada* (New York: Routledge, 2002), 151.

10. David Cole and James X. Dempsey, *Terrorism and the Constitution: Sacrificing Civil Liberties in the Name of National Security* (New York: New Press, 2006).

11. Abdullah al-Arian, "Soul Survival: The Road to American Muslim Political Empowerment," *Washington Report on Middle East Affairs,* March 2004, http:// www.wrmea.org/2004-march/soul-survival-the-road-to-american-muslim-politi cal-empowerment.html.

12. RAND Corporation, "The Muslim World after 9/11," 2004, xviii–xxv, http:// www.rand.org/content/dam/rand/pubs/monographs/2004/RAND_MG246.pdf.

13. Ibid., xxi.

14. Ibid., xxii.

15. Samuel J. Rascoff, "Establishing Official Islam? The Law and Strategy of Counter-radicalization," *Stanford Law Review* 64, no. 125 (2012): 159–60.

16. Mamdani, *Good Muslim, Bad Muslim,* 24.

17. Tariq Ramadan, "Good Muslim, Bad Muslim," *New Statesman,* February 12, 2010, http://www.newstatesman.com/religion/2010/02/muslim-religious-modera tion.

18. Laurie Goodstein, "U.S. Muslim Clerics Seek a Modern Middle Ground," *New York Times,* June 18, 2006, http://www.nytimes.com/2006/06/18/us/18imams.ht ml?pagewanted=all&_r=0.

19. Mike Ghouse, "The Model Mosque of America," *Huffington Post,* June 29, 2016, http://www.huffingtonpost.com/entry/the-model-mosque-of-america-adams -center_us_57737840e4bod24f8fb51952.

20. Associated Press, "AP's Probe into NYPD Intelligence Operations," 2012, http://www.ap.org/Index/AP-In-The-News/NYPD; Glenn Greenwald and Murtaza Hussain, "Meet the Muslim American Leaders the FBI and NSA Have Been Spying On," *Intercept,* July 9, 2014, https://firstlook.org/theintercept/article/2014/07/09/ under-surveillance.

21. Muslim Public Affairs Council, "Vision and Mission," http://www.mpac.org/ about/vision-and-mission.php.

22. Junaid M. Afeed and Alejandro J. Beutel, "CVE Critics Are Right, and CVE Is Still Necessary," *Patheos,* July 27, 2015, http://www.patheos.com/blogs/altmus lim/2015/07/cve-critics-are-right-and-cve-is-still-necessary/.

23. Jenifer Fenton, "US Law Enforcement Accused of Using Entrapment to Ensnare 'Terrorists,'" *Al Jazeera America,* April 23, 2015, http://america.aljazeera .com/articles/2015/4/23/law-enforcement-entrapment-terrorists.html.

24. "Objections to DHS's Fiscal Year 2016 Countering Violent Extremism Grant Program," August 31, 2016, http://www.cair.com/images/pdf/2016-CVE-Grant-Pro gram.pdf.

25. Murtaza Hussain, "Lawsuit Demands Information on Shadowy 'Countering Violent Extremism' Programs in U.S.," *Intercept,* February 12, 2016, https://theinter cept.com/2016/02/11/lawsuit-demands-information-on-shadowy-countering-violent -extremism-programs-in-u-s/.

26. Affinis Labs, "Haqqathon," http://www.affinislabs.com/hackathon-case-study .html.

27. Ibid.

28. Muslim Public Affairs Council, "Safe Spaces Initiative," http://www.mpac .org/safespaces/.

29. Rabia Chaudry, "Countering Violent Extremism Requires Law Enforcement and Muslims to Partner," *Common Ground News Service,* April 30, 2013, http://www .commongroundnews.org/article.php?id=32894&lan=en.

30. Wajahat Ali, Eli Clifton, Matthew Duss, Lee Fang, Scott Keyes, and Faiz Sha-kir, "Fear, Inc.: The Roots of the Islamophobia Network in America," Center for American Progress, August 26, 2011, http://www.americanprogress.org/issues/reli gion/report/2011/08/26/10165/fear-inc/.

31. Omid Safi, "The Asymmetry of Interfaith Dialogue," *On Being,* 2015, http:// www.onbeing.org/blog/omid-safi-the-asymmetry-of-interfaith-dialogue/8076.

32. Rabia Chaudry, "Jerusalem: Full Disclosure," *Patheos,* June 2014, http://www .patheos.com/blogs/splitthemoon/2014/06/jerusalem-full-disclosure/.

33. Sana Saeed, "An Interfaith Trojan Horse: Faithwashing Apartheid and Occu-pation," *Islamic Monthly*, July 1, 2014, http://www.theislamicmonthly.com/an-inter faith-trojan-horse-faithwashing-apartheid-and-occupation; Ali Abunimah, "Islamo-phobia Bankroller behind Organizer of Israel Junket for US Muslim Leaders," *Elec-tronic Intifada*, January 4, 2015, https://electronicintifada.net/blogs/ali-abunimah/ islamophobia-bankroller-behind-organizer-israel-junket-us-muslim-leaders.

34. Kamal Abu-Shamsieh, "A Palestinian's Journey towards Healing," *Huffington Post*, May 22, 2015, http://www.huffingtonpost.com/kamal-abushamsieh/a-palestin ians-journey-to_b_7339586.html?utm_hp_ref=tw.

35. Zareena Grewal, "Zionism, BDS, and American Muslim Leadership," *Jada-liyya*, July 30, 2014, http://www.jadaliyya.com/pages/index/18733/zionism-bds-and -american-muslim-leadership.

36. Tom Metcalf, "Gates Foundation Sells Stake in U.K. Prison Operator G4S," *Bloomberg News*, June 6, 2014, http://www.bloomberg.com/news/2014-06-06/gates -foundation-sells-stake-in-u-k-security-company-g4s.html; Associated Press in Detroit, "Presbyterian Church Votes to Divest Holdings to Sanction Israel," *The Guardian*, June 21, 2014, http://www.theguardian.com/world/2014/jun/21/presbyterian-church -votes-divest-holdings-to-sanction-israel; Sally Quinn, "Israeli Ambassador Breaks Fast with Muslims and Jews, but to What Effect," *Faith Street*, July 19, 2013, http:// www.faithstreet.com/onfaith/2013/07/19/israeli-ambassador-breaks-fast-with -muslims-and-jews-but-to-what-effect.

37. Joe Bradford, "I'm Not a Palestinian, I Can't Tell You about Palestine," Janu-ary 30, 2015, http://www.joebradford.net/im-not-a-palestinian-i-cant-tell-you-about -palestine; "Say No to Faithwashing: Boycott Muslim Leadership Initiative," Boycott Muslim Leadership Initiative, January 19, 2016, http://www.amchainitiative.org/ wp-content/uploads/2016/01/Say-No-to-Faithwashing_-Boycott-Muslim-Leader ship-Initiative-_2.pdf.

38. Haroon Moghul, "Why I Went to Israel," *Huffington Post*, January 21, 2015, http://www.huffingtonpost.com/haroon-moghul/why-i-went-to-israel_b_6507540. html/.

39. David Horovitz, "Everything You Always Wanted to Know about Islam, but Were Afraid to Ask," *Times of Israel*, September 9, 2015, http://www.timesofisrael .com/everything-you-always-wanted-to-know-about-islam-but-were-afraid-to-ask/.

40. Embassy of the United States of America, "American Muslims," Bureau of International Information Programs, U.S. Department of State, http://photos.state .gov/libraries/amgov/30145/publications-english/American_Muslims.pdf.

41. Saba Mahmood, "Secularism, Hermeneutics and Empire: The Politics of Islamic Reformation," *Public Culture* 18, no. 2 (2006), 323–47.

42. David Kaplan, "Hearts, Minds, and Dollars: In an Unseen Front in the War on Terrorism, America Is Spending Millions . . . to Change the Very Face of Islam," *U.S. News and World Report*, April 5, 2005.

43. Arun Kundnani, "No NSA Reform Can Fix the American Islamophobic Sur-veillance Complex," *The Guardian*, March 28, 2014, https://www.theguardian.com/ commentisfree/2014/mar/28/nsa-reform-american-islamophobic-surveillance -complex; Greenwald and Hussain, "Meet the Muslim American Leaders"; Spencer Ackerman, "No-Fly List Used by FBI to Coerce Muslims into Informing, Lawsuit

Claims," *The Guardian*, April 23, 2014, https://www.theguardian.com/world/2014/apr/23/no-fly-list-fbi-coerce-muslims; Adam Goldman and Matt Apuzzo, "With Cameras, Informants, NYPD Eyed Mosques," Associated Press, February 23, 2012, http://www.ap.org/Content/AP-In-The-News/2012/Newark-mayor-seeks-probe-of-NYPD-Muslim-spying; Paul Harris, "Fake Terror Plots, Paid Informants: The Tactics of FBI 'Entrapment' Questioned," *The Guardian*, November 16, 2011, https://www.theguardian.com/world/2011/nov/16/fbi-entrapment-fake-terror-plots; Glenn Greenwald, "The Real Criminals in the Tarek Mehenna Case," *Salon*, April 12, 2012, http://www.salon.com/2012/04/13/the_real_criminals_in_the_tarek_mehenna_case/; American Civil Liberties Union, "Blocking Faith, Freezing Charity: Chilling Muslim Charitable Giving in the 'War on Terrorism Financing,'" ACLU, June 2009, https://www.aclu.org/report/blocking-faith-freezing-charity-chilling-muslim-chari table-giving-war-terrorism-financing?redirect=human-rights/report-blocking-faith -freezing-charity; Jane Hamsher, "One of More Chilling Post 9-11 Political Prosecutions, Case of Sami al-Arian, Appears to Have Ended," *Shadow Proof,* July 2, 2014, https://shadowproof.com/2014/07/02/one-of-more-chilling-post-911-political -prosecutions-case-of-sami-al-arian-appears-to-have-ended/; Alia Malek, "Unlawful Detention on US Soil," *The Nation*, December 22, 2011, https://www.thenation.com/article/unlawful-detention-us-soil/; Keven Gosztola, "Communication Management Units: BOP's Lack of Process Allows for Targeting of Muslims, Political Speech," *Shadow Proof,* April 24, 2014, https://shadowproof.com/2014/04/24/communica tion-management-units-bureau-of-prisons-lack-of-process-permits-targeting-of -muslims-political-speech/.

3

Duplicity and Fear

Toward a Race and Class Critique of Islamophobia

STEPHEN SHEEHI

In August 2011, the Center for American Progress (CAP) released a study titled *Fear, Inc.: The Roots of the Islamophobia Network in America*. The report attracted an impressive degree of attention in the progressive and mainstream media, as it outlines that Islamophobia in North America is a product of "a small, tightly networked group of misinformation experts guiding an effort that reaches millions of Americans through effective advocates, media partners, and grassroots organizing."[1] The origins of Muslim hating in the United States, according to the authors, can be traced to a clique of five pernicious ideologues: Steven Emerson of the Investigative Project on Terrorism, Frank Gaffney at the Center for Security Policy, Daniel Pipes at the Middle East Forum, Robert Spencer of Jihad Watch and Stop Islamization of America, and David Yerushalmi at the Society of Americans for National Existence. These five provide the modus operandi for Islamophobia in the United States, which is then disseminated by a small army of, what I have called elsewhere, rogue intellectuals, hack journalists, native informants, and professional opportunists.[2]

By 2011, authors and journalists had mapped the ideological network between Islamophobic ideologues, think tanks, media outlets, activists, interest groups, and politicians at all echelons of power in the United States.[3] However, the CAP report's contribution to the topic of North American Islamophobia is tracking "a small group of conservative foundations and wealthy donors [who] are the lifeblood of the Islamophobia network in America."[4] By citing tax records, *Fear, Inc.* specifically links the "direct funding of anti-Islam grassroots groups" to a series of right-wing, nonprofit foundations. These funding sources are Donors Capital Fund, Richard Mellon Scaife Foundation, Lynde and Harry Bradley Foundation, Newton D.

& Rochelle F. Becker Foundations and Charitable Trust, Russell Berrie Foundation, Anchorage Charitable Fund and William Rosenwald Family Fund, and Aubrey Chernick's Fairbrook Foundation.[5] These seven "charitable organizations" provided $42.6 million to right-wing think tanks, most of which are headed by the aforementioned five leading Islamophobes.

Visually highlighting the amounts, sources, and destinations of this funding, the report is replete with personal profiles and colorful charts and diagrams that outline the interconnected web of ideologues, media outlets, foot soldiers, politicians, think tanks, and their funding sources. This neatly circumscribed web is termed the *Islamophobia network*. The argument, illustrated by diagrams and powerful information gleaned through the Internal Revenue Service, weaves a narrative of the Right's concerted effort to generate and disseminate "misinformation" about Islam. As a direct consequence, the report asserts that, "due in part to the relentless efforts of this small group of individuals and organizations, Islam is now the most negatively viewed religion in America."[6]

The CAP follow-up *Fear, Inc. 2.0*, released in 2015, follows the discourse of religious tolerance, noting that news media and conservative organizations, such as the American Conservative Union, repudiated and rejected "experts" like Frank Gaffney as contrary to American values. Noting that the 2011 report was "misconstrued" by some foreign and domestic actors as evidence for "widespread public antipathy toward the Muslim community in the United States," *Fear, Inc 2.0* reassures its readers that Islamophobia is "not indicative of mainstream American views" and is the view of a small "fringe" ever seeking to penetrate into the mainstream.[7] Not only do these two reports assert that Islamophobia is the purview of a radical fringe in U.S. polity but they understand it as an issue of religious rights and "fundamental values" *divorced from race*.

In this chapter, I focus on the 2011 *Fear, Inc.* report. While valuable documentation of the money trail between high-profile Islamophobes and right-wing funding sources, *Fear, Inc.* obfuscates the more damning racial and class structure of Islamophobia. The CAP's report—like the work of its authors, among them Wajahat Ali and Reza Shakir—offers an assimilationist narrative that comes as part of a long tradition of Muslim American and Arab American communities' collective, communal collaboration with white America and the U.S. government. I would argue, as well, that this quiescence and racial *ressentiment* leave space for Islamophobia to flourish and, indeed, have resulted in the election of a president too reliant on key Islamophobic tropes. I hope to offer a double critique of Islamophobia, understanding the targeting and profiling of Muslim and Arab Americans as racialized subjects while, simultaneously, identifying these communities' complicity with race and class privilege in the United States.

MECHANICAL PROBLEMS: CONTAINMENT

The CAP report was timely. Osama bin Laden had been killed. Candidates were gearing up for the 2012 elections and positions were solidifying around Islamophobia, although not with the intensity of the 2016 election. The Pew Research Center published demographic information about the Muslim American community announcing that despite discrimination and racial targeting, Muslim America is not a hotbed of homegrown extremism.[8] Additional scholarly reports were attracting media attention, further discrediting the theory of "homegrown" Muslim terrorism with facts such as "the number of [Muslim American] individuals plotting against domestic targets" in 2010 was only ten.[9] Journalists like Glenn Greenwald and Max Blumenthal were confronting public displays of Islamophobia in the progressive media.[10] Concurrently, blatant displays of Islamophobic sentiment were being discussed in the mainstream media outlets.[11] One might optimistically argue that, by 2011, Islamophobia as a mass phenomenon had taken a turn as even *USA Today* was critically remarking on the prominence of Islamophobia in the ramping up for the presidential elections.[12] Along with the election campaign, high-profile events, such as the Park51 Mosque and Terry Jones's Qur'an burning, along with productions such as *24* and *Homeland* had pushed middle America to begin discussing Islamophobia publicly and critically, albeit tepidly. Within this context, the strategy of *Fear, Inc.* becomes clearer.

The CAP report explains that Islamophobia emanates from the extreme right donors, insisting that "the importance of this funding cannot be overstated. This money enables a very small and tight-knit group of radical right-wing scholars, experts, and grassroots organizers to craft and share reams of misinformation about Islam and American Muslims."[13] The discussion does not address how Islamophobic tropes, stereotypes, and narratives find traction within the American Right. In fact, the report assiduously veers away from any discussion of Islamophobia that would link it to a larger cultural and political agenda in the United States, let alone to issues of race, class, or foreign policy.

The report works diligently to avoid alienating any element of the political mainstream and explicitly exonerates neoconservatives, not to mention Democrats, from responsibility or culpability in generating the atmosphere of hate, hysteria, and fear that surrounds the lives of Muslim American communities. For example, the report goes out of its way to distinguish "a variety of mainstream conservative groups, none of which are Islamophobic," such as the American Enterprise Institute, the Project for a New American Century, the Hoover Institution, and the Institute for American Values, from the handful of "Islamophobic" organizations like the Freedom Center, the Center for Security Policy, and Pipe's Middle East Forum.[14] By the logic of the report, that Bill Kristol, Robert Kegan, Reuel Marc Gerecht, Norman Podhoretz, Frank Gaffney, and Francis Fukuyama are associated with the Project for the New American Century does not necessarily mean that the D.C. think tank is a hub of Islamophobia.

The climate of the 2016 election showed how this tact was a tragic miscalculation. Parsing the "Islamophobia network" from an alleged non-Islamophobic network of conservative think tanks, commentators, politicians, and organizations perhaps intended to drive a wedge between the Beltway's Republican establishment and the Tea Party base that was driving the party. The report's refusal vindicated the ideological core of the Republican Party, who rely on think tanks like the American Enterprise Institute to provide them white papers on issues from energy to immigration, which allowed Islamophobic tenets to incubate within the Republican base and become a key mobilizing plank of Donald Trump's presidency.

Approaching Islamophobia as a discrete phenomenon of specific acts and actors, the CAP's report serves a poignant ideological purpose. *Fear, Inc.* isolates and *contains* the "origins" and propagation of Islamophobia. The report, like the politics of the CAP, sanitizes Islamophobia as a mass cultural, racist phenomenon that cuts through all strata of American mainstream political culture. It depoliticizes Islamophobia, removing the discourse from race and class to an issue of religion and "American values."

The relationships that are drawn out in *Fear, Inc.* between donor groups and think tanks and their members, along with the relationships between think tanks and "media," politicians, and Islamophobia "enablers," are portrayed asymmetrically. Islamophobic funding sources find their Islamophobic operatives, who, in turn, mobilize their Islamophobic foot soldiers, toadies, and peons to spread lies among talking heads and political cronies. In the process, Islamophobic campaigns targeting mosques and invoking "creeping shari'a" are launched with no real political intent other than to stigmatize Muslims and question their loyalty. Without differentiating between these institutions and players within this "network," the reader is left with the incorrect impression that David Yerushalmi's bush-league Society of Americans for National Existence shares the same prominence as the Project for a New American Century.

To be certain, *Fear, Inc.*'s network of hard-core Islamophobes, their organizations, and their funding sources is not inconsequential, as these have worked in tandem with other forces within the Republican Party to mainstream unprecedented Islamophobic policies and discourse. However, allotting exclusive blame to this small, rather repugnant "network" distracts us from the larger implications of politics in Washington as well as the depths to which Islamophobia is rooted in congenital forms of racism in the United States that cut across the base of both political parties.

On the most mechanical level, the method of locating the origins of Muslim hating in five individuals and seven funding sources ignores the true nature of American politics. The *issue* of Islamophobia, on this technical level, functions like any political issue, for example, the issue of climate change. Single-issue organizations are allied with larger political players and institutions to form a true network of interests organized *within* a political movement or party. In other words, these single-issue organizations function as representatives of particular planks within the overall platform of a party. It is not coincidental, therefore, that organizations like Donor Capital, Fairbrook, or the Bradley Foundation provide millions of dollars to noncontroversial, mainstream conservative think tanks such as the Heritage Foundation, the Hudson Institute, or the Washington Institute for Near East Policy. The CAP's report exculpates these conservative institutions as "not Islamophobic," despite the fact that they accept funding from sources that bankroll the public relations campaign against Muslim Americans.[15] The logic is skewed. For example, clearly, massive funding by the Koch brothers reveals an ideological affinity between the Cato Institute and the American Enterprise Institute, even though the two might push slightly differing agendas.[16]

In other words, politics in the United States works synergistically, mechanically, and holistically. The "fringe" Right within the Republican Party in 2012 served mainly to activate its most stalwart core, which could be contained by the party establishment. Before 2015, the GOP consistently froze out the Islamophobic fringe when it became a liability, as was the case with Pamela Geller and the Conservative Political Action Conference (CPAC).[17] The CAP's report shielded the larger American political establishment, the Obama and George W. Bush administrations, mainstream public opinion, and Muslim and Arab American community groups themselves from their culpability in refusing to identify Islamophobia as an issue of racism. Therefore the "findings" and method of *Fear, Inc.* distract us from the more pernicious origin, histories, and realities of Islamophobia.

IDEOLOGY AND RACE

Fear, Inc. suggests ways in which Islamophobic ideologues, think tanks, and Internet jockeys insinuate themselves into media, Congress, and local politics, which are otherwise ideologically clean places, holding no preconceived apprehensions about Muslims either in the United States or the world, including the many countries that the United States has invaded and occupied since 2001 that just happen to be Muslim. We are made to believe that a small number of committed, maleficent activists can spawn campaigns that generate a belief that Islam and Muslims imminently pose a threat to the United States. However, it is just as egregious to locate Islamophobia within a coterie of small-time, right-wing militants as it is facile to locate the origins of Muslim and Arab hating within the pro-Israel lobby or even within a larger, more "credible" network of big-time players.

Fear, Inc.'s failure to provide a working definition of Islamophobia seems peculiar in light of the fact that the Runnymede Trust provides a simple and matter-of-fact definition in its pioneering report released in 1996. Runnymede's report maps "Islamophobia's main features and the main dangers it poses."[18] Some of these Islamophobic precepts—precepts that clearly predate 9/11—are a reconfiguration of Orientalist tropes that see Islam and Muslims as "inferior," "static," "monolithic," "aggressive," "undifferentiated," and anti-Western and oppositional to modernity.[19] These tropes and narratives of Islamophobia are similar in the United States, although they have a different historical pedigree. On a governmental level, these Islamophobic talking points have organized policies on "homeland security" and foreign policy since the George W. Bush administration (if not before), reinforced by myriad "academics," journalists, activists, and policy wonks.[20]

In the United States, these Orientalist tropes were repurposed to serve particular ideological needs at the end of the Cold War. And while these narratives are closely associated with the neoconservative Right, the Islamophobic and anti-Arab narratives cut through the language, platform, and agenda of both parties, including the Democratic Party. *Fear, Inc.* sidesteps intentionally issues of race, racial history, white privilege, and American political and economic global power. Approaching Islamophobia as a racial phenomenon requires us to understand it as an ideological formation. Just as other forms of racism, Islamophobia as an ideological formation is enacted through acts of power by the state and *its dominant culture*. Islamophobia is not limited to the rants of Islamophobes or white supremacists but, rather, is a general cultural phenomenon that sees Muslim Americans as racial others and that facilitates a "security discourse," in local, state, and federal policies, predicated on Muslims as a potential and imminent threat to civic order and national security. Understanding Islamophobia as a widespread cultural formation rooted in U.S. racial history explains why the CAP investigators overlook the sustained continued "distrust" of the American mainstream with their Muslim neighbors.[21]

Islamophobia is not only a set of misrepresentations and misunderstandings. It is not a campaign or even a trope. Islamophobia is an ideological formation that provides pretexts for American power but also protects the privileges of Americans that rest on that power. It exists in a culture that might simultaneously decry the overtly racist talk of Pamela Geller, while also supporting how the Department of Justice instituted "special administrative measures" to deprive Muslim "terror" victims (and, increasingly, Black inmates) of basic human rights or how the Democratic President Obama and Congress proposed and passed the National Defense Authorization Act, which gives legal license to the Departments of Justice and Defense to incarcerate indefinitely any citizen or noncitizen, in the United States or abroad, without trial if he is suspected of "terrorism" or "material support" for it.[22] Of course, none of this is to mention the extreme and extremist Islamophobic policies and language of Donald Trump and his followers. When we are to sidestep the notion of race, power, and privilege, we are bound to be surprised that 60 million Americans voted for Trump despite his explicitly dehumanizing and incendiary Islamophobic language and vision of the United States. When we take race and white privilege out of the analytic equation, we may be surprised that anywhere between 42 and 52 percent of those surveyed approved of Trump's Muslim ban in its most egregious form.[23]

Islamophobia as a Racial Project

Islamophobia is a "racial project."[24] It is not a result of thousands of years of struggle between the East and West, of a "clash of civilizations," or of the animosity between Islam and Christianity from the Crusades. This "cult talk," as Mahmoud Mamdani states, indicates that Islamophobia and the questions of who Muslims are and what Islam is precisely emerge out of a particular moment and also serves, precisely, to dismiss our understanding it as a political phenomenon.[25] Matthew Frye-Jacobson highlights that the concepts of race and racial identity need to be studied as a "mode of perception contingent on the moment," as an "organizer of power whose vicissitudes track power relations through time," and as "the product of specific struggles for power at specific cultural sites."[26] Rather than being a prepackaged analysis deployed simply to serve a particular party or the latest form of racial vomiting from the white supremacist fringe, understanding Islamophobia as a form of race perception that became salient in the 1990s reveals larger, historically contingent structures of race, class, and power in the United States.

Islamophobia is a reworked progeny of Orientalism with roots not only in colonialism but also in the Cold War. Some, such as Junaid Rana, show how religion has been an operative notion in the origins of racism, indeed, showing how Islamophobia, anti-Semitism, and racism share a common genealogy.[27] Others, such as Nadine Naber, have argued that "within the post-9/11 moment of crisis, the racialization of an 'Arab–Middle Eastern–Muslim' Other has been constituted by a dual process of cultural racism and the racialization of national origin."[28] Whether Muslim and Arab American identity started to be constituted in racial terms before or after 9/11, it is obvious that the legal, law enforcement, legislative, cultural, and political developments in the United States since 9/11 have articulated, or "reorganized," Muslimness in terms of race and in terms of an American Other. If these developments created a "psyche of internment" among Muslim and Arab Americans, as Naber suggests, that psyche was formed through a comprehensive and sustained racial project where civil society's racist paradigms dovetailed neatly and conveniently with state policies in redefining "national interests" and "homeland security."

The *possibility* that Bernard Lewis and others could "rearticulate" Orientalist tropes into a "discursive reorganization" in the 1990s indicates a particular social need to reach into the racial index of American culture to reinterpret "ideological themes"—racial tropes that already existed in American culture—to justify new power relations in a unipolar, globalized, neoliberal world. Islamophobia is larger than a pernicious and ugly campaign launched by a small network of committed, boisterous, and shameless right-wing operatives. To the contrary, Islamophobia can still thrive in a culture where the cable media finds the ravings of such as Terry Jones and Pamela Geller, or President Donald Trump (or his cabinet), for that matter, distasteful or in a culture where right-wing libertarians defend the civil liberties of Muslims by opposing the government's "kill list" and drone assassination program, which have been policy since Presidents Obama and George W. Bush.[29]

We are therefore better served to understand Islamophobia as a racial project that involves a multitude of social participants, factors, and histories. Attacks on Muslim Americans as well as the defense of "them" are *"simultaneously an interpretation, representation, or explanation of racial dynamics, and an effort to reorganize and redistribute resources along particular racial lines."*[30] For example, it can be strongly argued that President Obama has exercised considerable discretion in avoiding Islamophobic rhetoric and discourses. He has avoided the term *radical Islam*. He has been discreet following domestic acts of violence, such as the Boston Marathon bombing, the San Bernardino shootings, and the Orlando nightclub attack. He maintains the inclusiveness of the United States to "all faiths" and has reached out to the Muslim American community. However, simultaneously, his administration's national counterterrorism strategy differs little from his predecessor's. The online *National Counterterrorism Guide* under Trump is the same that was issued under Obama. It is filled with images and information about a number of different explosives, the effects of anthrax, and the radius blast of an improvised explosive device, associating them with a list of terrorist groups, which are almost exclusively Islamic groups. Not one far-right-wing group or individual is named. We may not be surprised to learn that the Trump administration has decided to cut federal funds for investigating and combating white supremacist and white nationalist groups. But he has also kept Obama's appointee Nicholas Rasmussen as the director for the National Counterterrorism Center. Throughout his tenure, Rasmussen has continued to collapse "extremist violence" and "homegrown violent extremists" with political Islam and not rightwing, white supremacist, anti-abortionist, radical Christian, or antigovernmental organizations.[31]

Even before the rise in violence against Muslims, Jews, people of color, and women with the ascendancy of Trump, hate acts and hate speech against Muslim Americans had become daily occurrences in the United States.[32] I could elaborate on the increased number of legislative and legal developments that use Islamophobia as a foil to justify a plethora of civil liberties violations against Muslim Americans, not to mention the institutionalization of a draconian surveillance program, a drone program, the National Defense Authorization Act, illegal forms of torture, and secret prisons, all under the aegis of protection from the threat of (Muslim) "terrorism." *Fear, Inc.* skirts the relationship between systemic Islamophobia and state policies, in particular policies instituted, legalized, and prosecuted by President Obama's Defense, Homeland Security, Treasury, and Justice

Departments—policies wholeheartedly supported by both parties. The CAP's research ignores how "patterns observed in the racial logic of novels, films, and print journals" reflect the racial patterns of dominant culture and serve as the space where tensions are worked out to re-form syncretism of white and class privilege.[33] Films and television series such as *24*, *Argo*, *The Siege*, *Three Kings*, *All-American Muslims*, *The Tyrant*, *Homeland*, and *Shahs of Beverly Hills* are all confined within a similar but dynamic racial logic regarding Muslim and Arab otherness.[34]

Locating Islamophobia within the intersection of race and class in contemporary America allows us to understand them not as fixed but rather as highly dynamic concepts that involve more than othering, victimization, defense, and inclusion by majoritarian culture. This intersection invites us to explore how Muslim and Arab American communities uphold racial and class hierarchies themselves.[35] *Fear, Inc.* can be positioned as a point of "friction," in Frye-Jacobson's words, whereby we explore the "creation and formation" of racialized identities.[36] Therefore the trickle of books entering into the American mainstream explaining Islam to Americans, demonstrating how "we" are just like "you," and attempting to disassociate "radical" (read anti-West) Muslims from "good" (educated, middle-class American) Muslims speaks to the consolidation of Muslim American otherness into a self-view as a minority but one desperately hoping to demonstrate its class and racial solidarity with white middle America.

DUPLICITY

There is no Islamophobia in the United States without an American culture and history from which to arise or particular economic and social (read race privilege) purposes to serve. The sheer number of reports, polls, and studies by media, private pollsters, and academics repeatedly attesting to the civic mindedness and industry of Muslim Americans stands less as a vindication of Muslim Americans than as an indictment of the built-in racism of the mainstream that repeatedly needs massive amounts of empirical research to prove that Muslims are not a threat.[37] As the case of Khizr Khan's speech and presence at the 2016 Democratic National Convention demonstrates, Muslim Americans are repeatedly hailed to verify that they are "with us" on the "global War on Terror." Evelyn Alsultany points to a new wave of "complex" plots in American film and television that operate along a dichotomy of good Muslim–bad Muslim, as Mahmoud Mamdani has noted.[38] Jaspar Puar has recognized the process whereby American nationalist ideology hails the LBGTQ citizens to identify with dominant ethnonationalist normativity and state power.[39] Muslim Americans frequently argue about their own otherness in terms of "sameness," proving that they are "Muslim but still American."[40] Innumerable authors and Muslim American groups serve as interlocutors between Muslimness and Americanness, highlighting that Muslim values are American values. Splitting between "good Muslim" and "bad Muslim," Muslim Americans often fall into the trap of defining themselves vis-à-vis the bad jihadi, which itself has roots in the United States' own racial history.[41] Non-Black Muslim Americans, and certainly Americans, fail to locate themselves in this racial history, because doing so would force them to locate themselves on the race spectrum in the United States.[42] The position of many Arab and South Asian Muslim Americans matches or outpaces that of the white middle and upper middle class in terms of employment, education, and income.[43]

The CAP report's approach to Islamophobia is indicative of a larger collaborationist strategy found within most Muslim and Arab American civil rights groups that refuse to confront how the racist structure and history of the United States merges with class privilege. Sherman Jackson calls this "racial agnosia," where non-Black American Muslims "have traditionally been dubious about recognizing race as a feature of the American sociopolitical landscape."[44] Building on Jackson's observation, I would add that dissociating from Black America and Black Americans, whether Christian or Muslim Black Americans, was a conscious class act on behalf of Muslim and Arab Americans. While commentators constantly allude to the diversity of Muslim Americans in their defense against Islamophobia's broad swaths of racial profiling, this "diversity" means ethnic and racial diversity. This speaks to that fact that the United States is divided into subtle and sometimes not so subtle racial hierarchies, where identity is a dynamic process of racial differentiation.[45] However, the Muslim American community is far less diverse in the case of class. When one considers Middle Eastern (including Iranian) and South Asian Muslim Americans, who compose 45 percent of Muslim Americans, their middle- to upper-middle-class affiliation becomes even more coherent.[46]

Naber's ethnographic research reveals a discrepancy among Muslim Americans in their relationship to the state and society based largely on class. In discussion of feelings of isolation under the post-9/11 atmosphere of fear, she notes that working-class Muslim immigrants "speak about themes such as racial discrimination in the process of seeking employment or housing, fear of FBI investigations, detention, or deportation" less frequently than middle- and upper-class Muslims. Furthermore, when under attack, "middle–upper class individuals were more protected by legal aid and socialization within white middle class cultural norms (such as dress and speech) than their working class counterparts."[47]

This small demographic detour reveals a salient point underlying *Fear, Inc.* and the political posture of Muslim and Arab American groups. That is, the end of the Cold War, and certainly 9/11, heralded the age when Muslim Americans were jerked out of their "racial agnosia." This agnosia, or what I would rather call duplicity in white supremacist American culture, has historical roots that I can only briefly theorize here. Racial duplicity among Arab Americans was an active social project and legal campaign sponsored and organized by the Arab American community.[48] Christian Arab Americans consolidated their whiteness after the 1920s (Johnson Reed Act of 1924) as well as a series of state legal battles declaring them white. Indeed, socially, "Syrian" (Syrian, Lebanese, and Palestinian) immigrants assiduously worked for assimilation into the white Christian mainstream, facilitated, no doubt, by the expanded plurality of Catholics, which eventually constituted the largest religious voting block by 1965.[49] The integration of Christian Arabs into "whiteness," into "passing," was also facilitated by increased social mobility and financial success within white America.[50] Twentieth-century Arab Americans made a racial contract with white America. Arab Americans would not upset the racial or class order if they were considered "not Black" (not a small order in the Jim Crow South, especially when one is also Catholic) and were therefore allowed access into privileged white economic spaces.

The influx of Muslim Middle Eastern and South Asian immigrants put social–racial pressure on the racial matrix that undergirded this contract. However, Muslim American immigrants' higher than average educational level and social economic status also permitted them honorary entry into white privilege, especially if their political and class solidarities rested clearly with white America against Black and Brown America. However, this racial détente was fragile as the influx of Muslim Arab, Iranian, and South Asian immigrants in the 1980s coincided with the United States' rise to unipolar power and the fruition of its new global hegemony.

Fear, Inc. answered a challenge put forth to Muslim and Arab Americans by Islamophobes to rewrite the racial contract that was breached by the U.S. profiling of Muslims. The CAP report replicates the agenda of assimilationist "civil rights" organizations like the Arab American Institute, Arab American Anti-Discrimination Committee (ADC), Muslim Public Affairs Council (MPAC), and Council on American-Islamic Relations (CAIR), who work to maintain their access to white privilege by assuring the majoritarian culture (and the ruling class) that their own nonwhiteness is not only nonthreatening but better for the longevity of American society. The work of Sumbol Ali-Karamali, Eboo Patel, James Zogby, and Dalia Mogahed, among others, assured middle-class (read white) America of the civic mindedness and affluence of the American Muslim community.[51] Historically, nonwhite assimilationist groups stabilized whiteness by assuring them that their otherness would not detract from the privileges that white majoritarian culture ensures.[52] In affirming "the experiences of Muslim American experiences as American experiences," these groups in no way critically interrogate the racial history and class hierarchy of the United States nor the process by which Arabs, for example, lobbied to "become white" and protested not the ripping of that veil as much as the loss of their racial privilege.[53] As many Arab Americans voted Republican (probably more, because one-fifth are "independent" and "swing" votes) as voted Democrat even in 2000, when the majority voted for George W. Bush.[54]

The rise of Islamophobia in the United States has wedged the largely non-Black, middle-class Muslim Americans between their class privilege and the erosion of race privilege, which, through collusion with the racial order in the United States, has allowed them easily to share all of the benefits of the former. When I say collusion with the racial order, I allude to Arab and Muslim Americans' historic tendency not only to pride themselves on being the "ideal American immigrant community" but also to laud how their traditional, conservative "family values" make them a natural ally of the Republican Party, which is otherwise losing their vote.[55]

Sherman Jackson's pronouncement on "racial agnosia" taken from within the Arab and Indo-Pakistani Muslim American communities takes on new weight. "Muslim immigrants in the United States, especially after 9/11, are not only socially non-white," he states, but "they are legally and socially non-black!"[56] Some Arab American and Indo-Pakistani American groups and artists, such as poet Suheir Hammad, punk band the Kominas, music producer Fredwreck, rapper the Narcicyst, and advocacy group Desis Rising Up and Moving, highlight Muslim Americans' racialized identity, invoking racial solidarity with Black America while acknowledging its "difference" and specificities, especially within post-9/11 America. Likewise, a small number of CAIR chapters nationally have come out in support of the Black Lives Matter movement, understanding the connection between police brutality and surveillance. The considerable number of young Muslim Americans supporting Bernie Sanders indicates a generational shift.

However, these examples are the exception, not the rule. Islamophobes work to highlight racial difference and speculate these differences as insurmountable, insoluble, and antithetical to "American," Judeo-Christian (read white) identity. While baseless and laughable, at times, their racialized hysteria scratches at the dissonance between Muslim Americans' class and racial status. Pam Geller, Robert Spencer, and, indeed, Donald Trump previously have targeted Hillary Clinton's aide Huma Abedin, if not Barack Obama himself, as an Islamic fundamentalist.[57] Such paranoia about infiltration and "sleeper cells" speaks to the repressed issue of race in the United States and the Muslim American community. This anxiety lies at the heart of the efforts of Muslim and Arab American organizations, authors, and activists to reassure Main Street that "ethnic" differences are not threatening. In fact, we are continually reassured through these voices that Muslim Americans, especially those from immigrant communities, carry with them patriotism, civic mindedness, and "mainstream values."[58] Indeed, James Comey, while the FBI director, praised Muslim American cooperation with law enforcement in self-surveillance programs, even after the agency spied on two hundred Muslim American leaders.[59] More important, groups such as the Islamic Society of North America's (ISNA) and CAIR's national chapters actively work to assure the American public that Muslim Americans are patriotic, civilly engaged, philanthropic, and politically active (especially as voters). They routinely salute American Muslims' participation in the U.S. armed forces and recognize how Muslims historically "have played an integral part in defending the homeland and fighting for the American government's geopolitical interests."[60] These Muslim American organizations have rarely taken on controversial issues regarding race relations or poverty and economic issues in the United States. Rather, as "civil rights" groups, they aim at educating Muslim Americans about their legal rights but also reassure Muslim and non-Muslim Americans that they regularly issue news releases condemning terrorism and that ISIS recommends its sympathizers and applaud Republican officials when they break rank with their president's explicit Islamophobia.[61]

It should be noted that over the past few years, the ADC has attempted, with some pushback from its older and more conservative members, to centralize the issue of race and racism with the Arab American community. Of all Arab and Muslim American civic organizations, they have come out most vocally in support of the Black Lives Matter movement, and they have strongly advocated for "lawfare" against issues that they clearly identify as political issues informed by structural racism. ISNA, MPAC, and CAIR, however, remained largely conservative and cautious on the issue of race until the Trump era. More recently, local chapters of CAIR have come out in support of Black Lives Matter. However, it must be noted that these organizations remain concerned largely with mainstream politics, supporting Muslim American candidates, registering voters, highlighting the civic activity of Muslim Americans, and featuring "successful" Muslim Americans. Indeed, their membership and their projects remained centered on middle- and upper-middle-class (largely non-Black) Muslim Americans, focusing on developing business opportunities, social networks, and institutionalizing Muslim Americans into mainstream American politics without disturbing its racial and class structure in any substantial way. While CAIR, for example, has criticized Trump on a number of occasions for his role in the mainstreaming of the white supremacist agenda, virtually all of their critical and public interventions by the national headquarters regarding race are linked, in some way, to Islamophobia and how that racism affects "good" Muslim Americans. While Islamophobia means to stabilize whiteness for conservative majoritarian American culture, works like *Fear, Inc.* stabilize a racial hierarchy by defanging any threat of Muslim otherness and displacing it to the realm of religious tolerance. In other words, Islamophobia works to codify that matrix *outside* the realms of white majoritarian privilege, while assimilationists work to reconstitute that matrix *within* mainstream society as to further shore up the system of capital, power, and concomitant class and race privilege.

Conclusion

The purpose of this chapter was not to rip down the findings of *Fear, Inc.*, which are useful. The purpose is to properly identify Islamophobia and its origins and how we all participate in and perpetuate it, including Muslim and Arab American communities and well-intentioned liberal think tanks. *Fear, Inc.* offered an American readership a scapegoat. Such a tack may seem productive, even healing, in a world under attack by Donald Trump's mindless xenophobic prattle that does not distinguish between refugees, "illegals," and "radical Islam."

It offers an America that is "stronger together" when "accepting" Muslim Americans into the mainstream political fold without accepting responsibility for security discourses and policies based on Islamophobia or acknowledging Muslim Americans as racialized subjects. For Muslim Americans, it provides a convenient way to maintain a sense of ethnic belonging while also benefiting from the class privileges that are firmly rooted in middle-class white America. By reproaching and isolating a small fringe element, Muslim Americans are allowed to be brown and white at the same time.

The present critique of Islamophobia encourages us to approach it as an ideological formation and a racial project in which Muslim Americans actively collude to protect their own class positions and social relations. Speaking of racial formations, we acknowledge that racial identities are not fixed. They are open to "many types of agency, from the individual to the organizational, from the local to the global."[62] The theory draws together the multiple layers of agency and sources of power that inform race. What we are witnessing in the post-Obama era is a reorganization of white and nonwhite, including Muslim American, identities that are informed by U.S. political and economic power. This reorganization is resulting in a further consolidation of Muslim identities into North American identity, one that is simultaneously contested by President Donald Trump, his Islamophobic cabinet members, former Tea Party/Freedom Caucus legislators, the evangelical Right, and much of the Republican base. One could argue, in fact, that the 2016 election was precisely the "Muslim question" (linked with the browning of the United States) that forced a reconsolidation and counterrevolution of whiteness.

CAP and the Democratic Party it represents operate on similar discourses that deploy imminent Muslim otherness to justify policies and practices that have established a surveillance–police–corporatist–carceral state. The Democratic narrative calls for "religious tolerance," recognizes American Muslim patriotism (i.e., serving in the military), and invites Muslim Americans who "love America and freedom" and "hate terror," in Bill Clinton's words, "to stay here and help us win and make a future together."[63] At the same time, Muslim American civil rights groups, namely, CAIR and ISNA, coyly confront these policies by invoking the patriotism of Muslim Americans, leaving intact the very roots of Islamophobia, namely, U.S. racial and class hierarchy and the exceptionalism of American democracy, freedom, and economy.

Notes

1. Wajahat Ali, Eli Clifton, Matthew Duss, Lee Fang, Scott Keyes, and Faiz Shakir, *Fear, Inc.: The Roots of the Islamophobia Network in America* (Washington, D.C.: Center for American Progress, 2011), i.

2. Stephen Sheehi, *Islamophobia: The Ideological Campaign against Muslims* (Atlanta, Ga.: Clarity Press, 2011), 66–89.

3. Ibid. See also Nathan Lean's now landmark *The Islamophobia Industry: How the Right Manufactures Fear of Muslims* (New York: Pluto, 2012) and Deepa Kumar's fine primer *Islamophobia and the Politics of Empire* (Chicago: Haymarket, 2012).

4. Ali et al., *Fear, Inc.*, 13.

5. Ibid., 3.

6. Ibid., 6.

7. Matthew Duss, Yasmine Taeb, Ken Gude, and Ken Sofar, *Fear, Inc. 2.0: The Islamophobia Network's Efforts to Manufacture Hate in America* (Washington, D.C.: Center for American Progress, 2015), 1.

8. Within two weeks of the release of the Center for American Progress's report, the Pew Research Center published a study, "Muslim Americans: No Signs of Growth in Alienation or Support for Extremism. Mainstream and Moderate Attitudes," published on August 30, 2011, http://www.people-press.org/2011/08/30/section-1-a-demographic-portrait-of-muslim-americans/.

9. For example, see Charles Kurzman, "Muslim American Terrorism since 9/11: An Accounting," Triangle on Terrorism and Homeland Security in North Carolina, February 2, 2011, 1; and "Muslim American Terrorism Further Declining," Triangle on Terrorism and Homeland Security in North Carolina, February 1, 2013; also found at http://tcths.sanford.duke.edu/documents/Kurzman_Muslim-American_Terrorism_final2013.pdf.

10. For an example at this time, see Glenn Greenwald's discussion of the South Park–Muhammad controversy in *"The New York Times'* Muslim Problem," *Salon,* April 26, 2010, http://www.salon.com/2010/04/26/douthat_4, and Max Blumenthal, "The Great Islamophobic Crusade," *Huffington Post,* December 20, 2010, http://www.salon.com/2010/04/26/douthat_4.

11. For example, a segment by ABC's *Prime Time,* titled "Would You Stop Islamophobia?," became the topic of discussion online and in the blogosphere. John Quinones's segment "What Would You Do?" staged a scene where a worker at a roadside bakery was abusive and openly discriminated against a woman wearing a hijab (head scarf) to measure bystanders' reactions. See "What Would You Do," February 26, 2008, http://abcnews.go.com/WhatWouldYouDo/video/step-stop-islamophobia-11952548.

12. Amy Sullivan, "The Sharia Myth Sweeps America," *USA Today,* June 10, 2011, http://www.salon.com/2010/04/26/douthat_4.

13. Ali et al., *Fear, Inc.*, 23.

14. Ibid., 16.

15. Ibid., 22.

16. For a discussion of the Koch brothers' funding of an array of issues bound by a larger right-wing agenda, see Bill Press, *The Obama Hate Machine: The Lies, Distortions, and Personal Attacks on the President—and Who Is behind Them* (New York: St. Martin's, 2012), 176–236.

17. The CPAC barred Pamela Geller in 2013 as it has done in recent years. This is because the crude language of hate she deploys has become a political liability, especially in the post-2012 elections. Furthermore, the sensationalism of her campaign distracts from the higher priorities of the GOP, namely, issues of taxation, "entitlements," and the size of government championed within CPAC by Geller's rival, Grover Norquist. See, e.g., Jillian Rayfield, "Pamela Geller: CPAC Is

'Enforcing the Sharia,'" *Salon*, May 7, 2013, http://www.salon.com/2013/03/07/pamela_geller_cpac_is_enforcing_the_sharia.

18. See the Runnymede Trust, *Islamophobia: A Challenge for Us All* (London: Runnymede Trust, 1997), 1.

19. Ibid., 4.

20. For example, I have discussed elsewhere how such rogue scholars and journalists like Bernard Lewis, Fareed Zakaria, or Thomas Friedman *did not generate* but certainly helped reengineer anti-Arab, Orientalist tropes into political narratives that fit the needs of the United States in the Unipolar world. For an example of critiques of Lewis, Zakaria, and Friedman vis-à-vis Islamophobia and American empire, see Sheehi, *Islamophobia*, 67–84; Belén Fernández, *The Imperial Messenger: Thomas Friedman at Work* (London: Verso, 2011); and Shahid Alam, "Scholarship or Sophistry: A Review of 'What Went Wrong' by Bernard Lewis," *Studies in Contemporary Islam* 4 (2002): 51–78.

21. Despite empirical and statistical evidence to the contrary, several polls over the past ten years have continued to show that Americans are "skeptical" about Muslims in the United States; see, e.g., Eric Marrapodi, "Poll: Many Americans Uncomfortable with Muslims," CNN, September 6, 2011, http://religion.blogs.cnn.com/2011/09/06/poll-many-americans-uncomfortable-with-muslims, or Jon Cohen, "Poll: Americans Sceptical of Islam and Arabs," March 8, 2006, http://abcnews.go.com/US/story?id=1700599; or the Pew Research Center's report "Views of Islam Remain Sharply Divided," September 9, 2004, http://www.people-press.org/2004/09/09/views-of-islam-remain-sharply-divided. For a longitudinal survey of this distrust and the "cold" feelings toward Muslim Americans, see *The Bridge Initiative: Two Decades of Americans' Views on Islam and Muslims* (Washington, D.C.: Waleed Bin Talal Center for Muslim-Christian Understanding, Georgetown University, 2015).

22. See Sohail Daulatzai's writing on the logic of the carceral state in *Black Star, Crescent Moon: The Muslim International and Black Freedom beyond America* (Minneapolis: University of Minnesota, 2012), 109.

23. Ariel Edwards-Levy and Grace Sparks, "HUFFPOLLSTER: How Many Americans Support the Travel Ban? Depends on the Poll," *Huffington Post*, February 3, 2017, http://www.huffingtonpost.com/entry/polls-trump-executive-order-travel-ban_us_589479a4e4b0c1284f255570.

24. Michael Omi and Howard Winant, *Racial Formations in the United States: From the 1960s to the 1990s* (New York: Routledge, 1994).

25. See Mahmoud Mamdani, *Good Muslim, Bad Muslim: America, the Cold War, and the Roots of Terrorism* (New York: Three Leaves Press, 2005).

26. Matthew Frye-Jacobson, *Whiteness of a Different Color: European Immigrants and the Alchemy of Race* (Cambridge, Mass.: Harvard University Press, 1994), 11.

27. Junaid Rana, *Terrifying Muslims: Race and Labor in the South Asian Diaspora* (Durham, N.C.: Duke University Press, 2011), esp. 25–48.

28. Nadine Naber, "The Rules of Forced Engagement: Race, Gender, and the Culture of Fear among Arab Immigrants in San Francisco, Post-9/11," *Cultural Dynamics* 18, no. 3 (2006): 236.

29. See, e.g., Rand Paul's attack on the devolution of constitutional rights in the United States, "Rand Paul's Drone Filibuster Shakes Up Republicans," *Christian*

Science Monitor, March 7, 2013, http://www.csmonitor.com/USA/DC-Decoder/2013/0307/Rand-Paul-s-drone-filibuster-shakes-up-Republicans.

30. Omi and Winant, *Racial Formations*, 56, emphasis original.

31. See the "Counterterrorism Guide" at https://www.nctc.gov/site/index.html#. For an example of Nicholas Rasmussen language, see his speech to the NYPD at https://www.nctc.gov/docs/NYPD_Shield_Conference.pdf.

32. See, e.g., Wadie Said, *Crimes of Terror: The Legal and Political Implications of Federal Terrorism Prosecutions* (Oxford: Oxford University Press, 2015); Natsu Saito, *From Chinese Exclusion to Guantanamo Bay: Plenary Power and the Prerogative State* (Boulder: University of Colorado Press, 2007); Elaine Hagopian, *Civil Rights in Peril: The Targeting of Arabs and Muslims* (London: Pluto, 2004); or NYU's Center for Human Rights and Global Justice's report *Targeted and Entrapped: Manufacturing the "Homegrown" Threat in the United States* (New York: CHRSJ, 2011).

33. Frye-Jacobson, *Whiteness of a Different Color*, 11.

34. See, e.g., Amaney Jamal and Nadine Naber, *Race and Arab Americans before and after 9/11: From Invisible Citizens to Visible Subjects* (Syracuse, N.Y.: Syracuse University Press, 2008), and Steven Salaita, *Anti-Arab Racism in the USA: Where It Comes from and What It Means for Politics* (London: Pluto, 2006).

35. Tariq Ramdan, who was prevented from assuming an academic position at Notre Dame University by the George W. Bush administration, suggests that some Muslims in the West do not move beyond the politics of victimization and Islamophobia to justify their own complacency or "guilty passivity." See his *What I Believe* (Oxford: Oxford University Press, 2010), 59.

36. Frye-Jacobson, *Whiteness of a Different Color*, 3.

37. These reports and polls are too numerous to account. In addition to the many studies by Charles Kurzman and Triangle on Terrorism and Homeland Security in North Carolina, Zogby International's many polls partnering with the American Arab Institute, academic institutions like Georgetown, and mainstream media sources such as ABC News, one can look at the number of reports on Muslim Americans by the Pew Research Center over the past decade, including "The World's Muslims: Unity and Diversity," August 9, 2012, http://www.pewforum.org/Muslim/the-worlds-muslims-unity-and-diversity-executive-summary.aspx; "Muslim Americans: No Signs of Growth in Alienation or Support for Extremism: Mainstream and Moderate Attitudes," August 30, 2011, http://www.people-press.org/2011/08/30/section-1-a-demographic-portrait-of-muslim-americans; and "Muslim Americans: Middle Class and Mostly Mainstream," May 22, 2007, http://www.people-press.org/2007/05/22/muslim-americans-middle-class-and-mostly-mainstream.

38. Evelyn Alsultany, *Arabs and Muslims in Media: Race and Representation after 9/11* (New York: New York University Press, 2012), 28–29.

39. Jasper Puar, *Terrorist Assemblages: Homonationalism in Queer Times* (Durham, N.C.: Duke University Press, 2007).

40. For an example of the Muslim-as-normative American genre, see Sumbul Ali-Karamali, *The Muslim Next Door: The Qur'an, the Media, and That Veil Thing* (Ashland, Oreg.: White Cloud Press, 2008); Mucahit Bilici, *Finding Mecca in America: How Islam Is Becoming an American Religion* (Chicago: University of Chicago Press, 2012); Dalia Mogehed, *Who Speaks for Islam? What a Billion Muslims Really Think*

(New York: Gallup, 2007); Eboo Patel, *Sacred Ground: Pluralism, Prejudice, and the Promise of America* (Boston: Beacon, 2012); and Faisal Abdul Rauf, *What's Right with Islam Is What's Right with America* (New York: HarperCollins, 2004).

41. See Jacqueline O'Rourke, *Representing Jihad: The Appearing and Disappearing Radical* (New York: Zed, 2012).

42. Besheer Mohamed, *Democratic and Economic Profile of Muslim Americans* (Washington, D.C.: Pew Research Center, 2011).

43. See 2010 census information, "Demographic Portrait of Muslim Americans," Pew Research Center, August 30, 2011, http://www.people-press.org/2011/08/30/section-1-a-demographic-portrait-of-muslim-americans.

44. Sherman Jackson, "Islam, Muslims, and the Wages of Racial Agnosia in America," *Journal of Islamic Law and Culture* 13, no. 1 (2011): 6.

45. Frye-Jacobson, *Whiteness of a Different Color*, 143.

46. Mohamed, *Democratic and Economic Profile of Muslim Americans*.

47. Naber, "Rules of Forced Engagement," 245.

48. Sarah Gualtieri, *Between Arab and White: Race and Ethnicity in Early Syrian American Diaspora* (Berkeley: University of California Press, 2009).

49. Frye-Jacobson, *Whiteness of a Different Color*, 8.

50. Jackson, "Islam," 9.

51. For example, Dalia Mogahed's life work seems to intend to prove that Muslims are not a threat and that they live the "American dream" and have contributed to American society. See her report on the Muslim world "The Battle for Hearts and Minds: Moderate vs. Extremist Views in the Muslim World," http://media.gallup.com/WorldPoll/PDF/ExtremismInMuslimWorld.pdf, or *Who Speaks for Islam?*

52. Frye-Jacobson, *Whiteness of a Different Color*, 9.

53. Melody Moezzi, *War on Error: Real Stories of American Muslims* (Fayetteville: University of Arkansas Press, 2007), xviii.

54. James Zogby, "How Arab Americans Vote and Why," Arab American Institute, December 18, 2000, http://www.aaiusa.org/dr-zogby/entry/w121800/.

55. See, e.g., Zainab Mohammed, "US Muslims to GOP: If You're Trying to Lose Our Votes, You're Doing a Good Job," *Mother Jones*, December 7, 2012, http://www.motherjones.com/mojo/2012/12/muslim-americans-plea-gop-clean-your-act.

56. Jackson, "Islam," 10.

57. One only need read the conservative Internet media to see the degree to which Obama's race and politics are conflated into being a Muslim Brotherhood sympathizer. See, e.g., Mark Levin's rant "The Muslim Brotherhood Has Infiltrated Our Government: It's Called Barack Obama," *Real Clear Politics*, January 31, 2013, http://www.realclearpolitics.com/video/2013/01/31/mark_levin_the_muslim_brotherhood_has_infiltrated_our_government_its_called_barack_obama.html. Apart from Trump calling Obama a "cofounder" of ISIS, Abedin has been targeted as a Muslim Brother operative and responsible for the Clinton e-mail scandal, despite the fact that her husband, Anthony Weiner, was a staunchly pro-Israel congressman with a hawkish national security and foreign policy record.

58. It is hardly coincidental that articles reporting and commenting on polls, studies, and reports appeared even in the business media, such as in *Forbes* magazine. For one example, see John Zogby, CEO of the polling company Zogby International

and brother of James Zogby, founder of the Arab American Institute and arguably the most prominent Arab American community "leader" in the United States, in his weekly *Forbes* column "American Muslims Have Mainstream Values," *Forbes*, August 26, 2010, http://www.forbes.com/2010/08/26/muslims-polls-mosque-opin ions-columnists-john-zogby.html, as well as other articles in business-oriented Internet media, such as "Pew: Muslim Americans Are Diverse, Share American Values," *Marketing Vox*, May 23, 2007, http://www.marketingvox.com/pew-mus lim-americans-are-diverse-share-american-values-029889.

59. See Glenn Greenwald, "Meet the Muslim American Leaders the FBI and NSA Have Been Spying On," *Intercept*, July 9, 2014, https://theintercept.com/ 2014/07/09/under-surveillance. For James Comey's praising of Muslim American community in cooperating with the FBI, comments addressed after the Orlando shootings and in response to Trump's accusations to the otherwise, see "FBI Direc- tor Schools Trump on American Muslims," *Informed Comment* (blog), June 19, 2016, http://www.juancole.com/2016/06/director-schools-american.html. For a report regarding Muslim Americans' cooperation with federal authorities in moni- toring and preventing "home grown" terrorism, see their report Charles Kurzman, Ebrahim Moosa, and Daniel Schazner, *The Anti-Terror Lessons of Muslim Americans*, Triangle on Terrorism and Homeland Security in North Carolina, January 6, 2010, http://www.sanford.duke.edu/news/Schanzer_Kurzman_Moosa_Anti-Terror_Les sons.pdf. For an example of its warm reception in the mainstream media, see Bobby Ghosh, "Threat of Homegrown Terrorism May Be Exaggerated," *Time*, Janu- ary 6, 2010, http://www.time.com/time/nation/article/0,8599,1952009,00.html.

60. Published on CAIR-Florida's website at https://www.cairflorida.org/blog/ saluting_muslim_american_patriots.html; originally appearing as Craig Considine, "Saluting Muslim American Patriots," *Huffington Post*, June 10, 2015, http://www .huffingtonpost.com/craig-considine/saluting-muslim-american-patriots_b_70398 66.html.

61. See their "Condemnation of Terrorism" tab on their "About Us" page, http:// www.cair.com/about-us/cair-anti-terrorism-campaigns.html. For a recent example, see the local Iowa chapter of CAIR's praise for the Iowa Republican Party for not endorsing an Islamophobic event organized by the Pottawattamie County Republi- can Party. See "CAIR Applauds Iowa GOP for Stance on Anti-conspiracy Theorist Who Allegedly Assaulted Minnesota Sheriff," September 19, 2017, https://www.cair .com/press-center/press-releases/14604-good-news-alert-cair-applauds-iowa-gop -for-stance-on-anti-muslim-conspiracy-theorist-who-allegedly-assaulted-minn-sher iff.html.

62. Howard Winant, "Race and Race Theory," *Annual Review of Sociology* 26 (2000): 182.

63. "Bill Clinton's Full Speech at DNC (Full Text)," *Politico*, July 27, 2016, http:// www.politico.com/story/2016/07/full-text-bill-clinton-dnc-speech-226269.

4

Palestinian Resistance and the Indivisibility of Justice

RABAB IBRAHIM ABDULHADI

On November 29, 2012, sixty-five years after the United Nations (UN) Partition of Palestine, 138 member states of the UN voted in favor of recognizing Palestine as a "non-member observer state" to the international body, with nine opposing votes and forty-one abstentions. Israel, Canada, and the United States were among the three negative votes.[1]

Worldwide, supporters of Palestinian rights saw the successful campaign for UN recognition and the vote itself as a reminder of the international consensus on Palestine on official state and, more importantly, grassroots levels. It showed once again that the United States, Israel, and their allies in the Global North (or Global South states who were coerced into voting against Palestine) were the exception, not the norm, of the international community's stand on Palestine. It was a testament to the broadening international support for Palestine in the face of intensive Israeli and Zionist campaigns to discredit the Palestinian struggle. The Palestinian reaction was another matter. The Palestinian Authority (PA) and official Palestine Liberation Organization (PLO) circles were enthused about the driving dynamo of the UN campaign, yet a majority of Palestinian organizers and activists, within and outside of organized political groups (in Palestine and throughout the Palestinian diaspora), were critical of this move. They welcomed this sign of international reaffirmation and support for the Palestinian right to self-determination, including statehood, but were not in favor of dedicating Palestinian efforts to yet another campaign for UN recognition.

There were several reasons for such a lukewarm Palestinian reaction. First, the UN had already recognized Palestine. This took place following the adoption of the Declaration of Palestinian Independence by the Palestinian National Council at its meeting in Algiers in 1988,[2] less than a year

56

after the start of the 1987 Intifada.[3] By the end of 1988, more than eighty countries had recognized the Palestinian Declaration of Independence. The UN and its various agencies, as well as other international bodies, such as the Non-Aligned Movement,[4] the Organization of African Unity,[5] and the Organization of Islamic Summit,[6] had already renewed their recognition on multiple occasions, passing numerous resolutions that affirmed Palestinian self-determination and condemned the creeping Israeli annexation of Palestine.[7] More importantly, especially given limited Palestinian political and financial resources, critics of the UN recognition campaign saw it as a diplomatic maneuver through which the PA aimed to pressure Israel to return to the Oslo framework of bilateral negotiations, at a time when all Palestinian efforts should have been focused on ending the Israeli occupation and restoring Palestinian rights.

There was a qualitative difference between the 2012 Palestine UN statehood bid and the 1988 international recognition of the Palestinian Declaration of Independence. The 2012 bid made Palestine eligible to join several international bodies, most significantly the International Criminal Court (ICC), which Palestine did in 2015.[8] The ICC has teeth and could bring Israeli war criminals to justice, as it did those in Rwanda, Bosnia, and Herzegovina. Most Palestinians, however, were not confident that the PA or the Mahmoud Abbas–led PLO would exercise such a right based on their consistent pattern of bowing to Israeli threats and pressures. Another difference between the two UN recognitions lies in that, while the 2012 bid was more focused on state building, the Declaration of Independence was adopted during the 1987 Intifada, which was reflective of the movement's optimism.

What do these political developments mean for the Palestinian people's quest for liberation, justice, and peace? This chapter discusses strategies of resistance and liberation, arguing for the need to frame a Palestinian anticolonial discourse, the mechanisms necessary for such a strategy, and the sort of alliances and relations the Palestinian anticolonial liberation movement should build with regional and international forces. This chapter emphasizes that Palestinian discourses and actions must be rooted in an indivisible sense of justice.

Regrettably, the UN bid was not developed as an integral part of a Palestinian strategy of liberation; it was rather launched as a reaction to Israeli intransigence. The PA ignored history, which instructed the colonized never to put down their weapons or abandon other means of resistance, however modest, as long as their colonizers carried theirs, as the cases of the Algerians and the Vietnamese show. The Vietnamese and Algerian struggles also

underscore the necessity of not relinquishing any demands ahead of nego-
tiating a political settlement, especially what the Palestinians have referred
to as the minimal red lines, such as an end to the 1967 occupation, an end
to racism against Palestinians in Israel, and the right of return for Palestinian refugees. However, a few weeks before the UN vote, Palestinian president Mahmoud Abbas gave up his right as a Palestinian refugee to return
to his family's home in Safad, declaring in an interview with Israeli TV
Channel 2 that he would be satisfied with visiting but not demanding to live
there because the property now belonged to Israel.[9]

Abbas was neither pushed nor cornered into making this statement
but opted to use his TV appearance to address the Israeli public when he
abandoned the Palestinian right of return, instead of mobilizing his own
people.[10] It is unclear whether he gave any thought to how his own constituency, the Palestinian people, would react to such a pronouncement.
During the 1993 signing of the Oslo Accords on the White House lawn,
Palestinian leadership also selected to address the Israeli (and U.S.) publics, thus joining then Israeli prime minister Yitzhak Rabin, who directed
all his remarks to the Israeli public, in "assuaging the Israeli fears" as if the
constructed Israeli discourses of victimhood, or colonizers' angst, were at
the heart of the issue. No one spoke to the Palestinian people or sought to
explain to this oft-marginalized people the why and the how of the Oslo
Accords, or what they meant for the restoration of their rights. The focus of
Israel and Western backers has been and continues to be on Israeli security
and safety, ignoring Palestinian rights to peace and security.

At its best, Oslo would offer a mini demilitarized state in which the West
Bank and Gaza would be connected by a corridor, controlled and guarded
by Israel. Israel would also maintain control of sea and air spaces as well as
all other border crossings, deciding when and who is allowed or denied
entry. A small number of Palestinian refugees[11] would be allowed entry and
residence in the Palestinian mini state, but the majority of the millions of
stateless Palestinians would not be allowed to return to the original homes
of their ancestors, lest they disrupt the demographic balance of the Jewish-
exclusivity-seeking Israel.

DEFINING THE CONTEXT:
SETTLER COLONIALISM OR POLITICAL DISPUTE?

Had the Palestinian leadership offered a clear strategy to advance Palestinian self-determination, including sovereignty, the return of the refugees

from exile, and an end to structural Israeli racism against 1948 Palestinians, the 2012 statehood bid could have been meaningful and would have constituted an integral part of a comprehensive strategy of resistance to Israeli colonial rule. However, this was not the case, which might explain why the Palestinian leadership has not for a long time addressed its constituency, the Palestinian people, with clarity and transparency. The Palestinian leadership has moved a great distance from the days of the 1960s liberation movement to the Oslo era. These contradictions between the historical Palestinian struggle and the pragmatism of the current leadership have to do with how the PLO today defines the context in which it operates and how it acts based on that definition.

Unlike most scholars who attribute Palestinian leadership's abandonment of Palestinian national goals to the 1993 Oslo Accords, I trace the shift to the twelfth meeting of the Palestinian National Council (PNC), held in Cairo in 1974. At that time, the PNC adopted the ten-point program, calling for the establishment of a national authority "over every part of Palestinian territory that is liberated," with the aim of "completing the liberation of all Palestinian territory."[12] The national consensus broke down around this staged or interim program. Palestinians began to debate whether the first goal, establishing a "national authority," would lead to the second, the liberation of historic Palestine. As time went by, the interim program took on a permanent character, while the longer-term vision began to fade away; in its place, a new discourse was emerging that began to refer to the anticolonial Palestinian vision as utopian, unrealistic, infantile, or adventurous.

This paradigmatic shift was not divorced from the desire of the dominant PLO leadership to present itself internationally more as statesmen and less as militant guerillas, a shift coinciding with the 1974 historic address, later labeled as "the gun or the olive branch,"[13] given by PLO chairman Yasser Arafat at the UN General Assembly. The pouring of petrodollars into the bank accounts of some Palestinian factions, especially of the dominant group, Fatah, was no small factor in expediting this process of how Palestinian leaders saw themselves and their historic role.[14] Additional factors contributed to the shift in the PLO political program. This included the attacks against the PLO in the 1970s and 1980s in Jordan and Lebanon, along with the direct or indirect collusion of right-wing and nationalist Arab regimes, such as Syria, Saudi Arabia, Egypt, and Libya. The 1978–79 Camp David Accords between Israel and Egypt, the expulsion of Palestinian fighters from Lebanon following the 1982 Israeli invasion, and the relocation of PLO headquarters to Tunisia and other sites farther away from historical Palestine deepened this shift and reinforced the interim program to the point that it became the dominant discourse of the Palestinian leadership.

Conceptually, the root of the shift centers on how Palestinians define what they are struggling for or against; this definition informs Palestinian discourses, strategies, and actions. The main question since 1974 has been whether to focus on liberating Palestinian lands occupied in 1967 or on all of historic Palestine, including those lands colonized in 1948. This question manifests in how Palestinians in the 1948 areas are imagined by the Palestinian leadership—are they an organic part of the Palestinian people or a distant kin with whom alliances around short-term goals can be built? If the setting up of a state on parts of the West Bank, Gaza, and East Jerusalem while accepting the existence of Israel as a legitimate Jewish state is the end goal, then Palestinians in the 1948 areas would qualify more as allies, provided that they accept such a diminished role in Palestinian liberation or the perception that they do not belong to Palestinianness.

Aside from the central definition of what Israel constitutes and how its creation has impacted the indigenous Palestinian population, the framework of settler colonialism/anticolonial resistance allows for the inclusion of all Palestinians in the liberation movement, whether they reside in the West Bank and Gaza, in 1948 areas, or in the refugee camps in surrounding Arab countries and throughout the Palestinian diaspora. Here the experience of Palestinian Nazarene journalist Abir Kopty is instructive. In an interview,[15] Kopty discussed a meeting she attended in Ramallah, during which presumably one of the West Bank participants suggested that Palestinians tell Israel, "Don't build in the [West Bank] settlements; build inside." For Kopty, however, inside meant the areas where 1948 Palestinians live: "For us, the whole land is colonized, not only the West Bank."

A PALESTINIAN STRATEGY OF RESISTANCE

A Palestinian strategy for resistance was devised following the takeover of the PLO by Palestinian militant groups in the late 1960s.[16] This strategy has not been fully implemented, or more accurately, it has not been allowed to see the light of day primarily because of the adverse impact of petrodollars on the Palestinian movement that (1) influenced parts of it, especially the largest faction, Fatah, toward adopting a stand of neutrality vis-à-vis Arab oppositional and liberation movements and the regimes that crushed them and (2) qualitatively eclipsed the revolutionary spirit of anticolonial resistance among recipients of petrodollars, including leftist factions,[17] whose silence at times regarding the brutality of the regimes with which they were allied was deafening.

Obviously the old strategy, including armed struggle, cannot be easily replicated, nor was it perfect. Armed struggle was never and could not be the only strategy to liberate Palestine or any other colonized people. Resistance to settler colonialism, legitimized by the UN Charter, is often the only course of action (or the weapons of the weak, to borrow from James Scott) available for the powerless, who do not have unlimited options or the luxury of choice at their disposal; the terms of battle are usually imposed upon the colonized by their colonizers.[18]

Today, Palestinians are engaged in different anticolonial resistance strategies. They include the most basic but also one of the most powerful statements of resistance—and that is to simply stay put and refuse to leave one's land, one's home, or one's tent, such as the Sheikh Jarrah community struggle demonstrates.[19] *Staying put* has transformed each Israeli step aimed at erasing Palestinian rootedness into a costly venture in material and immaterial terms, including the rising cost in public relations—a most valuable commodity for Israel.[20] Thus Palestinians have combined an eclectic mix of strategies of resistance rather than presenting them in either/or dichotomous terms—a major contributing factor to the victory of the people's struggle against apartheid South Africa after whom the Palestinian Boycott, Divestment, and Sanctions (BDS) movement has modeled itself.[21]

The 2005 Palestinian civil society call to the international community to adopt BDS has been a major strategy of resistance.[22] This call has rallied thousands of people around the world to isolate Israel and hold it accountable for its brutalities and violations of Palestinian rights. However, BDS has often been misrepresented as a condemnation of Palestinian armed resistance or disavowal of those who sacrificed their lives in the struggle. Increasingly, however, Palestinians began to overtly and deliberately avoid ranking methods of resistance or modes of disengagement from Israel's colonial rule, especially in the aftermath of the 2014 Israeli assault on Gaza and the refusal of Gazans to distance themselves from the Palestinian resistance—another goal of the Israeli 2014 war.

As a powerful vehicle for isolating Israel, the BDS campaign has been until 2014 more of a strategy for the international community to express its solidarity with the Palestinian people and its opposition to Israeli practices than a strategy for Palestinians to resist Israel. While the Boycott National Committee (BNC) has not (rightly so) proposed itself as an alternative leadership for the Palestinians,[23] the PA's limited boycott of settlement products[24] has pushed the BNC as a body and the civil society forces it represents to come together to devise an effective and long-term BDS strategy around which Palestinians could mobilize. The PA's boycott was "symbolic" and "not punitive,"[25] calling for a temporary and voluntary boycott with an expiration date that is determined, not by an end to Israeli colonial rule or the occupation of the West Bank, but by the Israeli release of Palestinian tax revenues, withheld by Israel as a punishment for the 2012 statehood bid in 2012 and for joining the ICC in 2015. The PA call for settlement-only boycott basically attempted to hijack the initiative of the colonized, in this case Palestinian civil society, and hand it over to colonizers, the Israeli state, while maintaining the status quo of Palestinian economic dependency. Hamas also showed signs of the trappings of the Oslo framework. In what sounded like a marketing strategy to lure Israel to loosen its siege of Gaza, Hamas spokesman Taher al-Nounou said in 2012 that "Israel is aware now that it will lose a lot financially if it doesn't sell its goods to the consumers in Gaza."[26] Apparently oblivious of the imperative of boycotting Israel, al-Nounou's words were reflective more of a neoliberal business-as-usual economic model than of a group that opposes Israeli settler colonialism.

The PA continued to refuse to embrace the comprehensive BDS campaign and has insisted instead on limiting its boycott to goods made in West Bank settlements. During his visit to South Africa for the funeral of Nelson Mandela in 2013, Palestinian president Mahmoud Abbas reiterated his opposition to a total boycott of Israel and insisted on the limited boycott. The impact of such a policy is evident in the position adopted by allies such as South African president Jacob Zuma, who told the 2014 conference of the African National Congress Youth League that South Africa did not have to abide by the full BDS campaign because the Palestinian president told him that the boycott was limited to settlement goods.[27] Furthermore, the PA has continued to receive international guests who have violated and opposed BDS, especially the campaign for the Academic and Cultural Boycott of Israel (ACBI). For example, the PA hosted presidents of U.S. universities and other prominent figures primarily from the United States who visited Israel on Zionist-sponsored delegations or who signed statements against academic associations and individuals who adopted ACBI.[28]

By contrast, the Palestinian Campaign for Academic and Cultural Boycott of Israel (PACBI) has refused to meet with those who cross the intellectual picket line, refusing to provide them with a cover that absolves them of their complicity in the Israeli occupation, such as the Native American feminist poet Joy Harjo. Harjo had rejected repeated appeals from fellow indigenous scholars, such as J. Kēhaulani Kauanui and Robert Warrior,[29] urging her to cancel her appearance and decline a residency at Tel Aviv University. Palestinian BDS activists have also escalated their pressure on the PA to stop meeting with delegations hosted by Israeli institutions or sponsored by world Zionist organizations, such as the Jewish Community Relations Council (JCRC).[30]

In short, Palestinians began to formally[31] develop a boycott strategy at the core of which is a consistent praxis of "no business as usual" with colonialism rather than a strategy that is subjected to Israel's short- and long-term political agenda. This includes an end to joint Palestinian–Israeli business ventures, a refusal to launder Israeli money through the Palestinian economy, and the substitution of Israeli partnerships with Arab and international economic and industrial interests. To actualize such a campaign, the BNC dedicated its 2013 conference to discussing, devising, and coordinating the Palestinian boycott inside the West Bank, Gaza, and the 1948 areas and in the Arab world as well as to linking Palestinian and Arab campaigns with those of international forces that have been leading boycott campaigns throughout the world.[32]

The Indivisibility of Justice: A Strategy of Liberation

My discussion has focused thus far on a Palestinian strategy of resistance that, although related, is not identical to a strategy of liberation. A major debate in the Palestinian movement has centered on whether Palestinian energies should focus on justice for/in Palestine or on liberating Palestinian lands and attaining sovereignty, irrespective of whether such a goal entails constructing a more just and equitable society. Thus the question emerges of what justice for/in Palestine would look like. Historically, the Palestinian liberation movement was split down the middle regarding the question of its priorities. Some argued that the liberation of the land of Palestine should be the top priority and that all other struggles against structural inequalities (based on class, race, gender, sexuality, age, ability, etc.) should be addressed secondary to liberation; others, among whom I count myself, continue to insist that the liberation of people and land is inseparable. The idea here, which crystalized in the articulation of the Palestinian militant Left after 1967, is not to advocate a liberal agenda or propose an opportunistic sense of, for example, incorporating women and other marginalized groups because half of the society should not be left idle; this formulation implies that if women (or persons belonging to any other marginalized group) are not visibly involved in conventional political forms, then they are not involved in the anticolonial resistance. Nor is the idea that women should be visible to satisfy some Orientalist or colonial feminist notion and present Palestinians as "modern" and fit to belong to "civilized" societies.[33] I am arguing, rather, that if Palestine is about justice, then Palestinians can't demand justice for themselves and disregard it when it becomes inconvenient. Consistency is a necessary ingredient in Palestinian discourses and actions. What does the indivisibility of justice in/for Palestine look like, then?

Debates abound in the Palestinian political community regarding the meaning and intentions of the Palestinian National Charter.[34] The original charter called for a "secular democratic state in Palestine" and defined the Palestinian as one whose father (or mother[35]) is a Palestinian.[36] The main question that comes up in this context centers around what the content of this Palestinianness is today, what a secular democratic state in Palestine entails, and what place Jews will have in a future Palestinian political space.

To address these questions, I return to Palestinian history and the ways in which the Palestinian movement of the 1960s and 1970s attracted most of my generation. First, this movement was imagined by Palestinians and allies alike as a revolution against all forms of oppression, one that did not prioritize the liberation of land over liberation of the people, nor did it present Palestine as exceptional, more oppressed, or more deserving of freedom and justice than other movements or people. The imagined Palestinian community (to borrow Anderson's concept[37]) at the time was an inclusionary movement based on an indivisible sense of justice for all humanity. Moreover, as I've argued elsewhere,[38] Palestinians, especially under Israeli rule, have practiced (and still do) what Ernest Renan calls "a daily plebiscite,"[39] or referendum, on the extent of their allegiance to the liberation movement, the PLO, despite harsh Israeli retaliation. It is this vision of Palestinian anticolonial liberation as a prime example of the praxis of the indivisibility of justice that the Palestinian movement needs to reclaim today.

Second, the indivisibility of justice calls for struggling for a society that provides for its own members, in terms of shelter, food, education, health care, and other social needs—a society that does not tolerate the fact that a substantial percentage of families live on less than $2 per day,[40] while others, with ties to the PA,[41] receive a monthly income in the tens of thousands of dollars. This implies resisting neoliberal policies while holding the

PA as well as the huge network of nongovernmental organizations accountable and transparent. As well, arriving at a more equitable tax system that taxes the wealthiest in the Palestinian society and allocates those funds to alleviate the hardship of the majority of the population, including working families and Palestinians living under the poverty line, is a must.

Third, an indivisible sense of justice entails combating ethnocentrism that presents Palestine as an exceptional case of suffering and liberation. The notion of exceptionalism and uniqueness needs to be erased from the discourses of Palestinian leaders, and Palestinians must acknowledge that theirs is not the only people, nor are they the last, to experience occupation. More recent occupations include the U.S. occupation of Afghanistan, the Indian occupation of Kashmir, and Guantánamo Bay in Cuba. Palestine is also not the only site of settler colonialism. The Americas, New Zealand, and Australia are but some examples. There are also other, more recognizable colonized "territories," such as Hawai'i, Puerto Rico, and Guam.

Fourth, the indivisibility of justice demands as well that Palestinians engage in serious internal debates over the need to open up or broaden the public space for a multiplicity of views and ideologies, not in neoliberal multiculturalism but in a real, material sense—a challenge because of the interests and relations in which people are either embedded or implicated even for those who are officially positioned outside the Oslo structure that permeates every aspect of Palestinian life under (and outside) Israeli colonial rule.

As far as the "secular democratic state" is concerned, two issues are crucial in my view. First, when the slogan was initially adopted, the term *secular* did not share the same heritage as with what I call today's secular fundamentalists inside and outside Palestine would like to claim, that is, tracing the genealogy of the term back to the European Enlightenment, with all the trappings of Orientalism[42] and Islamophobia[43] that accompanied the European (and settler) colonial projects. Rather, the future state of a liberated Palestine was envisioned as a place for all Palestinians, including Muslims, Christians, and Jews[44]—an inclusionary alternative to the exclusionary framing and practices of Zionism. In other words, the secular democratic state was intentionally devised as an antidote to Zionism's racism. A major challenge has been to broaden the imagined Palestinian space so that it becomes more hospitable to all religious and spiritual diversities, including those with materialist nonreligious belief systems.

In fact, the Palestinian articulation of creating a secular democratic state in all of historic Palestine goes beyond the notion of liberal equality, a Western/U.S. model of governance that only focuses on elections; rather, the Palestinian consensus incorporates both participatory democracy and proportional representation so that governance is inclusive and broad based.

Rather than being a political slogan for public relations consumption, the PLO's call for the creation of a secular democratic state meant that the Palestinian movement practiced what it preached, while it always had a small number of Jewish members who were not originally Palestinians. The question, then, was not whether but how large a number of Israeli Jews can become involved in and see the Palestinian liberation movement as their own.

At this point, anti-Zionist Jewish Israeli citizens who do not identify with Israel and its Zionism and racist settler colonial project, such as Uri Davis,[45] see themselves (and have been historically seen by a majority of Palestinians) as potential citizens of a future Palestinian state in the similar manner as white South Africans like Joe Slovo or Ronnie Kasrils saw their destiny connected to that of Nelson Mandela, the African National Congress, and the majority of Africans. Back in the mid-1980s, Uri raised this question to me: "I was born in 1943 but my sister was born after 1948. Would this mean that I get to stay but she has to leave?"[46] The question arises out of statements attributed to Ahmed Shukairy, the first chair of the PLO,[47] who was falsely quoted as saying that "we will throw them into the sea," referring to the Zionist Jews who colonized Palestine. The statements, however, were clarified many years later and shown not to have been said by Shukairy but to have been magnified in Israeli and Zionist discourses to defame the Palestinian anticolonial struggle and label it as anti-Semitic.[48]

To return to the question Uri Davis raised, there are a few points worth noting here. First, since the late 1960s takeover of the PLO by militant groups, Palestinians have repeatedly said that Palestine belongs to all those who live there, including Jews who were descendants of Zionist colonizers who forcefully settled on Palestinian land and expelled its indigenous population. Second, historically speaking, 1948, the year Israel declared statehood, should not be defined as the demarcation date that determines which Jews can stay and which ones should leave, assuming we are operating under the erroneous notion that Palestinians wanted to expel Zionist settlers from Palestine. Historical records indicate that Zionist immigration to Palestine had begun earlier in the century.[49]

Finally, the relationship between the liberation of Palestine and Arab liberation has been much debated throughout Palestinian history as well. This question became more critical when the Jordanian monarchy, aided by the United States and Israel, launched a war of extermination against the Palestinian movement and its allies in the Jordanian democratic, anti-colonial, and national movement in 1970,[50] leading to the forced relocation of Palestinian militants to Lebanon. The Palestinian–Arab tensions escalated when then Lebanese right-wing forces, also supported by the United States and Israel, waged a bloody attack against the Lebanese anticolonial nationalist movement and the Palestinian resistance fighters. The Israeli invasion of Lebanon in 1982 cemented the impact of the Lebanese civil war and resulted in the evacuation of PLO fighters from Lebanon and their dispersal to several Arab countries (Tunisia, Yemen, Sudan, Algeria, Libya, and Syria). The Palestinian leader George Habash, founder of the Arab National Movement in 1952 and later the Popular Front for the Liberation of Palestine (PFLP) in 1967, was the first to argue that the path to the liberation of Palestine must go through (liberated) Arab capitals.[51] Habash's argument was supported by Palestinian militant leftists across the spectrum, ranging from the Democratic Front for the Liberation of Palestine (DFLP), Saiqa, and the Arab Liberation Front[52] to radical intellectuals within the largest Palestinian group, Fatah. Having coined this concept, the PFLP greatly underplayed it later on, especially at the height of the Palestinian "nationalist" phase during the 1987 Intifada. Today, and in view of the 2011 wave of Arab uprisings and the counterrevolutionary attacks seen in Egypt and led by Saudi Arabia, and combined with the central place Palestine continues to occupy in the hearts and minds of Arabs[53] at the grassroots level as well as on the platforms of the Arab groups with the most radical vision for social transformation, the question is not only relevant; it is timely and necessary. What's the basis for Palestinian relations with the leadership and grass roots of Arab revolutionary forces? Arab oppositional movements should not be seen as affinity groups or mere optional or tactical allies; rather, they must be supported on the basis of the indivisibility of justice, and their victories must be viewed as Palestinian victories.

Conclusion

Grounded in the most recent Palestinian historical and political context, this chapter has discussed the development as well as the factors contributing to the rise, weaknesses, and challenges facing the Palestinian movement for self-determination. In so doing, I have argued for the need to frame a Palestinian anticolonial discourse and discussed the mechanisms necessary for a Palestinian strategy of resistance and liberation as well as the sort of alliances and relations the Palestinian anticolonial liberation movement must build with regional and international forces.

I have argued against the either/or dichotomous construction of the Palestinian call for BDS that is propagated by liberal supporters of Palestine. These supporters, situated mostly (but not exclusively) in the Global North, suggest that BDS is far superior to other forms of Palestinian resistance, thus dismissing the sacrifices thousands of Palestinians made prior to the 2005 BDS call. By contrast, I discussed a mix of Palestinian strategies of resistance against Israeli settler colonialism.

I have suggested the indivisibility of justice as a comprehensive framework for conceptualizing Palestinian anticolonial resistance and liberation. I've offered several ingredients that I find necessary for such a vision, including broadening the public space for a multiplicity of views and ideologies, the need to combat the neoliberal model of state building, and combating ethnocentrism that presents Palestine as an exceptional case of suffering and liberation or that prioritizes one struggle against structural inequalities over another.

I have also argued that the objective of creating a "secular and democratic" state in all of historic Palestine was intended as an antidote to the exclusivity of Zionism rather than as adherence to secular fundamentalism. Thus the vision of a liberated Palestine also entails the broadening of support for this emancipatory perspective for Israeli Jews who refuse to associate themselves with Zionism and the Israeli settler colonial project.

Notes

An earlier version of this chapter was presented at the second annual conference of Masarat: The Palestinian Center for Political and Strategic Studies, Ramallah, Palestine, January 17–18, 2013. The author wishes to thank Jaime Veve, Mira Nabulsi, and Heather Porter Abu Deiab for their valuable feedback on the most recent version of the chapter and Ghassan al-Khatib, Khalil Shaheen, and Hani Masri for comments on an earlier draft.

1. United Nations General Assembly, "General Assembly Votes Overwhelmingly to Accord Palestine 'Non-member Observer State' Status in United Nations," GA/11317, November 29, 2012, http://www.un.org/press/en/2012/ga11317.doc.htm.

2. United Nations General Assembly and Security Council, "Question of Palestine: Declaration of Independence," A/43/827 and S/20278, November 18, 1988, https://unispal.un.org/DPA/DPR/unispal.nsf/0/6EB54A389E2DA6C6852560D E0070E392.

3. The 1987 intifada has been canonically referred to as the First Intifada. I find this a very problematic term that implies that before 1987, Palestinians had never risen up against Israeli colonialism and violence.

4. United Nations General Assembly, "Communique of the Non-Aligned Committee of Nine on Palestine," A/43/950, December 14, 1988, https://unispal.un.org/DPA/DPR/unispal.nsf/0/961AB72B5F17E2C9852568B0006EC58F.

5. United Nations General Assembly, "Observer Status of National Liberation Movements Recognized by the Organization of African Unity and/or by the League of Arab States," A/RES/43/160, December 9, 1988, http://www.un.org/documents/ga/res/43/a43r160.htm.

6. United Nations General Assembly and Security Council, letter dated March 30, 1988, from the Permanent Representative of Jordan to the United Nations addressed to the Secretary-General, A/43/273 and S/19720, https://unispal.un.org/DPA/DPR/unispal.nsf/0/88A4A640A08DC75785256B6C006FED67.

7. Non-Aligned Movement, "Report of the Outgoing Chair on the Activities of the Non-Aligned Movement during Its Full Term as Chair, September 1998–February 2003," February 28, 2003, https://unispal.un.org/DPA/DPR/unispal.nsf/0/0D8998B28B10F7A185256DB2004DC88F.

8. International Criminal Court, "Palestine Declares Acceptance of ICC Jurisdiction since 13 June 2014," January 5, 2005, https://www.icc-cpi.int//Pages/item.aspx?name=pr1080, and International Criminal Court, "The State of Palestine Accedes to the Rome Statute," January 7, 2015, https://www.icc-cpi.int//Pages/item.aspx?name=pr1082_2.

9. Ali Abunimah, "There's Nothing New in Mahmoud Abbas' and the PLO's Renunciation of Palestinian Refugee Rights," *Electronic Intifada,* November 4, 2012, https://electronicintifada.net/blogs/ali-abunimah/theres-nothing-new-mahmoud-abbas-and-plos-renunciation-palestinian-refugee-rights.

10. Ibid. For the full interview, see http://www.presstv.com/detail/2012/11/04/270325/mahmoud-abbas-interview-with-israels-channel-2-provokes-controversy/.

11. At one point, the figure of one hundred thousand refugees was mentioned by Mohammed Rashid, at the time the financial advisor to the late Palestinian chairman, Yasser Arafat.

12. Palestinian Liberation Organization Statements, June 8, 1974, http://www.icjs.org/sites/default/files/%27%27Palestinian%20Liberation%20Organization%20Statements%27%27%20June%208,%201974.pdf.

13. D. Hirst, *The Gun and the Olive Branch: The Roots of Violence in the Middle East,* 3rd ed. (New York: Thunder's Mouth Press, 2003).

14. Edward W. Said, "Palestinians in the Aftermath of Beirut," *Journal of Palestine Studies* 12, no. 2 (1983): 3–9.

15. "Palestine under the Scope—On This Land," *Al Jazeera,* December 21, 2012, https://www.youtube.com/watch?v=3SaToGK8oJo.

16. H. Baumgarten, "The Three Faces/Phases of Palestinian Nationalism, 1948–2005," *Journal of Palestine Studies* 34, no. 4 (2005): 25–48.

17. Palestinian Left factions, such as the PFLP and the DFLP, also received petrodollars from Algeria and Libya. While also impacting the internal dynamics of the groups by strengthening the positions of the factions and individuals receiving the funds, Libyan and Algerian petrodollars did not have the same detrimental impact as Fateh both because the size of funds and groups were smaller and as a result of the balance of regional powers in which the United States, and thus its allies, dominated the region.

18. J. C. Scott, *Weapons of the Weak: Everyday Forms of Peasant Resistance* (Delhi: Oxford University Press, 1990).

19. J. Barker, dir., *We Will Stay Here: The al-Kurds of Sheikh Jarrah*, March 28, 2016, https://vimeo.com/160679644.

20. Reut Institute, "Building a Political Firewall against Israel's Delegitimization Conceptual Framework," March 2010, http://reut-institute.org/data/uploads/PDF Ver/20100310%20Delegitimacy%20Eng.pdf.

21. Palestinian Civil Society, "Palestinian Civil Society Call for BDS," July 9, 2005, https://bdsmovement.net/call.

22. Palestinian BDS National Committee, "Impact," https://bdsmovement.net/impact.

23. The BNC leadership does not seek to act as an alternative leadership either, as Omar Barghouti of the BNC confirmed to Noura Erakat in "Beyond Sterile Negotiations," February 1, 2012, http://www.Al-Shabaka.org/. Retrieved from https://al-shabaka.org/briefs/beyond-sterile-negotiations-looking-leadership-strategy/.

24. Isabel Kershner, "Palestinian Premier Calls for Boycott of Israeli Goods," *New York Times*, December 20, 2012, http://www.nytimes.com/2012/12/21/world/middleeast/palestinian-premier-fayyad-calls-for-boycott-on-israeli-goods.html.

25. Ibid.

26. Isabel Kershner, "Israel, in Shift, Lets Building Materials into Gaza," *New York Times*, December 31, 2012.

27. Embassy of the State of Palestine to South Africa and BDS South Africa, "Joint Media Statement: Embassy of the State of Palestine to South Africa and BDS South Africa," December 20, 2013, https://bdsmovement.net/news/joint-media-statement-embassy-state-palestine-south-africa-and-bds-south-africa.

28. Native American and Indigenous Studies Association (NAISA), Association for Asian American Studies, National Association of Chicana and Chicano Studies, the American Studies Association, the Peace and Justice Studies Association, the American Historical Association, and United Auto Workers Local 2865, which represents thirteen thousand graduate teaching assistants in all University of California campuses.

29. The campaign was led by indigenous scholars in NAISA and USACBI, the U.S. Campaign for Academic and Cultural Boycott of Israel. For more on this campaign, see PACBI's open letter to Harjo, http://www.pacbi.org/etemplate.php?id=2072; Ali Abunimah's writing on Robert Warrior's and J. Kēhaulani Kauanui's call to Harjo to cancel her event, http://electronicintifada.net/blogs/ali-abunimah/acclaimed-feminist-author-musician-joy-harjo-lands-tel-aviv-find-boycott-calls; and USACBI's petition to Harjo, https://www.change.org/p/joy-harjo-cancel-your-show-don-t-perform-for-israeli-apartheid?utm_campaign=autopublish&utm_medium=facebook&utm_source=share_petition&utm_term=17340401. Also see the USACBI's official website, http://www.usacbi.org/.

30. As an apologist for Israel, JCRC has been notorious for its campaigns to shut down and attempt to silence any criticism of Israel, including its relentless attack on the Arab and Muslim Ethnicities and Diasporas Studies Program at San Francisco State University and the author of this chapter, as well as its successful campaign to stop the *Gaza Children* exhibition at the Oakland Children's Museum.

31. Palestinians had been engaged in boycotting the colonial structures much earlier than the official 2005 civil society call for BDS. Such boycotts are documented

in the resistance to British colonial rule, including the great 1936–39 revolt. I've personally grown up with the idea of boycott of Israel as the normal state of affairs. This was the everyday practice under occupation. Although they cannot survive without patronizing Israeli goods, services, and state institutions, '48 Palestinians have resorted to shopping for groceries and medicine and even to filling up their cars at West Bank Palestinian businesses to reduce their engagement with the state.

32. Palestinian BDS National Committee, "Report on the Fourth National BDS Conference, 8 June 2013, Bethlehem," June 18, 2013, https://bdsmovement.net/news/report-fourth-national-bds-conference-8-june-2013-bethlehem.

33. Edward Said, *Orientalism* (New York: Pantheon Books, 1978).

34. My intention here is not to advocate depleting the charter from its historical content and the sense of unwavering anticolonial posture, as the post–Oslo charter did not, to alter the definition of who will live in these lands and what sort of a state Palestine will be.

35. In 1965, this was only applicable to the General Union of Palestinian Women. However, the Palestinian Legislative Council voted that both parents can give their children Palestinian citizenship.

36. Palestinian National Council, Palestinian Charter, August 1968, http://www.pac-usa.org/the_palestinian_charter.htm.

37. Benedict Anderson, *Imagined Communities: Reflections on the Origin and Spread of Nationalism* (New York: Verso, 1983).

38. R. Abdulhadi, "Palestinianness in Comparative Perspective: Inclusionary Resistance, Exclusionary Citizenship," PhD diss., Yale University, 2000.

39. Ernest Renan, 1882, reprinted in *Becoming National: A Reader,* edited by G. Eley and R. G. Suny (Oxford: Oxford University Press, 1996).

40. World Bank, "Four Years—Intifada, Closures and Palestinian Economic Crisis: An Assessment," October 2004, http://siteresources.worldbank.org/INTWEST BANKGAZA/Resources/wbgaza-4yrassessment.pdf.

41. "Corruption in the Palestinian Authority," *Middle East Monitor,* December 2013, https://www.aman-palestine.org/data/itemfiles/b2a7e241322895ba53fdd642 5a55c40a.pdf.

42. Said, *Orientalism.*

43. R. Grosfoguel and E. Meilants, "The Long-Duree Entanglement between Islamophobia and Racism in the Modern/Colonial Capitalist/Patriarchal World System: An Introduction," *Human Architecture: Journal of the Sociology of Self-Knowledge* 1 (2006): 1–12; J. Rana, "The Story of Islamophobia," *Souls* 9 (2007): 148–61; and W. Mignolo, "Islamophobia/Hispanophobia: The (Re) Configuration of the Racial Imperial/Colonial Matrix," *Human Architecture: Journal of the Sociology of Self-Knowledge* 5, no. 1 (2006): 13–28.

44. This call is inclusive of the three monotheistic religions, but it excludes by omission other, nonmonotheistic religiosities, such as Buddhists, Hindus, Sikhs, Baha'is, Zoroastrians, Yazidis, and Wiccans, as well as agnostics and atheists. This is interesting, because the framework of the charter includes Palestinian Marxists, who were not particularly religious.

45. Uri Davis, a longtime anti-Zionist Jew who denounced his Israeli citizenship, was elected at the 2009 conference of Fatah in Bethlehem as a member of its Revolutionary Council.

46. Uri was specifically referring to Palestinian demand that preceded the 1968 Palestinian Charter that Israeli Jews who had settled after the foundation of Israel in 1948 leave upon the liberation of Palestine. Since 1968, Palestinian militant groups have called for Palestine to be a country of its people, but this position, which has been reaffirmed on numerous occasions, has been ignored and invisibilized by imperialist and Zionist discourses, especially by those who are committed to Israel as a settler colonial project and an exclusivist Jewish state.

47. The PLO was formed by a decision of the League of Arab States, which sought to address the question of Palestine in a way that preserved their regimes and responded to the demands of the Palestinians and other Arabs at the grassroots level who were united around the goal of liberating Palestine.

48. Moshe Shemesh, "Did Shuqayri Call for 'Throwing the Jews into the Sea'?," *Israel Studies* 8, no. 2 (2003): 70–81.

49. Jewish Virtual Library, "Immigration to Israel: Jewish Immigration to Palestine (1919–1941)," http://www.jewishvirtuallibrary.org/jewish-immigrantion-to-palestine-1919-1941.

50. Jimmy Emerman, Linda John, Penny Johnson, and Paul Rupert, *Our Roots Are Still Alive: The Story of the Palestinian People* (New York: Institute for Independent Social Journalism, 1997).

51. "George Habash: A Profile from the Archives," *Jadaliyya,* September 27, 2012, http://www.jadaliyya.com/pages/index/7547/george-habash_a-profile-from-the-archives, and As'ad AbuKhalil, "George Habash's Contribution to the Palestinian Struggle," *Electronic Intifada,* January 30, 2008, https://electronicintifada.net/content/george-habashs-contribution-palestinian-struggle/7332.

52. Saiqa and the Arab Liberation Front were respectively closely allied with the Syrian and the Iraqi Baathist regimes.

53. Support for the Palestinian struggle is not limited to the Arab world. The centrality of Palestine and the support for the Palestinian struggle for self-determination are also widespread throughout Muslim communities and indeed among the majority of humanity.

5

"From Here to Our Homelands"

An Interview with Lara Kiswani on Radical Organizing and Internationalism in the Post-9/11 Era

SOHAIL DAULATZAI

SOHAIL DAULATZAI (SD): From my understanding, AROC emerged in 2007 out of the ADC-SF. Can you talk about the political context and necessity for the formation of AROC at that particular time?

LARA KISWANI (LK): In the years after September 11, 2001, we saw a wave of ICE raids in San Francisco and increased targeting of Arabs and Muslims by the FBI. A group of thirteen local immigrant rights organizations came together to form the first legal and education collaborative in San Francisco. We recognized a need for legal defense of our communities, and a need for that service to be provided by those from the community, and to be provided for free. In addition, we wanted to bridge that with organizing and education, recognizing that the community needed to be aware of what services were available, what their options were, and how they can fight back. At that point, we decided to shift from ADC-SF, primarily an advocacy organization, to AROC, providing direct legal service bridged with advocacy and organizing so that our community could fight back against the conditions that caused them to need the services in the first place.

SD: Can you talk about how you got involved in AROC, and what kind of political commitments drove you?

LK: As a student organizer, I was a board member and intern with ADC-SF and Sacramento. So I have a history with the organization and the movement work it was a part of. As a Palestinian growing up in the Bay Area, I learned at a young age that in order to assert my dignity, I had to confront power. AROC provides a space for our community to cultivate that type of resistance and find a space to feel connected to our community, and ourselves, without comprising who we are. The role that AROC plays in connecting and organizing around local struggles of Arabs and other Black and Brown communities and international struggles speaks to my own commitment as an internationalist, and to all those who see themselves as forcibly replaced from their homelands, to fight for liberation while living in a country that is responsible for much of the devastation globally. AROC is a vehicle to both understand those connections and to organize to change the oppressive conditions we all share.

SD: Despite the media attention given to the NYPD [New York Police Department] surveillance program, the West Coast has been the laboratory for these kinds of policing strategies, including the Muslim Mapping Program in Los Angeles in 2007 that then Chief William Bratton sought to enforce and, around the same time, the FBI surveillance of Muslim communities in the Bay Area. How have programs such as NSEERS, CVE, and FBI surveillance programs impacted the work that AROC undertakes? What kinds of strategies have you employed to challenge these policies and approaches?

LK: Surveillance and repression are common experiences in our community. Many of us in AROC recall the case of the LA 8 and the ways in which it was used to shape many of the current counterterrorism laws and policies. Arabs, Muslims, and Palestinian activists in particular face heightened repression. Given that we are unapologetically antiracist and anti-Zionist, many of our leaders are often at the receiving end of the attacks by surveillance programs. For these reasons, we see the fight against repression as one that is central to our work and integrate it as a core element in our day-to-day organizing. We were one of the main organizations in the Bay Area Committee to Stop Political Repression, where we helped develop resources and materials to help organizers and activists equip themselves with tools to defend against state repression.

We know that being Arab or Muslim while being outspoken and active in support of Palestine comes at the risk of being targeted by law enforcement, campus administration, and Zionist institutions. These repressive attacks are interwoven with the United States' War on Terror, so repression, surveillance, and the targeting of our communities are daily realities that we are compelled to grapple with.

SD: How has Palestine and BDS [Boycott, Divestment, and Sanctions] figured into the work you all have done?

LK: As an antiracist organization committed to the liberation of Arab people, we are inherently anti-Zionist. We completely reject the colonial state of Israel and its partnership with the U.S. government. We understand that

Israel plays an instrumental role in U.S. imperialism and understand our fight against apartheid Israel as a contribution to the global fight against imperialism everywhere. So just as we are committed to denormalizing racism, we are also committed to denormalizing Zionism, which is how we understand our BDS work. This plays into every aspect of our organizing, whether or not we intend it to. For instance, when we successfully led a campaign to have Arabic taught in SF Unified School District, we were attacked by the pro-Israeli interest group the Jewish Community Relations Council. The JCRC, with a history of targeting people of color–led organizations that support the liberation of Palestine, attempted to stop the Arabic language pathways from moving forward, smeared AROC in the media, and attempted to pressure the Board of Education not to allow us to continue our (voluntary) programming in public schools. This was not simply because we are an Arab organization. This was an attack on us because we are explicitly anti-Zionist. This happened following of some of our most successful BDS work. The success of our efforts and demonstration of our organizing power leading Block the Boat shocked many, including JCRC, who themselves tried to pressure police to crack down on us.

So we understand our work is impactful and threatens those in power. We also understand that our work on Palestine makes us especially vulnerable to targeted attacks. But that makes it that much more important not to sway on our position against racism, white supremacy, and Zionism and to continue building with our partners and allies to do the same. We have been successful in isolating Israel in the Bay Area, because we work in coalitions and across movements, all of whom are committed to antiracism. As a result, JCRC was not successful in stopping the Arabic language pathways. And despite the repression we face, AROC remains committed to exposing Zionism and racism everywhere. The repression we face only makes it clearer to us why it is that much more important to fight back against attempts to silence and criminalize Arabs.

SD: How does AROC organize around U.S. militarism and support of dictatorships in the Arab world? And in this vein, can you talk about the Arab Spring and the impact that this has had on your organizing? Has it been divisive, or unifying, or both?

LK: AROC's vision is centered on the dignity and self-determination of Arabs from here to our homelands, understanding that our liberation is inextricably tied to the liberation of all oppressed people. In that light, we understand all our struggles here in the United States in relation to our struggles in our homelands, which more often than not are experiences of war, militarism, and occupation. Even when we provide our legal services, we do so understanding that as part of our community self-defense work and as part of our work against forced migration and displacement. This can look a lot of ways in terms of organizing.

One more obvious example is the Block the Boat campaign. With the Israeli war on Gaza in 2014, many of us in the United States struggled with ways to respond. We held numerous protests and then began incorporating direct action in order to disrupt business as usual. Soon after, we decided to take it a step further and build on some of the relationships our community had built with the ILWU Local 10 over the years. We decided to target the largest Israeli shipping line, ZIM, and work with the rank and file of ILWU Local 10 and request that they not cross a community picket and not unload the ship. This was not simply a direct action or protest. This took weeks and months of organizing on the ground with our community, allies, and workers and coordinating across North America and with Palestinian workers in Palestine. For four days, the workers refused to unload the ship. It left soon after. And the two times it came a month after, we formed another community picket, the workers respected our picket, and the ZIM ship hasn't docked at the Port of Oakland since. In this instance, we were able to organize a local campaign that directly impacted our conditions in the Arab world. We isolated Israel culturally, politically, and economically, forcing it to have millions of dollars in losses.

A different but fitting example is that of Stop Urban Shield. Generally, this is a campaign against militarism. For us, this is also a campaign against global repression and Zionism, particularly given the role of agencies from repressive governments around the world such as Bahrain, along with Israel in particular. Our coalition, made up of over twenty-four organizations, is committed to ending Urban Shield, the largest weapons expo and SWAT training in the world, from happening in the Bay Area or anywhere. We are able to make connections with our Arab and Muslim community and organize them on this issue by exposing the collaborations between law enforcement. Arabs may or may not have a negative reaction to learning about police trainings, but they more often than not have a negative reaction when they hear about Israel or the FBI. Unpacking the relationships between various law enforcement agencies, and their impact locally, allows us to bring the cross-movement building we are committed to into our bases and broader community that otherwise wouldn't be moved by such a thing.

The political developments internationally naturally reflect locally. Whether it is the Arab Spring, sectarianism, war, economic devastation, or repression, our families and communities in the United States experience it, and it has a tremendous impact. When the Arab uprisings took place, we saw sectors of our community mobilize in ways we have never seen before. It brought people together across different ideologies, socioeconomic backgrounds. What resulted soon after, with the rise of the new dictatorship in Egypt and continued uprisings in Syria, definitely fragmented our communities. It was exceptionally demoralizing to see how things panned out in the coming months and years, and that impacted how people related to political work here in the United States. And Syria, in particular, became the most divisive of issues. The traditional Arab Left insisted that it was impossible to oppose imperialism and foreign intervention while opposing the brutality of the Asad regime. Many of those in support of the uprisings in Syria insisted we could not have valid critiques of the uprising while still opposing the dictatorship. Ultimately, we found ourselves being attacked by all sides simply for remaining committed to anti-imperialism and self-determination of the people of Syria. Syria proved to put to a test the sophistication of our movements and how we understand anti-imperialism in this day and age, how we understand people's movements and self-determination.

sd: How has the post-9/11 context—one of deep anti-Muslim racism—framed the work of AROC? Obviously there are significant numbers among your constituency that are not Muslim identified (whether they be Christians, atheists, etc.)—how does AROC organize around and through those kinds of differences?

lk: The post-9/11 context is why AROC evolved into a local grassroots organization. The criminalization of Arabs and Muslims required work intentionally focused on defending and organizing our local communities. The day-to-day violence against Muslims or those perceived to be Muslim, the targeting by law enforcement, the attacks on activists and our youth, moved us to examine how we can build up new grassroots leadership and use that power to make shifts in our local and regional conditions. We identify as an Arab and Muslim organization both because not all Arabs are Muslims and not all Muslims are Arabs and because there is a shared experience of racialization and criminalization that requires us to build together and fight back together. Our membership is extremely diverse, with Arabs and Muslims from across North Africa and West and South Asia, as well as members who are neither Arab nor Muslim but are people of color who are deeply connected to our movement work. We are committed to movement building, and that requires us to move beyond identity-based politics. And yet, as a grassroots Arab and Muslim organization, we are also committed to centralizing the leadership of those communities.

SD: AROC has been, and continues to be, involved in a range of campaigns, including arts and social justice workshops, QueeRoc, Urban Shield, Third World Resistance for Black Power, et cetera. Can you talk about these and why you see these as important?

LK: The diversity of campaigns and work that we take up is a reflection of our internationalist and anticapitalist politics. We cannot take up issues of racism without talking about policing and white supremacy; we cannot talk about marginalized communities without centering the leadership of those most marginalized in our own communities—LGBTQ, immigrants, youth, and the poor. We cannot talk about cross-movement building without building on the history of Third World solidarity and the tradition of internationalism that has brought us to the place that we are today. For many of us, it is impossible to disconnect our lived experience or racism and repression in the Bay Area from the history of colonialism and war in Palestine, Iraq, Yemen, or Syria. And we understand that history to be a result of Western imperialism and, as such, built on capitalism and white supremacy. For those reasons, we not only find it important to make those connections in all our work, we find it necessary to do so in order to be in integrity with our vision and mission. That is why we played a leading role in organizing Third World for Black Power and Stop Urban Shield.

SD: What are some of the challenges facing AROC with the emergence of Trump? How do you see his brand of racism impacting AROC and its strategies?

LK: The emergence of Trump has made our work that much more important. The main challenge we are facing is capacity. The need for grassroots organizing, legal services, and advocacy is more important and more in demand than ever. There is, of course, an unmasking of racism and state violence that lies at the foundation of this country. This unmasking of state violence has a direct impact on the daily lives of our members and community and, in that way, makes our work around community self-defense, movement defense, and security that much more important. Our strategies haven't shifted. Due to our political orientation, we have always faced attacks and repression and have intentionally engaged in security and community self-defense work. This puts us in a better position than some. We have also consistently worked against militarism and policing, and racism. So our campaign strategies will not shift. What have shifted for us are our priorities, our scale, and our pace. We are scaling up, we are often forced to move faster in order to be more responsive (as we did with the SFO shutdown), and we are prioritizing building up our internal leadership and organizational structure to be able to meet the needs for the long haul.

II

Decolonizing Geographies

6

Oppressed Majority

Violence and Muslim Communities in Multicultural Europe

Fatima El-Tayeb

Eléonore Pourriat's 2010 short film *Majorité opprimée (Oppressed Majority)* depicts a day in the life of Pierre, a white, middle-class stay-at-home dad who lives in a Paris in which gender roles are reversed.[1] From a female neighbor casually belittling him to catcalls and drunken insults from strange women, he goes through experiences that are part of the actual everyday life of European women. The situation escalates when he is attacked by a group of youths whose aggressive "advances" he had rejected, and it only gets worse afterward at the police station, where the female officer questions his account while ogling a young policeman. Even Pierre's wife, while initially sympathetic, loses patience with him and suggests that he should have dressed less provocatively. In 2012, after receiving positive but somewhat muted reactions to her piece, the filmmaker posted it on YouTube, raking in about twenty thousand views. The film went viral, however, after a version with English subtitles was published in February 2014, with more than ten million views within a year.[2]

Pourriat's feminist intervention provoked a debate on the effectiveness and accuracy of her topsy-turvy world approach, but with few exceptions, the discussion focused on issues of gender, isolating them from other factors shaping the narrative, albeit in less explicit ways.[3] Race, religion, and class clearly intersect in the representation of Pierre's two most explicit encounters with the misandry shaping his world. First, when dropping off his child at a day care center, he has a hushed conversation with the Muslim worker there, forced by his wife to cover his head with a balaclava (in addition to being clean shaven, making him look like a child, according to Pierre, who continues, "But you are a man!"). Pierre vainly tries to install a sense of independence in the nervous Nassir, and even though it turns out that Pierre's wife is not as enlightened as he thinks and he himself less sheltered from the effects of sexism, he clearly is nowhere as damaged as the dispossessed and infantilized Nassir. Later, when Pierre is attacked and sexually assaulted by a group of young women, the assailants are easily recognizable as working-class *beurs*, first-generation French of North African descent (or "second-generation migrants," to use the dominant European terminology).

The film uses easily recognizable tropes to achieve its effect; thus these portrayals, as well as the lack of critical discussion around them, indicate how much they reflect the most normalized image of European Muslims, an image that is centered on violence and sharply divided along gender lines: the oppressed, muted, and veiled Muslima is complemented by the hyperviolent, male, outer-city youth,[4] and both images combined contribute to a different notion of "oppressed majority," one that is arguably much more popular than Pourriat's version (though not entirely separable from it): that of the majority of liberal, civil, white, Christian Europeans oppressed by a rapidly expanding yet completely unassimilated Muslim minority.[5] Ironically, while the continent frequently defines itself around shared values of humanism, equality, and tolerance, there is an increasingly intolerant and repressive attitude toward migrants and racialized minorities—justified by their supposed threat to exactly these values, especially when they are identified as Muslim.[6] "Muslim culture" is constructed as not only fundamentally different from "European culture," leaving little to no common ground and erasing centuries of shared history,[7] but as forcing "Europe's evolution from a Judeo-Christian civilization, with important post-Enlightenment secular elements, into a post-Judeo-Christian civilization that is subservient to the ideology of jihad and the Islamic powers that propagate it."[8]

The normalization of the fear of the internal Muslim Other was made explicit in the declaration of the end of multiculturalism by, among others, British prime minister Cameron, French president Sarkozy, and German chancellor Merkel in 2010. This meant the end of tolerance for those never considered real Europeans in the first place, blamed for their failure to assimilate into a racialized system dependent on their exclusion,[9] justified by unfounded but thoroughly mainstreamed claims to the continent's imminent "Islamization"—while Muslims make up no more than 6 percent of the population in most European nations.[10] The reframing of Muslims as a threat to European core values is usually tied to 9/11 and the subsequent global War on (Islamic) Terror. However, the process began much earlier, namely, with the deindustrialization of the continent's prosperous northwest in the late 1970s. The shift to a postindustrial economy disproportionally affected Muslim communities, consisting largely of labor migrants employed in the European coal, steel, and car industries.[11] The collapse of state socialism in Eastern Europe and the subsequent continent-wide turn to neoliberalism enhanced existing housing segregation, unemployment, mass incarceration, and the collapse of the public school system.[12]

The result is the positioning of European Muslims as a racialized underclass, ascribed a cultural pathology that holds them responsible for their economic and social marginalization. Meanwhile, the material and ideological foundations for the production of racialized subjects remain largely unexplored, hidden behind a chain of binaries—Muslims versus women, Muslims versus Jews, Muslims versus queers—that in the end amounts to Muslims versus modernity, creating a sense of crisis that adds urgency to the discourse on Europe's universalist, secular identity being threatened by the particularist politics of the continent's Muslims who position themselves in opposition to twenty-first-century values of diversity, tolerance, and equality. Gender, along with sexuality, takes center stage in this cultural construct, while race and class remain largely unaddressed. The supposed incompatibility of Islam and Europe is framed as a conflict between progressive European humanism, committed to the protection of rights such as gender equality and sexual freedom, and an intolerant, foreign culture hostile to these values. Invisible in this construct are not only Muslims as European but also the continent's long history of racism. The latter system is often treated as particular to the U.S. context, not as a global structure, in which the U.S. model is one variation of many—what David Theo Goldberg called regional racializations[13]—with the European variant shaped by two factors often understudied in U.S.-focused analyses of race and racism: nineteenth- and twentieth-century European colonialism in Africa, Asia, and the Middle East and the tradition of what Mustafa Bayoumi called, referencing the post-9/11 United States, the racing of religion.[14] As a result of the refusal to engage with this history, attempts to point to the ongoing relevance of racism for European identity formations are frequently framed as enforcing an Americanized "political correctness" meant to silence necessary critiques of migrant communities.

What Europeans perceive as the American obsession with race is a reflection of a fundamental shift in U.S. society in the wake of the civil rights movement, resulting in legal, social, political, and discursive changes. This did not happen in Europe after the Holocaust and colonial wars had forced the collapse of the normalized system of white supremacy. Instead, there was an externalization of the history of race and racism, replaced by what Stuart Hall called Europe's "internalist story," which can acknowledge neither the profound interconnectedness of cultures at the heart of the rise of Europe, and of the very idea of Europe itself, nor how colonialism and the transatlantic slave trade shaped not only the new but also the "old world"—the latter is instead conceived of as constantly producing progress out of its own resources, shaping the world but never being shaped by it.[15] This internalist framework is applied to the reindustrialization of northwestern Europe after Word War II, which produced a massive need for unskilled industrial labor and led to organized recruitment of so-called guest workers from the continent's south and east as well as North Africa, the Middle East, and South/Southeast Asia (in the latter cases often intersecting with postcolonial migration to the recruiting nations), with Turkey being the largest national source of migrants.[16] Until the 1980s, discourses on migration were shaped by the belief that the vast majority of these "guest workers" would simply return home when their work was done.[17] This rhetoric rings increasingly hollow, however, when referencing the children and grandchildren of the first generation of postwar labor migrants whose home is Europe. Rather than being accepted as European, however, this group is framed as being in fundamental cultural opposition to everything Europe stands for. This affects other racialized groups, such as Black Europeans and Roma, but currently it is Muslim communities that are repositioned in and as Europe's exterior—even if this highly diverse population is constituted as an identifiable, homogeneous group only through this normalized racializing discourse.

In what follows, I briefly sketch the role of multiculturalism in the current racing of religion with regard to European Muslims and end by pointing to a tradition of radical cultural activism around sexual, ethnic, gender, and national European identity that originated in exactly the communities that in current European discourses remain firmly on the outside, an activism that, rather than trying to work within multiculturalism, shows its inherently violent nature and replaces it with a model that deconstructs Europe's internalist narrative of cultural purity. My focus will be on the relatively stable and prosperous European northwest as representing exactly those "European values" of tolerance, liberalism, and equality to which Muslim communities are assumed to have trouble adjusting.

The repression of the long history of Europe as a multiracial and multireligious continent, a history that began long before the 1950s (or the

1490s), produces the continent's contemporary "(post)multicultural" state—associated with visual markers of non-Europeanness, be it dark skin or a head scarf—as a novelty that requires adjustment in the best case and resistance in the worst and that can simply be declared to have "failed." Multiculturalism thus does not merely describe a reality that cannot be undone at will but represents a particular discursive means to manage and control this reality. As a number of scholars have shown, the rise of (neo)liberal multiculturalism as the new global order allowed for continued Western domination after World War II, this time under the leadership of the U.S. antiracist empire. Having liberated the world from fascism and overcome racial strife within its own borders, it now seemed predestined to enforce global democracy—or so the story goes.[18] Within this framework, the European Union came to symbolize the continent's successful reformation after the twentieth-century crises of totalitarianism confirmed its place as gatekeeper of universal human rights. Since the early 1990s, the two aspects of Western domination, U.S. military force and European human rights commitment (manifest in the location of the International Criminal Court, prosecuting genocide, crimes against humanity, and war crimes, in the Hague), increasingly intersect: "humanitarian" NATO interventions and succeeding international war crimes tribunals suggest that waging war and protecting human rights are not only not exclusive but in fact might need to go together—especially since the "enemy of freedom" has moved from the socialist East back to a Global South that has always been perceived as in the best case having nothing to offer to a global democracy and as actively trying to destroy it in the worst. This includes the Muslim world, neighboring and often intersecting with Europe, which makes it easy to frame the continent's fifteen million Muslims as posing an internal as well as global threat. The crisis of (neo)liberal multiculturalism is thus localized among a population already made vulnerable through economic marginalization and political disempowerment.

The discourse on European Muslims as unleashing a sudden, devastating violence at an unsuspecting, innocent public still hesitant to aggressively defend itself has been cemented in the public mind around three 2005 incidents: the London bombings in July, the Danish "cartoon controversy" in September, and the uprisings in the French outer cities that fall. While the events—a terrorist attack, religious protests, and marginalized youths revolting against police violence—seem to be rather different, they are tied together by two factors: Muslims and violence. Male Muslims in European discourse represent endemic, uncontrollable aggression, directed

against their own communities, as tyrannical patriarchs and abusive hus-
bands, and society at large, as terrorists, juvenile delinquents, and religious
fanatics. This erases female agency and homogenizes and stereotypes Muslim cultures, increasingly normalizing the notion that Islam is incompatible
with modern societies. It also creates a false unity among European nations,
erasing homophobia and sexism and hiding the bias of the secularism
argument evoked in relation to, and increasingly against, the continent's
Muslims: an important but usually unspoken source of current tensions
around the supposed "desecularization" of Europe by Muslims is the un-
resolved internal tensions around Christianity and their meaning for the
continent's identity.[19]

Meanwhile, the narrative of Europe as human rights haven is constantly
affirmed—in the designation of the European Union as the 2012 Nobel
Peace Prize recipient,[20] the 2013 Pew Institute study confirming that queer
people have it nowhere better than in Europe, or the United Nations Gender Equality Index annually showing that men and women are nowhere
as equal as in Scandinavia, Germany, and the Netherlands.[21] Europe does
not do as well, however, in studies addressing racism.[22] Right-wing movements are on the rise across the continent—from the Greek Golden Dawn
to the Belgian Vlamse Belang and the Swiss People's Party.[23] Their aggressive rhetoric, and frequently physical violence, is directed primarily at so-
called migrants, that is, communities of color, in particular Black, Muslim,
and Roma—all groups that, rather than being recent additions, have been
present in Europe for decades or even centuries, but are still perceived as
foreigners.[24] The northwest does not fare better than other parts of the continent in that regard; in fact, it might do worse. Starting in the 1990s, there
has been a stream of racist violence, from beatings to shootings and lethal
arson attacks.[25] Among the most recent examples is the so-called National
Socialist Underground (NSU) in Germany, a white supremacist group
whose contacts reached from the U.S. Ku Klux Klan to the very authorities
tasked with prosecuting them. The NSU murdered at least nine Muslim
men over a seven-year period, randomly picking and executing them simply
because they assumed the men to be Muslim.[26] In 2011 in Norway, Anders
Breivik slaughtered more than seventy people in proclaimed protest of the
"Islamization" of Europe—and exactly five years later, an eighteen-year-old
in Munich shot nine people, most of them Muslims, directly referencing
Breivik.[27]

Nearly as disturbing as the regularity with which these incidents occur
is their perception by politics, media, and the general public: right-wing

violence is not qualified as (racial) "terror" but as isolated acts committed by disturbed individuals or fringe groups—in stark contrast to the perception of the violence by, say, Michael Adebolajo, who, in 2013, murdered a British soldier, or Mohammed Merah, whose 2012 killing of seven people in Toulouse immediately fit the framework of "Islamic terrorism" threatening Europe's core[28]—a terrorism that in turn is seen as indicative of "Muslim culture" threatening Europe's stability and identity—in a way that racist violence is not seen as indicative of dominant European culture and threatening its racialized populations. Rather, if these communities face violence and exclusion, it must be because they are doing something wrong—such as producing a pathological masculinity that can only end in terrorism. The current consensus on the "failure of multiculturalism," which is blamed on the inability of "immigrants" of the third or fourth generation to live up to European standards—standards to which they remain completely external—is an expression of this. The economic, social, and political marginalization of in particular European Muslim communities is not deemed a worthy subject of antiracism, because these communities failed to subscribe to the European project of liberal multiculturalism and are therefore not only responsible for their marginalized state but have in fact failed "Europeanness."

Explicitly racist, anti-Muslim and anti-immigrant political parties are on the rise in all of Europe.[29] These successes go hand in hand with a mainstreaming of repressive policies that goes beyond the oft-discussed hijab bans: from the elimination of pork substitutes in French public school lunches in Front National majority districts to the male circumcision debate in Germany, the minaret ban in Switzerland, and anti-halal laws in Denmark.[30] In all these instances, the measures are framed as a defensive action, a last-ditch attempt to defend "European values" against the barbarians. This fits into the larger narrative of Europe as always being already on the defense against the foreign, erasing it as producing initial structural violence, be it colonial or in the material living conditions of racialized communities permanently stuck in deteriorated "temporary" housing projects created for guest workers decades ago. The continental European Left fails to effectively challenge or even analyze this process, because it is too implicated in it, from an Enlightenment universalism that produced the white European as the paradigmatic human to a continental Marxist theory still ignoring race as a fundamental analytical category, viewing it as particularist distraction from the universally relevant category class—which is ironic, because class is deeply racialized in Europe. In the final section,

I suggest that productive answers to these questions come from the very groups targeted in the (post)multiculturalist order.

Scandinavia is frequently presented as the perfect embodiment of liberal multiculturalism: egalitarian, tolerant, and progressive—and yet incapable of integrating a foreign population hostile to these values. Denmark in particular became a key site of the perceived failure of multiculturalism in the infamous 2005 "cartoon affair," supposedly dividing Europeans, committed to free speech, and Muslims, in the West and outside of it, who place religion above civil, democratic rights. Unlike Breivik's terror attack in neighboring Norway some years later, this event fit the dominant narrative: Denmark appears as a small, progressive nation in which Christianity peacefully coexisted with a tolerant secular state that granted freedom of religion to all its citizens. The model worked as long as Danish society was largely homogeneous, but the nation's newly arrived Muslim migrants, the narrative goes, proved incapable of adapting to the secular-liberal lifestyle of northwestern Europe, leaving the nation's tolerance overstrained with a population irresponsive to values such as free speech and gender equality. The tension finally exploded through something that should not have been an issue in a democratic society, namely, the exercise of the freedom of the press in the form of a depiction of a religious prophet in a way that could be perceived as blasphemous by his followers, leading to an excessively violent reaction from the latter.[31]

However, a closer look provides a somewhat different picture: years before tensions erupted internationally when the nation's largest daily *Jylland's Posten* commissioned a number of cartoons, some depicting the prophet Mohammed as a terrorist, Denmark had been the first nation in Europe's reputedly progressive north to shift toward a populist, draconian anti-immigrant stance, pushed by a coalition between an explicitly Christian political right and an equally explicit liberal secularism. As a result of the 2001 elections, the nation limited benefits for migrants, closed homeless shelters to anyone without permanent residency, curbed family reunification, and forced Danish citizens marrying noncitizens to post a substantial bail in addition to raising the required minimum age to twenty-four years.[32] The climate in which the cartoons appeared thus was far from peaceful or comfortable for the nation's Muslims. Nor was *Jylland's Posten*'s publication motivated by a neutral commitment to free speech as evidenced in the paper's refusal in 2003 to print cartoons depicting Jesus, so as not to offend Christian readers.[33] Also not fitting with the image of Muslim overreaction to secular freedom of speech is the fact that rather than taking to the streets, eleven Danish Muslim organizations reacted to the publication by filing claims against the paper based on antidiscrimination regulations (the claims were rejected by the public prosecutor[34]). Their spokesperson was twenty-three-year-old Palestinian Danish Asmaa Abdol-Hamid, an outspoken feminist, socialist, and Muslim. An activist since her teenage years, in the tradition of women-of-color feminism, Abdol-Hamid draws strength from her community while simultaneously pushing its limits. She insists on embodying supposedly exclusive positionalities, such as wearing the hijab and being a radical socialist feminist, and most importantly on the right and ability of European Muslimas to speak for themselves. This has made her an extremely controversial figure in her home country.

The controversy, unsurprisingly, focused on her head cover. Treated as a visualization of the subjugation of Muslim women, a subjugation supposedly incompatible with Western values, the hijab receives an inordinate amount of attention in European discourses on migration, to the extent that is has become *the* symbol of Muslim Otherness, as evidenced in anti-hijab laws in France, Germany, and Belgium and much public debate about similar laws across the continent (usually not including the voices of women wearing hijab).[35] Considering that the majority of European Muslimas do not cover their heads and that only a tiny minority wears the niqab, the laws seem quite disproportionate. The focus on the veil makes more sense, however, if it is seen as resistance to accepting Islam as a permanent *European* religion, that is, to accepting its public presence, in the shape of mosques, halal butchers, or hijabs. The importance of these symbols of Muslim presence becomes evident when one turns to Frantz Fanon's assessment in "Algeria Unveiled" of nationalism as a scopic politics often symbolized by the clothing of female bodies. The veil during the Algerian war for independence from France in Fanon's analysis becomes a symbol for Algerian culture to both colonizers and colonized; its bearer, the Algerian woman, thus moves to the center of a symbolic politics that denies her agency exactly because she is positioned as the bearer of an intrinsic culture. Within this constellation, Muslim women faced pressure from both sides without being granted an autonomous voice in the conflict, and Fanon implies that this reflects the positioning of women within all nationalisms.[36]

Applied to the contemporary European context, the veil becomes the symbol of Europe's inability to tolerate visual markers of Otherness once they threaten to move from the periphery to the center, once the veil's bearer threatens to leave the symbolic space assigned to her. The sites of

Figure 6.1. This Swiss People's Party poster for the 2009 anti-minaret referendum combines all prevailing stereotypes in one image: the minarets turn into phallic missiles, and the veiled woman appears more sinister than oppressed.

conflict are national institutions—schools, courthouses, the police force, hospitals—in which Muslimas with hijab had been present en masse for decades as cleaners, that is, in their designated role of insecuritized labor force. As long as the head scarf signified class as much as religion, there was no conflict, no push for bans, and dismay about the female workers' domestic oppression was conspicuously absent from mainstream debates around migration. In other words, the hijab became the symbol of Muslim inability to adapt to modernity, aka Europe, only once it was associated with class mobility and once women wearing hijab threatened to enter positions where they represent the state/the nation/Europe. The head scarf affairs thus signify the collapse of boundary between Europe and its racialized Others rather than an unbridgeable culture gap. The hijab as a sign becomes both threatening and illegible when it is combined with a claim to European-ness or, in the case of Abdol-Hamid, combined with a radical intersectional critique of dominant constructs of nation, religion, and gender.

Her role in the failed attempt by Danish Muslims to mobilize state laws against hate speech was not Abdol-Hamid's last intervention into national politics from a position that simultaneously claimed Islam, Danishness, and progressive politics. In 2007, after making history as the first Danish talk show host wearing hijab, Abdol-Hamid became a candidate for the socialist Unity List. The ultimately unsuccessful candidacy provoked cri-tique not only from the Right but also from members of the socialist party, expressing the belief that Christianity, but not Islam, is compatible with secularism, feminism, and socialism.[37] Unwilling to fit predesigned cate-gories, instead creating new ones, Abdol-Hamid works on intersections that represent the potential of a fusionist "Euro-Islam." She does not pit Islam against Enlightenment and Europe against the Middle East; instead, she insists on combining her identities as Muslim, feminist, socialist, and European, affirming that all those identities are legitimately owned by her. Women like Abdol-Hamid represent an image that is unacceptable within European discourse (be it progressive, conservative, or mainstream), be-cause they show that Islam and commitment to "Western values" like gen-der equality are compatible and because they are representative of a larger group: feminist activism has been part of migrant and minority communi-ties for decades, and these grassroots activists often face resistance from ethnic communities, dominant feminist organizations, and the state alike. Their insistence on addressing simultaneous oppressions makes their work important and effective but also prevents them from gaining a prominent place in debates about their fate, exactly because of what they have to say about these intersectionalities.[38]

Continental Europe is a fruitful site for nontraditional diaspora scholarship from a transnational perspective, if one extends the notion of diaspora to describe a population that does not necessarily share a common origin, however imaginary it might be, but a contemporary condition. Shared histories of colonialism, racism, and migration create intersections and overlaps between, in particular, Black and Muslim but also Roma communities, resulting in shared spaces, cultures, and positionalities. These connections are suppressed in dominant policy-producing discourses that assign each group a distinct representational function: Muslims appear as the internal threat posed by migration, the Other that is already here but remains eternally foreign, whereas "Africans" (including seven million Black Europeans) represent the masses not yet there, pushing at the borders, the demographic, and racial, Goliath threatening to run over the European David.[39] The continent's twelve million Roma, the quintessential European minority of color, with a five-hundred-year history that includes slavery and genocide, continue to face extreme violence, poverty, and exclusion, while being largely absent as a recognized presence in contemporary Europe.[40] The discursive separation of these groups is symptomatic for the ways in which de facto intersections of communities of color—with each other and with white Europe—are negated within the ideology of multiculturalism, which cannot allow for porous boundaries and instead has to continuously produce distinct and homogenous communities whose hierarchical relationship is managed but not challenged. The ongoing perception of racialized Europeans as outsiders who need to integrate into a culture to which they have contributed nothing is also reflected in European scholarship, which continues to exclude scholars of color and much of the theory they produce. This results in the absence of intersectional analyses and in an intellectual paucity that severely limits continental Europe's ability to address its self-created problems—as Aimé Césaire noted half a century ago—but more than that, it allows an ongoing intellectual and political amnesia that is actively maintained through the erasure of the history of European racializations or, in the case of colonialism, its externalization, refusing responsibility for the violence of Europeanness, while discursively—and at times literally— erasing the possibility of a nonwhite, non-Christian European identity.

But structures of domination cross spaces separated by theory, and it is important to trace and validate these intersections and the coalitions they produce and to explore their potential impact on comparative studies of racialization. The ongoing unequal but intimate connections between Europe and Africa across the Mediterranean not only challenge an African diaspora theory that tends to marginalize contemporary Africa but also point to the complex negotiations of race within the Muslim diaspora. These negotiations have been all but erased within the dominant Hegelian model of sub-Saharan Africa as the "real," Black Africa and the resulting whitening of the "Arab" North. It is thus important to remember that it is nothing more than that—a working model, not a reflection of realities. The regional, religious, continental, and racial identifications of Africans affect internal as well as external group relations in ways that cannot be approached with a methodology inattentive to these complexities.

This becomes very obvious when we return to our starting point, Paris, where the 2005 uprisings in the outer cities brought into focus a largely Muslim North and West African–descended population that is neither ethnically nor racially homogeneous. Rather, the French system produced a homogenized, racialized economic underclass based on certain markers of "foreignness," centered on but not restricted to Islam.[41] This racialization forms the basis for the French Parti des Indigènes de la République (PIR), the Indigenous of the Republic, a decolonial movement formed in early 2005. The activists, mostly Muslims of North African descent, ground their decolonial politics in the experience of "the indigenized" of France (and Europe more broadly), which they consider to continue to be a colonial state. Indigeneity thus describes the positionality of a diverse population racialized by a system that is inseparable from European colonialism. PIR shows that colonial violence always took place in the metropole as well as the colony—and that it is not over. Their understanding of indigenized includes groups like the Roma, whose undertheorized oppression shares many markers with that of populations exposed to European settler colonialism.[42] PIR radically breaks not only with the notion that colonialism (and the indigenous it produced) is not part of Europe's internal(ist) past but that it is not part of its present. This also implies the refusal of the narrative of universal humanitarianism as justifying ongoing Western domination. Rather than confirming Muslims' and others' ability to adapt to Western universalism (or pointing out how these groups have contributed to it), PIR claims a positionality grounded in the subjugated position that universalism assigned racialized subjects, rejecting inclusion into a still racist global multiculturalism (as PIR founder and spokeswoman Houria Bouteldja put it, "We abhor anything that seeks to integrate us into whiteness"), instead asking for a global liberation project that acknowledges structural differences.[43]

Like Asmaa Abdol-Hamid, the queer activists of Strange Fruit, SUSPECT, SAFRA, and many others,[44] Bouteldja represents a new, distinctly European, Muslim diasporic activism invested in a coalitional politics that invokes a different kind of oppressed majority within and beyond the borders of Europe.

NOTES

1. *Majorité opprimée,* http://www.youtube.com/watch?v=kpfaza-Mw4I.

2. *Oppressed Majority,* http://www.youtube.com/watch?v=V4UWxlVvTiA (contrary to the French original, the subtitled version is age protected).

3. See, e.g., Paula Cocozza, "Oppressed Majority: The Film about a World Run by Women That Went Viral," *The Guardian,* February 11, 2014, http://www.the guardian.com/lifeandstyle/womens-blog/2014/feb/11/oppressed-majority-film -women-eleonore-pourriat; Alissa J. Rubin, "French Film Goes Viral, but Not in France 'Oppressed Majority' Provokes Debate on Internet," *New York Times,* April 6, 2014, http://www.nytimes.com/2014/04/07/movies/oppressed-majority-provokes -debate-on-internet.html?_r=0. For exceptions, see Ashan Jafar, "Overlooking the Oppressed Minority in 'Oppressed Majority,'" *Inside Higher Ed,* February 23, 2014, http://www.insidehighered.com/blogs/university-venus/overlooking-oppressed -minority-oppressed-majority#sthash.lEvG46rT.vdomiXiC.dpbs; Richard Seymor, "Feminism Can Save France from Islam: That's the Real Message of Majorité Opprimée," *The Guardian,* February 13, 2014, http://www.theguardian.com/com mentisfree/2014/feb/13/feminism-france-islam-majorite-opprimee-racism.

4. In France, and many other European nations, it is the neighborhoods far from the city center with its strong infrastructure, the outer, not the inner cities, that house marginalized, racialized populations. See Trica Keaton, *Muslim Girls and the Other France: Race, Identity Politics, and Social Exclusion* (Bloomington: Indiana University Press, 2006).

5. One of the most tragic outcomes of this stereotyping is the case of Egyptian pharmacist Marwa al-Sherbini, who, in 2009, while living in Germany with her husband, a scientist at the Max Planck Institutes, took a man to court after he, in reference to her head scarf, had insulted her as "Islamist, terrorist, and slut." Right after the sentencing, the man stabbed al-Sherbini, who was pregnant, to death and severely wounded her husband, who tried to protect her. Police entering the scene immediately assumed the husband to be the attacker and shot him, an assumption that was later justified as reasonable. "Maximum Sentence for Racist Murderer: Dresden Courtroom Killer Gets Life," *Der Spiegel Online,* November 11, 2009, http:// www.spiegel.de/international/germany/maximum-sentence-for-racist-murderer -dresden-courtroom-killer-gets-life-a-660730.html.

6. "Identified as Muslim," since this ascription is less a matter of religious practice or self-identification than of culturalist assignments that assume the existence of a homogeneous version of Islam shaping the cultural, rather than religious, identity of all members of communities originating in majority-Muslim nations.

7. It is exactly this shared history that creates the need to artificially separate Europe from its Others and has produced race and religion as markers of non-Europeanness. See Talal Asad, *Formations of the Secular: Christianity, Islam, Modernity* (Stanford, Calif.: Stanford University Press, 2003); Leeram Medovi, "Dogma-Line Racism: Islamophobia and the Second Axis of Race," *Social Text* 111 (2012): 43–74.

8. While Jews arguably became "European" post–World War II, the increasingly popular reference to Europe's Judeo-Christian identity, primarily evoked in response to the disruption represented by the contemporary Muslim presence, works to discursively erase the exclusion and persecution of the racialized Jewish minority by the Christian majority that characterized much of Europe's "Judeo-Christian" history. Bat Ye'or's "Eurabia," which identifies a widespread conspiracy between European leaders and the Arab world aimed at the United States and Israel, but victimizing white Christian Europe on the way, is one of the key texts of this narrative. Bat Ye'or, *Eurabia: The Euro-Arab Axis* (Cranbury, N.J.: Fairleigh Dickinson University Press, 2005).

9. This understanding of racialized communities as eternal newcomers is implemented quite literally in parts of the continent: Germany, Austria, Italy, and Switzerland traditionally practice a *ius sanguinis* that makes "blood," that is, descent, the only or primary factor in acquiring citizenship, excluding residents of "foreign blood" for generations, while making naturalization harder by denying dual citizenship. See Rogers Brubaker, *Citizenship and Nationhood in France and Germany* (Cambridge, Mass.: Harvard University Press, 1992). After the collapse of the Soviet empire, a number of Eastern European nations have returned to similar laws. The largest national group affected by this are the roughly four million Europeans of Turkish descent.

10. Conrad, Hackett, "5 Facts about the Muslim Population in Europe," Pew Research Center, January 15, 2015, http://www.pewresearch.org/fact-tank/2015/01/15/5-facts-about-the-muslim-population-in-europe/.

11. Muslim communities across the continent still face above average unemployment rates, housing discrimination, and lower educational achievements. See European Monitoring Centre on Racism and Xenophobia, *Muslims in the European Union: Discrimination and Islamophobia* (Vienna: EU Agency for Fundamental Rights, 2006); European Commission Directorate-General for Employment and Social Affairs, *Improving the Tools for the Social Inclusion and Non-discrimination of Roma in the EU* (Luxembourg: Office for Official Publications of the European Communities, 2010); European Commission, *Migrants in Europe: A Statistical Portrait of the First and Second Generation* (Luxembourg: Publications Office of the European Union, 2011).

12. European Commission, *Migrants in Europe*; European Monitoring Centre on Racism and Xenophobia, *Muslims in the European Union*.

13. David Theo Goldberg, "Racial Europeanization," *Ethnic and Racial Studies* 29, no. 2 (2006): 331–64.

14. Moustafa Bayoumi, "Racing Religion," *New Centennial Review* 6, no. 2 (2006): 267–93.

15. Stuart Hall, "Europe's Other Self," *Marxism Today*, 1991, 18.

16. European Commission, *Migrants in Europe.*

17. See, e.g., Germany's unsuccessful 1982 attempt to halve the nation's "Turkish" population—a plan based on the assumption that millions of "guest workers" and their descendants had not become part of German society and that a monetary incentive would thus be sufficient to make them give up the life they had established over decades in order hastily to return "home." See C. Hecking, "Secret Thatcher Notes: Kohl Wanted Half of Turks out of Germany," *Spiegel Online International,* August 1, 2013, http://www.spiegel.de/international/germany/secret-minutes-chan cellor-kohl-wanted-half-of-turks-out-of-germany-a-914376.html.

18. See Neda Atanasoski, *Humanitarian Violence: The U.S. Deployment of Diversity* (Minneapolis: University of Minnesota Press, 2013); Jodi Melamed, *Represent and Destroy: Rationalizing Violence in the New Racial Capitalism* (Minneapolis: University of Minnesota Press, 2011); Chandan Reddy, *Freedom with Violence: Race, Sexuality, and the U.S. State* (Durham, N.C.: Duke University Press, 2011).

19. José Casanova, "Religion, European Secular Identities, and European Integration," *Eurozine,* July 29, 2004, http://www.eurozine.com/articles/2004-07-29-casa nova-en.html.

20. The prize was awarded for "over six decades contributed to the advancement of peace and reconciliation, democracy and human rights in Europe" (http://www .nobelprize.org/nobel_ prizes/peace/laureates/2012/), ignoring colonial wars and the EU's less than stellar role in the war in Yugoslavia—an important chapter in the recent history of European Muslims often ignored. See Neda Atanasoski, *Humanitarian Violence: The U.S. Deployment of Diversity* (Minneapolis: University of Minnesota Press, 2013).

21. Pew Institute Global Attitudes Project, "The Global Divide on Homosexuality," 2013, http://www.pewglobal.org/2013/06/04/the-global-divide-on-homosexu ality/; United Nations, "Gender Equality Index," 2012, https://data.undp.org/data set/Table-4-Gender-Inequality-Index/pq34-nwq7.

22. Stephan Loewenstein, "UNHCR: Deutschland bricht Völker- und Europarecht," *Frankfurter Allgemeine Zeitung,* August 10, 2007; European Network against Racism, *Racism in Europe: ENAR Shadow Report 2011–2012,* http://www.enarfoun dation.eu/news/article/new-shadow-report-on-racism-in?news=oui.

23. Tony Patterson, "Hungary Election: Concerns as Neo-Nazi Jobbik Party Wins 20% of Vote," *Independent,* April 7, 2014, http://www.independent.co.uk/ news/world/europe/concerns-as-neonazi-jobbik-party-wins-20-of-hungary-vote-92 44541.html; Human Rights First, "Far-Right Parties in the European Elections: Fact Sheet," May 2014, http://www. humanrightsfirst.org/resource/far-right-parties-euro pean-elections.

24. European Monitoring Centre on Racism and Xenophobia (1994–2014), *Country Monitoring Work,* http://www.coe.int/t/dghl/monitoring/ ecri/library/pub lications.asp.

25. Paul Iganski, *Racist Violence in Europe* (Brussels: European Network against Racism, 2011); European Network against Racism, *Racism in Europe.*

26. Ben Knight, "Germany's Neo-Nazi Investigation Exposes Institutional Racism." *The Guardian,* November 13, 2012, http://www.theguardian.com/commentis free/2012/nov/13/germany-neo-nazi-investigation-institutional-racism.

27. Andrew Brown, "Anders Breivik's Spider Web of Hate," *Guardian*, September 7, 2011, http://www.theguardian.com/commentisfree/2011/sep/07/anders-brei vik-hate-manifesto; Fisher 2016.

28. Dominic Casciani, "Woolwich: How Did Michael Adebolajo Become a Killer?" *BBC News*, December 19, 2013, http://www.bbc.com/news/magazine-25424290; Edward Cody, "Mohammed Merah, Face of the New Terrorism," *Washington Post*, March 22, 2012, http://www.washingtonpost.com/world/europe/mohammed-mer ah-face-of-the-new-terrorism/2012/03/22/gIQA2kL4TS_story.html

29. In 2014 alone, the Hungarian Jobbik Party, among other things advocating detention camps for Roma, achieved 20 percent in national elections; the French Front National gained 25 percent; and the conservative Christian Danish People's Party secured 27 percent in the European parliament elections. Tony Patterson, "Hungary Election: Concerns as Neo-Nazi Jobbik Party Wins 20% of Vote," *Independent*, April 7, 2014, http://www.independent.co.uk/news/world/europe/concerns -as-neonazi-jobbik-party-wins-20-of-hungary-vote-9244541.html; Gavin Titley, "Pork Is the Latest Front in Europe's Culture War," *The Guardian*, April 14, 2014, 32; Human Rights First, "Far-Right Parties in the European Elections," Fact Sheet, May 2014, http://www.humanrightsfirst.org/resource/far-right-parties-european -elections.

30. Fatima El-Tayeb, "Time Travelers and Queer Heterotopias: Narratives from the Muslim Underground," *New Germanic Review: Literature, Culture, Theory* 88, no. 3 (2013): 305–19; Leo Benedictus, "Denmark Starts Meaty Argument over Animal Slaughter," *Guardian*, February 19, 2014, http://www.theguardian.com/lifeand style/shortcuts/2014/feb/19/denmark-meaty-argument-animal-slaughter-halal-ko sher-food; Gavin Titley, "Pork Is the Latest Front in Europe's Culture War," *Guardian*, April 14, 2014, 32.

31. See Klausen 2006

32. William L. Adams, "A Blow to Europe's Far-Right: Denmark Reshapes Its Immigration Policies," *Time*, October 6, 2011, http://world.time.com/2011/10/06/a -slap-to-europes-far-right-denmark-reshapes-its-immigration-policies/.

33. See Jytte Klausen, "Rotten Judgment in the State of Denmark," www.salon .com, February 8, 2006.

34. Kate Østergaard and Kristin Sinclair, "Danish Muslims, the Cartoon Controversy, and the Concept of Integration," *Global Dialogue* 9, no. 3/4 (2007), http:// www.worlddialogue.org/content.php?id=414.

35. The German law, prohibiting the hijab, but not other religious symbols, for teachers, was recently declared partially unconstitutional by the nation's supreme court. Timothy Jones, "Constitutional Court Strikes Down Absolute Headscarf Ban," *Deutsche Welle*, March 13, 2015, http://www.dw.de/constitutional-court-strikes-down -absolute-headscarf-ban/a-18313377.

36. Frantz Fanon, "Algeria Unveiled," in *A Dying Colonialism*, 35–64 (New York: Monthly Review Press, 1965). The 2016 local French laws banning burkinis, justified as a response to Islamist terrorist attacks and violently enforced, prove the ongoing relevance of Fanon's point. See Alissa J. Rubin, "Penalizing Women for Covering Too Little, and Then Too Much," *New York Times*, August 28, 2016, A5.

37. Fatima El-Tayeb, *European Others. Queering Ethnicity in Postnational Europe* (Minneapolis: University of Minnesota Press, 2011).

38. The feminist Muslima is in a position of impossibility comparable to that of the queer Muslim, whose very existence is erased in another European clash with its Others, in which implicitly straight Muslim and implicitly white queer community are pitted against each other. See Suhraiya Jivraj and Anisa de Jong, "The Dutch Homo-Emancipation Policy and Its Silencing Effects on Queer Muslims," *Feminist Legal Studies* 19, no. 143 (2011): 1–16; Fatima El-Tayeb, "'Gays Who Cannot Properly Be Gay': Queer Muslims in the Neoliberal European City," *European Journal of Women's Studies* 19, no. 1 (2012): 79–95.

39. The prevalence of metaphors along these lines helps to normalize the extremely high death toll the EU migration regime produces on its external borders—about two thousand per year since 2005 and recently more, most of them African Muslims, complemented by a rapidly growing (and increasingly privatized) regime of mass incarceration of undocumented migrants.

40. European Commission, *Improving the Tools for the Social Inclusion and Non-discrimination of Roma.*

41. See Keaton, *Muslim Girls.*

42. A small example of these shared positionalities: both PIR founder Houria Bouteldja and Hungarian Roma activists defending themselves against racist attacks have been charged with (and in the case of the Roma, sentenced for) "anti-white racism." See Parti des Indigènes de la République, "Procès contre Houria Bouteldja," June 8, 2012, http://indigenes-republique.fr/proces-contre-houria-bouteldja-en-anglais-espagnol-portugais/; Hungarian Civil Liberties Union, "Romas Sentenced for Hate Crime against Hungarians," July 13, 2012, http://tasz.hu/en/node/2786.

43. PIR thus demands of white allies to replace universal humanitarianism with "'domestic internationalism'; to understand that a fraction of the colonial empire is today within France's continental borders, that the colonial/racial divide is a structural internal divide inside France, and that now is not a time for solidarity with the immigrants and their children, but it is a time for constructing alliances that respect our mutual autonomies." Houria Bouteldja, "Dieudonné through the Prism of the White Left, or Conceptualizing a Domestic Internationalism," trans. Samir, Parti des Indigènes de la République, March 1, 2014, http://indigenes-republique.fr/dieudonne-through-the-prism-of-the-white-left-or-conceptualizing-a-domestic-internationalism/.

44. See Bacchetta Paola and Jin Haritaworn, "There Are Many Transatlantics: Homonationalism, Homotransnationalism and Feminist-Queer-Trans of Color Theories and Practices," in *Transatlantic Conversations: Feminism as Traveling Theory,* ed. K. Davis and M. Evans (Aldershot, U.K.: Ashgate, 2011), 127–43, and Fatima El-Tayeb, *European Others: Queering Ethnicity in Postnational Europe* (Minneapolis: University of Minnesota Press, 2011), for a more detailed discussion of some of these activist groups.

7

Atlanta, Civil Rights, and Blackamerican Islam

ABBAS BARZEGAR

In certain quarters, it has become a tired refrain to discuss nationalism as a by-product of myth and (his)tory. However, in the "Black Mecca" of Atlanta, the heart of the "New South" where I have had the privilege to study and teach over the last decade, celebrating the civil rights movement is not only a customary civic instinct but a nationalist enterprise as well. Streets and monuments proudly remind visitors and local residents of (and teach them) the names of the city's local heroes: Andrew Young International Boulevard, the Maynard Jackson Terminal at Hartsfield International Airport, Hosea Williams Drive, Hank Aaron Drive, and, of course, Martin Luther King Jr. Boulevard. Just off the main highway at the heart of downtown, a giant portrait mural of civil rights icon and congressman John Lewis shouts "HERO" to drivers throughout the day. In his pithy and lasting *Arcades,* Walter Benjamin critiqued the ubiquitous ideological force of the intersection between myth, material culture, and memory in the very streetscapes of Paris, drawing attention to the discord between the rhetoric of a city's self-image and the reality of the socioeconomic contradictions its residents encounter.[1] Similarly, as Atlanta basks in the post–civil rights narrative of racial reconciliation and national progress, it grinds through the pitfalls of promises unmet. After all, the city has become one of the country's most infested sex trafficking hubs.[2] Its public transportation system has been stunted because of racial politics, and its public education sector has been the subject of national embarrassment.[3] The city's de facto residential segregation as seen in its history of white flight and gentrification puts a final seal on the enduring structural[4] racism that has marked its existence since the antebellum period.[5] Atlanta's experience in boasting a narrative of freedom and progress along with perpetuating structures of systemic inequality, however, reflects a larger national disconnect between historical memory and current politics.

Simply to point to the power of nationalist mythology to endure such contradictions is an admittedly tautological, if necessary, academic exercise. However, during the contemporary political moment of deeply polarized social and political fields domestically and rapidly growing disenfranchisement internationally, deconstructing the discursive inertia that authorizes and engenders the myths of American exceptionalism and perpetual progress becomes a political act. It is in such spirit that I offer a few comments in this essay on Atlanta, civil rights discourse, and the city's Blackamerican Muslim legacy. As the city positions itself to be the custodian of America's civil rights narrative, along with the rest of "the country," it does so at a time when our current social and political moment uncomfortably resembles the very historical era that—according to the all but official narrative—should have been overcome. The senselessness of the Vietnam War justified by a theopolitical battle against communism parallels a similarly exacerbated theopolitical war against Islamist insurgencies and transnational military organizations such as al-Qaeda and ISIS. These imperial ambitions, then and now, also justify feeding the insatiable appetite of the American security state through pernicious government programs and policy initiatives such as COINTELPRO, the USA PATRIOT Act, and Countering Violent Extremism.[6] The muzzling of political dissent, as seen in the prosecution and/or persecution of activists and whistle-blowers such as Edward Snowden, Julianne Assange, and Sami Al-Arian, also recalls a not so distant past when political leaders were targets of state violence. To speak of the civil rights movement as a thing of the past without addressing the actual encroachment of civil liberties today is but a ritual of nostalgic inebriation. It is in this context, then, that the present volume rightfully summons an intellectual praxis that is robustly grounded in self-reflective and politically relevant historical scholarship.

Writing as I am from Georgia State University, which is literally engulfed—by way of its physical location in the downtown district—by Atlanta's civil rights mytho-history, I provide a perspective on how local, but nationally connected, Blackamerican Muslim histories disrupt conventional narratives of not only the city's but the country's triumph over social discord, racial polarization, and political inequality. I begin by discussing how two major additions to downtown Atlanta's landscape—the creation of the National Center for Civil and Human Rights (NCCHR) and the Atlanta

Streetcar—function as material extensions of the myth of American exceptionalism and, moreover, literally and rhetorically efface alternative discourses and memories of Atlanta as site of Black social empowerment. Thereafter, I outline the ways in which Blackamerican Muslim discourses are firmly rooted in a larger tradition of Black internationalist political thought that also connects to global discourses of Muslim transnational liberation. In doing so, I highlight the social and discursive space that two distinct Black Muslim organizations occupied in Atlanta, namely, the Dar al-Islam and the Islamic Party of North America (IPNA).

In closing, I make the case for the preservation and archiving of Black Muslim oral histories, literary sources, and documentary materials as a means of recovering a critical social discourse that can enrich contemporary strategies to manage the enduring discursive structures of the American imperial apparatus. I should also mention, at the outset, that my use of terms such as *Blackamerican, Black Muslim, African American Muslim,* and so forth is a strategic, ethical choice intended to help navigate the very discursive hegemony that we address in this essay. That is, throughout my writing here, and elsewhere, I consciously use markers and labels interchangeably in ways that few of my peers would. The primary reason for this choice is simply to reflect the diversity of usage existent within the communities I've worked with to help tell this story. While there is a heated tradition of debate within certain academic and advocacy circles about the importance of using the term *Black* over *African American,* for example, I have found it significantly less present and relevant among the community interlocutors who undergird the After Malcolm project. My use of multiple, even antagonistic terms is intended therefore to reflect the instability and limited scope of such debates as well as more accurately represent the discursive fluidity present in multiple communities' self-representations. Using and interchanging even contradictory terminology is one of the many ways I attempt to allow a multiplicity of voices to disrupt conventional narratives of this history.

More than a Streetcar

In a gesture to honor the fiftieth anniversary of the Civil Rights Act and other commemorations from the period, the city of Atlanta opened the NCCHR in June 2014. Located in Centennial Olympic Park, which also hosts CNN headquarters, the Coca-Cola Museum, and the city's aquarium, the new museum cements the city's self-image as a center for social and economic progress. It does so even as the neighborhoods just west of down-town undergo an aggressive postrecession gentrification and real estate development boom that exemplifies the city's troubled relationship with its past. This includes the construction of a controversial new stadium. That is, on one hand, the presence of a number of corporate headquarters and improvements in middle- and upper-income housing demonstrates just how far the city has come from the 1960s, but on the other hand, the visible presence of vagrancy, open-air drug markets, and depressed housing just a few miles from shiny apartment developments suggests an uneven story of development. The NCCHR, like other ideological projects, has trouble capturing such contradiction in a coherent narrative.

Nonetheless, the NCCHR is but one example of the ways in which the city's public planning mirrors the ideological commitments that the post–civil rights narrative demands. By positioning itself as a "national" institu-tion dedicated to human and civil rights simultaneously, the NCCHR seeks to connect Atlanta's civil rights history to a larger narrative of post-racial American reconciliation in particular and American exceptionalism, by extension, in general. In this way, the jagged histories of America's Civil War and Blackamerican liberation legacies become sublimated into a larger framework of America's moral hegemony abroad. Consider, for example, the NCCHR's mission statement:

A UNIVERSAL MISSION: The mission of The National Center for Civil and Human Rights is to empower people to take the protection of every human's rights personally. Through sharing stories of courage and struggle around the world, The Center encourages visitors to gain a deeper understanding of the role they play in helping to protect the rights of all people.

The National Center for Civil and Human Rights harnesses Atlanta's leg-acy of civil rights to strengthen the worldwide movement for human rights. Atlanta played a unique leadership role in the American Civil Rights Move-ment. Through harnessing Atlanta's legacy and galvanizing the corporate, faith-based, public-sector and university communities, The Center serves as the ideal place to reflect on the past, transform the present and inspire the future.[7]

The statement, as unapologetic and confident as it is, is boldly creative in its storytelling. For example, in the 1960s, the language of human rights was actively summoned as an anti-thesis to civil rights by Malcolm X and others who sought legal redress to the problem of Black suffering outside of the scope of the American legal framework. That is, the discourse of human rights was an oppositional framework during the civil rights era. In this context, "America" was never a project worthy of rhetorical, material, or mythological investment to anti-institutional political activists and community leaders invested in visions of Black freedom that went beyond the American nation-state. To make an equation between civil and human rights, therefore, is a rather remarkable memory-making achievement, as subtle as it is coercive. Not only do such equivalences invoke particular memories over others but they demand suppression or revision of marginal, alternative renditions.

Furthermore, that African American civil rights can find "resonance" on every group on every continent assumes a monolithic understanding of freedom as simply a matter of recognition achieved through the granting of particular legal rights. Here legal rights equal recognition. What of dignity, historical redress, material reparations, political and economic self-determination, and other explicit goals of various freedom struggles around the world? By articulating freedom in terms of legal rights, alternative visions of social and political freedom are elided and excluded from the local, national, and universal conceptions of liberation proffered under the umbrella of American exceptionalism.

However, an even greater implication of the "every group, every continent" claim to universalism lies in its coalescence with ideas of American exceptionalism and national covenant. And herein lies the ideological power of Atlanta's civil rights mythology: even as it tells the story of overcoming the historical consequences of centuries of African enslavement, economic exploitation, and political disenfranchisement, it grounds itself in the same notions of progress, universalism, and freedom upon which the larger American mytho-national project is built. The net political outcome, therefore, is the maintenance and perpetuation of America's imperialist and universalist ideological project in the contemporary world in which the United States' political and economic global hegemony is underwritten by a transcendent mythology. In doing so, the narrative of the White Man's Burden of Euro-America's civilizing mission becomes the unlikely mechanism through which even the heirs of the colonized can advanced themselves.

The mission statement's explicit espousal of nonviolent collaboration also doubles as an endorsement of the politics of multiculturalism and racial tolerance in a way that ignores or is dismissive of more radical strands of Black political thought and practice that were philosophically, culturally, and religiously revolutionary. This practice of discursive elision finds further material manifestations in the city's physical landscape as well. For example, in the midst of the construction of the NCCHR, Atlanta mayor Kasim Reed undertook the construction of a federally funded streetcar transportation project that would link the Martin Luther King Center with the downtown district ending at Centennial Olympic Park and thus provide convention goers and tourists quick and easy access to the renowned sacred site of America's post-racial patron saint. Developers maintain that the project is primarily intended to spur economic development and facilitate local transportation in depressed areas of downtown and the Old Fourth Ward district, where vagrancy, drug trafficking, and prostitution remain. While the streetcar project could be hailed as a positive development in a city that has long suffered from racialized transportation barriers, it is easy to recognize that the net impact and target of the project serve a tourist rather than resident population.

Ultimately, the streetcar project elides the historical roots of inequality in Atlanta and the persistence of the structural disenfranchisement in the name of capital progress. In doing so, it also continues to marginalize alternative narratives of Atlanta as a center for African American empowerment. For example, the depressed Old Fourth Ward neighborhood that is connected to the downtown commercial and tourist districts through the streetcar project was home to the 1906 race riots and the 1917 Great Atlanta Fire that saw the destruction of the city's thriving Black business district. The same neighborhood is currently witnessing a massive influx of capital investment and gentrification practices that have community advocates and long-term residents concerned that the city's historical appeal to African Americans will continue to be systematically diluted. Indeed, well before the 2008 economic banking fiasco, the *New York Times* raised the issue of gentrification in Atlanta to a national level: "Even the Old Fourth Ward, the once elegant black neighborhood where Martin Luther King Jr. was born, is now less than 75 percent black, down from 94 percent in 1990, as houses have skyrocketed in value and low-rent apartments have been replaced by new developments."[8] Since the so-called economic recovery, gentrification trends in Atlanta have continued along their original tracks. As a professor of Georgia State University, it also behooves me to mention that my university's rapid growth trajectory has been one of the major drivers of gentrification in this part of the city in the last two decades.[9]

While the gentrification of entire neighborhoods, building of new museums, and construction of transportation projects are obvious and explicit indicators of the city's priorities, both at the level of planning and in a wider stakeholder network, they simultaneously obfuscate the Atlanta's not-so-conventional narratives of progress and social change. Just as the NCCHR hegemonically articulates the legitimate boundaries of what freedom, progress, and liberation mean to Atlanta residents and thereby dismisses alternative visions of human political and social fruition, so too does the streetcar project—by privileging the Old Fourth Ward and the King Center—demand that one forget other neighborhoods central to the story of Black empowerment and liberation over the course of the last half-century.

For example, the West End district just southwest of downtown has been home to a range of Black social, political, and religious movements that do not conform to the civil rights narrative, American myths of exceptionalism, or the politics of respectability that have dominated discussions of social change in "the city too busy to hate." The West End hosts a range of locally owned Afrocentric bookstores, gift shops, and organic health care outlets. It also is home to the Shrine of the Black Madonna and a popular vegan restaurant owned by community members of the Black Hebrew Israelites. It is also home to Imam Jamil Al-Amin's West End Community Mosque, which serves as the center of the current national community and its affiliates that is an outgrowth of the Dar al-Islam movement. The Blackamerican[10] Muslim experience in Atlanta is but one of many that has articulated an alternative and at times contrarian view of the social change as compared to that conventional rendition offered by city elites. It is also one of the most undocumented and least understood. In the next section, I turn my attention to the many ways in which exploring this historical tradition of Blackamerican Islam informs current discussions on American social polarization and material demands of dreams unfilled.

AFTER MALCOLM: ALTERNATIVE VISIONS OF FREEDOM

Since 2012, along with Dr. Bilal King of Morehouse College, I have had the privilege of codirecting an oral history and document preservation research project titled "After Malcolm: Islam and the Black Freedom Struggle," which attempts to explore the many ways African American Muslims have cultivated Islamic practices, beliefs, and symbols in the multifaceted quest for freedom and dignity. The primary output of the work of this team can be seen in the construction of an open-source online digital archive that houses the organizational documents, personal papers, and recorded oral histories.[11] Recording oral histories and crowdsourcing original audio and visual materials are absolutely necessary if future historians and educators want to speak authoritatively on African American Muslim life during these years. It also goes without saying that as scholars and cultural workers around the country reflect upon the contested legacies of civil rights and Black Power, Blackamerican Muslim visions of social empowerment, freedom, and justice deserve their rightful place in the historical record. And finally, it is imperative to note that these historical traditions serve to enrich existing discourses of political praxis.

The bulk of the group's work concentrates on the period between 1965 and 1985, and although it is focused on the history of Atlanta, the highly networked nature of Muslim communities has drawn in participants from around the country. Our team focuses on the "after Malcolm" period for a number of reasons. First and foremost among them is that documentary materials from this period are scarce and need to be preserved, especially as many figures who shaped this historical moment have already passed on or are entering their twilight years. The antiestablishment posture of many of these communities—a direct result of FBI efforts to undermine them and other Black empowerment groups—has also significantly contributed to the dearth of documentary material from this period. We have found, however, that in working with grassroots networks, local historians, and community leaders in addition to providing a high level of transparency in the collection process, barriers of mistrust are rather easily overcome. To date, we have drawn participants from the national network of mosques falling under the general leadership and inspiration of W. D. Muhammad's teachings, the National Community of Imam Jamil Al-Amin, including affiliated communities of the Dar al-Islam movement, the IPNA, the Mosque of Islamic Brotherhood in New York City, and individuals from decentralized Sunni communities across the United States.

As a praxis-oriented research project, we recognize that the study of African American Islam has largely unfolded in academic silos and been left out of a wider conversation about American empire and its domestic reverberations. Given the increasing inability of American society—by which I mean the dominant media culture and political institutions—to manage its current encounter with the "Muslim world," we argue that this void comes at the peril of our own national and democratic consciousness. To put it simply, African American Muslim experiences are uniquely positioned to contribute to contemporary cultural and political conversations about Islam, democracy, and global justice precisely because they have sat at the intersection of domestic and international dimensions of the Euro-American imperial project.

In addition, our team looks to the period as one that can critically inform cultural and pedagogical praxis in the contemporary political moment. It is during this period that the Cold War entered a heightened phase of intensity, the civil rights movement waned, and strategies for Black empowerment began to take on more radical postures. Civil rights narratives today, which often exclusively champion the dimensions of nonviolence and judicial recourse in the struggle for justice, often gloss over these moments of U.S. history. The period of 1965 to 1985 in Black radical thought does not lend itself to neat, moralistic narratives of national memory. Rather, it offers an avenue through which to better understand the contemporary moment of continued ideological and cultural polarization as well as economic inequality rooted in the historical legacies of American political and social inequality.

The contrast and tension between contested legacies of Black Power and civil rights, then, provides the context for the materials gathered and analyzed by the After Malcolm research team. Sohail Daulatzai, whose thesis in *Black Star, Crescent Moon* has deeply informed the scope of our work, comments on the politics of narrative concerning the post–civil rights period:

> The narrative of Civil Rights has tremendous purchase and traction in the United States, because it has been used to rewrite the 1960s, underwrite the white backlash and the "culture wars" of the 1980s and '90s, and cement the politics of the New Right, which assumes that race has been transcended and that the United States has fulfilled its national destiny. Most important, the Civil Rights narrative has assumed that Black freedom could be achieved within the legal frameworks and political institution of the United States.[12]

If the mainstream civil rights narrative that has grown dominant, and solidified especially in a post-Obama period, is a source of historical revisionism, it also elides the individuals, organizations, and ideas that offered an alternative vision for freedom and dignity in the United States. This is especially the case for Blackamerican Muslims, whose individual and community building enterprises largely unfolded in ways counter to mainstream religious, legal, and political practices. As Imam Furqan Muhammad of Masjid al-Furqan, located on Hank Aaron Drive just behind Braves Field, said, "We have been deliberately written out of Civil Rights history!"[13] Most poignantly, the overwhelming majority of Blackamerican Muslim movements overtly rejected the notion that freedom, equality, or dignity could be achieved within the framework of American social and political life, or any secular national state or identity, for that matter.

In contradistinction to civil rights discourses that sought both spiritual and political redemption in the promise of inclusion in, and recognition by, American exceptionalism, Blackamerican Islam touted a universal humanism hermeneutically derived from global international traditions of Islamic civilizations and culture coupled with a fierce anticolonial sociopolitical mandate born from local African American experiences. It is in the context of global anti-imperial solidarity that Blackamerican Muslim movements throughout the twentieth century, but more particularly those emerging after the assassination of Malcolm X, can be counted among the larger traditions of Black radical and international thought. Daulatzai, again, provides context:

> But while Civil Rights has assumed that Black freedom is attainable within U.S. legal frameworks and political institutions, critical Black internationalists have historically questioned that assumption, seeing white supremacy as a global phenomenon and looking to international struggles in the Third World as lenses for their own battles with white power, exploring the tactics and strategies of those struggles, and also seeking solace and solidarity by expanding their racial community of belonging. And while Civil Rights has assumed that the United States has been a force for good in the world, whether it be through fighting and eradicating communism or any other perceived threats to U.S. national security, Black internationalists have been skeptical and have even outright challenged U.S. foreign policy, viewing it as similar to European colonialism, as an extension of Manifest Destiny and a racist logic that it practices at home.[14]

The After Malcolm project has sought to engage with those quarters of the African American freedom struggle that explicitly rejected the notion of American exceptionalism and defined freedom in ways radically divergent from their civil rights counterparts. It has done so precisely to provide historical depth to national conversations currently unfolding, which continue to revolve around problems concerning American imperialism, institutionalized racism, and socioeconomic marginalization. The remainder of this essay demonstrates the continued relevance of Blackamerican Muslim traditions to contemporary domestic and international political problems. It does so by outlining two distinct Blackamerican Muslim social institutions in Atlanta and showing how they both converge and diverge from mainstream civil rights narratives and offer a way to enrich historical discourses that inform contemporary political possibilities.

MEMORIES AFTER MALCOLM

In this section, I review two distinct Blackamerican Muslim traditions: (1) the IPNA and (2) the West End Community Masjid spearheaded by Imam Jamil Al-Amin. It should be noted that although members of these organizations often share deep institutional, personal, and often familial ties, the groups during the period of review were nonetheless in deep rivalry with one another. This was a result of predictable competitive tendencies found in all social movements but was also due to adversarial political and theological orientations that were exacerbated by the vacuum left by the collapse, delegitimation, and disintegration of the Nation of Islam. Traversing these movements has required sensitivity to this tension but has also allowed us to discover common threads of discourse that unite actors in this space in ways that are often otherwise overlooked.

In the course of building its digital archive, the After Malcolm research team was loaned the only existing full run of the newspaper *al-Islam: The Islamic Movement Journal* published by the IPNA.[15] Founded by Atlanta born and raised Yusef Muzaffaruddin Hamid, IPNA was formally active between 1970 and 1978 in Washington, D.C. It boasted a network of affiliates and members across the United States, which positioned the group as a formidable adversary to the Nation of Islam and rival to the Dar al-Islam. Although the organization did not formally survive for more than a decade, it played an extremely important role in the formation of African American Muslim thought and practice in the post–Malcolm X period, given that a number of influential American Muslim leaders over the last forty years were either official members or active affiliates of the organization.[16]

IPNA as seen in its main publication outlet, *al-Islam,* represents a Blackamerican Muslim tradition that overtly challenges not only the quest to achieve civil rights but the very foundations of secular liberalism and its attendant conceptions of democracy, citizenship, and individual freedom. In doing so, IPNA thought and practice can be firmly placed within a global tradition of Islamic internationalist political activism invested in both the betterment of African American communities in the United States and those fallen victim to Euro-American imperialism abroad.

Over the course of his lifetime, Muzaffaruddin Hamid traversed geographic, ethnic, sectarian, and ideological lines across five continents in his lifelong quest to manifest Islam as a holistic revolutionary movement.

Inspired by Muslim revivalists across the world, Hamid, who was raised in Atlanta and of Guyanese heritage, eventually returned to the city in the late 1970s, when he moved the central branch of the organization from the neighborhood surrounding Howard University in Washington, D.C., to the Atlanta suburb of Conyers on the eastern corridor of the now sprawling metropole. The organization was unable to successfully transition and dissolved within two years of the leadership's move. However, Hamid applied his organizing skills in the Caribbean and Central and South America, where he set up a number of small communities that shared IPNA's mission and vision but took a different name. Like the Dar al-Islam, the W. D. Muhammad communities, and the Nation of Islam, IPNA's connection to the city of Atlanta is a reflection of larger African American and African American Muslim social currents unfolding in the country in the late 1960s and 1970s.

The editorials of *al-Islam,* which were often authored by Hamid himself, exemplify the discourse of Black internationalism that African American Muslims espoused in the post–Malcolm X period. On the first page of the fall 1972 edition, which is also dated as 1392 in reference to the Islamic Hijri calendar, the editorial page has two parallel columns: one side is titled "Zionist Terrorism," the other "Police Brutality." Both articles draw attention to the historical and social contexts of the issues and are discussed through an Islamic framework. The murder of eleven Israeli athletes at the Munich Olympics is juxtaposed with the "24-year-old Zionist usurpation of Palestine" and argues in capitalized letters that "THERE WILL BE NO PEACE IN THE MIDDLE EAST UNLESS JUSTICE IS DONE TO THE PALESTINIAN PEOPLE." The editorial is framed as a persecution of Muslims, as can be seen in the reference to Palestinians' "1,400-year-old heritage" in the land.

On the subject of police brutality, a heightened sense of urgency leads the article, arguing that that trend of "cruel and brutal dealing with youths from the oppressed communities . . . has increased in intensity, resulting in the deaths of at least three teenaged men in a two-week period in three different cities." The article then proceeds to discuss the breakdown of social and family infrastructure in oppressed communities as a root cause of criminal activity that is exploited by law enforcement tactics such as entrapment and surveillance. The solution to the problem of police brutality and juvenile delinquency, the article argues, is to provide the youth "with meaningful family situations where love, moral, emotional and ideological needs are satisfied." Coupled with a "unified community" wherein "neighbors are true brothers and sisters," institutional structures of law enforcement can be challenged. The article concludes, "Islam is the only ideology that can supply such benevolent rules to the people and provide them with the proper guidelines for family and community development." By articulating Islam as an ideological force, Hamid places himself and IPNA firmly within a global tradition of Islamic political revival, a finding that contradicts standing academic perspectives on the relationship between Blackamerican Islam and the so-called ideological trend of Islamism.[17]

Palestinian oppression and U.S. support of Israel have long been a medium through which social justice movements in the United States have framed their own claims. In fact, solidarity with the Palestinian struggle was a marker of anticolonial movements around the world and thereby provided another conduit through which Black internationalists articulated their claims against U.S. imperialism at home and abroad. For example, the American Indian Movement and the Black Panther Party made ideological and institutional connections with the Palestinian Liberation Organization at various phases of their own development, demonstrating that IPNA's identification with Palestinian struggle was simply one of many threads in a tapestry of revolutionary internationalist political thought.

This multilevel solidarity, however, also applied domestically for IPNA leadership as well as others in the post–Malcolm X Blackamerican Muslim milieu. For example, one photograph preserved in the archive shows Hamid proudly shaking hands with an unidentified American Indian leader. Likewise, the intermittently published newspaper of the Mosque of Islamic Brotherhood—the institutional heir to Malcom X's Muslim Mosque Inc.—titled *The Western Sunrise,* features its founding imam El-Hajj Ahmad Tawfiq meeting with Sioux activist Keith Demarais on the cover of its 1976 edition.[18]

The staying power of this Black internationalist paradigm in general and the theme of Palestinian and American Indian solidarity can be seen in the contemporary moment as well. In January 2015, a delegation of racial justice activists composed primarily from the leadership of the Ferguson Black Lives Matter network visited Palestine to draw attention to the similarities between the plight of Palestinians facing occupation and African American communities suffering from institutionalized structures of racism. In the words of Cherrell Brown, one of the delegates, "our oppressors are literally collaborating together, learning from one another—and as oppressed people we have to do the same."[19] Hamid and Tawfiq's solidarity with the American Indian Movement is also a political precursor to current African American Muslim expressions of solidarity with current indigenous

American struggles. For example, Imam Zaid Shakir, cofounder of the Zaytuna Institute (and a former IPNA affiliate who lived as a child in Atlanta) penned an eloquent statement on the interconnectedness of the Sioux battle for land rights in the Standing Rock campaign and the Islamic ritual imperative of "standing" at Arafat during the Hajj Pilgrimage—a letter he wrote just before he physically joined the protests himself.[20] Since Imam Zaid's visit, along with those of other prominent American Muslim activists, such as Linda Sarsour, the Standing Rock platform became one with which Muslims around the United States expressed solidarity. The Islamic Party's platform, though now out of the sight and memory of most historians, can be seen as part of a continuous trend in Black internationalist thought that intersects with a spectrum of global Muslim discourses of anticolonial solidarity. Blackamerican Islam, then, may be seen as a radical political cosmopolitanism that continues to surface at various points in American political thought and find resonance in contemporary practices of resistance today.

Another genealogy of African American Muslim experience in Atlanta can be found in the activities of the Dar al-Islam, which has had a formidable impact on the tone and style of Blackamerican Sunni Islam since the 1960s. Its radical, anti-institutional posture drew supporters from the Black nationalist movement and the wider milieu of Blackamerican Muslims in search of a theological and social platform that did not accept the peculiarities of Elijah Muhammad's Nation of Islam. Established in 1962 by Yahya Abdul Karim, the Dar built a decentralized network of mosques around the country that sought to establish Sunni orthodoxy as the dominant Islamic practice among African Americans. In doing so, the Dar, like other Blackamerican Muslim movements, espoused a political theology of holistic liberation marked by a strident commitment to self-determination and self-governance. This included, for example, the establishment of businesses, the purchase of properties, and especially systematic mechanisms for collective self-defense. Like IPNA, the Dar represents a strand of Black radical internationalism that diverges significantly from the domestically oriented civil rights discourse that reigned over mainstream African American politics at the time. In the same way, its radical posture and institutional location produced a legacy that is paradoxically pervasive and hidden at the same time. That is, while the Dar helped shape Blackamerican Muslim religious sensibilities in contradistinction to the Nation of Islam, by the mid-1980s, internal fragmentation, political marginalization, and state persecution demanded that its legacy be systematically recovered and highlighted to recognize its continued significance.

The original delegation of the Dar al-Islam came to Atlanta in 1969 under the leadership of Imam Mutawaf Shaheed, who spearheaded the Islamic Revivalist Mosque in Cleveland, which became one of the earliest members of the larger network of the Dar. Imam Mutawaf, who has been a principal supporter of the After Malcolm archive, traces his entry into Islam through multiple avenues, including international travel, Black liberation politics, and jazz music.[21] Cleveland was home to a number of active Black national-ist movements, including the Republic of New Libya of Ahmad Evans, who engaged in a deadly shootout with police in the city in 1968. This occurred only two years after the Hough Riots, which also ended in bloodshed and came on the heels of rising racial tensions in the city. Cleveland was also home to an early Islamic presence among both African Americans and immigrants, including an early chapter of the Ahmadiyya Movement and the First Cleveland Mosque of Wali Akram.

It is in this context that Imam Mutawaf discusses his gradual immer-sion into not just the Dar but the wider global network of Muslim social and spiritual activists it invited. In this sense, it is worth mentioning that Imam Mutawaf and his small group of early converts had participated in the outreach activities of the Tablighi Jamaat, the well-known South Asian Deobandi group that focuses on calling upon lay Muslims to increase their pious commitments and religious dedication. Unsatisfied with the group's apolitical orientation, Imam Mutawaf and his small group began develop-ing their own strategies of spreading Islam and establishing small commu-nities dedicated to building a national movement of social and spiritual change based on the basic structure of the Tablighi Jamaat practice of trav-eling for sustained periods of time in active recruitment. This nucleus of individuals would go on to establish mosques in Tennessee, Florida, Ala-bama, and Kansas.

Despite Imam Mutawaf and the Cleveland community being responsi-ble for establishing the first mosque in Atlanta, it is the infamous SNCC chairman and Black Power leader who went into prison as H. Rap Brown in 1971 and came out Imam Jamil Al-Amin who is most commonly associ-ated with the Dar al-Islam's activities in Atlanta. According to oral history interviews with Karima Al-Amin, Imam Jamil's wife, who is an accom-plished lawyer and civil rights activist in her own right, prominent Black leaders in Atlanta, such as Andrew Young and Shirley Franklin, supported H. Rap Brown's family's application to have him paroled in Atlanta upon release from prison. Imam Jamil took up residence with the small commu-nity of Dar members who had established their base in the West End, the neighborhood mentioned earlier known for its diverse array of African American cultural institutions. Imam Jamil's small storefront shop situated directly across from the West End Park quickly became a symbol for the transformative potential of Blackamerican Islam. His burgeoning community began to buy homes in the community, establish a mosque and community center, and build businesses. However, among the most important dimensions of Al-Amin's relocation to Atlanta is the way he and his group of followers systematically rooted out criminal activity in their immediate areas of influence. This was done through a not-so-subtle combination of negotiation and intimidation.

Similar to Hamid of IPNA, Al-Amin also exemplifies the Blackamerican Muslim internationalist tradition with its simultaneous focus on transnational Islamic solidarity and commitment to the empowerment of Muslims as a collective force in the United States. By the early 1980s, Imam Jamil had risen as the recognized leader of the national Dar al-Islam movement, which had undergone significant cleavages and fragmentation. The network of mosques throughout the country—and even some in the Caribbean—was now renamed simply "the Community" or "al-Ummah." Imam Jamil's community represented, it was said, upward of ten thousand members, which demanded that he be recognized as one of the country's national Muslim leaders, a fact that placed him on significant national Muslim platforms and within institutions. In addition to working toward long-established Blackamerican Muslim goals of spiritual revolution and social liberation, Imam Jamil was influential in participating in the Bosnia Task Force, a pan-Islam network that included prominent American Muslim networks and institutions. His community was, then, naturally involved in the resettlement of a number of Bosnian refugees to the small community of Clarkston just outside of Atlanta in the mid- to late 1990s.

Today, Imam Jamil's successor in Atlanta is Imam Nadim Ali, a practicing therapist known for helping both Muslims and non-Muslims with personal, familiar, and marriage struggles. His calm and steady demeanor is a trademark of a life of disciplined spiritual transformation that translates into a continuation of Imam Jamil's steady approach to social change. Imam Nadim is a regular member of Atlanta-wide Muslim institutions, supporting causes both domestically and internationally. Like Imam Jamil, he and his community have largely steered away from the street protests and political struggles that mark the contemporary moment in favor a much longer term set of goals based on a platform of holistic and collective empowerment.

DISREMEMBERING AND DISREGARDING

The central argument of this essay has been that triumphant narratives of civil rights history not only obscure the objective historical record by privileging discourses that buttress the American imperial project but also cloud intellectual capacity in the contemporary context to manage the challenges of social polarization and practices of disenfranchisement that mark the American political landscape. Moreover, I have argued that the dominance of the civil rights cum American nationalist narrative has also led to a vacuum of scholarship on alternative narratives of political, social, and spiritual freedom that have been articulated by a long tradition of Blackamerican Muslim thinkers. This vacuum is not only a deliberate result of a particular political posture but the active site of contested visions on how to manage both the past and the present. In a poignant demonstration of this phenomenon, I close with an example of Randall Kennedy, the well-known Harvard law professor and public intellectual whose early clerkship with the towering figure of Thurgood Marshall places him firmly within a critical tradition of legal racial politics in American history.

In a brief commentary published in the *Boston Review* in March 2015 titled "Protesting Too Much: The Trouble with Black Power Revisionism," Randall Kennedy argues stridently that the recent rise in scholarship surrounding figures in the Black Power movement, such as Malcolm X, Huey Newton, and Stokely Carmichael, by formidable historians, such as the late Manning Marable and Peniel Joseph, are irredeemably flawed. He says that such historical works "seek to elevate the reputations of black power radicals. But their efforts are subverted by sloppy argumentation and insistent adulation. In each of these books, analysis is overshadowed by hagiography."[22] Kennedy is hardly original in pointing out that historical memory is always incomplete, selective, and moralistic. Despite the irony, neither is he the first to avoid the application of that criticism on his own portrait of the past. What distinguishes Kennedy's criticism is that he unapologetically makes the case that figures from the Black radical tradition simply do not deserve to be remembered—that Malcolm was a poor leader, that SNCC was destroyed under the leadership of Stokely Carmichael and H. Rap Brown, and that their projects never contributed to the betterment of Black life in this country. For him, it is only the legal and mainstream institutional framework of American politics that can offer any lasting influence on the lives of Black Americans. I am not interested in challenging Kennedy's views given the long history of criticism that has come from his own peers and even mentors, such as the late Derrick Bell, who preceded him at Harvard.

Rather, I would simply like to point out how the hagiographic civil rights discourse he embodies so thoroughly alienates him and others who hold this view from the contemporary unfolding political resistance against structural racism and its attendant discourses.[23]

For example, Kennedy's article was published just months before heightened national tension surrounding police brutality, lack of government responsiveness, and increasing white supremacist violence. The murder of Freddie Gray in Baltimore on April 12, 2015, for example, set off weeks of civil unrest that demonstrated the volatility of the political environment in the city. Just two months later, Sandra Bland was found dead in police custody on July 13 in a Texas jail. However, the murder of nine members of the Emanuel African Methodist Episcopal Church in Charleston by Dylann Roof, a young white supremacist, was the most forceful reminder that the embers of hate and racial discord permeated all capillaries of society.

During this season of social unrest, it is important to note the presence of African American Muslim networks, leaders, and organizations actively contributing to the national conversation on justice and equality. In addition, a national online campaign spearheaded by Faatimah Knight, a young Black Muslim graduate of Zaytuna College—which was cofounded by Imam Zaid Shakir—managed to raise more than $100,000 in response to the burning of multiple churches in summer 2015. In Baltimore, as the riots began to settle, Mayor Stephanie Rawlings-Blake thanked the Nation of Islam, saying that the organization had "been very present in our effort to keep calm and peace in our city." Conservative figures and media outlets nationwide fiercely criticized her for her praise of the organization, but many familiar with the local context recognized the powerful stabilizing force the Nation of Islam has played in Baltimore for generations. Mayor Rawlings-Blake knew that the Nation of Islam had the capability to help city leaders manage the unrest because of the tremendous political capital it had amassed, in part because of its "radical" messaging and programming of self-determination and community empowerment.

The contrast between Mayor Rawlings-Blake's engagement with a living tradition of Black radicalism and Kennedy's disavowal thereof is indicative of the larger pattern in the disjuncture between national nostalgia and the demands of contemporary politics. The collapse of Atlanta's civil rights myth, for example, was palpable in 2016 as Atlanta activists, led by the Black Lives Matter movement, managed to shut down a major highway in the heart of the city in response to the shooting of Alton Sterling in Baton Rouge. Mayor Kasim Reed endorsed the protestors' right to civil disobedience but invoked the mythical patron saint as a nonagitator who didn't risk the safety of his supporters: "We hear this generation's concern, and the protest tonight, but we're going to have to do it in a King-ian fashion. . . . We're going to have to make sure that people remain safe," he said.[24] National observers were shocked by Reed's claim that MLK "would never take a freeway."[25] The gulf between grassroots activists and Black Lives Matter was especially apparent when the iconic Ambassador Andrew Young categorically dismissed the political demands of the protestors, referring to them as "unlovable brats." These comments, in addition to his meeting to show support of police officers, drew uncharacteristically harsh comments from the NAACP, which effectively called for his retirement.[26]

It should be conceded by thought leaders, scholars, and political actors that the civil rights narrative, and its attendant liberal framework of human rights, is utterly unequipped to manage the contemporary political challenges unfolding in the both domestic and international spheres. Rather, as political actors mobilize their material and intellectual resources to challenge the abuses of empire abroad and the structures of disenfranchisement domestically, they would be strengthened to understand their struggles in a larger historical tradition of resistance. In particular, cultivating and curating the radical tradition of Blackamerican Muslim thought and practice may help lend insight into how to navigate the current political moment fraught with domestic polarization and international uncertainty.

Notes

1. Walter Benjamin, *The Arcades Project,* trans. Rolf Tiedemann (Cambridge, Mass.: Belknap Press of Harvard University Press, 1999); Graeme Gilloch, *Myth and Metropolis: Walter Benjamin and the City* (Cambridge: Polity Press, 2013).

2. Kimberly Kortla, "Domestic Minor Sex Trafficking in the United States," *Social Work* 55, no. 2 (2010): 181–87; Raisa Habersham, "FBI Arrests 21 Accused in Georgia Sex Trafficking Sting," *Atlanta Journal Constitution,* October 18, 2016.

3. Jason Henderson, "Secessionist Automobility: Racism, Anti-urbanism, and the Politics of Automobility in Atlanta, Georgia," *International Journal of Urban and Regional Research* 30, no. 2 (2006): 293–307; Alan Blinder, "Atlanta Educators Convicted in School Cheating Scandal," *New York Times,* April 1, 2015.

4. Kevin M. Kruse, *White Flight: Atlanta and the Making of Modern Conservatism* (Princeton, N.J.: Princeton University Press, 2007).

5. Ibid.

6. Natsu Taylor Saito, "Whose Liberty—Whose Security—the USA PATRIOT Act in the Context of COINTELPRO and the Unlawful Repression of Political Dissent," *Oregon Law Review* 81 (2002): 1051; Khaled A. Beydoun, "Islamophobia: Toward a Legal Definition and Framework," *Columbia Law Review Online* 116 (2016): 108.

7. https://www.civilandhumanrights.org/about-us/.

8. Sheila Dewan, "Gentrification Changing Face of New Atlanta," *New York Times*, March 11, 2006, http://www.nytimes.com/2006/03/11/us/gentrification -changing-face-of-new-atlanta.html?_r=0.

9. Charles Rutheiser, "Making Place in the Nonplace Urban Realm: Notes on the Revitalization of Downtown Atlanta," in *Theorizing the City: The New Urban Anthropology Reader*, ed. Setha M. Low (New Brunswick, N.J.: Rutgers University Press, 1999), 317–41. For a timely master's thesis on this subject, see Dominique Wilkins, "The Effect of Athletic Stadiums on Communities, with a Focus on Housing," International Development, Community and Environment, 2016, http://com mons.clarku.edu/idce_masters_papers/88/.

10. I borrow the term *Blackamerican Islam* from Sherman A. Jackson's seminal work *Islam and the Blackamerican: Looking toward the Third Resurrection* (Oxford: Oxford University Press, 2005).

11. http://sites.gsu.edu/am.

12. Daulatzai, *Black Star, Crescent Moon: The Muslim International and Black Freedom beyond America* (Minneapolis: University of Minnesota, 2012), xi.

13. Imam Furqan's oral history can be found at http://sites.gsu.edu/am/oral -histories/.

14. Daulatzai, *Black Star, Crescent Moon*, xii.

15. For a brief introduction to this collection, see Abbas Barzegar, "Seeing and Reading *al-Islam*: The Visual Rhetoric of the Islamic Party of North America's Newspaper (1971–78)," *Liquid Blackness*, 72–84, http://liquidblackness.com/publi cations/fluid-radicalisms/.

16. Khalid Griggs, "Islamic Party in North America: A Quiet Storm of Political Activism," in *Muslim Minorities in the West: Visible and Invisible*, 77–106 (Walnut Creek, Calif.: Alta Mira Press, 2002).

17. See, e.g., Edward Curtis's article "Islamism and Its African American Muslim Critics: Black Muslims in the Era of the Arab Cold War," *American Quarterly* 59, no. 3 (2007): 683–709, which argues that African American Muslim critics largely eschewed global Islamist politics. For a robust discussion on the consequences of the analytic category of "Islamism," see Richard Martin and Abbas Barzegar, eds., *Islamism: Contested Perspectives on Political Islam* (Princeton, N.J.: Princeton University Press, 2009).

18. This document is available at http://digitalcollections.library.gsu.edu/utils/ getfile/collection/Islam/id/1937/filename/1918.pdfpage/page/1.

19. Kristian David Bailey, "Dream Defenders, Black Lives Matter and Ferguson Reps Take Historic Trip to Palestine," *Ebony*, January 9, 2015, http://www.ebony .com/news-views/dream-defenders-black-lives-matter-ferguson-reps-take-historic -trip-to-palestine#axzz3WpK47TtB.

20. Article available at https://www.newislamicdirections.com/nid/notes/stand ing_at_arafat_standing_with_standing_rock_standing_in_the_need_of_pray.

21. His oral history can also be found at http://sites.gsu.edu/am/oral-histories/.

22. Randall Kennedy, "Protesting Too Much," *Boston Review*, March 23, 2015, http://bostonreview.net/books-ideas/randall-kennedy-protesting-too-much-black -power-revisionism.

23. Derrick Bell, "The Strange Career of Randall Kennedy," *New Politics* 7, no. 1 (new series), whole no. 25, Summer 1998.

24. "Atlanta Mayor Kasim Reed's Protest Performance Draws Praise," *Atlanta Journal Constitution*, July 9, 2016, http://politics.blog.ajc.com/2016/07/09/atlanta-mayor-kasim-reeds-protest-performance-draws-praise/.

25. See, e.g., Jeanne Theoharis, "MLK Would Never Shut Down a Freeway, and 6 Other Myths about the Civil Rights Movement and Black Lives Matter," *The Root,* July 15, 2016.

26. Richard Halicks, "Andrew Young Apologizes for 'Unlovable Little Brats' Remark," *Atlanta Journal Constitution,* July 12, 2016.

8

Like 1979 All Over Again

Resisting Left Liberalism among Iranian Émigrés

ARASH DAVARI

I had a wild imagination. I wasn't anything more than eleven years old, yet I somehow managed to think about the Islamic Republic of Iran in fantastic terms. In stories of family members' long-gone political activism, I found an explanation for the discordance of immigrant life in the United States. It was romantic and simple: my family was here because they had stood up against the U.S. government's support of a dictator. In stories about family members' persecution, I entertained a terrifying possibility. Imagining myself to be a political prisoner in Iran, I'd convince myself to eat foods I didn't like, as if my ability to swallow the remainder of my grandmother's haphazardly cooked soup in a dimly lit apartment in Los Angeles could secure the survival of a fledgling political faction in a country I hadn't visited since infancy. The world was made to make sense somewhere between these inherited vestiges of romance and terror.

I was the child of displaced Marxist activists—which, to me, meant I had access to truths others weren't ready to hear. More often than not, our leftist imagination was defined in opposition to life in the Islamic Republic. The distant yet constant presence of Iran helped us navigate the turbulent waters of migration. We had found ourselves in a United States where the dissident spirit of the 1960s and 1970s seemed to have been replaced by a consensus around Ronald Reagan's presidency—where the promise of organized activism seemed to have given way to neoliberal social policies. In that unfamiliar and unwelcoming environment, our shared imagination was a life raft, ordering the chaotic memories of the past while providing direction for what might come to pass.

Despite our best efforts, stability proved fleeting. There were moments when the past made an unexpected appearance in our lives, provoking a sense of panic bordering on rage. I remember the day my aunt received a phone call that left her in tears. Her cousin had been executed. I remember the night a family friend paced the sidewalk in front of our home, hitting himself as my parents attempted to calm him down while I peered through the blinds. I was told something about a nervous breakdown. I remember tones changing—uncles and aunties discarding their normally sweet cadence for clumsy curse words. In the 1980s and early 1990s, these crises folded themselves into our routines.

Things always seemed to be worse when we talked about Islam. If someone so much as hinted at a sympathetic portrait of Islam in a political context—an increasingly common conversation in leftist circles after September 11, 2001—reactions were fierce. There were those who maintained an anti-imperialist posture, finding resistance to American ventures in Afghanistan and Iraq in Islamist social movements. But the majority stood at the opposite corner of family gatherings. They included longtime exiles who had spent the 1990s following the ups and downs of Iran's domestic politics through Sunday morning news broadcasts on KCET as well as recent migrants—young people increasingly closer to my age, touting the authority of authentic experience from years of personal and professional disappointment. They responded to the slightest hint of sympathy for Islamist movements with condescension. They had already experienced what "radical Islam" could do firsthand, well before anyone cared to listen. Once Islam mixed with politics, they had been telling the world, it couldn't be reasoned with. This was like 1979 all over again. "We told you so," they said.

How has a previous generation's left politics become today's liberal consensus? How does this consensus coalesce with an anti-Muslim attitude, one that precludes our critiques of empire? What of the Iranian Left in an age defined by the "War on Terror"? What of the Left in any number of similarly migrant or exilic populations from Muslim majority nation-states?

In our political climate, these Iranian émigrés may unwittingly become a new breed of native informant. Buoyed by a sense of historical injury, the effort to think critically about politics in Iran from abroad has dovetailed too neatly with efforts to define human rights against manifestations of collective political resistance. To be sure, the predilection is not limited to assessments of Islamism. But it rears its head most forcefully when Islam is mentioned. It undermines any effort to entertain the possibility that Islamist movements could make legitimate claims to political power by asserting the backwardness of Islam in general.

The assertions are said to make sense because they are spoken by those who claim to know them to be true, viscerally: an older generation of Iranians who suffered real historical wrongs in the wake of the 1979 revolution, now living in exile as a result; a younger generation who experienced similar feelings of hope and despair over the course of postrevolutionary Iran's various social movements. For years, the most forceful proponents of this position among my parents' generation had little to rely on but regret for perceived past mistakes. When younger activists came along, they became exemplars of what social change should be: purer manifestations of the "nonpolitical" and "nonideological" commitments underlying a shared liberal ideal.

In the unqualified affirmation of that ideal, a range of possible struggles for dignity and justice are rendered illegible—not debated and refuted on points of merit but simply silenced wholesale. The blind spots are part of a broader logic that refuses to understand why, after the revolution in Iran, anyone would consider rallying against the U.S. government under the banner of Islam. The U.S. government couldn't agree more.

Left Liberal Melancholia

Left liberalism is a political disposition. It channels leftist rhetoric, energies, tactics, and affectations in the service of liberal ideals. Unlike the liberal Left—for whom liberalism contains and supplements the excesses of leftist politics—left liberalism deploys radical ideas to reassert the status quo. Among émigrés[1] from the greater Middle East, left liberalism poses a unique political challenge. Politics cast in this register can readily align with anti-Muslim sensibilities in Europe and the United States. Among Iranian émigrés in particular, left liberalism acts as a point of convergence between yesterday's revolutionaries (an older generation of disillusioned leftists) and today's reformists (a younger generation of recently migrated activists and artists).

Like all revolutions, the 1979 revolution in Iran had its "losers"—political actors who failed to secure power and instead suffered the violent consequences of state consolidation. The sense of loss felt by yesterday's revolutionaries only affirms the self-righteousness found among today's reform-minded youth.[2] Younger reformists cite admissions of past failure and culpability by yesterday's revolutionaries as adequate justification for the need to turn away from revolutionary politics altogether. Loss fuels the fires of left liberalism. How might we temper those flames by addressing the loss that brings us together? If left liberalism is a prevalent disposition among

Iranian émigrés and loss our shared emotional bond, an acknowledgment of past disappointments might help us avoid the minefields underlying the current political consensus.

In an effort to theorize the political stakes of loss, Wendy Brown describes left melancholia as a disavowal of the present in favor of the past. Its paradoxical nature derives from a displaced and disproportionate love for the ideals that previously promised to change the world; we hold on to these past ideals with such ferocity and passion that our attachment blinds us to the now. Brown presents the concept to explain reactions against identity politics and poststructuralism by those holding on to the promises "signified by the terms *Left, Socialism, Marx,* or *the Movement.*"[3] As neoliberalism and post-Fordism took root, the European and American Left turned to traditionalism, in effect associating all forms of political and economic change with Thatcher and Reagan. The unresponsive and unchanging solutions adopted as a result—maintaining the promises of the New Deal and protecting civil liberties at all costs—prevented the Left from considering new alternatives engaged with the existing world. In the imaginary of the left melancholic, it is because of the divergence from the ideal of left unity by other leftists that the ideal has been lost, not the inapplicability and disappointment of the ideal itself.[4]

While there very well may be Iranians who fit Brown's description to the letter, the more pernicious challenge facing Iranian émigrés requires revisions to her thesis. There is a difference between left melancholia and left liberal melancholia—a difference on display in community events across Southern California where the largest population resides.[5] To be sure, in an echo of Brown's description, small contingents of activists attend and often disrupt proceedings when their tenor hints at any semblance of reform. They flash the anti-imperialist rhetoric of the 1970s as a way to vilify a much larger group who have since embraced the language of liberal democracy and human rights.[6]

Yet despite pretensions to reform and progressive evolution, the larger group's vision is fettered by the past too. The opposing sides in these community events are mirror images of one another, even if their shared characteristics are not readily apparent. Many in the larger group have jettisoned Marxist critique for commerce and capitalism. Many long ago suffered what Hamid Naficy calls an "identity crisis," turning their attention from politics to culture.[7] Yet these substantive ruptures were accompanied by an attachment to past reflexes in practice. Or rather, left liberal melancholia is constituted by the eager rejection of past principles through the continued performance of past practices. In left melancholia, as Brown argues, one disavows the present by embracing a past ideal of left unity. In left liberal melancholia, while pretensions to left unity are forgotten in exchange for new ideas, there nevertheless remains a refusal to relinquish the practice of believing in a utopian promise—one that might animate universal change in the future. The previously cherished objective of Marxist revolution becomes the pursuit of human rights.[8] That newfound utopian ideal is projected backward in a manner that parallels the left melancholic's attachment to left unity. In the imaginary of the left liberal melancholic, it is because of divergences from secular liberalism that the 1979 revolution was lost, not the inapplicability and disappointment of secular liberalism itself. At its worst, the crudest form of old left politics can shape the left liberal émigré's pursuit of human rights: the act of imagining a utopian world and employing whatever means necessary to achieve it.

We must not forget that the liberalism distinguishing the ideology of these democratic activists emerged out of a direct encounter with revolutionary politics. Unlike the European and American Left, these are people who lived the promises and disappointments of an actual revolution. Their lost ideal is not figurative. It is the physical absence of fellow activists who died. Under these conditions, when one debases the ideological, one debases one's past selves. In the wake of what is now perceived to have been political excess, revolutionary activism and revolutionary thought are set aside in favor of a much more palatable liberal ideology of nonideology.

For this reason, left liberal melancholia's unintended consequences are tragic. Former student activists, today's left liberals had once worked up the courage to risk life and limb in protest against the Pahlavi state for its dependence on Western powers. And yet, many of these exiles' lives have since been tied to the protections afforded by the very liberal democratic regimes they challenged. Former student activists, today's left liberals spent the 1970s marching in solidarity alongside Ethiopians, Vietnamese, Palestinians, Chileans, and Black Americans. And yet, despite its covert attachment to the past's utopian promise, left liberalism's overt denial of the past inadvertently parallels the national myth advanced by the Pahlavi state.

Denying the cosmopolitan roots of Iranian national identity in practice,[9] that myth linked modern Iranians to an ancient self-designation as *ariya*. The link, however, was not direct. Confusing shared linguistic roots with race, twentieth-century Pahlavi nationalists' efforts to draw a link to *ariya* were mediated by contemporaneous European conceptions of "Aryan" identity—which, of course, projected whiteness as racial superiority. The result was the term *ārīyāyī*, a "self-Orientalizing" understanding of Iran and Iranians as Europeans geographically misplaced in a sea of (inferior) Arab nation-states.[10]

The *ārīyāyī* concept has endured in exile, partly because its anti-Arab qualities provide easy fodder for reactionary politics in response to the outcome of the 1979 revolution. For many of Iran's monarchist exiles, the privileges lost through the experience of the revolution and the privileges gained through honorary whiteness relative to other immigrant populations have only further encouraged it.[11] For left liberal Iranian émigrés, a shared target of opposition has allowed a slippage into similar rhetorical patterns.[12] Elder family members tell young men to shave their beards because they resemble "Hezbollāh." Uncles mock university students for taking Arabic language courses, justifying an argument against education by suggesting that Arabs never contributed anything to "civilization." These former leftists exude an idyllic love for Iran's secular letters.[13] These former leftists exude an idyllic love for human rights, drawing a mythical link between contemporary rights discourse and the Cyrus Cylinder.[14] These former leftists exude an idyllic love for the cosmopolitan, only if and when the cosmopolitan appears European.

Their seemingly innocent preferences teeter at the edge of a precipice. Just over that edge, left liberal melancholia turns into anti-Muslim vitriol, threatening to place a commitment to social justice in the service of today's American military ventures. I've spoken with a handicrafts salesman who travels across Europe for business carrying five editions of the Qur'an in five separate languages, each marked in a color-coded fashion to identify statements he claims contradict human rights principles. He had been raised in a working-class religious household in Iran; he had turned to Marxism as a student activist just before the revolution; he had watched as friends and family were imprisoned, then executed, in the years that followed. He now lives as an exile in Europe, where he champions the virtues of social democracy and *laïcité*. At a time when secularism facilitates war, the otherwise innocent act of sharing one's anger and frustration with strangers—an act that disavows contemporary configurations of power in the persistent effort to acknowledge past traumas—inadvertently functions as proselytization for European and American violence against people racialized as Muslim.

THE PITFALLS OF LIBERAL POLITICS
BETWEEN IRAN AND ITS ÉMIGRÉS

Short of calling a political opponent "counterrevolutionary," the worst label one could muster in 1979 Iran was "liberal." Immediately after the revolution, a provisional government ruled from February until November 1979. It drew the majority of its cabinet members from the Society for the Defense of Freedom and Human Rights (Jimā'at-i Difā az Azādi va Hūqūq Bashar)—an opposition group formed in late 1977 to take advantage of political openings afforded in response to the Carter administration's newly adopted rights agenda. The provisional government's prime minister, long-time activist Mehdi Bāzargān, was a founding member of the Liberation Movement of Iran—an offshoot of the National Front intent on combining liberal ideals with Islamist politics to affirm the democratic promise underlying the 1905 Iranian Constitution.

The provisional government and the equally liberal first draft of the Islamic Republic's constitution were regularly challenged and excoriated by various groups of radical leftist activists. The sentiment continued well into the Iran–Iraq War. To counter the rising tide of support for groups advocating continued revolutionary activity, the Revolutionary Council and, later, the Islamic Republican Party pivoted toward an anti-imperialist position. Ezzatollāh Sahābi, one of the first directors of the Planning and Budget Office in postrevolutionary Iran and a prominent advocate of the effort to separate political considerations from the exercise of technocratic expertise, recounts young "Hezbollāhis" blocking his attempts to leverage popular support for the war in order to wean the country off its reliance on oil production. Out of fear for the challenge posed to state consolidation by radical leftist groups, populist reason triumphed over technocratic expertise.[15]

Nearly twenty years later—when revolutionary consolidation was well on its way, the war had come to an end, and leftist forces had become a negligible force in global politics—Sahābi's position reemerged. Its return to prominence was ironically facilitated by many of those same young "Hezbollāhis." The September 11 attacks in the United States occurred in the midst of a significant upheaval in Iran's domestic politics. Mohammad Khatami's unexpected presidential election in 1997 and the ensuing parliamentary victory of Reformist candidates in 1999 inaugurated a series of political battles between the revolution's internal factions.[16] The newly minted Reformists were the same left-leaning economic nationalists who had dominated public office in the 1980s. At the time, Ayatollah Ruhollāh Khomeini's ability to maneuver the differences between various factions allowed these left-leaning economic nationalists to coexist alongside a socially and economically conservative judiciary. The former faded from the public eye just as the Cold War came to an end. Khomeini's death in 1989, the end of the Iran–Iraq War (lasting from 1980 to 1988, during which time state subsidies were popular), and the attempt to usher in free-market economic policies as part of postwar reconstruction all contributed to the Islamic Left's diminishing ideological, geopolitical, and economic influence.

The Reformist movement reintroduced yesterday's leftist factions to sanctioned political competition. The turn of events set a precedent for future mobilizations. People who had climbed Iran's social ladders by virtue of the welfare state now became its critics.[17] In accordance with the neoliberal logic that came to define the language of global justice after the 1970s, Reformists translated the appeal for social change into an appeal for human rights and democracy. Whereas political actors shied away from liberalism in the past, liberalism became the ideology of resistance in our present. A commitment to state subsidies was set aside in favor of an emphasis on rights pertaining to the rule of law. This language of rights—women's rights, labor rights, the rights of free speech and association, and above all human rights—dominated the new agenda, now focused on intervening in the political sphere by creating changes in civil society.

The brief success of the Reformist movement in Iran inspired a new cycle of hope and despair among Iranian émigrés. The by-now fading dreams of counterrevolution held by many critics of the regime abroad found renewed voice in its vocabulary. The idea emerged that working within the system presented a tangible alternative for the time being, if not a pathway for lasting change. But Khatami's limitations and eventual failures provoked a renewed sense of disillusion—a sense that began to set in as early as his reelection in 2001. Many émigrés set Khatami aside as a leader not up to the task of standing against the establishment. Others saw him as a stooge of the regime, deliberately sent to appease liberal aspirations while preserving the fundamental structure of the state. Because their sense of disillusion focused on a rejection of the individuals who led the Reform movement, it allowed the ideological principles that underwrote the movement to linger. The promise of liberalism remained.

That promise contains important political possibilities when it manifests as *means*. Individuals in Iran and abroad shrewdly navigate the ambiguities afforded by "nonpolitical" modes of social action—in art, public policy, the preservation of historical memory, the provision of social services, technological innovations, and theology. These realms need not directly engage contentious politics but nevertheless create opportunities for politically laden interpretations and yet-to-be-defined social transformation.

Yet when that liberal promise becomes an *end*, its pitfalls are more pronounced. The pitfalls prove especially true for the left liberal émigré. For its part, left liberal melancholia involves a continued (albeit disavowed) attachment to leftist politics as its means. It retains a sense of sacrifice for a utopian ideal even as it jettisons utopianism (in name) and a broader leftist project (in practice). Its objective, or *end*, is the "nonpolitical" itself.

Take discussions of ideology. Left liberal émigrés reject the emphasis they once placed on ideological debates. Their regret becomes the basis for outward critique—that is, instead of dwelling in the uncertainty of past loss, the melancholic debases a substitute object. In one iteration, émigré scholars strive to understand why the Left lost the revolution. They respond by presenting the Left as ideologically outmaneuvered by its political opponents, and they explain why an Islamic ideology was more resonant for Iran's revolutionary mass. In effect, one rejects and ridicules one's previous belief that Marxism could have appealed to Iranians in 1979, especially when retrospectively measured against charismatic appeals to Islam. Beneath the self-abnegation lies a subtle and more profound challenge to the political intelligence of the revolution's popular mass: every story of interpellation requires a mass to follow its (charismatic) leader. With this, left liberal scholars and pundits contribute to images of people from the Middle East moved by religion—not moving on their own, in a self-determined fashion.[18] Taken to its extreme, this perspective calls for a rejection of ideology altogether. Ideology, the émigré concludes, is quite simply counter to the promise of democratic coexistence. We cannot respond to contemporary political problems with ideological answers. We have already experienced what ideological movements do firsthand. It would be like 1979 all over again.

In this vein, left liberalism hews too closely to the status quo. By virtue of its continued reaction to the past, it makes us believe that certain political possibilities are impossible. What is more, by virtue of its continued attachment to the past, it aggressively argues for social transformation on terms that mirror the terms of Western military intervention in the greater Middle East: interventions made in the name of humanitarianism, democracy promotion, and individual human rights, interventions whose nonviolent aspirations have paradoxically generated more violence, death, and destruction in people's daily lives. It is for new voices of exile to dispute and disrupt that status quo—to shake a generation's worth of reaction and attachment to the past.

NOTES

I am grateful to Amirhassan Boozari, Sohail Daulatzai, Junaid Rana, and Solmaz Sharif for their helpful suggestions on earlier drafts.

1. I have deliberately chosen to use the term *émigré* instead of *exile, refugee,* or *expatriate* to describe communities of migrants from the greater Middle East (Iran, in particular) currently living in North America and Europe. This choice follows Edward Said's discussion of the differences between these terms in "Reflections on Exile," in *Reflections on Exile and Other Essays* (Cambridge, Mass.: Harvard University Press, 2000), 181. For Said, an *exile* is banished and cannot return home; the term carries a touch of "solitude and spirituality." The *refugee* lacks this affect. He or she is instead a product (and a victim) of the twentieth-century state. In contrast to both, the *expatriate* chooses to live in a foreign country. The term *émigré* reflects an ambiguity that may include "exile" (which many Iranian leftists as well as monarchists experienced) as well as more voluntary forms of economic migration. It also encompasses transitions from a status of exile to one of nation building—from powerlessness to power. In this sense, *émigré* better captures the range of migratory experiences undergirding parallels to anti-Muslim animus among certain groups of Iranians.

2. Hamid Naficy describes a "triple sense of loss" among leftist Iranian exiles. See *The Making of Exile Cultures: Iranian Television in Los Angeles* (Minneapolis: University of Minnesota Press, 1993), 12–15.

3. Wendy Brown, "Resisting Left Melancholia," in *Loss,* ed. David L. Eng and David Kazanjian (Berkeley: University of California Press, 2003), 460.

4. Brown's formulation draws from and develops earlier formulations by Sigmund Freud and Walter Benjamin. See Freud, "Mourning and Melancholia," in *General Psychological Theory: Papers on Metapsychology,* 161–78 (New York: Simon and Schuster, 1991); Benjamin, "Left-Wing Melancholy," in *Walter Benjamin: Selected Writings,* vol. 2, part 2, trans. Rodney Livingstone, ed. Michael W. Jennings, Howard Eiland, and Gary Smith, 423–27 (Cambridge, Mass.: Harvard University Press, 1999). In psychoanalytic terms, instead of coming to terms with its absence, the individual in love with an ideal develops a narcissistic identification, which serves as a substitute. This substitute is abused and debased, presenting itself as an object of hate. As a result, the individual may unload his disappointment with the ideal for having changed or disappeared while preserving the image of the ideal as it was in the past. Freud considers these dynamics in a situation where a lover loses her beloved to death. Instead of mourning (and accepting) the loss, the lover holds on to the beloved by falling into a state of self-deprecation. The lover identifies her own ego with the beloved; by beating herself up, she expresses her frustration at the beloved for leaving while holding on to an image of the beloved as infallible. With specifically *left* melancholia, however, Brown follows Benjamin's lead, extrapolating from the dynamic described by Freud to discuss a condition where the substitute object of hate becomes other members of the Left.

5. My observations are based on multiple ethnographic visits to associational meetings in Southern California in 2009–10, when the 2009 presidential election in Iran and the social movement that followed were a regular topic of conversation.

6. For a description of prominent and particularly disruptive examples of this practice—the 2000 Berlin Conference hosting prominent Reformists from Iran, which was disrupted by a cohort of leftist exiles, leading to considerable setbacks for the reform movement in Iran, and similar disruptions at the meetings of the International Women's Science Foundation over the course of the 1990s—see Halleh Ghorashi and Kees Boersma, "The 'Iranian Diaspora' and the New Media: From Political Action to Humanitarian Help," *Development and Change* 40, no. 4 (2009): 677, 681–82. Notably, not all left opposition groups were opposed to the Berlin conference. See Ziba Mir-Hosseini and Richard Tapper, *Islam and Democracy in Iran: Eshkevari and the Quest for Reform* (London: I. B. Tauris, 2006), 38. For a more sympathetic account of left exiles as a "Diaspora within a Diaspora," ostracized for their attachment to the past and consequently misunderstood, see Pardis Shafafi, "Long Distance Activism: Looking beyond Teaching Old Dogmatics New Tricks," in *Identity and Exile: The Iranian Diaspora between Solidarity and Difference*, ed. Resa Mohabbat-Kar, 80–90 (Berlin: Heinrich Böll Foundation, 2015). The distinction I draw between left melancholia and left liberal melancholia parallels Shafafi's distinction between "old dogmatics," on one hand, and, on the other, commentators who bemoan a lack of cohesion in the Iranian diaspora because of ideological differences, accusing the former of outdated rigidity.

7. Naficy, *Making of Exile Cultures*, 53–54. Ghorashi and Boersma present this development as a shift from exilic to diasporic patterns of identity—from political action in a posture of resolute opposition against the Islamic Republic to "humanitarian help" and charity efforts based on distinctions between various groups in Iran and a related ambivalent attachment to one's homeland. See "'Iranian Diaspora' and New Media," 667–91.

8. For a related discussion of European and American activists' turn to individual human rights as a "last utopia," see Samuel Moyn, *The Last Utopia: Human Rights in History* (Cambridge, Mass.: Belknap Press of Harvard University Press, 2010).

9. For discussions of these cosmopolitan roots, see Hamid Dabashi, *Iran: A People Interrupted* (New York: New Press, 2007), and Dabashi, *Iran without Borders: Towards a Critique of the Postcolonial Nation* (London: Verso, 2016). For a complementary account that emphasizes material conditions—specifically, territorial land and geography—see Firoozeh Kashani-Sabet, *Frontier Fictions: Shaping the Iranian Nation, 1804–1946* (Princeton, N.J.: Princeton University Press, 1999).

10. Reza Zia-Ebrahimi, "Self-Orientalization and Dislocation: The Uses and Abuses of the 'Aryan' Discourse in Iran," *Iranian Studies* 44, no. 4 (2011): 445–72. For a discussion of "dislocative nationalism" as a dominant ideology with appeal across the political spectrum, see Reza Zia-Ebrahimi, *The Emergence of Iranian Nationalism: Race and the Politics of Dislocation* (New York: Columbia University, 2016). For a much-needed and well-crafted critique of recent collaborations between Iranian American proponents of an Aryan myth and the alt right, see Amy Tahani-Bidmeshki, M. Shadee Malaklou, Nasrin Rahimieh, and Parisa Vaziri, "An Open Letter to Iranian/American Academics and Scholars in the United States," *Medium*, September 14, 2017, https://medium.com/@amytahanimadain/an-open-letter-to-iranian-american-academics-and-scholars-in-the-united-states-3c25bd1f7051.

11. For a discussion of anti-Muslim sentiment in cultural production by monarchist exiles during the 1980s and 1990s, see Naficy, *Making of Exile Cultures*, 83. For a study of Iranian Americans' strategic identifications with whiteness in the public sphere, see Nilou Mostofi, "Who We Are: The Perplexity of Iranian-American Identity," *Sociological Quarterly* 44, no. 4 (2003): 693–97. A status of honorary whiteness came to conflict with many Iranian immigrants' lived experiences after 9/11—what Neda Maghbouleh calls "the limits of whiteness." The state had granted recognition through whiteness, and yet the lived experience of discrimination after 9/11 indicated otherwise. The racial paradox played out across generational divides—an older generation of immigrants willingly identifying as white and a younger generation of Iranian Americans resisting the label—as well as changes across time: an older generation coming to see themselves as nonwhite through their children. See Maghbouleh, *The Limits of Whiteness: Iranian Americans and the Everyday Politics of Race* (Stanford, Calif.: Stanford University Press, 2017).

12. This slippage may be unique to Iran's modern history. In Afshin Marashi's assessment, unlike liberation movements where nationalist elites were able to form an alliance with subaltern classes, the 1979 revolution was "populist-subaltern." This was a product of a semicolonial condition in the nineteenth century, later manifest in the twentieth century through a "surrogate colonial state" exercising a monopoly over the discourse of nationalism. As a result, nationalist intellectuals were unable to act as a vanguard in Iran's revolutionary movement. See Marashi, "Paradigms of Iranian Nationalism: History, Theory, and Historiography," in *Rethinking Iranian Nationalism and Modernity*, ed. Kamran Scot Aghaie and Afshin Marashi (Austin: University of Texas Press, 2014), 18–19. On these terms, I would suggest, opposition to the Islamist outcome of the 1979 revolution allows for unlikely yet not unprecedented parallels between activists previously mobilized on behalf of nationalist liberation, on one hand, and purveyors of the Pahlavi national myth, on the other.

13. Naficy, *Making of Exile Cultures*, 15–16, 132–33. In this vein, a number of short stories by modern Iran's most celebrated prose author, Sadeq Hedāyat, exhibit antireligious, specifically anti-Muslim and anti-Arab, sentiments. A representative example, "Seeking Absolution," tells the story of a group of pilgrims en route to visit the holy Shi'a city of Karbala. Hedāyat's story suggests that the pilgrimage allows unchanged sinners to reconcile their guilt without transformation or accountability. The journey to Karbala is said to parallel traversal through "the corridors of hell" *(dalān-i jahanam)*; the Arab inhabitants of the city are portrayed as *chirk* (dirty), *pāchih-varmālīdih* (ragged), and speaking in a "guttural Arabic" that came "from the depth of the throat and entrails deafening the ear." See Sādiq Hidāyat, "Talab-i Āmūrzish" [Seeking absolution], in *Sih Qatrih Khūn* [Three drops of blood], 73–86 (Stockholm: Arash, 1988). For an English translation, see Sadeq Hedāyat, "Seeking Absolution," trans. Minoo Southgate, in *Modern Persian Short Stories*, ed. Minoo Southgate, 3–12 (Washington, D.C.: Three Continents Press, 1980). For a critical assessment of the story's move from Orientalist social realism to a general indictment of Islamic religion and culture, see Michael Beard, *Hedayat's Blind Owl as a Western Novel* (Princeton, N.J.: Princeton University Press, 1990), 24.

14. The Cyrus Cylinder is an ancient artifact trumpeted by many Iranians as the first declaration of human rights. These broad historical gestures overlook circumstantial variations between modern declarations of rights (1789 and 1948, in particular)—not to mention the vast differences in historical context and legal doctrine between these declarations and the cylinder itself. For a critique of these claims, see Zia-Ebrahimi, *Emergence of Iranian Nationalism*, 73–74. On the myriad appropriations of the Cyrus Cylinder by Iranian émigrés in Los Angeles, see Arash Saedinia, "O, Cyrus," 2014, https://vimeo.com/125550050.

15. See Bahman Amūī, *Iqtisād-i Sīyāsī-yi Jumhūrī-yi Islāmī* [The political economy of the Islamic Republic] (Tehran: Gām-i Naw, 1382/2003–4), 40. These developments have led Iranian émigré scholars and pundits to advance a highly polemic "hijacking" thesis in the effort to narrate the history of the revolution. For two prominent iterations, see Janet Afary and Kevin B. Anderson, *Foucault and the Iranian Revolution: Gender and the Seductions of Islamism* (Chicago: University of Chicago Press, 2005), and Said Amir Arjomand, *After Khomeini: Iran under His Successors* (Oxford: Oxford University Press, 2009). Arjomand notably characterizes postrevolutionary state consolidation as a "coup d'etat" where Khomeini, through "demagogic manipulation," channeled leftist designs against a liberal state into the "smooth passage of Iran's theocratic constitution." For accounts of the revolution and of postrevolutionary state consolidation that directly refute these arguments, see Ervand Abrahamian, *Khomeinism: Essays on the Islamic Republic* (Berkeley: University of California Press, 1993); Behrooz Ghamari-Tabrizi, *Foucault in Iran: Islamic Revolution after the Enlightenment* (Minneapolis: University of Minnesota Press, 2016); Behrooz Ghamari-Tabrizi, *Islam and Dissent in Postrevolutionary Iran: Abdolkarim Soroush, Religious Politics, and Democratic Reform* (London: I. B. Tauris, 2008); and Kevan Harris, *A Social Revolution: Politics and the Welfare State in Iran* (Oakland: University of California Press, 2017).

16. For a detailed account of postrevolutionary factional politics, see Mehdi Moslem, *Factional Politics in Post-Khomeini Iran* (Syracuse, N.Y.: Syracuse University Press, 2002).

17. See Kevan Harris, "A Martyrs' Welfare State and Its Contradictions," in *Middle East Authoritarianism: Governance, Contestation, and Regime Resilience in Syria and Iran*, ed. Steven Heydemann and Reinoud Leenders, 61–80 (Stanford, Calif.: Stanford University Press, 2013).

18. Studies of the role of ideology and legitimacy in the Iranian revolution are many. Not all of them inform what I am calling left liberalism, but they certainly reflect a shared historiographical trend among scholars of Iran (many of whom are émigrés). For representative examples, see Said Amir Arjomand, *The Turban for the Crown: The Islamic Revolution in Iran* (Oxford: Oxford University Press, 1988); Peter Chelkowski and Hamid Dabashi, *Staging a Revolution: The Art of Persuasion in the Islamic Republic of Iran* (New York: New York University Press, 1999); Hamid Dabashi, *Theology of Discontent: The Ideological Foundation of the Islamic Revolution in Iran* (New Brunswick, N.J.: Transaction, 2006); Ghamari-Tabrizi, *Islam and Dissent*; and Theda Skocpol, "Rentier State and Shi'a Islam in the Iranian Revolution," *Theory and Society* 11 (1982): 265–83. For arguments against the centrality of an Islamic ideology (or any ideology, for that matter) in analyses of the revolution, see

Harris, *A Social Revolution*; Charles Kurzman, *The Unthinkable Revolution in Iran* (Cambridge, Mass.: Harvard University Press, 2004); and Misagh Parsa, "Ideology and Political Action in the Iranian Revolution," *Comparative Studies of South Asia, Africa, and the Middle East* 31, no. 1 (2011): 53–68. For an effort to write the cultural histories of the 1979 revolution beyond either interpellation or the outright rejection of ideology, see Arash Davari, "Indeterminate Governmentality: Neoliberal Politics in Revolutionary Iran, 1968–1979," PhD diss., University of California, Los Angeles, 2016.

9

The Only Good Muslim

Immigration Law, Popular Culture, and the Structures of Acceptability

VIVEK BALD

> Listening to the public discourse after 9/11, I had the impression of a
> great power struck by amnesia. . . . President Bush moved to
> distinguish between "good Muslims" and "bad Muslims." At the same
> time, the president seemed to assure America that "good Muslims"
> were anxious to clear their names and consciences of this horrible
> crime and would undoubtedly support "us" in a war against "them."
> But this could not hide the central message of this discourse: unless
> proved to be "good," every Muslim was presumed to be "bad." All
> Muslims were now under obligation to prove their credentials by
> joining in a war against "bad Muslims."
>
> —MAHMOOD MAMDANI, *Good Muslim, Bad Muslim*

During the U.S. presidential election of 2016, Muslim and South Asian
Americans found themselves in a familiar bind. The Republican candidate,
Donald Trump, targeted and demonized "Muslims"—a broad category that
in the minds of his followers extended to anyone Brown and "Middle Eastern looking"—explicitly and repeatedly. At one rally after the next, Trump
conflated Muslim immigrants, citizens, and refugees with the Islamic State
(ISIS). He promised that he would require all Muslims within U.S. borders
to register with the government and carry special identification. At different
points in his campaign, he proposed that incoming Muslim immigrants
be either subjected to "extreme vetting" or banned outright. His rhetoric
contributed to a surge in anti-Muslim, -Arab, and–South Asian violence
that continued throughout 2016 and reached a level not seen since the
months immediately following the attacks of September 11, 2001.[1]

Trump's opponent, Hillary Clinton, took what on its face was an opposing position. Clinton celebrated the achievements of Muslim Americans,
insisting that they were an important part of the American national fabric.

This theme reached its apogee when the Clinton campaign gave the stage of the Democratic National Convention to the parents of Humayun Khan, a Pakistani American U.S. Army captain killed in the George W. Bush administration's war in Iraq. For many South Asian and Muslim Americans, it was a powerful thing to see this couple in their sixties, so familiar that they could have been our own aunt and uncle, step into the center of the national spotlight to challenge directly the racism, xenophobia, and Islamophobia of Trump, his policies, and his followers. Khizr and Ghazala Khan did this with an inspiring fearlessness at the convention and in ensuing interviews and public statements.[2]

But here was the bind. In one party's rhetoric, Muslims and South Asians were always and forever foreign and retrograde; they were all potential terrorists who needed to be surveilled, policed, and, ideally, excluded and expelled from the nation. The other party's message was more subtle, but it was, to many of us, no less clear: America will accept—and even praise and celebrate—Muslims and South Asians *if* they unequivocally prove their loyalty to the nation. Humayun Khan proved his Americanness by giving his life in service of U.S. military, geopolitical, and economic pursuits in the Middle East. Other Muslims, Clinton made clear in a series of debate appearances, could demonstrate their Americanness by becoming "partners" in the state surveillance of their own communities. To be recognized as Americans, the Clinton campaign implied, Muslims and South Asians should not exercise the right to criticize their government's foreign and domestic policies toward other Muslims and South Asians but must help prosecute those policies.

It was something quite new to see Khizr Khan excoriating Donald Trump for his hateful xenophobic rhetoric on live national television. Yet there was nothing new about the bind presented to Muslim and South Asian Americans in that singular moment of the U.S. presidential campaign. This was precisely the bind that Mahmood Mamdani identified operating at the center of the Bush administration's detention and deportation regime in the years following 9/11: "All Muslims were now under obligation," Mamdani wrote, "to prove their credentials by joining in a war against 'bad Muslims.'"[3] I want to suggest, however, that this formulation of the "loyal citizen" (or "model minority") versus the "terrorist" goes back much further than 2001. Since at least the late nineteenth century, the racialization of Muslims and South Asians in the United States has depended precisely upon positing us as simultaneously threatening and desirable, and for over a century, this racialization has functioned like a carrot and stick, making us want to perform and prove our desirability, and thus disciplining us into becoming particular kinds of Americans.

XENOPHOBIA AND INDOPHILIA

Mohammed Ismail arrived in the United States just one year into the new century. He was told that he would be providing personal security for a wealthy employer from his native Karachi, with whom he would travel to London, then Toronto, and then New York, before returning home. It seemed a good prospect, an opportunity to see some of the world outside and bring money back to his working-class family in the Sindhi city. But Ismail had been deceived about the work he would be doing here; he was, in fact, being brought to New York to work in the kitchen of an Indian restaurant—one that would be run by two Americans whom he had never met or even heard of. Ismail's wealthy employer from Karachi was simply a middleman, someone who was helping the two Americans establish a new food trend in the city: upscale adaptations of traditional North Indian cuisine, served in plush surroundings and geared toward New York's business elites. Not only was Ismail being misled about his work but he arrived in the United States as the country was in the grip of an anti-immigrant frenzy in which men from his part of the world were increasingly demonized and suspect.

The partners who hatched their plan for a haute Indian restaurant in Manhattan did such a bad job of it that Ismail and a group of other men who had been recruited in Karachi ended up in deportation proceedings just a few months after arriving in the United States. The restaurant fell through, the workers never received any wages, and they were rounded up for violations of the immigration laws. A year after being recruited in Karachi, Ismail was deported, but only as far as London, where he was stuck in conditions only nominally better than the detention center where he had been held in New York. He had no resources, little in the way of English language skills, and no one to whom he could turn for help. All he wanted was to return to his family, but with every day, this prospect seemed more remote.[4]

The year could have been 2002, but it was 1902. Mohammed Ismail was part of an obscure episode in the history of U.S. immigration that helps to illuminate the century that followed and the present in which we now find ourselves. Roland and Stanley Conklin, the men who bankrolled what would have been the United States' first Indian restaurant in 1901, had sought to bring Ismail and more than twenty other Indian workers into the

United States to give their New York establishment exotic flair. The restaurant was not a far-fetched business venture; at the turn of the century, "India" was all the rage among American elites. Roland Conklin appears to have gotten the idea for a restaurant after becoming acquainted with a curry chef who was employed at Louis Sherry's, the upscale Manhattan restaurant and hotel where Conklin had lodgings. This young man from Karachi, who went by the name "Ranji Smile," was already a celebrity of sorts; he had created a stir when Louis Sherry brought him to New York in 1899 and touted him in the press as "America's First India Chef." Conklin eventually decided he would hire Smile away from Sherry and open his own Indian establishment along a prime stretch of Fifth Avenue. So, in 1901, Conklin and his brother sent Smile to India to initiate their plan: the curry chef would hire cooks, waiters, musicians, and a dancing girl; purchase rugs, draperies, and elaborate furnishings; and then return to New York to help turn their restaurant—the Omar Khayyam—into a kind of Orientalist dream world.[5] This scheme depended on the Conklins'—and Ranji Smile's—ability to do two things: (1) to manipulate American fantasies of the exotic East and (2) to circumvent the era's tightening anti-Asian immigration laws.

Smile was already skilled at playing to his Western customers' fantasies of who and what a "Hindoo chef" should be. From the moment he arrived at Louis Sherry's, Smile relished the press interviews that Sherry set up for him. During the first of these, published in the *Los Angeles Times* in late October 1899 and reprinted in papers across the country, Smile flirted with the interviewer, preparing her an elaborate meal, tying a colorful turban on her head, and declaring to her readers, "If the women of America will but eat the food I prepare, they will be more beautiful than they as yet imagine. The eye will grow lustrous, the complexion will be yet so lovely and the figure like unto those of our beautiful Indian women."[6] Smile was an expert at what we might now call "self-Orientalizing"; he knew how to turn others' fantasies toward his own notoriety and financial gain.

For their part, the Conklin brothers were skilled at making money at the edges of legality and the frontiers of American imperial power. They had made their initial fortune as mortgage brokers; they used the money of distant British investors to make loans to the homesteader families buying Midwestern land in the wake of the 1880s Plains Indian wars. When an economic depression hit the United States in the 1890s, and the land business dried up, they declared bankruptcy but somehow managed to move their assets—including hundreds of thousands of dollars of their investors' funds—through shell companies into a new venture based in New York City. They escaped a series of ensuing fraud claims in the 1890s, and their new venture, the North American Trust Company, was appointed as the U.S. government's financial agent in Cuba. Theirs was the first U.S. company to set up in Cuba after the Spanish–American War, when the United States assumed control over the island. The Conklins made a second fortune there, setting up banks, sugar refineries, and railroads to exploit Cuba's vast resources.[7]

The main obstacle to the Conklin brothers' 1901 restaurant scheme was, no doubt, minor compared to those they had surmounted in their previous business dealings. The Conklins' plan to bring Indian workers into the United States violated the terms of the 1885 Alien Contract Labor Law. The 1885 law had been enacted as a means of tightening the regime of immigrant exclusion that the United States had initiated with the 1882 Chinese Exclusion Act. Specifically, the 1885 law forbade U.S. employers from "importing" foreign laborers under contract to work in the United States. The Conklins were prohibited from bringing into the United States precisely the "native" cooks, waiters, and performers whom they needed to create the fantasy world of their planned Indian restaurant. Unbowed, the Conklin brothers came up with a plan to outsmart the Contract Labor Law by exploiting one of its "exceptions": while American employers were forbidden from bringing overseas workers into the country, traveling foreign dignitaries, including royalty, were allowed to enter the United States along with an unlimited number of servants and staff.[8]

So Roland and Stanley Conklin dialed up Smile's performance of Eastern fantasy. Ranji would go from being a dashing curry chef to being an Indian prince. On arrival in Karachi, and then on his return voyage and reentry into the United States, Smile would claim to be a son of the Amir of Baluchistan, traveling with a retinue of servants, cooks, musicians, and a dancing "nautch girl" on a tour of the United States. It was a seemingly perfect ruse; it played to Western fantasies about the wealthy and mysterious princes of the East, while it also enabled the Conklins to bring their restaurant workers into the United States through a loophole in the Contract Labor Law.[9]

THE PRINCE AND THE DANCING GIRL

However obscure it might be, the story of Ranji Smile, the Conklin brothers, and the Omar Khayyam restaurant illuminates the ways that a bifurcated set of racial ideas about South Asians and Muslims took shape and took root in the United States at the turn of the twentieth century. The story of Mohammed Ismail demonstrates the stakes of these ideas. When Ismail arrived as part of Ranji Smile's "princely retinue," the United States was emerging simultaneously as (1) an imperial power that both emulated and competed with Great Britain; (2) a society of mass production, marketing, and consumption; and (3) a "nation of immigrants"—and immigrant exclusion. In this moment, U.S. laws worked together with mass cultural representations to ascribe a set of apparently contradictory characteristics to South Asians and Muslims. South Asians and Muslims were *desirable* to the extent that they confirmed, performed, and delivered upon Western colonial understandings of certain types of mysterious and exotic "Orientals"—princes, swamis, magicians, acrobats, and dancing girls. They were also desirable to the extent that they provided American consumers with goods that conjured the fantasy world of the colonial Orient—rugs, embroidered textiles, perfumes, hookahs, scimitars, tea, spices—and that had consequently become signs of worldliness, sophistication, and imperial identity. At the same time, South Asians and Muslims were *undesirable* to the extent that they *failed* to deliver upon these fantasies or provide these goods—that is, to the extent that they were simply "Hindoo," "Mohammedan," "Arab," or "Asiatic" workers.[10]

Workers from British India were arriving in the United States in steadily increasing numbers from the 1890s through the 1910s and were predominantly Sikh and Muslim men. The discourse that grew up around these men in American newspapers simultaneously drew upon ideas and images rooted in European colonial literature and built upon the United States' own evolving racialization of Chinese and other Asian workers; the "Hindus" were sinister, unpredictable, unclean, and, like other men from Asia, inscrutable and threatening. In 1900, the *New York Post* described the Indian and Malay ship workers who moved in and out of boardinghouses near the southern tip of Manhattan in terms that summed up the era's broader sentiments: "[They] are peaceable and orderly up to a certain point, and then they lose all self control and resort to the knife."[11] These ascribed characteristics—both the "positive" (exotic, romantic) and "negative" (dangerous, heathen)—not only defined Americans' understandings of South Asian and Muslim immigrants at the turn of the century but also shaped these immigrants' claims for entry at U.S. borders and their attempts at social inclusion once they were here.

When the Conklin brothers directed Ranji Smile to impersonate a Baluchi prince in 1901, they were tapping into one of the most potent "positive" fantasy images of the East—one that had, in previous decades, permeated the United States' expanding mass culture. The specific visual trope upon which they sought to capitalize—the grand maharajah, sultan, or amir, lounging on a divan, atop an Oriental rug, smoking a hookah, surrounded by fan-waving attendants, and watching the snakelike dance of one or more of his scantily dressed young "harem girls"—had cohered in European and American popular consciousness over the course of the eighteenth and nineteenth centuries. The image had first circulated widely in European art and literature; it was both a discursive by-product of and an ongoing justi- fication for British and French colonial incursions into North Africa, the Middle East, and South Asia.[12]

In the 1860s and 1870s, Oriental potentates, odalisques, and dancing girls were subjects of numerous works by European painters—Jean-Léon Gérôme, Jean-Auguste-Dominique Ingres, Mariano Fortuny. At the same time, a group of American artists—expatriates in Europe and in some cases students of Gérôme—brought the obsessions and imagery of Orientalist painting to galleries and exhibitions in the United States. Some of the Americans also found a market for their work beyond such elite spaces, in the realms of mass culture and commerce. The Boston-born artist Edwin Lord Weeks, for example, gained notoriety for his colorful large-scale paint- ings of Oriental street scenes and royalty, which became features of the yearly Paris Salon throughout the 1880s and 1890s. In the United States, he not only brought his work to similarly elite galleries and exhibitions but developed a relationship with the U.S. periodical *Harper's Monthly*. Starting in 1890, Weeks published a series of illustrated travelogues for *Harper's* about his artistic excursions through North Africa and India. The black- and-white sketches that Weeks presented in *Harper's* made their way into the homes of hundreds of thousands of Americans. Here, in the minds of this broad U.S. readership, Weeks's images and text reified and gilded European Orientalist views of India. Weeks's "India" consisted of decaying "ancient" architecture (mosques, temples, palaces); chaotic market scenes (shops, stalls, buyers, and sellers); grand Indian royalty (rajahs, Mughals, royal processions, hunts, elephants, horses, retinues); and exotic Indian women (bathers, water carriers, and nautch dancers). Weeks's choice of imagery was market driven: he delivered, visually, the Orient that Ameri- cans had encountered in European Orientalist literature—*The 1001 Nights, Lalla Rookh, The Rubaiyat of Omar Khayyam*—all tales that had been pub- lished in U.S. editions throughout the nineteenth century.[13]

Weeks's bridging of high art and literature, on one hand, and popular magazines, on the other, was part of a larger shift; in the 1890s, Orientalist ideas and imagery moved firmly into the arena of American mass culture, and especially into the realms of marketing and entertainment. As Holly Edwards, William Leach, and others have asserted, American branding and advertising underwent a paradigm shift in the closing decades of the century. While manufacturers and retailers previously sought to win customers by describing the strengths of their products, they now began to lure customers through images and inferences. Products were not sold on the basis of their own inherent qualities but on the basis of the qualities they could impart to the consumer. The fantasy image of the Oriental palace, potentate, hookah, and harem, with its suggestions of power, sophistication, and sex, was perfectly suited to the new American style of marketing.[14]

This image took a particularly deep hold on American men's smoking culture. In what Edwards has described as "the most sustained campaign to capitalize on oriental motifs," American tobacco companies made the fantasy of the palace and harem central to the branding and advertising of a wide range of their products. Smokers were offered a plethora of American-manufactured tobacco products branded and marketed with "Near Eastern" names—Mecca, Red Kamel, Fatima, Bagdad—or explicitly East Indian ones. Americans could fill their pipes with Hindoo brand tobacco, smoke Royal Bengal cigars, or buy packs of Mogul cigarettes. Across the United States, advertisements for these products filled the visual landscape with images of dancing girls, bearded turbaned potentates, hookahs, and scimitars, set against the backdrop of alluring Oriental palaces and desert landscapes. Wealthy American men—the likes of the Conklin brothers—took this imagery further by furnishing their parlors and smoking rooms in lush Oriental style. These rooms brought to life the fantastical harem and palace interiors made popular by Weeks and other Orientalist painters; here successful American businessmen—a new imperial ruling class—could smoke in surroundings replete with their own thick-pile Persian and Afghan rugs, divans, and hookahs; tiger skins and elephant tusks; and the swords and other weaponry of the vanquished rulers of the East, hung upon the walls.[15]

At the same time, the figure of the "Oriental dancing girl" was too alluring, and too profitable, to remain confined to paintings and advertising images. From the late nineteenth century through the beginning of the twentieth, light-skinned, dark-haired women performed the Indian "nautch dance" and the Arab "danse du ventre": from the sensational introduction of "Little Egypt" at the 1893 Chicago World's Fair to the early appearances of Isadora Duncan in Newport, Rhode Island; from the "barefoot" dancers in the brothels of New Orleans's Storyville to the Broadway performances of a bejeweled and sari-clad Ruth St. Denis; from elite bachelor parties to Coney Island sideshows; and from the multiple stagings of Oscar Wilde's *Salome* to the grand spectacle of the Ziegfeld Follies, the "Oriental dancer" took hold of American mass (and elicit) entertainments.[16]

Given this context, it is not surprising that Roland and Stanley Conklin directed the chef, Ranji Smile, to pose as a "real Indian prince"—traveling with a young "nautch girl" for his entertainment and a retinue of servants and cooks to attend to his daily needs—as a cover for importing "native" workers to staff their Indian restaurant. As "Prince Ranjit of Baluchistan and party," these travelers from the East were eminently desirable to Americans; they were embodiments of the fantastical images of India that had circulated in American mass entertainment and consumer culture and entered the nation's popular consciousness. However, there was another, even more compelling reason that the Conklins devised this particular ruse, and it was rooted in the era's evolving *legal* mechanisms for distinguishing desirable from undesirable immigrants, includable from excludable aliens.

LAWS OF EXCEPTION

In her 2016 book *The Good Immigrants,* historian Madeline Hsu asserts that the anti-Asian immigration laws of the 1880s–1920s were not simply and straightforwardly "exclusion laws." A closer examination of these laws reveals a more nuanced picture of the ways racialized state power was, and continues to be, exercised against varied immigrant groups. In fact, every immigration law of the so-called Asian Exclusion Era contained provisions that defined *some* groups of Asian immigrants (such as the students and intellectuals upon whom Hsu focuses) as exceptional and admissible to the United States. In effect, Hsu argues, the logic embedded in these laws was not one of exclusion but of selection. From the nineteenth century onward, the U.S. state institutionalized distinctions of class, education, and professional skills in such a way that some Asians were defined as desirable even as others—the majority—were defined as undesirable.[17]

The key to this understanding lies in the exceptions, or "provisos," of each Immigration Act. Section 1 of the Chinese Exclusion Act of 1882, for example, specifically identifies Chinese workers as the target of exclusion:

"The coming of Chinese laborers to the United States . . . is hereby, suspended; and during such suspension it shall not be lawful for any Chinese laborer to come, or having so come . . . to remain within the United States." Section 13, however, exempts "diplomatic and other officers of the Chinese Government" and their "body and household servants" from the provisions of the law. Even more significantly, Section 13 allows for the continued entry of Chinese migrants and travelers who had been defined as admissible to the United States two years earlier under the Angell Treaty of 1880, specifically, "Chinese subjects . . . proceeding to the United States as teachers, students, merchants," or tourists.[18]

In 1885, the United States passed the Alien Contract Labor Law in large part as a means of strengthening the Chinese Exclusion Act and expanding its provisions to other foreign workers from Asia and southern Europe. Once again, the main provision of the law specifically singled out laborers for exclusion: "It shall be unlawful for any person, company, partnership, or corporation, . . . [to] in any way assist or encourage the importation or migration of any alien or aliens . . . into the United States . . . under contract or agreement . . . made previous to the importation or migration of such alien or aliens . . . to perform labor or service of any kind in the United States." And once again, the law contained a series of exemptions that allowed the entry of specific classes of foreigners into the United States: the "private secretaries, servants, or domestics," of foreign citizens, "temporarily residing in the United States, either in private or official capacity"; "skilled workmen . . . provided that skilled labor for that purpose cannot otherwise be obtained" in the United States; and "professional actors, artists, lecturers, or singers."[19]

The 1917 Immigration Act vastly expanded the number of immigrants who would be barred from entering the United States. Indeed, on its face, the 1917 act appears to have completed and secured the exclusion of Asian immigrants from the United States, and the law has largely been understood as having done so. However, it also expanded and more closely specified the types of immigrants, Asians included, who would be exempted from the law's exclusions and allowed to enter the country. The act defined as inadmissible "all idiots, imbeciles . . . epileptics, insane persons . . . persons with chronic alcoholism; paupers; professional beggars; vagrants; persons afflicted with tuberculosis . . . [or] any loathsome or dangerous contagious disease," felons, polygamists, anarchists, prostitutes, procurers, contract laborers, and all migrants from a swath of the globe defined as the "Asiatic Barred Zone," which stretched from the Eastern Arabian peninsula through

Afghanistan and across almost all the rest of South, Southeast, and East Asia. (The United States had already negotiated restrictions on migration from Japan and Japanese-controlled portions of China under a separate treaty.) Yet the 1917 act once again delineated categories of Asian migrants who were *acceptable* as entrants to the United States: "government officers, ministers or religious teachers, missionaries, lawyers, physicians, chemists, civil engineers, teachers, students, authors, artists, merchants, and travelers for curiosity or pleasure."[20]

Between the late nineteenth and early twentieth centuries, in other words, the U.S. government continually refined and sharpened its laws and practices in an attempt to define, identify, and exclude the "undesirables" among the rapidly increasing number of immigrants at the nation's borders while allowing the entry of those deemed valuable and desirable. While this period was later mythologized as an "age of immigration" in which the United States was guided by the principles set out by the poet Emma Lazarus—"Give me your tired, your poor, / Your huddled masses yearning to breathe free"—it was more accurately an age in which the U.S. state put in place a system of strict distinctions between acceptable and unacceptable groups of incoming immigrants, guided not by lofty principles but by the immigrants' race, religious practices, political beliefs, education, skills, and perceived physical and mental "fitness." Throughout this period, the U.S. government sought to control and police the entry of immigrants—to distinguish between those who were "desirable" as either short-term residents or potential citizens and those who were not.

U.S. immigration laws of this era quite unabashedly used race and national origin as one of the primary bases for such distinctions; "Asiatics"—whom white nativists insisted were a scourge and a danger—were to be kept out of the country. At a deeper level, however, the United States was also making distinctions *within* the racial category of "Asiatic"—distinctions based upon class, occupation, and profession. This second level of distinction had as important an effect on Asian immigrants as the first. It not only determined which Asians were allowed to enter the United States and which were not but shaped what and who Asian immigrants claimed to be in order to *gain* entry into the United States—and, just as important, what kind of "Asianness" they would need to embody, prove, or perform in order to stay.

As an "edge case," Chinese, Indian, and Arab peddlers illustrate just how narrow and precarious the distinction was between "acceptable" and "unacceptable" for "Eastern" immigrants at the end of the nineteenth century, in the wake of the 1885 Alien Contract Labor Law. To enter the country legally to sell their wares, these migrants had to prove to the immigration inspectors at Ellis Island and elsewhere that they were members of one of the allowed categories; specifically, they had to assert that they were independent "merchants" or "businessmen" rather than workers entering the United States to sell some other merchant's goods. Although many peddlers successfully claimed "merchant" status and were able to enter the United States, this was by no means a sure thing. The era's newspapers are littered with articles about peddlers who were detained and deported because examiners had decided that they "peddle goods not their own [and are thus] held to come under provisions of the Contract Labor Law."[21] For those peddlers who did successfully enter the United States, their value on U.S. streets and in U.S. markets—and, crucially, the value of their goods—depended upon their ability to perform Western fantasies of the Hindoo, the Arab, or the "Chinaman." They were selling the "exotic East," and therefore the authenticity and worth of their goods were tied to how well they fulfilled Western expectations of the "exotic Easterner."[22]

THE SCHEME AND ITS FAILINGS

In 1901, this was the situation of the curry chef Ranji Smile and of the two wealthy Americans who wished to install Smile as the main feature of their new restaurant on Manhattan's Fifth Avenue. In the Conklin brothers' scheme, popular–cultural and legal constructions of Indian "desirability" were tightly entwined. The success of the restaurant venture depended upon how "authentic" a world the Conklin brothers could create within the four walls of their establishment. This entailed furnishing the restaurant with a wealth of Oriental goods—the plush hand-woven rugs, draperies, wall hangings, brass work, hookahs, and scimitars that had become the markers of an imagined Eastern palace—and, of course, with real Indians. At a time when "Asiatic laborers" were under attack in the United States for purportedly taking away jobs and bringing crime and disease, the Conklins needed Asiatic laborers to give their elite New York clientele the illusion of entering an exotic, imperial space, as if they were the British or Mughal rulers of Orientalist literature and popular fantasy. The Conklins' restaurant, Ranji Smile, and the workers would be culturally desirable to the extent that they could create such an illusion.[23] Yet, the immigration laws of the day shaped the personae of Smile and his workers as much as the era's popular–cultural fantasies. As foreign workers whom the Conklins aimed to employ in an American establishment, Ranji and the others were precisely the "alien contract laborers" that the 1885 law aimed to bar from the country. As an Indian prince and his retinue, they were something quite different; they were acceptable, even desirable, as entrants into the United States. So this is how they arrived. They set out for New York via London and Montreal, Ranji Smile and thirty others, including Mohammed Ismail, in October 1901.[24]

The Conklins would likely never have come up with their plan to game the immigration laws were it not for the fact that Ranji Smile, like the Indian, Chinese, and Arab peddlers of his day, was such a skilled performer of Western fantasies of the Orient. For Smile, as much as for the peddlers, the mastery of such performances was a condition of their mobility across and within imperial spaces and a condition for the success of their work. Mrs. A. M. Brisbine, the author of Smile's 1899 profile, had completely fallen for the young man's flash and flair. He appeared at her table, Brisbine wrote, "immaculately arrayed in a heavy white linen India costume with a gorgeous turban of white all outlined in gold braid, with a broad smile, which show[ed] all his gleaming teeth, and with the . . . seductive manner that pleases the public so much." Smile had explained that on special occasions, he wore grander attire: "a long black satin coat . . . magnificent embroidered white sash, pointed slippers, white trousers and a blue silk turban, on which the Maharajah of Coochbehar has pinned a handsome design in recognition of Smile's services to him."[25]

The turban—an item that would in just a few years become the maligned symbol of an Indian immigrant "invasion" of the U.S. West Coast—was an especially popular aspect of Smile's appearance. After watching the chef tie a turban and place it "upon one very pretty young woman's head," Brisbine had asked if he could do the same for her and discovered that he had "made several turbans for prominent people on the stage, usually placing a sweeping feather to one side, to give it the usual jaunty touch." Ranji served Brisbine her food with equal panache: "[He] lays before you a silver dish. . . . [He] makes a cunning little circle on your plate, with deftness of long practice, of the whitest, flakiest, curried rice, in the center of which he places a bit of chicken. All this time, he is telling you in his gentle way that his one hope is this may be only the first of many dinners he is to serve you." It was in this guise that Roland Conklin had first encountered Ranji Smile at Louis Sherry's, and in this guise, no doubt, that Conklin saw the potential to capitalize on his skills as a purveyor of fantasy.[26]

What is most instructive about the Conklins' scheme, however, is the way it failed. The plan began to unravel only when the popular–cultural desires shaping Ranji's performance began to work at cross purposes to the contours of acceptability laid out in the immigration laws. Neither Smile nor the Conklins appear to have anticipated the excitement that would take hold of New Yorkers when news reports came in from London and Montreal that a real-life traveling Indian prince and "nautch girl" were about to visit their city. Such excitement was surely what the Conklins were hoping for in the long term, after they opened their restaurant. But in the short term, to get Smile and the workers across borders to the United States, they needed the group simply to pass as a foreign dignitary and his servants and quietly slip into the country. Any extra scrutiny of Smile and the workers was unwelcome and put the plan at risk. In the end, however, they could not control the attention. From the time that Smile and the others arrived in London and holed up in a hotel, American reporters ran with the story of the Indian prince who was on his way to New York. In a front-page story, the *New York Times* announced, "Prince Ranjit, Mystery of London, Coming Here—He Is Accompanied by a Suite of Twenty-Three Attendants—Lived in Oriental Splendor in a London Hotel." The *Tribune* announced, "A Dusky Oriental Potentate Now on His Way to This Country." "Mysterious Prince Exciting Great Curiosity," proclaimed South Dakota's *Aberdeen Daily News*, "Like a Character in Arabian Nights He Has Many Servants and Unlimited Gold."[27]

After "Prince Ranjit" arrived in New York City and disappeared to an unknown location, it took less than twenty-four hours for local reporters to track him down and recognize that he was, in fact, the young Ranji Smile, whom they had written about just two years earlier when he arrived in the city as Louis Sherry's new cook. The stories the next day were as unforgiving as they are revealing: the *New York Times* granted Smile neither a prominent place in the paper nor even his prior status as a dashing upscale curry chef. On page sixteen, under the headline "Ex-waiter, Not a Prince," an indignant *Times* wrote, "This Hindu [*sic*], with his . . . retinue of fourteen servants, and his weird musicians, who was reported to be at least the son of a Rajah, now turns out to be a former servant in a Fifth Avenue restaurant." The *New York World* made clear the full significance of Smile's ruse: "Lucky, indeed, will [he] be if the United States authorities do not swoop down upon him and harass him for violation of the alien labor laws. . . . [He] went to India early in the summer with the intention of hiring real Indians to act as waiters and cooks. . . . As members of the 'retinue' of the 'Prince' these cooks and waiters were imported without question."[28]

In its collapse, the Conklins' plan revealed both the structure and the contingency of "acceptability" for South Asians in the United States at the turn of the twentieth century. Over the course of twenty-four hours, Ranji Smile went from being a celebrated and eagerly anticipated "real Oriental prince" to being the denigrated and ridiculed "servant" of the restaurateur Louis Sherry. Not long thereafter, when the involvement of the Conklin brothers was revealed, Ranji Smile was described as "the Conklins' prince." But, most significantly, Mohammed Ismail and the rest of the workers, who had been the most deceived and exploited in this plan, were stripped of both their cultural desirability and their legal acceptability as the "retinue" of an Indian prince. In an instant, they were transformed into "alien contract laborers." In an instant, their presence in the United States was rendered "illegal." In less than a year, the majority were rounded up, placed in detention, and deported.[29]

THE TRAP OF ACCEPTABILITY

Donald Trump spent the first six months of his presidency attempting to impose a "Muslim ban" by executive order. Two such attempts were swiftly blocked by federal district courts. On June 26, 2017, however, the Supreme Court of the United States allowed a portion of Trump's second executive order to go into effect on a temporary basis. According to the Court, the U.S. government could bar from entering the country anyone from the six Muslim-majority countries specified in the order who could not prove a "bona fide" relationship to someone who was a current legal resident of the United States. Most refugees from these six countries could be barred as well, at least until the Supreme Court could hear full arguments for and against the constitutionality of the executive order. Although this was only a partial and short-term "victory" for Trump, the president issued a celebratory statement; he touted the ruling as a step toward his goal of admitting only those people who do not wish to "do us harm," people who "can love the United States and all of its citizens, and who will be hardworking and productive."

By this point in 2017, Trump had already proved to be more crude and overt in his xenophobia, Islamophobia, and racism than almost any other mainstream American politician of the early twenty-first century. Yet, the underlying logic of Trump's statement here was essentially the same as what undergirded George W. Bush's and, for that matter, Barack Obama's and Hillary Clinton's approaches to Muslim immigrants, residents, and citizens—Muslims were required to prove their acceptability as Americans by some singular measure of value and allegiance to the economic, geo-political, and racial projects of the U.S. state. As a fallback from his propos-als for an outright ban, Trump insisted that Muslims prove that they were worthy of U.S. residency through "hard work," "productivity," and (implic-itly unequivocal and uncritical) "love for" the nation. Clinton, Obama, and Bush had used criteria that were not so far removed from this. They had insisted, for example, at different times and in different language, that American Muslims prove or perform their worthiness by becoming part-ners and participants in the fight against global and domestic terrorism—acquiescing, in this case, to overseas wars in Iraq, Afghanistan, and Yemen, while acting locally as the eyes and ears of the FBI. And none of these criteria were that far from those that had defined the acceptability and admissibility of South Asian and other Asian entrants in federal immigration laws stretch-ing from the 1882 Chinese Exclusion Act to the 1885 Alien Contract Labor Law to the 1917 Asiatic Barred Zone Act, and right up until the 1965 Hart–Cellar Act. The first three of these four barred working-class Asian immi-grants (and, by 1917, political radicals) but made exceptions for the educated, merchants, and professionals; the 1965 act "opened the gates" to Asian immigration but used "preferences" to ensure roughly the same categories of "desirables" were allowed entry, while leaving few openings for others.

While it is true that every modern nation imposes standards and cri-teria for immigrant entry, residency, and naturalization, four points are important here. First, in the case of Muslim and South Asian immigrants to the United States, these criteria have, since the nineteenth century, been bound inextricably with class- and gender-based racial ideas, ideologies, fears, and desires. Second, these racial ideas have invariably taken the form of binaries of the kind described by Mamdani. His "good Muslim–bad Muslim" has many variants: model minority–terrorist, exotic–fearsome, spiritually elevated–dirty and profane. That is, Muslims and South Asians have not been wholly dismissed and excluded but assigned sets of seem-ingly opposite and contradictory characteristics. Third, these binaries have undergirded the cultural and legal distinctions—acceptable–unacceptable, desirable–undesirable, admissible–inadmissible—through which we have either been allowed to enter and remain part of the U.S. nation or been vilified and excluded. Fourth, and most crucially, these distinctions form a structure of discipline for Muslim and South Asian communities; through a set of rewards and risks, they direct us toward becoming particular kinds of citizens—they encourage us to shape ourselves, to present ourselves, to act and to strive, in particular prescribed ways.

Just as surely as Ranji Smile was rewarded for performing the role of the dark, handsome, and exotic curry chef at Louis Sherry's in 1899, and (briefly) for embodying a fantastical Baluchi prince in 1901, present-day South Asians and Muslims are rewarded—socially, culturally, and economically— for performing the role of the model minority, the "immigrant entrepreneur," the "moderate" or "secular" Muslim, or the anti-Muslim "native informant." And perhaps even more than they were for the members of Ranji's retinue, the dangers are very real for those South Asians and Muslims in the present-day United States who do not or cannot play these roles, who remain undocumented and contingent; who labor in the service economy; who live in hypersurveilled urban working-class neighborhoods and worship in these neighborhoods' mosques, gurdwaras, and temples; who retain accents, speak in "broken" English, or merely converse publicly in "foreign" languages: Arabic, Farsi, Urdu, Hindi, Bangla; who wear the outer signs of their faith and ethnicity: beards, turbans, hijabs, kufis, saris, salwar kameez; or who openly criticize and protest U.S. domestic and foreign policies—who are, in Mamdani's words, not willing to "support 'us' in a war against 'them.'" The "good Muslim–bad Muslim" and the "model minority–terrorist" binaries, in other words, are not just ideas that circulate in the arena of media representation—in films, on television, in political rhetoric. They define our acceptability, direct our actions, structure the ways we present ourselves in society and interact with the state.

In 1923, the case of an Indian immigrant, a World War I veteran and University of California, Berkeley PhD named Bhagat Singh Thind, went before the Supreme Court. Thind and his lawyers had argued in the lower courts that he had a right to naturalize as a U.S. citizen, despite the Asian exclusion laws of the day. Thind's case is, by now, well known. At the time he sought to become a U.S. citizen, the laws only allowed two categories of foreign-born people to do so: "free white men" and "persons of African descent." These categories—and Western racial "knowledge"—directly shaped Thind's claims upon the state: Thind and his lawyers used the "scholarship" of nineteenth-century European anthropologists and racial scientists to claim that as a "high-caste Hindu," Thind was Aryan, and therefore Caucasian, and therefore a "white man" eligible for U.S. citizenship.[30] This acceptability claim ultimately failed, and when we look back on it one hundred years later, we most often regard the ruling as a failure of the *state*; this was an injustice, in other words, that the United States eventually got around to correcting when it scrapped race-based criteria for citizenship.

But what if we see the Thind case as a failure of Thind himself to see and to challenge the logics, choices, and structures of citizenship that he faced? We know that Thind was a supporter of the Indian independence movement, a movement for justice and self-determination. We know that after a decade in the United States, Thind would have been very well aware of the limitations to full citizenship—to justice and self-determination—that "persons of African descent" faced in the United States. We know that the Indian nationalist literature produced by Thind's contemporaries in the U.S.-based Ghadar Movement openly discussed the injustices to which native peoples were subjected in the United States. What if, instead of seeking citizenship, Thind simply stayed in the United States to fight simultaneously the injustices meted out against Indians by the British and the injustices meted out against indigenous peoples and African Americans in the United States? What if this work was grounded neither in claims for subjecthood within the British Empire nor in claims for citizenship in the United States but in calls to a higher sense of justice, humanity, and belonging that transcended both the British Empire and the U.S. nation-state?

These are, of course, hypotheticals grounded in the present, rather than the past, that ignore the historical specificities of Bhagat Singh Thind's circumstances, choices, and era. I raise them, however, precisely to think about the present, to ask whether there is a way of moving forward politically outside and against the categories that have confined us for the past decade and the past century, of escaping the trap of acceptability.

NOTES

1. American Civil Liberties Union, "The Trump Memos," July 13, 2016, https://action.aclu.org/sites/default/files/pages/trumpmemos.pdf; Eric Lichtblau, "Hate Crimes against American Muslims Most since Post-9/11 Era," *New York Times*, September 17, 2016, https://www.nytimes.com/2016/09/18/us/politics/hate-crimes-american-muslims-rise.html; Brian Levin, *Special Status Report: Hate Crime in the United States* (San Bernardino, Calif.: Center for the Study of Hate and Extremism, California State University, 2016); Bridge Initiative, "When Islamophobia Turns Violent: The 2016 U.S. Presidential Elections," May 2, 2016, http://bridge.georgetown.edu/report/when-islamophobia-turns-violent-the-2016-u-s-presidential-elections/; Alexis Okeowo, "Hate on the Rise after Trump's Election," *The New Yorker*, November 17, 2016, http://www.newyorker.com/news/news-desk/hate-on-the-rise-after-trumps-election.

2. Paul Owen, "Fallen Muslim American Soldier's Father Scolds Trump: 'Have You Even Read the Constitution?,'" The Guardian, July 29, 2016, https://www.theguardian.com/us-news/2016/jul/29/khizr-khan-democratic-convention-constitution-trump; Khizr Khan's speech to the 2016 Democratic National Convention,

ABC News, August 1, 2016, http://abcnews.go.com/Politics/full-text-khizr-khans
-speech-2016-democratic-national/story?id=41043609.

3. Mahmood Mamdani, *Good Muslim, Bad Muslim: America, the Cold War, and
the Roots of Terror* (New York: Pantheon Books, 2004), 15.

4. United States v. Roland R. Conklin, Stanley L. Conklin, and Joe Ranji Smile,
United States Circuit Court, Southern District of New York, 1902, Testimony of
M. Ismail, 3–12.

5. Ibid.; A. M. Brisbine, "A Chef from India," *Los Angeles Times*, October 15,
1899, 25; "Oriental Cookery in New York," *Harper's Bazaar*, October 28, 1899,
32; "Evil Days for Ranji Smile," *New York Tribune*, May 21, 1902, 1; "To Deport
Prince—He Is Accused of Violating Contract Labor Law," *New York Daily People*,
May 23, 1902, 1; "The Conklins's Prince," *New York Sun*, February 23, 1904, 9.

6. Brisbine, "A Chef from India," 25.

7. Peter Hudson, "Dark Finance: An Unofficial History of Wall Street, American Empire, and the Caribbean, 1893–1933," PhD diss., New York University, 2008,
73–79.

8. The Alien Contract Labor Law came, as Adam McKeown has argued, amid a
global effort by white settler nations to close their borders to "Oriental" workers.
Adam McKeown, *Melancholy Order: Asian Immigration and the Globalization of Borders* (New York: Columbia University Press, 2008), esp. chapter 5, "Experiments
in Border Control, 1852–1887," 121–48, and Chapter 6, "Civilization and Borders,
1885–1895," 149–84; Immigration Act of 1917, 39 Stat. 874 (1917).

9. See note 5.

10. Kristin L. Hoganson, *Consumers' Imperium: The Global Production of American Domesticity, 1865–1920* (Durham, N.C.: University of North Carolina Press, 2007),
26–29; Joan M. Jensen, *Passage from India: Asian Indian Immigrants in North America* (New Haven, Conn.: Yale University Press, 1988), 42–56, 101–20; Vivek Bald,
Bengali Harlem and the Lost Histories of South Asian America (Cambridge, Mass.:
Harvard University Press, 2013), 12–15, 50–51.

11. "New York Has a Malay Colony," *New York Post*, November 22, 1900; Her-
man Scheffauer, "The Tide of Turbans," *The Forum*, no. 43 (1910): 616–18. See also
Mai Ngai, *Impossible Subjects: Illegal Aliens and the Making of Modern America* (Princeton, N.J.: Princeton University Press, 2003), 40–41.

12. Holly Edwards, *Noble Dreams, Wicked Pleasures: Orientalism in America, 1870–
1930* (Princeton, N.J.: Princeton University Press, 2000), 11–13, 42–43, 128–34.

13. Ulrich W. Hiesinger, *Edwin Lord Weeks: Visions of India* (New York: Vance
Jordan Fine Art, 2002); Edwin Lord Weeks, "Street Life in India," *Harper's New
Monthly Magazine*, August 1890, 455–69; Weeks, "Lahore and the Punjaub," *Harp-
er's New Monthly Magazine*, October 1894, 651–72.

14. Edwards, *Noble Dreams*, 40–43; William Leach, *Land of Desire: Merchants,
Power, and the Rise of a New American Culture* (New York: Vintage Books, 1994),
9–10, 16–21.

15. Edwards, *Noble Dreams*, 42–43. For examples of the era's Egyptian-, Turkish-,
and Indian-themed tobacco branding and advertising, see the online Tobacco
Advertising Database compiled by Stanford Research into the Impact of Tobacco

Advertising at http://tobacco.stanford.edu/tobacco_main/subtheme.php?token=fm_mt027.php.

16. Bald, *Bengali Harlem*, 16–18.

17. Madeline Hsu, *The Good Immigrants: How the Yellow Peril Became the Model Minority* (Princeton, N.J.: Princeton University Press, 2015), 2–5, 12–16.

18. *An Act to Inaugurate Certain Treaty Stipulations Relating to Chinese*, 47th Cong., sess. I, chap. 126, 22 Stat. 58 (1882).

19. An Act to Prohibit the Importation and Migration of Foreigners and Aliens under Contract . . . , 48th Cong., sess. II, chap. 164, 23 Stat. 332 (1885).

20. An Act to Regulate the Immigration of Aliens to, and the Residence of Aliens in, the United States, 64th Cong., H.R. 10384; Pub.L. 301; 39 Stat. 874 (1917).

21. "Hindoo Peddlers Not Admitted," *New York Times*, June 27, 1897, 23. See also "Rug Peddlers Detained," *Baltimore Sun*, July 23, 1890, 1.

22. I further elaborate upon this point in Bald, *Bengali Harlem*, 50–51.

23. U.S. v. Conklin, Conklin, and Smile.

24. Ibid. See esp. the testimony of C. Ganglee, 239–51.

25. Brisbine, "A Chef from India," 25.

26. Ibid.; U.S. v. Conklin, Conklin, and Smile.

27. "Mysterious Prince Ranjit," *New York Tribune*, October 27, 1901, 4; "Prince Ranjit, Mystery of London, Coming Here," *New York Times*, October 27, 1901, 4; "Mysterious Prince Exciting Great Curiosity," *Aberdeen Daily News* (Aberdeen, S.D.), November 1, 1901; U.S. v. Conklin, Conklin, and Smile.

28. "Ex-waiter, Not a Prince—'Ranjit of Baluchistan' Is Well Known to Sherry's Patrons," *New York Times*, November 8, 1901, 16.

29. Ibid.; "Evil Days for Ranji Smile," *New York Tribune*, May 21, 1902; "Smile's 'Retinue' to Go Today," *New York Tribune*, May 24, 1902, 3; "The Conklins's Prince," *New York Sun*, February 23, 1904, 9.

30. United States v. Thind, 261 U.S. 204, 213–15 (1923).

10 Charlie, National Unity, and Colonial-Subjects

Selim Nadi

By exploding the former colonial reality the struggle uncovers unknown facets, brings to light new meanings and underlines contradictions which were camouflaged by this reality.

—FRANTZ FANON, *Wretched of the Earth*

As he conveyed his best wishes to the media on January 20, 2015, French prime minister Manuel Valls declared that there will exist a "before and an after 7 January 2015." In the same way, the French journal *Le Monde* titled its January 9 edition "The French 9/11." If these formulas are mainly meant to impress people, French colonial-subjects have experienced the truth of these words. By *colonial-subjects,* one should understand *indigènes.* Indeed, the English translation "indigenous" is far from perfect; the concept of "colonial-subject" seems closer to the French concept. I cannot cover the whole history of these struggles in this chapter, but I quickly evoke a certain continuity in the relation of the French colonial-subject to politics. In his book *Pour une politique de la racaille,* Sadri Khiari comes back to "indigenous status" relating to the colonized Algerians set up in 1865, giving French nationality to the colonial-subjects but still excluding them from political life (as they had no political or civil rights). But, Khiari wrote, "all this does not only belong to history. A whole part of the population, living and working in France, is still deprived of citizenship."[1] In the same way, the descendants of migrants, who have French citizenship and have more rights than their parents, still stay outside of political life, and as a result, their political priorities are never taken into account. Thus I use this term to stress the fact that racism is not just about prejudices or ideological issues. Racism is a political and social system—resulting from colonialism— that should be analyzed as such when one aims at analyzing the political consequences of events like the attacks on *Charlie Hebdo.* Hence, even if the word *indigenous* exists in English, it is more accurate to use the concept of colonial-subject to speak about nonwhite people in France. The French word *indigene* is a political category that has a profound actuality, even if, of course, the situation has evolved since colonialism, and there is a certain social and political continuity. The concept of "colonial-subject," even in a "postcolonial world," is useful in pointing out the specificity of racism people with an immigrant background face, and this racism is deeply rooted in the colonial Republic.

Hence, for colonial-subjects in France, the consequences of January 7, 2015, can be compared to the consequences of September 11, 2001. To sum up, besides the emotional aspect of the *Charlie Hebdo* and the Hypercacher attacks, these events will have a strong impact on the way colonial-subjects will be treated in France, and in Europe. One of the consequences of these attacks will be the attempt to pull down antiracist and decolonial movements. Indeed, the decolonial struggle in France has made much progress in the last few years, especially on the political level.[2] However, the call to national unity by the state through a major social response, as well as the accusations against antiracist organizations of being morally associated with these attacks, is a part of a violent backlash against the antiracist block that has emerged in the last ten years in France. A good example of this is how the term *free speech* was used to muzzle the French antiracist movement. Thus the possibility of the survival of antiracism will, after the "*Charlie* effect," reveal the capacity, or not, of political antiracism to survive in an explicitly hostile environment. Of course, the French state has not waited for these attacks to organize the marginalization of and fight against antiracism, but the reactions to the attacks are a new step in the state's fight against antiracism as well as a new step in the colonial counterrevolution dressed up as the holy "Republican pact."

Even if one cannot explain French racism only through "ideological content" (the Republic) and should also be aware of the very material roots racism has in European and American societies, it is important to stress the French specificity of republicanism. Concerning the "Republican pact," French philosopher Alain Badiou explains very well the role it plays in the counterrevolutionary strategy of the state:

> This "republican pact" to which so many former leftists have rallied—including *Charlie Hebdo*—has always suspected that trouble was brewing in the suburbs, the factories on the periphery and the gloomy banlieue hang-outs. It has always sent big police battalions into these areas, and under countless

pretexts filled its prisons with the suspect, ill-educated young men who lived there. It infiltrated its snitches and grasses into these "gangs" of youths. Moreover, the Republic carried out a vast array of massacres and implemented new forms of slavery in the interests of keeping order in its colonial empire, torturing "suspects" in the smallest African or Asian village police station. Indeed, it was Jules Ferry—who was without doubt, a fighter for the republican pact—who outlined the programme of this bloodsoaked empire, exalting France's "civilising mission."[3]

Hence it is obvious that republicanism played a large role in French colonialism and racism. After the *Charlie Hebdo* attacks, "republicanism" appears in its very contradictions: as a political weapon against colonial-subjects. Even some "moral antiracists" played the Republic card to say that one should not confuse terrorists, who are against the Republic, with the vast majority of French Muslims, who accept the Republic and its rules. But one cannot—as many humanist-republicans have done—just say "stop amalgams!" because what happened in France goes much further than just an amalgam between Muslims and terrorists. In this article, I question the reasons why there will be a "before and an after 7 January 2015" for colonial-subjects in France. In this, I first analyze the immediate reactions of the state to the attacks and the new step in the colonial counterrevolution, then I recall why, now more than ever, it is urgent to build a strong decolonial movement in France.

A New Step in the Colonial Counterrevolution

In his book *La contre-révolution coloniale en France*, Sadri Khiari writes,

> Every single revolution is accompanied by a counter-revolution. It is almost a law of history. The problem is that we can never know from where the counter-revolution will come. Neither when.[4]

This is exactly what the attacks on *Charlie Hebdo* represent: the beginning of a new phase of the colonial counterrevolution whose aim is to annihilate every form of decolonial resistance. These attacks have caused a large emotional wave in France that has had a disastrous effect on the way these attacks were handled, because it is the affective handling of the attacks that caused a peak in the muzzling of the colonial-subject and in the institutionalized violence that struck them. The day after the *Charlie* attack, President Hollande decreed a national day of mourning, and every French school observed a minute of silence. Of course, everybody knew that some pupils would not respect this minute of silence. Going further, we could say that this minute of silence was a kind of "test" to measure the attachment of nonwhite pupils to the French state. For many politicians, the rage, the incomprehension, and the doubt the pupils expressed were unbearable. Najat Vallaud-Belkacem of the Ministry of National Education affirmed in her answer to UMP deputy Claude Goasguen in the French parliament that "there were too many questions coming from pupils." The denunciations of nonwhite pupils to the police and the accusations of an "apology of terrorism" became more and more recurrent. Thus, in the expressions of anger of Muslim teenagers in France, with all the discrimination, stigmatization, and oppression coming from their condition, the French state saw only a pure and simple "apology for terrorism." To say it more crudely, what do twelve dead people represent to a young colonial-subject who, since his birth, has seen the Congolese, Iraqi, Palestinian, Afghan, and Nigerian mortuaries became more and more filled in widespread indifference? It is difficult to understand why the French Republic was surprised by their reactions. French politicians were unable to analyze their reactions, which meant placing them in the historical, political, and social configurations in which the colonial-subject lives.

But besides in schools, French justice was mobilized to track down every person who could possibly be suspected of an "apology for terrorism" or, more simply, everyone who "is not Charlie." Indeed, on National Channel France 2, on January 12, the journalist responsible for the political service of the channel, Nathalie Saint Cricq, said, "We have to find those who are not Charlie, those who, in certain schools, refuse to make the minute of silence, those who 'snitch' on social media and those who did not understood why this fight is their fight. Well, we should find, treat, integrate or re-integrate these people in the national community."[5] And indeed, this is exactly what was done: a large denunciation network hunted down and arrested those who did not want to be integrated into the national union. This arsenal of repression, organized by the state, was the first part of this new step of the colonial counterrevolution. The second aspect was the way in which the media treated the attack: in a totally nonpolitical way. German activist Volkhard Mosler notes that nobody—neither politicians nor journalists—have questioned the deeper causes of the attacks.[6] Instead of questioning the link between the group that organized the attacks and Euro-American imperialism, most French journalists focused their accusations on those who accused *Charlie Hebdo* of being Islamophobic. Thus

Jeannette Bougrab—former secretary of state under Nicolas Sarkozy, who presented herself as the partner of Charb, who was killed in the attacks—went on every TV channel to accuse several political groups and activists of being complicit in the attacks. The "companions" of terrorism were the journalist Rokhaya Diallo, former member of *Charlie Hebdo* Olivier Cyran, the antiracist group Les Indivisibles, the website LMSI.net, the Parti des Indigènes de la République, and several other antiracist activists or organizations. After the attacks of January 7, 2015, the fight against Islamophobia became suspect not only among mainstream journalists and politicians but also among certain people on the Left. In 2009, Sadri Khiari had already written,

> The République is an Islamophobic religion. Islamophobia does not fight against the Muslim as a Muslim but . . . against the Muslim as a potential threat to the white order, and this is why every single Muslim is a potential fundamentalist or terrorist. Islamophobia does not develop itself in the field of "religious intolerance" but in the field of racial struggle. Thus, she is only a part of the colonial counter-offensive made against every colonial-subject and, more specifically, against the space of their resistances, the working-class suburbs where the different aspects of the "security policies" express themselves.[7]

This is exactly what happened in reaction to the attacks against *Charlie Hebdo*: every attempt at resistance coming from colonial-subjects against the racism of which they were victims was delegitimized. Thus Christophe Ramaux, a member of the left-wing group Économistes atterrés, published a press-box on the website of *Le Monde,* in which he asked,

> How did we come this far? How can we explain that some leaders of ATTAC, of the NPA, some journalists from Politis and others—who organized with the *Indigènes de la République* and Médiapart, a day against Islamophobia on December 13th 2014—have served this infamy?[8]

This former Trotskyist, who took part in founding the Parti de Gauche, did not accuse French imperialist policy of participating in the birth of the groups who attacked *Charlie Hebdo,* but he attacked those who struggled against French Islamophobia. In his opinion, it was the antiracist struggle that encouraged these attacks. The abstract call to "freedom of expression"—

embodied in the famous slogan "Je suis Charlie"—completely muzzled the struggle against the privilege structuring the racial system in France. The irony of this is that "freedom of speech" is part of white privilege, and in this, it is part of the racialization of Muslims (who find its roots in the very economic and social systems of France). Indeed, the invocation of "freedom of speech" was just a pretext to shut down every discourse not in line with the official one. Remember that, a few months before the attacks, in summer 2014, the racial state ideology banned the demonstrations in support of Gaza.[9] But after the attacks of January 2015, the statement "freedom of expression" became a holy expression in front of which one had to be quiet. Thus this formula has joined the long list of the blurred vocabulary of the French state: *République, laïcité,* and so on. The French philosopher Elisabeth Badinter—who supported the law against hijab in schools in 2004—made a comparison between *Charlie Hebdo* and Voltaire:

> We treated them as provocative. Would one say that Voltaire was provocative when he fought against every religious fanaticism? We owe a part of the history of freedom of speech to Voltaire and, 250 years later, to the journalists of *Charlie Hebdo*.[10]

Besides the fact that Voltaire was well known for a virulent anti-Islam theater play, *Le Fanatisme ou Mahomet le Prophète* (1736), it is intriguing to note how the question of freedom of speech is totally unhistoricized. How can one compare the critique of the Church, which was a state religion, to the diatribes against the members (or presumed members) of a subaltern religion? Because this is the real point—the relation to the state—when one speaks about freedom of speech. Indeed, when in his "Lettre à d'Argence" (1763) Voltaire declared that "Christianity is the most infamous superstition that has ever befuddled people," he was taking a risk in attacking the state religion, unlike the journalists of *Charlie Hebdo*, who attacked Muslims with the complicity of the state. Of course, needless to say, this does not justify the attacks on the journal, but it is a true indicator of how the defender of "freedom of speech" unhistoricizes everything and how this type of approach permitted the hunting down of those who simply did not "feel Charlie."

Yet the murder of the *Charlie Hebdo* journalists cannot be understood without taking into account the European and American imperialism that indirectly produced this type of event, exactly as French structural racism provides "fighters" to these groups. But the emotional treatment of these types of events does not provide any political analysis of them. Besides the indirect complicity of European imperialism, these events should be analyzed in light of the incapacity of the white Left to grasp the racial question in France. Because, in France, a certain part of the Left analyzes the racial question as a "pure" class struggle, the racism of a whole part of the white working class is just seen as a false consciousness by the radical Left or as an abstract antihumanist attitude by the French social democracy. The new step in the colonial counterrevolution ongoing in France is thus also a consequence of the turbulence that has shaken the colonial order there. Even if political antiracism is not that strong in France, it has produced a large pro-Palestinian solidarity movement, it has put Islamophobia at the center of public debate, and it has developed diverse mobilizations among the descendants of postcolonial immigration, breaking with the dominant parties. This is why national unity and the use of "Je suis Charlie" were necessary to the French state. This *"union sacrée"* looks like the description that was made of it in the "MPs' chamber" (Chambre des députés) by Raymond Poincaré on August 4, 1914:

> In the war that arrives, France . . . will be heroically defended by all its sons who are fraternally and patriotically together outraged in seeing this aggression. Today nothing will break the *union sacrée* in front of the enemy.[11]

The difference between the *union sacrées* of 1914 and 2015 is that in 1914, it was an outside enemy—Germany—whereas today, it is an inside enemy: the colonial-subject. This is why, today, among the white Left, many debate whether one should support meetings against Islamophobia, instead of questioning why the *"marche républicaine"* for national unity, on January 11, 2015, counted only very few nonwhite people; the state and most of the white political organizations preferred to condemn the refusal of colonial-subjects to bow down before the national union.

While the antiracist and decolonial political bloc, which has emerged in France in the last ten years, is today questioned by these attacks, it is—now more than ever—urgent to assume our positions and to continue elaborating an antiracist strategy and movement. Indeed, the colonial counterrevolution uses these attacks to break the basis of the decolonial struggle in France. The "war against terror" by the French government is mainly directed against Muslims, and this is why the attack should be answered politically.

AFTER THE ATTACK ON *Charlie Hebdo*, THE DECOLONIAL
STRUGGLE IS MORE THAN EVER A NECESSITY IN FRANCE

In an interview with Stella Magliani-Belkacem and Félix Boggio Éwanjée-Épée, Sadri Khiari explains that political "autonomy is part of the balance of forces":

> Any organizational action we take, any thinking independence we have, it's only a certain balancing of power that enables us not to be subjected to the will of others.[12]

The political moment that began after the January 2015 attacks made clear the necessity of playing a role in the balances of power to direct the power toward the antiracist camp. Building a political countermovement is thus more necessary than ever.

But an obstacle to building this countermovement was the attitude of the French Left. Indeed, even when the Left rejected the strategy of the "clash of civilizations" (the conservative strategy), it refused to give to the racial polarization that structured society a real place in its political struggle. Even if the word *race* is not that shocking in France today, as it was a few years ago, it remains true that when a person speaks about race, he does not speak about it as a power relationship between white and nonwhite or as a social and political struggle between them, thus emptying the word of its meaning. It is frightening to see that the word *race* is completely depoliticized and has become a sort of leftist gadget. The fact that the race question is either ignored or depoliticized by the Left is truly revealing in the incompetence of the Left to grasp the racial issue in France and to contribute to building a larger antiracist grassroots political front. This attitude of the Left participates in feeding the new step in counterrevolution opened by the January 2015 attacks.

The state is the main oppressive force against the colonial-subject; this is why it is at the center of our political analysis. Racial stratification is constitutive of the nation-state. The history of the building of the nation-state is intimately linked to the apparition and evolution of the social-race struggle. Yet, in the present situation, it is not enough to abstractly call for a fight against the state; rather, it is necessary to fight to build a larger political bloc regrouping decolonial organizations as well as left-wing allies. One should thus overtake its punctual disagreement because building a decolonial movement should, especially today, be a priority of every organization that wants to break with imperialism and with French structural racism. Indeed, vague calls against the amalgams between Muslims and terrorists or the cry for grand humanist discourse are not enough and will not help us to face the political situation we are in.

Thus the shock provoked by the *Charlie Hebdo* attacks achieved the strong unification of white power and participated in a new step of the colonial counterrevolution. One can only hope that this situation will provoke the constitution of such a decolonial movement. We can only be optimistic regarding our struggles and the birth of a real decolonial strategy in France, even if we probably should be very patient.

NOTES

1. All translations herein are by the author. Sadri Khiari, *Pour une politique de la racaille. Immigré-e-s, indigènes et jeunes de banlieues* (Paris: Textuel, 2006), 53.

2. On this, see Selim Nadi, "Why Do We Need an Indigenous Party in France?," http://indigenes-republique.fr/why-do-we-need-an-indigenous-party-in-france/.

3. Alain Badiou, "The Red Flag and the Tricolore," http://www.versobooks .com/blogs/1833-the-red-flag-and-thetricolore-by-alain-badiou.

4. Sadri Khiari, *La contre-révolution coloniale en France. De de Gaulle à Sarkozy* (Paris: La Fabrique, 2009).

5. See https://www.youtube.com/watch?v=wW3viL_cJ7I.

6. Volkhard Mosler, "Der Krieg der Armen," *Marx21*, January 2015.

7. Khiari, *La contre-révolution coloniale en France.*

8. Christophe Ramauz, "Pour Christophe Ramaux, la gauche radicale a eu tort d'attaquer la prétendue islamophobie de 'Charlie,'" http://www.lemonde.fr/idees/ article/2015/01/09/la-gauche-radicale-a-eu-tort-dattaquer-la-pretendu-islamopho bie-de-charlie_4552848_3232.html.

9. See Richard Seymour, "March for Gaza banned in Paris after a week of tensions," http://www.leninology.co.uk/2014/07/frances-ban-on-pro-palestine-march .html.

10. Elisabeth Badinter, "On doit une partie de notre histoire de la liberté d'expression à Charlie Hebdo," http://www.lejdd.fr/Societe/Badinter-On-doit-une-partie-de -notre-histoire-de-la-liberte-d-expression-a-CharlieHebdo-711582.

11. Raymond Poincaré, "Le président de la République Raymond Poincaré et le discours de l'Union sacrée du 4 août 1914," http://14-18.crdp-limousin.fr/blog/2014/ 08/04/546/.

12. Houria Bouteldja and Sadri Khiari, eds., *Nous sommes les indigènes de la République* (Paris: Éditions Amsterdam, 2012).

11

"Nuts-and-Bolts Organizing, They Work Everywhere"

An Interview with Fahd Ahmed on Mass-Based Organizing and the National Security State

JUNAID RANA

JUNAID RANA (JR): Since its founding in 2000, DRUM [Desis Rising Up and Moving] has had as a central mission the organization of South Asian immigrants and youth in New York. What can you tell us about the model that was created through the work of DRUM? How has the organizing approach changed over the last decade and a half? Were there any significant turning points?

FAHD AHMED, EXECUTIVE DIRECTOR, DRUM: From its inception, DRUM was always intended to be an organization of working-class, immigrant, South Asian workers and youth. The idea was that it would be a mass-based organization, so it engaged large numbers of those people and supported them to be in leadership of the organization. When it started, initially it was a collective of working-class South Asian activists. And it took us some time to figure out how to engage actual community members who were not already politicized. This shift from an activist model to a mass-based model took some time. There was definitely a period immediately after 9/11, because we were the first and primary organization that was inside the prisons that located all of the people that were picked up and disappeared, we were engaged with a lot of those detainees and their families to get them involved in the mobilizations and in the actions, but the work was still centered around the activists. It really wasn't until 2003 to 2004 when we started shifting to create the infrastructure where our members became critically engaged and central to the decision-making process, the leadership process, to where the activists started taking a step back and started supporting the development of and the leadership of our members. That sort of model that has the nuts and bolts of organizing is pretty rare in our communities, whether they be Muslim communities, South Asian communities, or Arab communities. It's really through our partnerships and relationship with Black, Latino, and LGBTQ organizations that we learned how to deepen those models. Over the last decade and a half, we have been refining that model and an evolution of the issues that we work on.

Immediately in the period after 9/11, most of the work centered on the work of post-9/11 policies. And so we built the base of maybe about nine hundred people. And by 2003 to 2004, about 95 percent of those people had been deported. And so we realized that while we needed to confront those types of 9/11 policies, we really needed to build a base around bread-and-butter issues. Things that are everyday impacts where there are some concrete, tangible wins or policy changes to fight for. And we worked on those types of campaigns for a good six to eight years refining our model and refining the nuts and bolts of how do we do engagement and how do we do development. Once we had a really good model in 2011, we began experimenting with more risky campaigns around national security and NYPD [New York Police Department] surveillance. Now I think we have a good model that I think we can build on top of that we can tackle the issues that are coming up.

JR: How did you end up working with DRUM? What were the commitments that drove you to do this work?

FA: On a personal level, I came into DRUM because of being personally impacted, being from a working-class South Asian family, being undocumented for many years, having a brother who went through a deportation proceeding, having a cousin who was set up by the DEA and the FBI in one of the War on Drugs entrapment cases, and having gone to school in Oklahoma facing a lot of racial violence. So these incidents and moments in my life were politicizing. So by the time I graduated college and I moved to New York, I was what you would call an angry Brown kid. I had this anger and knew that if things weren't right with the world and something needed to be done, I didn't exactly know what to do and where to do it. I moved to New York in July of 2000, and in August of 2000, I found an old flyer from the very first action that DRUM had done. The flyer was already five years old. The flyer was from an action that DRUM had done when the officers who killed Amadou Diallo were acquitted. DRUM had done a community rally in Jackson Heights [Queens, New York]. I found this flyer and was intrigued by the idea that this was a working-class South Asian organization that openly talked about solidarity with Black and Latino communities, that openly talked about police abuse and violence. I reached out and called the number, and it was a pager number, which existed in those days. I got a call back two days later and met up with the folks. I've been active and involved ever since. It's become a home. For those of us who come from working-class communities, there are very few organizations where working-class people have political leadership and that are tailored to the needs, the voices, and the lived experiences of working-class communities. So that's how I stayed involved as a volunteer, as a full-time volunteer, as a staff person, as board member and staff member, and now as the executive director. Now, having done that, I fell in love with organizing work. The day to day of organizing, recruiting people, engaging people, building relationships with people and supporting their leadership, taking on campaigns and winning those campaigns. Three years ago, I had the opportunity to become the director of DRUM. This meant that I would not get to do the day-to-day organizing on my own. Stepping into the role, what became clear is that I became responsible for creating the space for other people to be able to do the day-to-day organizing work. And I think that is what got me grounded, because I am responsible for creating the space, providing resources, support, and training for people to go into their communities and organize for the issues they care about.

JR: More recently, DRUM, alongside other organizations, launched a successful campaign to convince the Obama administration to shut down the NSEERS, or Special Registration Program, launched by the George W. Bush administration in 2003. Why was this important? What does this policy tell us about patterns of deportation, detention, and surveillance?

FA: First, we were one of the lead organizations in fighting against Special Registration when it was launched in September 2002. We formed the New York City Coalition against Special Registration and recruited a lot of the Muslim, South Asian, and Arab organizations. That coalition was actually co-led by Black and Latino organizations that had been doing prison abolition, prison reform, or anti–state violence work. And so it allowed us to have a broader framing and a broader perspective that really saw special registrations as a continuity of past policies of state violence and targeting and surveillance and just seeing special registrations as the newest iterations. Through the policies, eighty-three thousand people were registered, thirteen thousand were put into deportation proceedings, and we were handling I think about four hundred of those cases, and these were people we got to know, people we had relationships with. And we had a direct expansion working with the people who were impacted at that time. And the impacts were, first, directly from the policies, in terms of people who went to go register, got detained, got interrogated, got humiliated, some of them were let back out. Most of them were put into deportation proceedings, and many of those folks were actually put into detention. And so you know, visiting folks inside of detention. Working with them like if they were put into deportation proceedings.

But then there were also the set of folks who didn't register who were just living in fear and asking what they should do. Many of those folks decided to cross the border and go over to Canada. And there was a moment when we were getting calls from the refugee centers on the border, saying, "There's all these Pakistanis in particular, that we have here. We've put them in tents in the middle of the cold, and they are waiting to cross over to the Canadian border." And once they crossed over, after a couple of years, they were usually deported back, so we also had to facilitate the process of bringing those folks back, integrating them back in, figuring out what happens with them once they are here, and what are the services and support they need.

And then there was a third aspect of the people who didn't register and how they were impacted, which was generally the families of the registrants. And so there were a lot of women who we had to help, those who mainly worked at home and now needed to go out and find jobs. We had conversations with fourteen- and fifteen-year-olds about dropping out of school so that they could support their families. Or that they could go and look after their siblings at home, while their mothers went off to work. And so you know, for us, it wasn't just the policy, it was really about the flesh-and-blood experiences of our communities and our people who we remembered from that period.

We worked with those families, and then trying to end NSEERS. The NSEERS program kind of went inactive by the mid-2000s, but we knew it was still on the books. And we wanted it to be formally closed. A lot of our members who had been impacted by special registrations were part of that work. When the Obama administration came in, we continued to push for them. And eventually the Obama administration formally closed down the program, but they left the laws on the books. They didn't take off the regulations. And we highlighted to them that if you don't take them off, the program can easily be reactivated. And the response we got was "that would never happen." And at that point, we said, "You never know what would happen, and it is better that it be taken off the books." So when the Trump campaign was talking about a Muslim registry program, we had in the back of our minds, could that really just be a reference to the NSEERS program?

And the day after the election, that became a reality. And so immediately, we started talking to our members, started talking to our allies. And we decided that was the moment to make a push for the Obama administration to actually take the regulations off the books, that they had to undo the regulatory framework that allowed that program to exist. That wouldn't prevent the new administration from being able to rebuild it again, but they would have to rebuild it from scratch. And that would create an opportunity for us to be able to intervene in that process. And the need to be able to do this became particularly clear when this meme and quote and idea of if there is a Muslim registration, we need white people to register, or like you know we as Jews will register, or we as Christians will register. And to us, that was alarming, because of having lived through the registration program and working with folks. One, there really is no way that other people can register on your behalf, but second, if that program is already running, then that's already millions and millions of dollars of jobs, infrastructure, policies that are already in motion, and so by that time, it is already too late. And we needed to do something that prevented it from getting to that point. And so the idea was, how do we get the Obama administration to undo the regulatory framework? And so we worked with Moveon.org to do an online petition. We worked with American Arab Anti-Discrimination Committee around meeting directly with the White House and then also working with activists in the D.C. area to do a local action to push the Obama administration. And through all the pressure, the Obama administration took steps to undo the regulatory framework, and now if the Trump administration wants to re-create that program, they would have to start from scratch. Which would mean that they would have to do public hearings or public comment periods. It is possible they may even have to go through Congress, we aren't sure about that. But it makes the process much more difficult for them, and then also makes it less likely for them to do it in the way that they intended.

And so I think the last thing that I would say is about what this tells us about the sweep patterns in American history. For example, what was done with indigenous peoples was in some ways, not like registrations in the formal way, but just collecting people, surveilling people, and then either them being massacred, or them being relocated or being interned. That goes back to the earliest periods of American history. What was done with Japanese communities, what was done in COINTELPRO [the FBI counterintelligence program], and what we understand is just the capacity of the American state to inflict violence on racialized communities within its borders. The second lesson is that these are the types of things where complacency is very dangerous and even ceding a little bit of ground is very dangerous. One of the conversations when special registrations started was like, OK, let's trust the government. Some of our advocacy organizations were saying that: "let's trust the government, let's register, let's see what happens." But the people who actually had to do that are the ones who bore the impact. For us, it's kind of like we can't really cede any ground. We have to be up front and confronting the current administration and these types of policies at every step every inch of the way. Because once you cede even a little bit of ground, the impacts of that are immeasurable.

JR: Relatedly, what is the impact of NYPD surveillance in Muslim neighborhoods throughout the New York area? What are your current campaigns around this, and what sort of role did this have on South Asian workers in New York? How did this change the models for organizing Muslim and non-Muslim South Asians?

FA: Immediately after 9/11 what we started to see were these massive numbers of sweeps and detentions of hundreds of people, mainly, almost all men from New York and New Jersey areas. Within a couple of days of 9/11, we put out a flyer across the city in South Asian neighborhoods with a toll-free hotline number saying if you experience a hate crime or discrimination or anything, please give us a call. That phone started ringing immediately, and it started ringing nonstop. The calls we were getting were from kids saying like, "Oh, my father left for work a couple of days ago and he hasn't come home." Or from women saying, "The police, immigration, and FBI came to my home last night and took my husband and I don't know where he is." We started getting them from workers saying a black van just pulled up in front of our store, grabbed a few people, and drove off. We were able to locate these folks who were largely held in county jails in New Jersey. After we started working with them, most of the people were being held incommunicado from their families and from any lawyers and anybody else. They picked up over twelve hundred men and the find was zero to have any connection to anything related to terrorism. A year after 9/11, when Special Registration started, they registered eighty-three thousand and put thirteen thousand into deportation proceedings, and they find of all of those people zero to have any connection to terrorism. By early 2002, before Special Registration, there were some questions and concerns in the media, from our communities, politicians, and some policy makers about "these people are being picked up and it's not producing anything." In early 2002, we started seeing law enforcement agencies adding a new tactic, which was coming to community members and community leaders and saying, "We want to work more closely with you to identify the bad people, and we want your help in this so we don't target people who are innocent." A lot of community leaders who at that time were living under a lot of fear, and their communities were devastated, were open to the idea. Having worked with Black and Latino organizations and Asian organizations and knowing that history, we said, "No, this is not a good idea." Because there was such a high level of fear and people thought, "what else could we lose?" they welcomed law enforcement into their organizations. Immediately after those community forums, after a day or two, we started getting reports saying, "Hey, I went and met with this officer the day after and they are asking me questions about the imam, they are asking me to collect license plate numbers at the masjid." So at that point, we immediately recognized that this community engagement was being used in broader covert surveillance through the use, at that time, of informants, and eventually we figured out also with undercover officers. This was happening with federal law enforcement agencies, and NYPD was also running its own programs doing surveillance.

From the 2003 to 2006 period, we knew that these things were happening. We would read about them in the news but weren't really working on these issues. In 2006, we started getting members who had been targeted by the surveillance programs, in particular, one family whose son had been targeted by an NYPD informant. The informant spent a year and a half building a relationship with him. After having gained his trust, he started showing him pictures, articles, and videos about U.S. atrocities in Iraq, Israeli atrocities in Palestine. And then having incited him emotionally, he then started poking: "what are you gonna do about this, you gotta do something." As soon as he said, "Yes, we should do something," he got arrested, put on trial, found guilty, and sentenced to thirty years in prison. His family became members of DRUM before the trial. Through that, because it was reflected in our membership, we started to address those issues more and more. We had been talking about how NYPD surveillance was playing out and that these entrapment cases were the extreme version of it but that there were actual undercovers and informants in our communities and what impact is that having and what does that do to communities. In 2011, when the Associated Press [AP] reports came out, we started to get a better picture of the lower-level impact of surveillance and the lower-level manifestation of surveillance. Which then explained some of the impact we were seeing in the community. So if entrapment is the highest manifestation, there is a medium level of like informants and undercovers engaging in the community by hooking them, prodding them, blackmailing them, pressuring them. On the lowest level is the quiet surveillance that is happening that people don't really feel but they kind've vaguely know about. Which explains why so many people in our communities have gone completely silent, stopped going to mosques or stopped having political conversations in the mosque. Or mosques started having these policies around not talking about those things, and a lot of those types of things are conversations that would be useful in our communities that were driven underground. That sort of impact at all three levels is still felt from NYPD and FBI surveillance.

In 2011, when the AP reports came out, we started a series of conversations with our members and with some community partners, a number of those who wanted to work with the NYPD, to consider that those moments of engagement were actually moments of surveillance and information collection. And those engaging in dialogue with law enforcement were also being surveilled. One of the main things that we did was to encourage the Muslim sector folks to partner with Black and Latino organizations that were working on issues of stop-and-frisk at that moment. Many of those organizations we had relationships with as early as 1999, before DRUM was formed. We pushed both sectors as the only organization that had relationships with both sectors, and as an organization that had a membership base impacted by both sets of issues, and encouraged them to come together and talk and work together. Through that work, the idea of an inspector general came about, with some sort of oversight over the NYPD surveillance program. That campaign was launched in 2012, and by 2013, we were able to pass the Community Safety Act, which created (1) an antiprofiling law and (2) an Inspector General's Office over the NYPD. Since then, we have been working with that Inspector General's Office to do investigations and reports on the NYPD surveillance program and put out a first report, which was more about record keeping and procedures. That report was put out last summer [2016], and we are continuing to engage them with additional investigations and reports.

The impact I already talked about concerns levels of fear and how fear impacts religious practice, political practice, and even social engagement. We did a survey of about five hundred New York City Muslims between 2011 and 2015, and we found people who said they were uncomfortable talking to or meeting new people within the community because of the feeling that "you don't know who is who." People talked about feeling uncomfortable about going to the mosque. Even if they are going to the mosque, they have anxiety about it and wonder about whether that will put them at risk. Young people talk about anxiety around becoming politically involved at their high schools, colleges, or workplaces. The impact has been on the level of fear, that then shapes the things that people will do, the activities they will engage in or will not engage in.

The intervention that we made was that we couldn't do this alone as a Muslim community, first, because a lot of the immigrant Muslim communities don't have the larger historical context of how the various manifestations of state violence and surveillance worked in the past, that this gap needed to be filled through ongoing dialogue with Black and Latino organizations that had been doing this kind of work for decades. Second, while there were several advocacy organizations from our communities, DRUM was the main organization that was mass based and active in South Asian and Muslim communities. And really the difference was in the leadership that was coming from our membership, straight-up South Asian working-class folks who were targeted by surveillance and were talking to the media, talking in city council meetings, meeting city council members or protesting outside of their offices, to really pressure and build the momentum to pass policy changes. That understanding of building the leadership of everyday people and that they are ones who should lead those campaigns is something I think we still need to build better recognition of. Too often, we rely on "community leaders" or religious leaders or advocates or lawyers. For us, it is really important that everyday people have the capability and are actually much more able to effectively and strongly organize.

JR: What are the challenges that are facing DRUM in the immediate future under a Trump presidency and administration? How will these policies

be connected to the previous Obama administration? For example, the
Obama administration's Countering Violent Extremism (CVE) program?

FA: In some ways, we have a lot of the same challenges: surveillance, dis-
criminatory street policing, immigration enforcement, undocumented
people, underfunded and overpoliced schools, worker exploitation—all
of those issues still exist. There is a realization that the state apparatus
that allowed those conditions to exist before is in the hands of people
who are a lot more aggressive and committed to targeting our communities. It's a difference in scale and magnitude. On these issues of surveillance and policing and enforcement of worker abuse and educational
justice, the stakes are ramped up. The onslaught is more aggressive
from multiple sides. The realization we have is that our communities
are not well organized enough to be able to withstand and be able to fight
back. We need to build deeper, broader, and stronger within our communities. We need more organized spaces and more well organized
spaces to confront these policies and these forces. That's really influenced how we do our work in this period, but it has also got us thinking
about how to support those capacities within our communities—South
Asian, Arab, Muslim—to be more organized in similar ways and models
so they are able to participate in the fight back.

For the CVE program, it immediately sounded like the conversation
from law enforcement agencies that was happening in 2002 of "hey, we
just want to work with you to figure out who are the right people that
we need to engage so we don't engage the wrong people." That set the
foundation for expansive surveillance and penetration of our communities. Similarly, CVE uses the language of youth engagement and an
expansive surveillance apparatus into services like health care and education. It made those services an extension of the surveillance apparatus.
That was meant to be subtle. Now that same apparatus is in the hands
of an administration that is openly and blatantly committed and makes
it even more weaponized and dangerous.

JR: Is New York exceptional as a place for social justice politics? Can you
describe the demographics of the membership base of DRUM in Queens
and some of the things that workers are dealing with? Are there strategies and models that might be adapted for use elsewhere?

FA: New York is exceptional in three ways that are notable. One, there are
more dense populations, and there are more dense populations of our
community. So it allows the outreach, recruitment, and engagement in a
much easier way. So I can walk down the street and there are a hundred

people I can talk to in a few hours. So that allows me to engage people and recruit them in the work more readily. Whereas in other places, where people are more scattered, that can be more challenging. It's doable, but it requires a little bit of a different approach. Having that density makes it easier to engage people, and the more you can engage people, the more you can plug them into social justice work.

The second is that there are more opportunities for getting resources for this kind of work in New York, in particular, being able to get non-profit funding. It allows you to have the resources to do institutional building, which sometimes can be harder in other places, with some exceptions in religious institutions.

The third aspect is that because there is funding available and because there's a history of social struggle here, there are other organizations and other models that people from our communities can see. And sometimes, when we try to engage people, they are kind of like, "Oh, I don't know, is it safe? I don't know exactly what we are trying to do." But when they go out and meet other organizations that are doing similar work, and when they meet members from other organizations or see them in action or march alongside them or protest alongside them or do media work alongside them, it gives them a sense of "oh, OK, other people are doing this work, and we are doing this along with them and doing it particularly for our communities." In those ways, I think it makes it a little bit easier to do this work in New York. That said, I think the issues and challenges that people face exist across the country. As organizers, we are trained in identifying where people are hurting, how we tend to that hurt, in a way that provides some relief but also provides some agitation for people to engage in struggle and social justice work. That part's doable, it just requires tailoring based on particular geographies and contexts.

Almost fifteen to sixteen years after 9/11, we are seeing that there are some similar models of communities organizing themselves or segments of communities organizing themselves that are trying to do things. I think probably most notably in Somali communities, especially in the Twin Cities [Minneapolis and St. Paul, Minnesota], where there are a lot of young people who are becoming organized themselves, and it's not just like an activist collective, it's broader engagement with everyday people in their communities, around how do we fight back against CVE, how do we fight back against media portrayals of our communities? And you know, that is a big source of hope in these moments.

The demographics of our membership are low-income people of South Asian descent, so that includes the diaspora, that includes people, particularly Indo-Caribbean folks from Trinidad, Guyana, Suriname, also folks from other parts of the diaspora, occasionally Malaysia and Fiji. And we are a majority women-led organization. We prioritize building the leadership of women. We also prioritize building the leadership of young people. Trying to undo some of the hierarchies that exist within our communities, understanding that young people and women are really best positioned to be in the leadership of this work because of the multiple ways in which they experience exploitation, marginalization, within our communities.

Models have to be tailored to particular contexts. But I think two things we would say are the basics of nuts-and-bolts organizing, they work everywhere. You know, the basics of getting out and talking to people, recruiting people, figuring out systems and infrastructure around how to engage them and how to give them ownership in the decision-making process, and providing the support to make that decision making happen, and then channeling folks into campaigns. You know those nuts and bolts of organizing apply everywhere. It just requires some tweaking to figure out how it would apply in a particular context.

The second thing we would say is that being able to do mass-based organizing work requires a particular orientation. Organizing can only happen when we believe in the power of people to be able to do for themselves, speak for themselves, not only individually but collectively. It doesn't happen spontaneously; we need to provide the support and resources to make that happen, but we really have to believe in the capacities of people to be able to do for themselves. And I think once people have that orientation, if we have that orientation as organizers, there's always issues that people can be organized around. It's just a matter of figuring out what are the issues that move them, what are the hurts that really resonate for them, and that there is an opportunity to engage them on it.

JR: In the conversation about the sanctuary movement, and more broadly the immigrant rights movement, the connection between immigrant families as Muslim and undocumented seems to not have much traction in the national conversation. Are there particular ways that DRUM approaches organizing faith-based communities? How might a faith-based approach that incorporates Muslims invigorate what we think of in terms of social justice movements?

FA: So DRUM is a secular organization, but we do recognize the important role that faith and faith-based institutions play in people's lives, both in positive ways and in challenging ways. We do build relationships with faith-based institutions, we do have relationships with them, we do try to engage them in the work when we can, in terms of mobilizing, in terms of advocacy. Because our primary focus is our own membership, we engage our members just on the basis of being DRUM members. The majority of our membership is Muslim, and so we do provide a space to be able to acknowledge that identity, but we don't organize people particularly as Muslims or from a faith perspective. And I think that's mainly because we are a secular organization that has a multireligious base or multifaith base, and so we want the space to be opening and welcoming for everyone. The majority of our membership is Muslim, almost half of our membership is undocumented, so the majority of our undocumented members are also Muslim. And many of them have been on the forefront of the immigrant rights struggle, locally and nationally. Because there are very few non-Latinx organizations that are doing work in undocumented communities, we have a prominent role on the national level. We are able to deeply engage, organize, and mobilize our folks despite being Muslim and being undocumented, as well as South Asians of other faith traditions, Sikh, Hindu, atheist, Buddhist.

Particularly around sanctuary, though, I think there have been conversations with faith-based institutions from our communities. In conversations with our own members, with our own communities, and with the faith-based institutions, our assessment is that sanctuary actually is, in the traditional sense of sanctuary inside of a faith home, not realistic within the faith institutions in our communities. First, for mosques, when they are so thoroughly surveilled and infiltrated by informants and undercovers, they are not safe places for people to take sanctuary. Or most mosques are not.

And then I think there is a second level, even beyond mosques. Whether law enforcement agencies, and ICE [Immigration and Customs Enforcement] in particular, would offer the same sort of respect to a mosque, to a mandir, to a gurdwara, that they seem to offer to the churches and synagogues, and I think there is a real big question around that. When a lot of interfaith institutions want to declare themselves as sanctuary, or want to proclaim it, for us it has been a conversation around "is this really useful?" Proclaiming is not enough. "What are we going to do afterward?" and can we actually provide the sort of safety and sanctuary that are necessary, and we think the answer to that is no.

And then I think another aspect that we have also found is at least in our conversations within working-class South Asian communities, the idea of people living inside of a faith institution for months or years actually doesn't seem very appealing. The largest response we've gotten is, "Wait so I will just be imprisoned inside of a faith institution. That doesn't really sound very useful, I might as well either deport myself or just live in hiding in my home."

It's become pretty popular for a lot of liberal to progressive elected officials right now to proclaim their cities as sanctuaries or become advocates for sanctuary. I think for us, cities that have taken steps to limit the interaction and relationship between local police and ICE or local agencies and ICE is always a good thing. But I think three questions that remain for us are, first, sanctuary can't really just be a declaration, it actually has to be something substantive, so what are those substantive steps that are being taken? Second, in those substantive steps, we can't talk about "police will not give information over to ICE" without talking about, well, what about police itself? What does aggressive policing mean for our communities, for poor communities, for targeted communities? And even if police aren't directly turning over information to ICE, if there is aggressive policing in let's say the Broken Windows policing model, that automatically channels people into the deportation pipeline. Third, when we say sanctuary, are we only talking about immigrant communities? What do sanctuary communities mean for Black communities, for queer communities, for Muslim communities, for women, for young people? And so for us, in this moment, when this administration is targeting not only immigrants but so many other communities, we can't stay limited to a notion of sanctuary that only talks about immigrants. It actually has to be sanctuary for all of our communities. And so it has to be all-encompassing and inclusive. And so that means conversations around, what do police look like? How do we get rid of Broken Windows policing? How do we create alternatives to policing to keep ourselves safe? What will our educational institutions be doing? What information do they collect? What information do they turn over? What does policing inside of schools look like?

You know, I think it is a moment that is really calling for us to expand the notion of sanctuary beyond immigrants and to be inclusive of all communities, going beyond sloganeering to really look at substantive policies and budgeting. What does it mean if New York City spends $400 million a year for school policing, yet our schools, some of our schools, still don't have books, don't have desks, are underfunded, and have leaky roofs. What does that say about how people are made to feel safe in their neighborhoods, in their schools, in their communities?

These are the questions that our membership have been asking since before the election, but particularly since the election. And for us, that's led to our current work being channeled into a strategy that we are calling "hate-free zones," which is really building a neighborhood-based defense system, around how we start to build safety on a neighborhood level. How do we build the relationships, how do we provide the training for people to be able to defend themselves individually, for people to be able to defend each other on the community level, for us to be able to leverage the community institutions that we have to be able to participate in the defense, but also to leverage their power? How do we start to do this not only in our communities but across communities, with other communities? How do we defend ourselves from policies of hate but also forces of hate that are currently being organized and are mobilizing to target our people?

JR: In the history of the United States, particularly when we think of the civil rights movement, there is a tendency to overlook the influence of religion on organizing such that figures such as Martin Luther King Jr. and Malcolm X are imagined in terms of their impact as leaders of the Black Freedom movement. Yet they represent a religious approach to organizing in which King might be imagined as part of a Christian Left, and while Malcolm X was averse to labels of Right and Left, he has certainly been influential to many of the Left. What is the advantage of thinking of the Muslim Left?

FA: I do think it is important to think of the worldview that is presented by a particular politics. What are the implications, who is included, how are they included, who is uplifted, and who is not? From that perspective, the Left is more inclusive, and thinking about systemic change and about creating a world for humanity as a whole. For me, that's an important factor. Regardless of what traditions people draw from, I think if people have a similar view that is encompassing and embracing of people, then that provides a foundation to work with people that while we may not have the minute details aligned, we are overall working in the same

direction. That sort of view allows us to get to the root cause of our problems and to understanding the root causes through capitalism, white
supremacy, and through imperialism.

People, whether they are Muslim, immigrants, or other communities, should think about what political worldview they subscribe to and
what the implications of that worldview are. The category of Muslim Left
would use it in different ways by different people, which might create
contradictions. One example might be that when we say Muslim Left,
is "Muslim" just an identity, and is "Muslim" bringing a politics, and is
that politics from Islam, and what understanding of Islam is it drawn
from?

On a personal level, those are questions that I've grappled with. Right
now, I'm so immersed in my day to day at DRUM, which is more of a
secular Left approach, that I don't have those questions at the forefront
of my mind. If I wasn't here and I wanted to organize in Muslim communities as a Muslim, I may have to grapple with them again. But it's
not so much a question for me now. In engaging in other people, it
does become a question. In the United States, where questions of Muslim identity are forced upon you by the state, society, and our communities, it makes the possibility of these conversations a lot more difficult.

Some of these struggles weren't even struggles; they were organic
conversations in our home countries. You look at Maulana Bhashani in
Bangladesh, who openly talked about communism and the manifestation of Islam as communism. And he had millions of followers. Khan
Abdul Ghaffar Khan in Pakistan, who wasn't a religious leader, but his
work with the Khudai Khidmatgar, that movement drew upon his understanding of Islam, and it was imbued with a spirit. There were secular
Left forces that challenged them and religious forces that didn't like
the mixing of Islam and left-wing politics that attacked them. But they
had large followings. It's a little questionable whether those same forces
could exist back home now, given how different religious movements
have grown strong in our home countries. It does seem that being both
Muslim and Left is a difficult terrain to navigate definitely in the United
States and, it could be argued, back home.

III

TECHNOLOGIES OF
SURVEILLANCE AND CONTROL

12

"A Catastrophically Damaged Gene Pool"

Law, White Supremacy, and the Muslim Psyche

SHERENE H. RAZACK

That each cluster of adjectives cancels out the other is of no moment since contradiction, incoherence and emotional disorder "fit" when the subject is black.

—TONI MORRISON, "The Official Story: Dead Man Golfing," in *Birth of a Nation'hood*

Poor prognosis is associated with being religiously devout. In other words, the more religious the person, the more poor the prognosis.

—MICHAEL WELNER, psychiatrist, expert witness for the prosecution in the sentencing hearing of Omar Khadr at Guantánamo about jihadists

Race thinking, Hannah Arendt wrote, turns on the idea that culture and character are inheritable traits.[1] Europeans imagined that they possessed an innate capacity for rationality while those whom they conquered and ruled over remained unable to move out of the state of nature. In *Casting Out: The Eviction of Muslims from Western Law and Politics,* I explored how race thinking persists today in security hearings where Muslim men detained without charge and witho ut full legal rights face a court that seeks to establish whether they will engage in terrorism against the state.[2] Race thinking is evident in these hearings when Muslims, Islamic extremists, and terrorists are collapsed into one category and are imagined to share cultural and social characteristics (of tribalism, fanaticism, and a commitment to violence) that are innate. Importantly, in this contemporary imaginary, people of European origin also share innate social and cultural characteristics, but their gene pool produces civility, rationality, the capacity to live as autonomous individuals, and the capacity to exercise free choice.

The racial Other who has yet to emerge out of the state of nature is neces-sary for the birth of rational man who knows of his triumph over nature, the triumph of mind over body, only through the existence of those beyond the boundary of humanity.

Race thinking thrives in a legal environment of secret evidence, deten-tion without charge, and diminished standards of proof. In the absence of law, as I have shown for security hearings, psychology has to do a great deal of work to provide coherency. The idea of the Muslim psyche as a privileged site of investigation has come to hold sway in a variety of legal fora, chief among them the hearings around who will engage in terrorism in the future. These legal processes are structured around racist ideas about Muslims as a race of premodern people who pose a threat to the West and who do not possess the capacity to become modern. Muslim savagery is read in the personality of the detainee and in his practices of religi-osity. Psychologists and psychiatrists serving as expert witnesses guide the court in understanding Muslims and their cultural predisposition for violence.

In this essay, I propose to illustrate race thinking in law through a close reading of the sentencing of Omar Khadr by a military commission at Guan-tánamo and specifically of the testimony of the psychiatrist Michael Wel-ner, testimony that was the core of the state's case against Khadr. Khadr, a Canadian, was held at Bagram and Guantánamo from the age of fifteen and accused of killing an American soldier, Christopher Speers, during a firefight in Afghanistan. In 2010, Khadr pled guilty as part of a deal to be returned to Canada. He was sentenced to forty years in prison for war crimes. The pretrial deal capped Khadr's sentence at eight years. Welner's testimony that Khadr was an unrepentant jihadist sealed his fate. Indeed, Canada gave as its official reason for delaying the transfer of Omar Khadr to Canada until September 2012 that it had not seen the videotape of Wel-ner's seven-hour interview and had formally requested an unredacted re-port in order to make the final decision about his repatriation.[3] Omar Khadr was released on bail in May 2015 to live with his Canadian lawyer, Dennis Edney. On February 18, 2016, the newly elected Liberal government dropped an appeal started by the previous government to revoke Khadr's bail. On July 7, 2017, the Canadian government apologized to Khadr and offered him a settlement of $10.5 million.

When considering the role of race thinking in the War on Terror, Khadr's case is especially instructive. Khadr, a thirty-year-old in 2016, became (and remains) particularly important as a liminal figure, someone who was a child when incarcerated but who was nevertheless always treated as an adult in law. As I have shown elsewhere, passionate pleas that Khadr be considered a child soldier (and thus under the Optional Protocol for child soldiers) long fell on deaf ears, despite the support of people like General Romeo Dallaire, Canada's most famous general (for his actions in trying to stop the Rwandan genocide).[4] The torture of a Canadian child at the Bagram and Guantánamo prisons has spectacularly failed to move both the Canadian population (polls suggest that 81 percent of Canadians do not want Khadr in Canada) and the Canadian government.[5] Neither of the West nor of the East, neither child nor adult, Khadr is the limit point of justice. To mark the place where terror lives (and thus where it does not), Khadr is someone who has to be shown to be the definitive Muslim terrorist. The case against him required a conceptual arsenal of white supremacist ideas about Muslims, chief among them the idea that Muslims carry the seeds of violence in their blood (culture/religion) and are deceptively normal until they strike. The notion of a worldwide Muslim conspiracy to wage jihad as the project of a cabal of violent jihadists in sleeper cells draws on long-standing racist ideas about Jews, an ironic historical connection given the contemporary utility of such ideas to Zionist groups. In examining closely what these ideas consist of, and how they were deployed to condemn Khadr, we can learn a great deal about the contemporary structure of anti-Muslim racism. These ideas install the Muslim as someone who is fanatical, unable to think autonomously, angry, and dysfunctional. White supremacist ideas have a wider appeal than is ordinarily imagined because they rest on the same liberal foundation of Western societies, namely, that people of European origin are rational individuals with an innate capacity to govern inferior races. In a hospitable legal environment, they blossom, upholding, and upheld by, a state of exception where legal rights are suspended for those considered outside the boundaries of humanity and citizenship.

A close look at how anti-Muslim racism operates in Khadr's case sheds light on two features of the War on Terror. First, the legal abandonment of Muslims relies upon even as it produces an understanding of Muslims as subhuman. As several scholars have shown, this mode of thinking is institutionalized and actively promoted by well-resourced groups, a feature that is fully in evidence in the Khadr sentencing hearing.[6] These individuals and groups successfully circulate the position that the origins of terrorism lie in Muslim culture and in Islam rather than in social and political contexts. Although, as Arun Kundnani suggests, conservatives stress that it is Islamic culture that is to blame and liberals emphasize that "the roots of

terrorism are not in Islam itself but in a series of twentieth century ideologues who distorted the religion to produce a totalitarian ideology—
Islamism—on the models of communism or fascism," in practice, the two
views are reconciled on the matter of a fatal attraction between Muslims
and terrorism.[7] The net result is that all Muslims are stigmatized. When
radicalism comes to be seen as a cultural and psychological predisposition,
we engage in race thinking where culture and character become innate and
inheritable traits.

The second feature of legal processes of the War on Terror follows
from the first. On squarely racist terrain, legal processes operate in the
manner that Toni Morrison has described for the law's treatment of Blacks.
Writing of the O. J. Simpson trial for the murder of his wife, Morrison has
shed light on the features of a legal process in which race shapes the outcome. In *Birth of a Nation'hood,* she considers that O. J. Simpson was widely
regarded in mainstream media as guilty. Of the media and the courtroom,
Morrison writes, "The language developing around him portrays a thought-
ful, meditating murderer capable of slick and icy-cold deliberations *and/or*
a mindless, spontaneous killer—a kind of lucky buffoon."[8] If the adjectives
cancel each other out—"contradiction, incoherence and emotional disorder
'fit' when the subject is black"—Morrison is clear about what transforms
incoherence into the coherence of a guilty verdict: "Illogic, contradiction,
deception are understood to be fundamental characteristics of blacks and
in judging them there need be no ground of reason for a contrary or more
complicated view."[9]

Reviewing Welner's testimony in Khadr's sentencing hearing, one cannot help asking how such ideas come to make sense in law and how they
continue to make sense when circulated widely in the media. How does a
far right, white supremacist message come to achieve respectability? If one
believes in Muslim irrationality, it is easy to follow and accept the many
contradictions and inconsistencies in Welner's white narrative. Racism
gives coherency where otherwise there is none, allowing us to bypass illogic,
contradiction, and duplicity to be rewarded with a world in which there are
two levels of humanity and two levels of law. Welner, and Nicolai Sennels,
on whom he relies, may be clearly visible as anti-Muslim, far right propa-
gandists, but in court at Guantánamo, they become men of science who
offer reasonable appraisals of Muslim degeneracy. Determining how this
transformation is effected in the military hearing is the task I set myself in
this chapter. As I discuss, the transformation of white supremacist zealots
into credible men of science is accomplished through the law's preservation

of a space of law without law. That is, Khadr is evaluated in a court of law, but it is one in which he does not enjoy the full right of facing his accusers. The legal environment at Guantánamo is such that processes such as cross-examination of expert witnesses are impeded by hidden forces. Khadr's lawyers claimed that prosecutors threatened to revoke Khadr's plea deal if they substantively challenged Welner's credentials.[10] Race thinking invests these otherwise Kafkaesque proceedings with legitimacy.

RELIGIOSITY AND FUTURE DANGEROUSNESS

As the expert witness for the prosecution, Michael Welner's task was to conduct a risk assessment of Omar Khadr to determine the likelihood of his reoffending, an evaluation, in his words, of "future dangerousness of a jihadi."[11] (Two psychiatrists for the defense, Stephen Xenakis and Kate Porterfield, were never invited to testify. Both concluded that Khadr did not exhibit terrorist tendencies.)[12] Importantly, Khadr is presumed at the out-set to be a jihadi. Although he had no knowledge of jihadis, Welner said that he was well versed in criminal recidivism and that he had developed a useful depravity scale that he hoped would assist courts in sentencing by providing a measure of the depravity of a crime. Welner refers to his scale as measuring evil.[13] Locating himself firmly within the school of thought that considers evil as the explanation for terrorism, Welner then easily moved to considering what the signs of evil are in jihadists and how we might be able to predict who is and is not evil and who might be reha-bilitated. As an expert for the prosecution, Welner assessed Khadr for "the risk for activities that would relate to violent or criminal expression of jihad," "the prospects for Omar Khadr's reintegration," and "whether there is a need for deradicalization with Omar Khadr or whether it can even be done with Omar Khadr."[14] In the absence of actuarial data, Welner clarified that he had to go about learning about the population of radical jihadists, beginning with the definition of radical Islam as distinguished from tradi-tional Islam.

It is important to pause here to follow the color line of the psychologi-cal radicalization model where Welner's assessment begins. Kundnani dis-cusses the ideas behind a psychological radicalization model in his book *The Muslims Are Coming!* In the post-9/11 climate, it soon was considered treasonous to consider the social and political roots of terrorism. Instead, terrorism was seen as originating in the "evil mind-set of the perpetra-tors."[15] While older forms of terrorism were understood to have political origins, Islamic terrorism was straightforwardly understood as originating in religious fanaticism. Kundnani suggests that although this first step matured into a broader consideration of how Islamic extremism develops, it was circumscribed by the demands of counterterrorism policy makers whose interests lay in explaining terrorism as a product of how Islam was interpreted and not as a product of specific social and political circumstances.[16] Psychology and theology provided a comfortable ground on which such analyses can rest. With an emphasis on the individual psyche, it was not long before a mini-industry of scholars, intelligence analysts, and policy makers grew around the idea that Muslims move to extremist views because of an underlying cultural predisposition. Identifying the historian Walter Laqueur (ironically a scholar who has written persuasively of the social and political factors that produced the Holocaust[17]) as someone who provided a bridge between older terrorism studies and the new focus on the psyche, Kundnani shows how Laqueur, a Washington insider with connections as Israel's representative to the CIA-funded Congress for Cultural Freedom, developed the idea that al-Qaeda emerged because of Muslim religious commandment to jihad.[18] For Laqueur, Muslim communities in Europe failed to integrate and wanted to preserve a separate religious identity. In this environment, the second generation, sexually repressed and aggressive, and angry at non-Muslims, turned easily to terrorism. As Kundnani notes, such explanations set the stage for a radicalization focus on religious beliefs, anti-Western attitudes, and youth alienation where extremism is seen as a kind of virus that some people can catch. Law enforcement has to prevent exposure but also look for indicators of the patterns and beliefs that indicate terrorist risk.[19] As I detailed for Canadian security cases in the first half of the decade, intelligence services seeking to detain Muslim men whom they believed had the potential to engage in terrorist activity needed only to make the case in court that the defendants had a profile that made them of use to al-Qaeda. Courts were by and large persuaded that those who held Muslim religious beliefs, who had certain histories (e.g., those who went to Afghanistan during the 1980s), and who appeared "normal" were simply waiting for the ideal time when their true natures would be revealed.[20] Omar Khadr presented Welner with an ideal opportunity to illustrate the psychological and theological foundations of the process known as Muslim radicalization. Because Welner was expected to assess whether Khadr could be deradicalized, a process understood as involving developing an alternative interpretation of Islam, his assessment had to explore whether Khadr exhibited the signs that scholars such as Laqueur invited policy makers to examine, namely, the presence of anger and aggression and disaffection as well as the extent and direction of his religious commitment. The incoherence that Morrison reminds us is a feature of racial explanations gave Welner free rein to articulate his theories and Guantánamo's feature, a space of law without law, restricted opportunities for challenging his views.

Omar Khadr was considered a violent jihadist because he threw a grenade that killed an American soldier. Khadr denies killing Speers but had to admit to it as part of the plea bargain for a lesser sentence and for the chance to return to Canada. The fact that he was fifteen and that the circumstances of the firefight in which Speers was killed are in doubt have no bearing on the outcome. Khadr, Welner reminded the court, was a convicted war criminal. In Welner's words, "Well, he's murdered. He has been a part of Al Qaeda, and we're still at war."[21] Moreover, "the war is not ending soon." Under these circumstances, the "prognosis" for rehabilitation was grim.

Welner considered whether Khadr was in a financial position to facilitate violent attacks and whether he was a leading figure who had the capacity to commit terrorist acts.[22] Since Khadr had no financial resources, Welner focused on his potential as a leader of jihad. It is here that the question of Muslim religiosity became central. A leader of jihad, for Welner, is someone who leads prayers and who inspires others through his increasing religiosity. Religious devotion in this formulation becomes a feature of radical behavior. To assess a radical jihadist, something Welner had not previously done, Welner turned to Nicolai Sennels, maintaining that Sennels was one of very few people in the world who had studied young Muslims in a correctional setting and who had treated them therapeutically. It is Sennels's articulation of the psychological radicalization paradigm elaborated earlier by Laqueur that becomes the foundation of Welner's analysis.

Sennels's views are frequently profiled on a large number of anti-Muslim and white supremacist blogs, something that was not brought out in court.[23] A young psychologist whose first job was working in a Danish youth prison, Sennels (who was fired for his anti-Muslim views) wrote a book titled *Among Criminal Muslims: A Psychologist's Experience from the Copenhagen Municipality.* In this book, he presented his findings about the psychological characteristics of Muslim youth in prison. In his three years at the youth facility, Sennels claimed to have conducted individual and group therapy with 150 Muslim and 100 Danish clients (the terms Muslim and Danish are incommensurate for Sennels). He concluded that anyone reared in a Muslim environment was likely to develop antisocial patterns because Muslim culture "supports the development of certain psychological characteristics."[24] Chief among these characteristics is the Muslim procliv- ity for aggression and anger, particularly when criticized or made fun of, as in the Danish cartoon controversy. Muslims are also unable to take responsibility and to act autonomously. In Sennels's phrase, their "locus of control" is outer-determined rather than inner-determined. That is, Mus- lims are unable to decide how to live their own lives and are guided instead by "a fearsome God, a powerful father, influential imams, [and] ancient but strong cultural traditions."[25] Given these characteristics, they are unable to integrate into Western society, and Sennels has spent considerable time pro- moting his views that Muslim immigration to Europe should be halted. He believes that Muslims will always refuse to integrate, will push for the Islam- ization of Europe, and will provoke a "continent wide civil war."[26] For Wel- ner, Sennels's work is especially pertinent because he compared Muslims to non-Muslims. Welner admired what he regarded as Sennels's humility. Sennels, he told the military court, was not afraid to admit that he had failed in his therapeutic work in curing young Muslims of their religious extremism. From Sennels, Welner concluded that remorse and Western- ization were the two factors that led to "a positive prognosis."[27] Westerniza- tion, in this view, is the opposite of religiosity, and the religiously devout Muslim has the poorest prognosis of all of reintegrating into society.

The First Sign: Memorizing the Qur'an

For Welner, that Khadr memorized the Qur'an revealed that Khadr became more religious while in prison. He also saw this achievement as Khadr's rejection of secular studies. Cross-examined, Welner did not recall that Khadr had also explained to him that he had memorized the Qur'an because he didn't have much else to do and also because, even though he wanted to study medicine one day, he found it hard to slog through the high school science and math curriculum unaided. Asked about leading prayers, Khadr noted that because he had been able to memorize the Qur'an while many others hadn't, he was able to lead the prayers.[28] Khadr represented his own religiosity as consisting of "living as strict as he can" and figuring out the meanings of the Qur'an by himself.[29] Admitting on cross-examination that radical and devout need not be the same thing, Welner insisted, nonethe- less, that "the problem is radicalized jihadists who happen to be devout, because the more devout they are, the more it increases the risk of a poor prognosis."[30] In this logic, radical jihadists, who are by definition devout because they believe in a holy war to establish shari'a, bear a special burden of showing that their religiosity is declining rather than increasing.

Religiosity has a major role to play in revealing the contours of the terrorist psyche. Drawing closely on Sennels, Welner concluded that Khadr's apparently increasing religiosity was a sign that he was fanatical, submissive to the will of others, and without remorse. Welner explained to the court what he derived from Sennels:

> His [Sennels's] best sense is that part of the observance and adherence to Islam is submission, submission to the Qur'an, submission to what the Imam says, submission to paternal and superior influences and while that may cultivate obedience and it may enhance structure and order in a certain context. At the same time what he finds, as a clinician, a drawback of that is that it makes it much more difficult for somebody to be introspective. The locust [sic] of control that someone has on their life is always someone else. It's always someone else's fault. It's someone else who has control. And in someone who is more introspective and more self-reliant, the person takes responsibility, takes ownership, takes a look at the predicament they are in and says "What can I learn from this? How can I go forward? How can I better myself? How can I develop? How can I grow?" That, from his experience, is the best explanation for the relationship between how devout a person is and how that devoutness actually increases a risk of poor prognosis.[31]

Although the argument is declared to be about violent jihadists, for both Sennels and Welner, the problem lies with Islam and with Muslim culture. Muslims "have a God that decides their life's course," Sennels has written, and clerics who tell them what to think and do.[32] Muslims, as unthinking fanatics who look to others for direction, only become more devout in prison and more devoted to the cause of jihad. Khadr is at particular risk of succumbing to what Welner never fails to represent as a disease with a poor prognosis. He lost his father and is particularly sensitive to "pseudo parents," "people who might be older and who might take him under their wing" and people who are ideologically hardened and mature, as are the detainees of Camp 4. Notably, here Khadr is considered a child, whereas throughout, he has been tried and sentenced for the crimes of an adult.

The Second Sign: The "Rock Star" Who Leads Prayers

Welner reported to the court that Khadr was considered by fellow detainees as a "rock star," with the capacity to inspire and lead them. He gleaned this information not from interviewing Khadr's fellow prisoners but from Khadr's interrogators and guards. Indifferent to the contradiction of a portrait of a rock star leader who is also submissive and seeking pseudo parents, Welner's argument about the detainees of Camp 4 as ideologically hardened jihadists who both follow Khadr and influence him runs aground quickly, as even the prosecution seemed to have recognized. Reminding Welner that Camp 4 detainees are supposed to be the most compliant of detainees (they are given the freedom to associate with each other), the prosecuting attorney Captain Eason asked Welner if their compliance might also mean that they were deradicalized.[33] Welner is able to navigate these contradictions through appeal to a long-standing racist idea of the sleeper cell with its population of patient, calculating, and duplicitous Orientals (as the term was first used during the Second World War) waiting to strike at an unsuspecting West:

> Radicalized Islam works at its own timetable just because it is a—it is a movement that dreams and at some times actually implements apocalyptic violence doesn't mean that it doesn't have the patience to wait for opportunity. And many people who are housed in Camp 4 have extremely destructive pasts and legacies but they are just smart enough to know to follow the rules, and keep themselves quiet and compliant, and they will have an uneventful incarceration. And so this is the example that is provided for Omar Khadr and it's an example that he follows and so he is well behaved in the custodial environment as are they, but it does not at all speak to their mission; it does not at all speak to their ideology. What it does speak to is that Mr. Khadr, when he chooses, has perfectly good impulse control and in a certain kind of risk of dangerousness assessment that would be relevant. That's not the kind of risk of dangerousness assessment that I am asked to do here. I did not do a psychopathy checklist. I did not assess whether he is a psychopath or not. He may be, he may not be, but were I to have done that assessment, impulsivity, which is one of the measures of the PCL-R [a psychopathy scale that is considered the single best predictor of violent behavior], his time in camp 4 reflects on him as someone who is not impulsive.[34]

Patient and calculating, and with "good impulse control," Khadr's good behavior and apparent rationality are only a cover until he can strike, an argument I have previously tracked in Canadian security cases where detainees are condemned for being too normal. A rock star, someone who has memorized the Qur'an, a murderer, the revered son of the famous Ahmed Khadr, and someone who has even spent time with bin Laden, Khadr is also fluent in English, multilingual, charming, good at sports, and someone who has attracted nongovernmental organization support. As Welner item- izes these qualities, he adds a few incidents that under cross-examination are revealed to be fabrications. For example, apparently wanting to check Khadr's interactions with non-Muslims, Welner tells the court that Khadr had a confrontation with an African American female guard, calling her a slut and a whore.[35] (He does not consider what might have provoked such an incident.) While Khadr acknowledged that he sometimes cursed at the guards out of frustration, it was also clear that he was not yet in Camp 4 when the incident with the guard took place. When they are revealed, such fabrications do not appear to damage Welner's credibility, a feature of legal processes that achieve their coherence from racist ideas.

Having entered the domain of religion, the violent jihadist can never emerge, a position that depends on race thinking, the idea that culture is innate and inheritable. Deradicalization, Welner explains, means changing one's interpretation of the Qur'an, and there is little chance that this can happen in Omar's case, because he has a family that is deeply radicalized.[36] Using a biological metaphor of "a fungating tumor" that requires a skilled surgeon, Welner declares that the level of skill required to do the operation simply doesn't exist.[37] In fact, there is nothing that could interrupt Khadr's journey of radicalism.

The Third Sign: Failure to Acculturate

The argument that violent jihadists have the capacity to seem otherwise carries the risk that we will not know one when we see one. Khadr gener- ates anxiety, an anxiety comparable to long-standing white supremacist anxieties about Jews who are regarded as deceptively white and normal and who are behind-the-scenes manipulators.[38] He is of the West but is not Western. How would we know whether a charming, apparently Western- ized boy from Toronto is a seasoned, adult killer, seeped in Muslim and non-Western culture and with the potential to lead a jihad? Khadr is the litmus test for jihadism precisely because he does not appear to be the fully formed Middle Eastern Muslim terrorist, and because he spent his child- hood in both the West and the East. The anxiety is mitigated through an old sociobiological idea: Khadr carries his potential for dangerousness in his history. As inheritance, Khadr's culture and religion can only condemn him to his fate. He may look and sound like he is of the West, but an Eastern cultural inheritance runs through his veins. He carries within him a predisposition for violence.

Welner is at pains to establish that while Omar Khadr is from the West, he is not Westernized.[39] Rather, he is the quintessential duplicitous Oriental whose duplicity is never as apparent when he appears most Western. It is not surprising, then, that any evidence that he is behaving as an ordinary Western teenager and then a young man of twenty-five becomes evidence that he is secretly a violent jihadist. The question of Khadr's acculturation is complicated by the fact of his personality. As Welner acknowledged, Khadr was charming and comfortable with everybody, and therefore "very different from the other al Qaeda folks who are more limited in their cultural experience."[40] He seems normal. He reads Harry Potter novels, for example, which helped him (in his own words) to "just get away, to not think about things." For Welner, Khadr's indulging in "escapist literature" only indicated a desire to avoid facing reality and to dissociate from his environment.[41] Khadr was very angry about being in custody, Welner reported, and "does not involve himself in the kinds of things that would acculturate him to this Western environment." Welner is not pressed to say what such things might be at Guantánamo, or whether Khadr, imprisoned at fifteen and tortured, might in fact have reason to be angry and reason to want to get away from it all, if only via a fantasy novel.

When, under cross-examination, Welner is asked to explain why Khadr also read books by Mandela and Obama, he refuses to reply on the grounds that he would need to see the exact place in the transcript of his interview with Khadr to comment. A rather transparent obstructionist tactic, Welner is never fully called to account for his selective use of the interview data. The same tactic serves him well when he is cross-examined about his conclusion that Khadr wishes to return to Canada not because it is his native country but because he wishes to replace civil law with shari'a law. As Khadr's defense counsel pointed out, Khadr communicated to Welner that he believed the opposite of what Welner alleges: in Khadr's words, "I can be a Muslim. You can be a Christian. It doesn't have to do with anything."[42] Welner again refuses to comment when Khadr's words are quoted until he can see the transcript. Since the defense cannot locate the exact page number for this quote, the matter is dropped after Welner offers an inchoate and rambling explanation for his belief that Khadr secretly wanted to establish shari'a:

Again, just as an example of the sort of cherry picking with one of the questions that had just come up only a couple of minutes ago about Mr. Khadr and—in which a question came up of whether he could be around Christians, the significance of that was I didn't even ask him that. But he was so coiled, and he was so calculated, and he was so ready for that question to come in that he took me to a different area. I merely wanted to ask him, "What's it like for you when you need to practice around people who don't share the same beliefs?" Not whether you're willing to live with anyone. I mean, look, there are Christians in Tehran. There are gays in Tehran. While the leader there wants to destroy the world, and it doesn't mean that you can't practice Christianity.

You know just because somebody espouses a theocracy, it doesn't mean that they're not aware or may even be friendly to people practicing something else, as long as they are submissive. You know, that's—and that's the way a theocracy would work. Now that's not a reflection on Mr. Khadr. He's devout in his belief. I just wanted to everybody around you is—can understand this sort of devout thinking, but my awareness t a feel for him [sic]. That's all I was after.[43]

The Miasma of Muslim Incoherence

"Difficult explanations," writes Morrison, "are folded into the miasma of black incoherence."

> A single, unarmed black man on the ground surrounded by twelve rioting police can be seen as a major threat to the police. A beaten up, sexually assaulted black girl wakes up in a hospital and is "convicted" of raping and defiling herself. To ask why? How? is to put a rhetorical question—not a serious one worthy of serious response.[44]

As when the subject is Black, things don't need to make sense when the subject is Muslim. Questions are rhetorical and logic is beside the point. Khadr wants to establish shari'a law in Canada but hides his true intentions with an apparent broadmindedness. His Westernized tastes are merely evidence of his deception. Legal procedures permit the incoherence to stand, as the attempts by the defense to point out Welner's selectivity and the contradictions of his claims come to naught because the appropriate pages of Welner's interview with Khadr were not marked and tagged in advance. The defense asks questions that remain rhetorical. The logical circularity of Welner's argument goes unchallenged. No one pursues how Welner knows that Khadr killed in order to martyr himself or how he knows that Khadr is "al-Qaeda royalty." There is no need for serious consideration of these matters, and they can be dealt with in sound bites gleefully consumed by the media and replayed for several years.[45]

Nowhere does the legal process seem more complicit in providing a platform for white supremacist beliefs than when Welner is challenged about his reliance on the work of Nicolai Sennels. Welner maintains that although he relies on Sennels, he really does not know a great deal about the man or his work. His knowledge of Sennels was mainly based on a telephone conversation with him. Cross-examination of Welner begins with the apparent inability of the defense to say Sennels's name correctly. Defense counsel Major Schwartz establishes that Welner has not interviewed other jihadists and had no prior experience with evaluating the future dangerousness of a jihadi.[46] Sennels, it seems, is Welner's only source of information. Asked about the peer review process and the details of Sennels's research (which Sennels himself has made clear in interviews was not a research project), Welner reiterates that he was impressed with Sennels because he acknowledged that he had failed to deradicalize jihadists (because they are beyond help). Sennels's research methodology, he elaborates, was simply that he worked with Muslim patients and treated them therapeutically. Research has no place in the military hearing when it involves Muslims.

The defense presented Welner with three short articles and an open letter to British prime minister David Cameron all written by Sennels or featuring interviews with him (and widely circulated on the Internet on a number of Islamophobic blogs and websites). The court is not told where these articles appear, and the vague discussion about peer review and its meaning only hints that Sennels does not do academic research. Welner is unable to confirm that he has read any of Sennels's work. He responds that he recognizes only some parts. He is surprised when he learns from the defense that Sennels is only thirty-three years old. He has never seen interviews with Sennels about his book, nor has he seen an open letter Sennels wrote to Prime Minister Cameron urging him to deny Turkey entrance into the European Union because Muslims are unable to integrate into European society. Welner recognizes some parts of Sennels's article on the psychological differences between Westerners and Muslims, but when asked about Sennels's opinions about Muslim inbreeding, in an article in which Sennels refers to the "catastrophically damaged gene pool" of Muslims, Welner repeats that he does not find these ideas relevant and so did not read them. Given time to peruse the documents over lunch, he is asked whether the articles have changed his opinion of Sennels. Confident to the end, Welner replied that the articles are "just a political comment from a political opinion," adding, "I believe I heard Chancellor Angela Merkel say something of the sort probably within the last 2 weeks."[47] The cross-examination ends with Welner maintaining that he agrees with a significant amount of the content of the work of Nicolai Sennels.[48]

CONCLUSION

Welner's views remained the key testimony about Omar Khadr's "risk of dangerousness." Those who disagreed with Sennels, notably the two psychiatrists for the defense, were never called to testify. As *Toronto Star* reporter Michelle Shephard reported, when forensic psychiatrist Marc Sageman rebutted Welner's professional expertise in the field of terrorism, the military judge presiding over Khadr's case "allegedly quipped to the defence that 'Dr. Welner would have been as likely to be accurate if he had used a Ouija board.'"[49] No one, it seemed, expected the sentencing hearing to make sense. In the strange ending to Omar Khadr's sentencing hearing, an avowed white supremacist Nicolai Sennels is held up as an expert, and his anti-Muslim rhetoric remains on record as scholarly research. Welner's lack of familiarity with Sennels, an ignorance that puts in doubt his own scholarly expertise and record, and his refusal to condemn Sennels for his extremist views nevertheless do not damage Welner's credibility. Instead, Welner feels free to state that after reading the materials on Sennels provided by the defense, "Dr. Sennels' work is actually more impressive than I ever gave him credit for."[50] If we are tempted at this point to believe that Khadr's sentencing hearing was meant to be farce, that impression is solidified when Welner closes his testimony with an opinion that now dispenses with the arguments around religiosity made earlier and stresses instead that it is Khadr's history and his family and his supposed capacity "to inspire and to be incendiary" that indicate his future dangerousness.[51] History, family, and an inherent deviousness make the case for future dangerousness. Blood, it seems, trumps all.

It is instructive to end this exploration of white supremacist views in Omar Khadr's sentencing hearing with a psychiatrist who worked with Khadr's defense team and who was not called to testify. A retired army brigadier general, and a child and adolescent psychiatrist who assessed Khadr and found that he shows no proclivity for committing terrorist acts, Stephen N. Xenakis wrote to the *Washington Post* expressing his outrage at Welner's testimony:

As I listened to the prosecution's expert testimony depicting Khadr's state of mind, I was reminded of psychiatry and the politicization of mental health under the Soviet regime. Those were the years when political dissidents were accused of insanity simply because they had the audacity to challenge the Soviet system. The medical profession, especially psychiatry, was a political instrument of control and repression.[52]

What I can add to this is that race thinking, the belief that Muslims carry the seeds of fanaticism and irrationality in their culture, helps to smooth the way to this repression. Psychiatry is best able to do the work that it does as a political instrument of repression when it is harnessed to ideas about humanity and sub-humanity.

NOTES

1. Hannah Arendt, *On the Origins of Totalitarianism* (New York: Harcourt, Brace, Jovanovich, 1975), 159.

2. Sherene H. Razack, *Casting Out: The Eviction of Muslims from Western Law and Politics* (Toronto: University of Toronto Press, 2008), 25–54.

3. Minister of Public Safety, "In the Matter of Omar Ahmed Khadr and the *International Transfer of Offenders Act,*" press release, September 28, 2012, Ottawa, Canada.

4. Sherene H. Razack, "The Manufacture of Torture as Public Truth: The Case of Omar Khadr," in *At the Limits of Justice: Women of Colour Theorize Terror,* ed. Suvendrini Perera and Sherene Razack, 57–85 (Toronto: University of Toronto Press, 2014).

5. Yahoo Canada Poll, October 1, 2012.

6. See Nathan Lean, *The Islamphobia Industry: How the Right Manufactures Fear of Muslims* (London: Pluto Press, 2012); Stephen Sheehi, *Islamphobia: The Ideological Campaign against Muslims* (Atlanta, Ga.: Clarity Press, 2011).

7. Arun Kundnani, *The Muslims Are Coming! Islamphobia, Extremism, and the Domestic War on Terror* (London: Verso Press, 2014), 11.

8. Morrison, "The Official Story: Dead Man Golfing," in *Birth of a Nation'hood: Gaze, Script, and Spectacle in the O.J. Simpson Case,* ed. Toni Morrison and Claudia Brodsky (New York: Pantheon, 2010), ix.

9. Ibid., ix–x.

10. Michelle Shephard, "Omar Khadr's Lawyers Question Pentagon's Star Witness," *Toronto Star,* April 18, 2011, http://www.thestar.com/news/world/2011/04/18/omar_khadrs_lawyers_question_pentagons_star_witness.html.

11. Dr. Michael Welner testimony, United States v. Omar Ahmed Khadr (October 26, 2010), ISN 0766 (Office of the Military Commissions, Guantanamo Bay), 4490, https://commons.wikimedia.org/wiki/File:Dr_Michael_Welner%27s_testimony_at_Omar_Khadr%27s_sentencing_hearing.PDF.

12. See Steven Xenakis's report, http://www.macleans.ca/news/canada/the-xenakis-report/, and Kate Porterfield's report, http://www.macleans.ca/news/canada/the-porterfield-report.

13. Michael Welner, "The Depravity Standard," https://depravitystandard.org/.

14. Welner testimony, 4392.

15. Kundnani, *Muslims Are Coming!*, 115.

16. Ibid., 117.

17. Walter Laqueur, *The Terrible Secret: Suppression of the Truth about Hitler's "Final Solution"* (New York: Penguin Books, 1982).

18. Kundnani, *Muslims Are Coming!*, 120.

19. Ibid., 122.

20. Razack, *Casting Out*, 25–58.

21. Ibid.

22. Welner testimony, 4394.

23. See, e.g., http://www.frontpagemag.com/2010/jamie-glazov/among-criminal-muslims/; http://gatesofvienna.blogspot.ca/p/nicolai-sennels.html; http://www.newenglishreview.org/Nicolai_Sennels/Muslims_and_Westerners%3A__The_Psychological_Differences/; http://europenews.dk/en/node/21789; http://www.islamist-watch.org/author/Nicolai+Sennels; http://www.jihadwatch.org/2013/09/nicolai-sennels-psychology-why-islam-creates-monsters; http://islamversuseurope.blogspot.ca/2013/05/psychologist-serious-consequences-of.html.

24. Jamie Glazov, "Among Criminal Muslims," interview with Nicolai Sennels, http://www.frontpagemag.com/2010/jamie-glazov/among-criminal-muslims/; http://gatesofvienna.blogspot.ca/p/nicolai-sennels.html.

25. Ibid.

26. Ibid.

27. Welner testimony, 4403.

28. Ibid., 4457.

29. Ibid., 4559.

30. Ibid.

31. Ibid., 4409.

32. Nicolai Sennels, "Muslims and Westerners: The Psychological Differences," http://www.newenglishreview.org/Nicolai_Sennels/Muslims_and_Westerners%3A__The_Psychological_Differences/.

33. Welner testimony, 4420.

34. Ibid., 4421.

35. Ibid.

36. Ibid., 4437.

37. Ibid., 4446.

38. Jesse Daniels, *White Lies: Race, Class, Gender, and Sexuality in White Supremacist Discourse* (New York: Routledge, 1997), 107.

39. Welner testimony, 4458.

40. Ibid., 4406.

41. Ibid., 4408.

42. Ibid., 4570.

43. Ibid., 4601.

44. Morrison, ix.

45. For an analysis of the how narratives about Khadr travel from the media to political and legal spaces, see Razack, "Manufacture of Torture as Public Truth."

46. Welner testimony, 4490.

47. Ibid., 4541.

48. Ibid., 4545.

49. Michelle Shephard, "Omar Khadr's Lawyers Question Pentagon's Star Witness," *Toronto Star*, April 18, 2011, http://www.thestar.com/news/world/2011/04/18/omar_khadrs_lawyers_question_pentagons_star_witness.html.

50. Welner testimony, 4600.

51. Ibid., 4603–5.

52. Stephen N. Xenakis, "Radical Jihadism Is Not a Mental Disorder," *Washington Post*, December 5, 2010, http://www.washingtonpost.com/wp-dyn/content/article/2010/12/10/AR2010121006997.html.

13

Death by Double-Tap

(Undoing) Racial Logics in the Age of Drone Warfare

RONAK K. KAPADIA

It is not just a more exhaustive reckoning with the past and present of imperialist violence that is needed but, more specifically, a non-juridical reckoning. For this, our starting point should be neither the law nor any desire for a "progressive" appropriation of the law, but the mounting dead for whom the law was either a useless means of defense or an accomplice to their murder.

——RANDALL WILLIAMS, *The Divided World*

No issue today so disturbingly illustrates the contemporary U.S. homeland security state's wretched relation to race and imperialism than the rise of its drone strikes and "extrajudicial targeted killings" in Pakistan, Yemen, Somalia, Libya, and beyond. The accelerated deployment of armed unmanned aerial vehicles (UAVs), or drones, in U.S. military campaigns of the so-called post–War on Terror era provides an important opportunity to reflect on shifting strategies, practices, and technologies of the U.S. homeland security state as well as their effects on contemporary political and legal life. What are drones, and why does their expanded application concern scholars and activists of race, war, and empire? How does the so-called unmanned future of warfare give rise to new ways of thinking about race and racialization—in both the distant, unseen battlefields of U.S. empire abroad and the hidden-in-plain-sight theaters of undeclared war closer to home? In this chapter, I identify how contemporary drone attacks in the "Af-Pak" borderlands region worked to destroy communal bonds among Afghan and Pakistani civilians and to what effect. I further ask how the global circulation of these weapons, and the broader aerial counterinsurgencies that they symbolize, not only sow the seeds for resentment across the "Muslim world" but also create the conditions for new communities of resistance, solidarity, and transnational affiliation in their wake.[1]

By foregrounding these questions, this chapter offers both a primer on the gendered racial logics of contemporary drone violence and an intervention into the emergent "drone talk" in Western cultural criticism. To date, the drone discourse has been unwilling or unable to reckon sufficiently with the gendered and racialized figure of the Muslim and its multiple rehearsals, which, as Sohail Daulatzai rightly observes, "haunts the geographic and imaginative spaces of American empire."[2] Our criticism of drone wars is impoverished without sufficient account for the livelihoods and experiences of those rendered most precarious by this mode of violence. As I will show, a more direct engagement with the racialized figure of the Muslim, one of the primary sites for the development of late modern tactics of killing and surveillance, advances a more complex portrait of the carceral, anti-Black, and colonial dimensions of the U.S. homeland security state.[3]

The increasing popularity of armed drones in U.S. counterinsurgency and counterterrorism efforts forces us to reckon with the uneven global distribution of life chances, risks, and rewards in the age of security and permanent war. A wide array of critics of late modern warfare have focused on the technoscientific dimensions of drone strikes. For instance, theorists have drawn attention to the implications of how these surveillance technologies produce "God-like vision" with video feeds from aerial platforms and how killing from a distance transforms the relation between the bomber and his targets.[4] Others have noted the historical legacies of modern airpower and visual surveillance across the twentieth century[5] or honed in on the ethical questions raised by the contemporary civilian and commercial adoption of drones.[6] What is most clear from a review of this growing literature is that the drone commentary has evolved as quickly as the technology itself. In lieu of an exhaustive summary of these findings, I choose to distill some recent insights in the following section to make visible (so as to better challenge) contemporary global circuits of U.S. imperial violence. But my chief concern in this chapter is less that the empire has new toys and more how unique aspects of these militarized technologies have transformed racialized social relations on the ground for those rendered most precarious by the buzzing beat of drones in the so-called lawless frontiers of U.S. warfare.

To illustrate this point, I focus on the controversial "double-tap" phenomenon, in which drone operators repeatedly strike a targeted terrain in quick succession, leading to a variety of dis-ordering and dehumanizing effects on the ground.[7] The double-tap phenomenon forces an ethical quandary in which one must decide between one's own life and the life of others in the decision to aid the wounded and to honor the dead, producing a kind of institutionalization of callousness as constitutive to drone strikes in the region. In this chapter, I illuminate how contemporary aerial warfare innovates new modes of racialization that attempt to manipulate, conflate, and destroy communal bonds among its targets, thereby further stripping away our sense of responsibility and our way of knowing each other and ourselves in times of war. And yet, even as the double-tap of drone warfare disorganizes and makes impossible previously existing forms of affective belonging, I contend that it also produces the conditions for the possibility of new affective connections and intimacies across time and space. To that end, I close with a consideration of the prospects of transnational and multiracial coalition building in the drone age and the mandate to challenge the official narratives and ethical common sense of Washington about the conduct of global surveillance and warfare. In sum, this chapter asks how activists and scholars can expose the greater "dronification of state violence" to further make visible the systemic continuities of imperial violence between the global War on Terror and the domestic carceral state.[8]

VISUALIZING THE IMAGINED GEOGRAPHIES OF U.S. EMPIRE

Drones are suddenly everywhere. Like many imperial technologies perfected in the colonial laboratories of empire, these unmanned flying objects have come home to roost.[9] Drones have been adopted in a variety of everyday settings beyond the U.S. military, from commercial aerial surveillance, filmmaking, sports, and photography to domestic policing, oil, gas, and mineral exploration, disaster relief, and scientific research.[10] Its zeitgeist is confirmed further by news that corporate giants like Amazon, Apple, and Facebook have all made plans to roll out drones into future offerings of goods and services.[11] Yet I am less concerned here with the mundane violence of consumer capital or the techno-fetish of the drone itself and more with the spectacular modes of violence that armed drones make possible as they become the centerpiece to a broader U.S. military strategy in the Middle East, South Asia, and North Africa.[12]

Drone weapon technologies represent the growing trend and preferred tool for U.S. military and security planners in Iraq, Afghanistan, Somalia, Yemen, and Pakistan.[13] Whereas some UAVs are controlled remotely from locations thousands of miles away from their bombing sites (including air-conditioned command centers for global surveillance in rural areas of Colorado and Nevada), other UAVs fly reconnaissance missions without human direction at all, preprogrammed instead with flight plans and complex automation systems. Yet all drones are invested in the "power to make the faraway intimate."[14] Since at least 2004, the CIA and the U.S. Air Force have carried out an illegal "targeted killing" program in Pakistan and Afghanistan, where people in the frontiers of violence deemed "enemies of the state" are murdered without charge or trial. The executive branch has claimed the unchecked authority to classify citizens and others on what it euphemistically terms a "disposition matrix," a secret capture/kill database of suspected terrorists and enemy combatants developed by the Obama administration "based on secret determinations, based on secret evidence, that individuals meet a secret definition of the enemy."[15] The most widely publicized example of this form of covert military innovation is the General Atomics MQ-1 Predator drone. First conceived in the early 1990s and in flight since 1995, the Predator has been deployed by the U.S. Air Force and the CIA in combat missions over Afghanistan, Pakistan, Bosnia, Serbia, Iraq, Yemen, and Libya. The Predator drone was first deployed as part of the newly branded "global War on Terror" in late 2001 from bases in Pakistan and Uzbekistan, designed for hitting so-called high-profile targets, including "terrorist leaders" in Afghanistan. As a vital symbol for the U.S. revolution in military affairs (RMA), the Predator has come to represent the military's technocratic aspiration for an automated, self-perpetuating future of calculated warfare in the twenty-first century.[16]

The CIA's use of these highly publicized, if officially covert drone attacks and aerial surveillance campaigns has sparked immense debate among defense experts and critics alike.[17] Their emergence raises questions about the ethics of civilian casualties, sovereignty and border disputes, and conventional and unconventional approaches to the waging of war.[18] Mainstream critics question the accuracy of drone targeting, the legality of these extrajudicial assassinations (including President Obama's targeted killings of U.S. citizens abroad), and the greater "collateral damage" of these bombings more generally, which are widely condemned as grave breaches of international laws of war like the Geneva Conventions.[19] Publicized news accounts have exposed the U.S.-led covert drone attacks in remote areas of northwest Pakistan since as early as 2004. The Pakistani drone strikes in the Federally Administered Tribal Areas (FATA) and Waziristan are particularly troubling given that the Pakistani government serves, at least ostensibly, as a willing partner and ally of the United States in its counterterrorism agenda, a fragile alliance that appears to be dissolving of late.[20] This fractured security consensus is not unlike the fate of Pakistan's own territorial integrity as the United States continues to bomb various targets along its border with Afghanistan without officially declaring war.[21]

"Af-Pak," as the rugged borderlands region between Afghanistan and Pakistan has come to be known within U.S. foreign policy circles, refers to a racialized state of exception. First coined by the late Richard Holbrooke, Obama's special adviser on the region, the neologism symbolizes "not just an effort to save eight syllables. It is an attempt to indicate and imprint in our DNA the fact that there is one theater of war, straddling an ill-defined border, the Durand Line."[22] Holbrooke's vision of a single battlefield of military operations to disrupt the transnational presence of al-Qaeda speaks volumes about the imagined geographies of U.S. empire. This ever-expanding map violates national sovereignty and international humanitarian law on a variety of fronts while simultaneously building on and advancing older legacies of European colonialism and racism that predate the U.S. encounter with the region altogether. "Af-Pak" today symbolizes the "lawless frontier" of lethal experimentation, a topography where, as Ian Shaw and Majed Akhter rightly observe, "uneven geo-legalities of war, state, and exception make drone warfare a reality in certain places and not others."[23]

The fact that certain geopolitical terrain is considered *more* hospitable to drone targeting than other sites begs an important question: why have drones become so popular now in the first place? While the technology has been in the works for decades, conventional explanations suggest that drone strikes were seen as an *antidote* to the messiness of Bush-era detention, rendition, and interrogation practices, spectacles widely conjured by the names of disparate carceral sites like Guantánamo, Abu Ghraib, Bagram, and other still secret centers of detention and misery around the globe. Military planners believed it to be easier to outright *target and kill* suspected terrorists than to *detain and interrogate* them. And yet, while some defense experts favor the use of drones for "surgical strikes" in this manner, others would still opt for the more expensive, labor- and time-intensive counterinsurgency operations seen in the Iraq and Afghanistan ground wars of the 2000s—where U.S. and allied combat forces "embed" within civilian populations in an effort to target their enemies. This so-called kinder and gentler mode of affective governance involves accessing sociocultural knowledge of the local occupied populace in an effort to shape "hearts and minds."[24] To date, the first seventeen years of the global War on Terror has reflected an ad hoc, flexible assemblage of biopolitical military strategies under both the Bush and Obama administrations, ranging primarily from rendition, indefinite detention, torture, and domestic surveillance in the Bush years to

Obama's steadfast "imperial commitment to cyberwar, digital surveillance, and a global 'targeted killing' (that is, assassination) program using both Special Forces and drones."[25] These tactics, as we have already witnessed, are not transforming for the better under the current presidential leadership.[26]

Finally, it is important to observe that the aerial view of the drone is particularly central to the "scopic mastery" desired by the United States as part of its RMA. The RMA is a blanket term to describe important transformations in the fantasies and trajectories of post–Cold War military sciences, which were increasingly aimed at advancing a high-tech, low-personnel vision of warfare after the fall of the Soviet Union. Drones became essential to this recalibrated vision since military and security planners imagined that they could provide a way of fighting perceived insurgencies without public scrutiny. The goals and outcomes of this "unseen war," however, were dubious at best. According to visual culture scholar Nicholas Mirzoeff, the objective is to "maintain a permanent state of crisis, rather than achieving a phantasmatic victory. In the game context in which war is now visualized, the point is less to win than to keep playing, permanently moving to the next level in the ultimate massively multiplayer environment."[27] Drone wars perfectly encapsulate this video game context of endless warfare with its "massively multiplayer" visualizations. The drone is further imagined in the terms of Derek Gregory as "an assemblage of force," because it combines "knowing (intelligence, surveillance, reconnaissance), sighting (targeting in movement and in the moment), and eliminating ('putting warheads on foreheads')."[28]

Scholars of visual culture have further pointed out that the process of racialization specifically operates through the visual targeting of suspected al-Qaeda affiliates.[29] These authors explore the gulf between what the drone operator sees and how she makes sense of what or who is actually on the ground. The subjective dissonance of drone targeting underscores a larger philosophical debate about the relationship between modern visuality, knowledge, and warfare.[30] Theorists have argued that visual and conceptual frames have contributed to the manufacture and obliteration of populations as objects of knowledge and targets of war.[31] From these critical studies, we learn that perspectival vision is in fact constitutive to the logic of surveillance and the materiality of war. As the eye became the privileged organ of knowledge and authority, the power to *see* became equated with the power to *know* and to *dominate*. Across the twentieth century, we see this enduring alliance between vision and war. As military fields increasingly became reconfigured as fields of visual perception, preparations for war were increasingly indistinguishable from preparations for making a film. As Rey Chow adds, "war would mean the production of maximal visibility and illumination for the purpose of maximal destruction."[32] We might conceive of the global War on Terror, then, not only as a struggle over "oil, water, and the resources of globalization but [also quite centrally over the] control of the global image and data worlds."[33] Thus, rather than the invisible, stealth, precision-targeting that U.S. security planners imagine, these military operations instead have produced devastating destabilizations in the region and insecurities for diverse populations brought together conceptually and violently in the "cross hairs" of drone strikes. In the discussion that follows, I turn to an underreported aspect of drone weaponry to illuminate why drones are crucial for theorizing U.S. state violence anew.

Double-Tap and the Disorganization of Collective Social Life

Whereas numerous critics have focused on how the covert drone war heralds the forefront of technological innovation in the U.S. military, my primary concern in the remainder of this essay is to explore how the racial logics of drones work by disaggregating targeted Muslim populations besieged by bombs. I see this practice itself as a novel mode of racialization, which is a term scholars use to describe the process of abstraction that hierarchically ascribes social value to bodies based on intersectional forms of racial difference.[34] Recently, lawyers and human rights activists have shed light on a particular practice of U.S. drone attacks that illuminates how war disorganizes and destroys communal bonds, namely, the "double-tap" phenomenon. A double-tap strike refers to when a Predator or Reaper drone targets a terrain multiple times with "hellfire" missiles in quick succession. There have been cases reported in northern Waziristan in late 2012, for example, where missiles of an unmanned drone slammed into a house, reducing it to shards. When villagers rushed to the scene minutes later to aid the injured, they were attacked again by another round of fire, with an even greater number of civilian casualties in the process.[35] Human rights lawyers have speculated that the double-tap phenomenon is less a military strategy and more a result of the "less-than-pinpoint-accurate technological capacity of the missiles."[36]

The "double-tap" phenomenon is alarming for a number of reasons. First, it reveals that the notion of a "surgical strike" is anything but precise. Drone proponents argue vociferously that the "bureaucractic, rational, even scientific nature of targeted killings replaces individual thought with machinic certainty."[37] The notion of a cleaner, gentler, more effective and bureaucratic form of war, which has been crucial to the public debate on drones, has been widely repudiated by numerous human rights reports and journalist accounts. An important 2012 report by legal experts at Stanford University and New York University (NYU), for instance, found that only *one in fifty* victims of "surgical strikes" in Pakistan were known militants.[38] The U.S. military makes ambitious claims about the so-called endurance, proximity, and precision of drone operations, but we must recognize now that in twenty-first-century asymmetric warfare, the line between civilians and militants, or what the U.S. government calls "affiliates," has been blurred to the point of oblivion.[39] These enemy targets are instead racialized in relation to algorithmic calculations of imminent threat to the U.S. homeland, a bureaucratic process that targets "patterns of life" and signals the emergence of a new mode of race war.[40] In Sepoy Mutiny's estimation, "there is no clarity in determining who anyone may be and what their purported sin may be."[41] What is clear, though, is that drone killings produce untold consequences and devastation on local communities in the borderlands of Af-Pak and other militarized sites across North Africa, the Middle East, and South Asia.

Second, these reports reveal that double-tap strikes have created a chilling effect on survivors of drone-targeted terrain because they dissuade civilians from rescuing the injured or coming to aid the dead. They have also stopped emergency humanitarian workers from providing crucial and urgent relief. One organization in northern Waziristan, for example, has instituted a six-hour mandatory delay.[42] Human rights reports detail countless examples of innocent civilians killed or injured when trying to rush to the aid of those injured and maimed. We should pause here to reflect on how the double-tap phenomenon freezes the basic functioning and organization of collective social life in regions targeted by drones, a mode of collective paralysis that has devastating and long-lasting effects. Legal experts have noted the impact on education, on health care, on community gatherings, and on cultural and religious practices related to burials and funerals in northern Waziristan. "Because drone strikes have targeted funerals and spaces where families have gathered to offer condolences to the deceased, they have inhibited the ability of families to hold dignified burials."[43] Key aspects of the burial process are furthermore impossible because bodies are so badly burned or torn apart as to be unidentifiable. We might speculate on the barbaric logic at work here among U.S. military planners—the civilizational ideology that those targeted by drones need not mourn their dead. This is an apt reminder that a crucial part of the logic of contemporary U.S. warfare is the racial dehumanization of its victims.

An even more troubling development related to the ongoing and ever-present fear of congregating has been the regional breakdown of the *jirga* system, "a community-based conflict resolution process that is fundamental to Pasthun society."[44] The Stanford and NYU report notes that the *jirga* is a crucial element of Pasthun legal and political life, as it provides "opportunities for community input, conflict resolution, and egalitarian decision-making. Hampering its functions could have serious implications for the communal order, especially in an area already devastated by death and destruction."[45] The targeting of community practices like the *jirga*, communal prayer in mosques, mourning at funerals, and wedding celebrations spells isolation for those whose lives are already rendered precarious by drone targeting. The interruption of collective ceremonies, rituals, and kinship ties is but one of many unseen, stultifying, and routinized effects of drone wars. This is part of my larger argument about the disorganizing and disaggregating effects of U.S. global counterinsurgencies and the opportunities for new communities of affiliation and transnational resistance that can respond to these practices of racial dehumanization and disorder.

Third, double-tap drone strikes have caused, perhaps predictably, a range of mental health outcomes for survivors and civilian populations. Reports testify to the experiences of posttraumatic stress disorder, stigmatization, anticipatory anxiety, and "diffuse and chronic" fear common in conflict zones, where "the buzz of a distant propeller is a constant reminder of imminent death."[46] In the words of one interviewee, "God knows whether they'll strike us again or not. But they're always surveying us, they're always over us, and you never know when they're going to strike and attack."[47] In her short documentary feature *Wounds of Waziristan,* journalist and scholar Madiha Tahir further details this sense of powerlessness produced by the indeterminacy of the drone: "Because drones are at a certain remove, there is a sense of uncertainty, a sense that you can't control this. Whether it's true or not, people feel that with militants there is some degree of control. You can negotiate. There is some cause and effect. But there is no cause and effect with drones. It's an acute kind of trauma that is not limited to the actual attack."[48] The lack of cause and effect produces its own perverse calculus to encode the debilitating racial logics of drone warfare and its right to kill and to maim civilian subjects.[49]

Fourth and finally, the "dissuasive effect" that the double-tap pattern of strikes has on first responders raises crucial moral and legal concerns. As legal experts from Stanford and NYU report, "not only does the practice put into question the extent to which secondary strikes comply with international humanitarian law's basic rules of distinction, proportionality, and precautions, but it also potentially violates specific legal protections for medical and humanitarian personnel, and for the wounded. As international law experts have noted, intentional strikes on first responders may constitute war crimes."[50] From multiple legal and ethical perspectives, then, the double-tap of the drone exponentially intensifies experiences of misery, isolation, debility, and pain in Af-Pak and beyond.

Conclusion: Challenging the Future of U.S. Drone Warfare

No rational response to drone proliferation appears efficacious to date. No serious debate in Washington has yet to emerge over the past two decades about the dramatic reorganization in fiscal, political, ethical, and affective priorities brought on by the buildup of the homeland security state. Despite the grotesque failures of U.S.-led counterinsurgency operations in Iraq, Afghanistan, Pakistan, Yemen, Somalia, and beyond, we might conclude that drones are here to stay and that their presence is symptomatic of the gendered racial violence and capitalist exploitation at the heart of U.S. empire. But perhaps the absolute focus on the drone confounds the larger underlying problems of the homeland security era. This weapon is the latest in a long line of technoscientific spectacles that inure us from the unseen and unsaid of contemporary U.S. imperial violence. Af-Pak presently serves as a frontier space of lethal experimentation on Muslim bodies. But we know that the technologies perfected in the distant theaters of war will soon give rise to new modes of surveillance, targeting, and elimination closer to home. News accounts already have begun to reveal the "drone creep," and the lines between U.S. military and police forces are blurrier than ever. As Priya Kandaswamy states succinctly, "the police and military are two faces of the same system of global repression and racism."[51] Blurred lines between militarism and policing are nothing new, of course, as students of and activists within the Black Freedom movement know all too well.[52] During the Cold War, for instance, global counterinsurgency tactics were perfected not only in Latin America, Africa, and the Middle East but on Black, indigenous, and racialized immigrant populations in the United States as well.[53] As such, when analyzing the vastly proliferating deployment of drone weaponry, we must also look to identify unlikely alliances and new communities of struggle that have emerged in response and in contestation. Despite the seeming omnipresence and permanence of the drone, I want to hold on to the idea that the spectacularly failed counterterrorism and counterinsurgency operations in the age of drone warfare create the conditions of possibility for new forms of solidarity, new movements, and new communities of resistance.

It seems especially urgent to refresh our political imaginations and be experimental in our tactics and strategies of resistance to both the global War on Terror and its domestic reverberations connecting to mass incarceration and police violence in the United States. In the words of Randall Williams, we need a "non-juridical reckoning" with these global circuits of U.S. state violence.[54] If affect refers to the glue that coheres social relations, the U.S. drone campaign has made various forms of affective belonging difficult or impossible to sustain through its violences, abstractions, and restrictions on the movement of bodies—not least of all through the double-tap tactics detailed earlier. At the same time, the U.S. global security state also conflates multiple groups of people into "terrorist lookalike" populations and evinces Manichean Cold War–style binaries that divide the world into those who are "with us" and those who are "against us" in the global War on Terror. This dominant map of U.S. empire, characterized by its fixity, schisms, and incoherences, has produced what Patrick Deer calls "a strategy that partitions, separates, and compartmentalizes knowledge, offering a highly seductive, militarized grid through which to interpret the world."[55] This grid not only creates partitions and separations when imagining peoples and geographies but also attempts to produce a coherent idea of the racialized "Muslim" figure out of disparate populations of Arabs and South Asians with divergent histories of race and class oppression in the United States.[56] According to Junaid Rana, this process of racialization is meant to construct "a visible target of state regulation and policing for consuming publics."[57] The great irony of this form of enemy production is that rather than celebrate the "richness of population historically forced together by conquest," as Randy Martin notes, U.S. empire instead treats this diversity as "a menacing entanglement from which imperial might must flee."[58] U.S. global counterinsurgency and security interventions are therefore not only about resource extraction or control over strategic territories but also about ways "to effect a separation from unwanted attachments and attentions—precisely what is meant by terror."[59]

I want to insist that there are unintended and potentially valuable consequences to these drone war conflations, abstractions, and estrangements for theorizing alternatives to the prevailing frames of security and warfare.

The tactics of the U.S. homeland security state have inadvertently produced new alliances between groups of people who might not have previously seen themselves in allegiance with each other or who might not have understood how they were involved in overlapping struggles against imperial policing, racialized punishment, and gendered militarism at home and abroad. An alternative map of diasporic affiliation and transnational solidarity has certainly been engendered among South Asians, Muslims, and Arabs in the United States, for instance, as a result of, and despite, the racializing practices of the global War on Terror. Thinking South Asian–Muslim–Arab concurrently thus names an alternative politics of belonging not circumscribed by the hostile categories conjured by U.S. security as it targets populations for discipline or dispersal.[60] Thinking comparatively about new activist formations produced in and through the global War on Terror thus refuses simply to reproduce the violences of U.S. gendered racialization, where a whole set of differences is reduced to a chain of equivalences under the sign of "Islam." Instead, our movements benefit from drawing connections between distinct but overlapping struggles. Resistance to global surveillance and the drone war provides ample illustration of how to build forms of solidarity that connect the domestic and international contexts of U.S. war making. This is especially crucial for activists and scholars interested in tracing the links between the unprecedented U.S. domestic policing and prison expansion project that disproportionately targets working-class people of color and the newly emergent global prison archipelago that is part and parcel of the U.S. global War on Terror.[61]

Finally, we need to challenge the ethical common sense in Washington that drones will solve our national security problems and, in so doing, that we might better expose the brutalities of late modern warfare. If our political imaginations are impoverished by the perverse calculus and prevailing logics of state security in discourses of terrorism, militarism, and war, then our mission must be to challenge the ethical common sense of U.S. state violence (founded, as it is, on perverse fantasies and ideological trajectories of settler colonialism, imperialism, cis heteropatriarchy, white supremacy, and anti-Black racism). As scholar activists committed to dismantling gendered racial domination and capitalist exploitation at the heart of U.S. empire, we should give ourselves the license to be as experimental as the state in our tactics and strategies, thereby investing in new expressions of as yet unimaginable sociality and solidarity.

In closing, this chapter has asked after the effects of the drone on the social relations of populations destroyed by U.S. imperial warfare. If the drone manipulates, conflates, and destroys communal bonds, stripping away our sense of responsibility and our way of knowing each other and ourselves in times of war, it then also produces the conditions of possibility for imagining alliances anew. We benefit from exploring this contradictory terrain created by U.S. security wars, breaking open the imperial frames of violence to develop a more expansive account of the drone, its gendered racial logics, and its targets. To do so would be to conjure the moment when, as Judith Butler says, "war stands the chance of missing its mark."[62]

Notes

1. My invocation of the "Muslim world" follows anthropologist Zareena Grewal's assertion that "rather than a foreign region, the Muslim world is a global community of Muslim locals, both majorities and minorities who *belong* to the places where they live and who, in their totality, exemplify the universality of Islam." See Grewal, *Islam Is a Foreign Country: American Muslims and the Global Crisis of Authority* (New York: New York University Press, 2014), 6–7.

2. Sohail Daulatzai, "Protect Ya Neck: Muslims and the Carceral Imagination in the Age of Guantánamo," *Souls* 9, no. 2 (2007): 135.

3. This chapter joins the growing scholarly activist effort to expose the ideological and material links between various sites of contemporary U.S. state violence. In this chapter, I place the global concept of "homeland security" in dialogue with seemingly more domestic concepts like "mass incarceration" and "police violence." I do so to underscore the blurring between the domestic and foreign fronts in the U.S. War on Terror and to call attention to the imaginative forms of coalitional activism that emerged in response. I use the concept of the homeland to describe a broader constellation of interests and ideologies that extend beyond the sovereign borders of the state. Following scholars like Amy Kaplan and Alex Lubin, "the homeland" refers to a transnational space that can include urban U.S. cities and distant battlefields in the global War on Terror. Similarly, "military urbanism" refers to the militarization of urban spaces. The idea explains how Western militaries and security forces have come to perceive all urban terrain as a conflict zone inhabited by lurking shadow enemies. Thus, if war, terrorism, and security are now the grammar through which collective social life is viewed and regulated across urban spaces in the United States, how do activists and scholars begin to resist and reimagine these militarized frames of war and the manifold forms of violence enacted in their name? This is the central animating question that this piece seeks to answer. On the homeland, see Amy Kaplan, *The Anarchy of Empire in the Making of US Culture* (Cambridge, Mass.: Harvard University Press, 2002), and Alex Lubin, "The Disappearing Frontiers of Homeland Security," *Jadaliyya*, February 26, 2013. On military urbanism, see Stephen Graham, *Cities under Siege: The New Military Urbanism* (New York: Verso, 2011).

4. Hugh Gusterson, *Drone: Remote Control Warfare* (Boston: MIT Press, 2016); Ian Shaw, *The Predator Empire: Drone Warfare and Full Spectrum Dominance* (Minneapolis: University of Minnesota Press, 2016); and Nicholas Mirzoeff, *The Right to Look: A Counterhistory of Visuality* (Durham, N.C.: Duke University Press, 2011).

5. Sven Lindqvist, *A History of Bombing*, trans. Linda Haverty Rugg (New York: New Press, 2003), and Caren Kaplan, *Aerial Aftermaths: Wartime from Above* (Durham, N.C.: Duke University Press, 2017). See also Priya Satia, *Spies in Arabia: The Great War and the Cultural Foundations of Britain's Covert Empire in the Middle East* (Oxford: Oxford University Press, 2008); "The Defense of Inhumanity: Air Control in Iraq and the British Idea of Arabia," *American Historical Review* 111 (2006): 16–51; "Attack of the Drones," *The Nation*, November 9, 2009, http://www.thenation.com/article/attack-drones/; and "Drones: A History from the British Middle East," *Humanity* 5, no. 1 (2014): 1–31.

6. Grégoire Chamayou, *A Theory of the Drone*, trans. Janet Lloyd (New York: New Press, 2014); Marjorie Cohn, ed., *Drones and Targeted Killing: Legal, Moral, and Geopolitical Issues* (Northampton, Mass.: Interlink, 2014); Caren Kaplan and Lisa Parks, eds., *Life in the Age of Drones* (Durham, N.C.: Duke University Press, 2017); Chris Woods, *Sudden Justice: America's Secret Drone Wars* (Oxford: Oxford University Press, 2015); Nick Turse and Tom Engelhardt, *Terminator Planet: The First History of Drone Warfare 2001–2050* (New York: Dispatch Books, 2012); Tom Engelhardt, "Air War, Barbarity and Collateral Damage," in *The American Way of War: How Bush's Wars Became Obama's* (Boston: Haymarket, 2010), 57–91; and Medea Benjamin, *Drone Warfare: Killing by Remote Control* (New York: OR Books, 2012).

7. Journalists began actively reporting on the "double-tap" phenomenon in 2012. See the groundbreaking work of the London-based Bureau of Investigative Journalism on covert drone wars, https://www.thebureauinvestigates.com/category/projects/drones/.

8. Ian Shaw and Majed Akhter, "The Dronification of State Violence," *Critical Asian Studies* 26, no. 1 (2014): 211–34.

9. Hannah Arendt, "Home to Roost: A Bicentennial Address," *New York Books*, June 26, 1975.

10. In August 2016, the ACLU revealed that the Baltimore Police Department has been subjecting that city to a vast and covert apparatus of aerial surveillance—one of a number of recent instances that demonstrate how the tactics and technologies of U.S. global counterinsurgency have been adopted for domestic social control. See Jay Stanley, "Baltimore Police Secretly Running Aerial Mass Surveillance Eye in the Sky," https://www.aclu.org/blog/free-future/baltimore-police-secretly-running-aerial-mass-surveillance-eye-sky.

11. See, e.g., Amazon's new "Prime Air" service, https://www.amazon.com/b?node=8037720011, and Facebook's new "Aquila" solar-power plane that aspires to "beam internet to remote parts of the world and eventually break the record for longest unmanned aircraft flight," https://www.facebook.com/notes/mark-zuckerberg/the-technology-behind-aquila/10153916136506634/.

12. The vastly proliferating deployment of drones should be contextualized in light of debates about the renewed importance of global counterinsurgency campaigns worldwide. Aerial bombardment is by no means a new phenomenon; its history stretches across British, French, and American occupations and late colonial wars. Recent scholarship has documented that aerial counterinsurgency was in fact invented in Iraq and the Afghanistan–Pakistan borderlands by the British Royal Air Force in the 1920s. Iraq was a target again in the early 1990s under the

Saddam Hussein regime, when bombing campaigns were crucial to the U.S. Persian Gulf War. See Priya Satia, *Spies in Arabia*; Michael Sherry, *The Rise of American Air Power: The Creation of Armageddon* (New Haven, Conn.: Yale University Press, 1989); and Spencer Weart, *Nuclear Fear: A History of Images* (Cambridge, Mass.: Harvard University Press, 1989).

13. Jane Mayer, "The Predator War," *The New Yorker,* October 26, 2009, and Seymour Hersch, "Up in the Air: Where Is the Iraq War Headed Next?," *The New Yorker,* December 5, 2005.

14. Ian Shaw, "Predator Empire: The Geopolitics of US Drone Warfare," *Geopolitics* 18, no. 3 (2013): 10.

15. Greg Miller, "Plan for Hunting Terrorists Signals US Intends to Keep Adding Names to Kill Lists," *Washington Post,* October 23, 2012. See also the ACLU's archive on targeted killings: https://www.aclu.org/issues/national-security/targeted-killing?redirect=national-security/targeted-killings. On the "disposition matrix," see Shaw, "Predator Empire."

16. On the "Revolution in Military Affairs," see Randy Martin, *An Empire of Indifference: American War and the Financial Logic of Risk Management* (New York: New York University Press, 2007). On "Predator Empire," see Ian Shaw, "Predator Empire." The terms *small wars, irregular warfare, asymmetrical warfare,* and *fourth-generation warfare* (4GW) all express anxiety within the military establishment about the blurring between civilians and soldiers in contemporary wars of the Global South. Coined in 1989, at the end of the Cold War, by William S. Lind to describe the nation-state's loss of monopoly on the use of violence and signaling the emergence of the violent "nonstate actor," some scholars suggest these terms merely signify a rebranding of the (counter)insurgencies of the "homeland security" era.

17. Reuters, "UN Investigator Decries US Use of Killer Drones," June 19, 2012. On the centrality and power of the secret to contemporary U.S. society and the security state, see Joseph Masco, *The Theater of Operations: National Security Affect from the Cold War to the War on Terror* (Durham, N.C.: Duke University Press, 2014).

18. Nasser Hussain, *The Jurisprudence of Emergency: Colonialism and the Rule of Law* (Ann Arbor: University of Michigan Press, 2003), and "Counterinsurgency's Comeback: Can a Colonialist Strategy Be Reinvented?," Boston Review, January/February 2010, http://bostonreview.net/BR35.1/hussain.php.

19. Ian Shaw, *Predator Empire,* and Lt. Col Dwight A. Roblyer, "Beyond Precision: Issues of Morality and Decision Making in Minimizing Collateral Casualties," Arms Control, Disarmament, and International Security Occasional Paper, April 2004.

20. There has been scant formal investigative journalism on the Pakistani government's collusion with the U.S. secret drone war campaign to date. See Steve Coll, "The Unblinking Stare: The Drone War in Pakistan," *The New Yorker,* November 24, 2014; Adam Entous, Siobhan Gorman, and Evan Perez, "US Unease over Drone Strikes," *Wall Street Journal,* September 26, 2012. See also Zakir Minhas and Altaf Qadir, "The US War on Terror and the Drone Attacks on FATA, Pakistan," *Pakistan Annual Research Journal* 50 (2014): 15–28; Ian Shaw and Majed Akhter, "The Dronification of State Violence," *Critical Asian Studies* 26, no. 2 (2014): 228; and Chris Woods, *Sudden Justice,* as well as his writings at the Bureau of Investigative

Journalism, for more details: https://www.thebureauinvestigates.com/2012/09/28/pakistan-categorically-rejects-claim-that-it-tacitly-allows-us-drone-strikes/.

21. The majority of drone attacks launched in Pakistan (with their leaders' tacit support) during both the Bush and Obama administrations have been on Pashtun villages in North and South Waziristan in the Federally Administered Tribal Areas along the Afghan border. See the work of Worldfocus, which has produced a devastating Google map outlining U.S.-led drone attacks in Pakistan since 2004: http://maps.google.com/maps/ms?ie=UTF8&hl=en&t=h&msa=0&msid=1139237083385
51641006.00047caa42cb2374421e4&ll=33.031693,70.587158&spn=1.611824,3.295
898&z=8&source=embed.

22. Holbrooke, as quoted in William Safire, "Wide World of Words," *New York Times,* April 23, 2009.

23. Shaw and Akhter, "The Unbearable Humanness of Drone Warfare in FATA, Pakistan," *Antipode* 44, no. 4 (2012): 1500.

24. Roberto J. González, *American Counterinsurgency: Human Science and the Human Terrain* (Chicago: Prickly Paradigm Press, 2009).

25. Joseph Masco, *The Theater of Operations: National Security Affect from the Cold War to the War on Terror* (Durham, N.C.: Duke University Press, 2014), 197.

26. Glenn Greenwald, "Trump's War on Terror Has Quickly Become as Barbaric and Savage as He Promised," *Intercept,* March 26, 2017, https://theintercept.com/2017/03/26/trumps-war-on-terror-has-quickly-become-as-barbaric-and-savage-as-he-promised/, and Benjamin Hart, "Report: U.S. Air Strikes Killing Far More Civilians under Trump," *New York Magazine,* July 17, 2017, http://nymag.com/daily/intelligencer/2017/07/u-s-air-strikes-are-killing-far-more-civilians-under-trump.html.

27. Nicholas Mirzoeff, *Right to Look,* 21.

28. Gregory, quoted in Elliott Prasse-Freeman, "Droning On," *The New Inquiry,* February 20, 2015.

29. For a nonexhaustive list of scholarly sources, see Derek Gregory, "From a View to a Kill: Drones and Late Modern Warfare," *Theory, Culture, and Society* 28, nos. 7–8 (2011): 188–215; Caren Kaplan, "Sensing Distance: The Time and Space of Contemporary War," *Social Text,* http://www.socialtextjournal.org/periscope/2013/06/sensing-distance-the-time-and-space-of-contemporary-war.php; Keith Feldman, "Empire's Verticality: The Af/Pak Frontier, Visual Culture, and Racialization from Above," *Comparative American Studies* 9, no. 4 (2011): 325–41; and Ronak K. Kapadia, "Up in the Air and On the Skin: Drone Warfare and the Queer Calculus of Pain," in *Critical Ethnic Studies: A Reader,* ed. Nada Elia, David M. Hernández, Jodi Kim, Shana L. Redmond, Dylan Rodríguez, and Sarita Echavez See (Durham, N.C.: Duke University Press, 2016).

30. On the nexus of visuality and war, see Paul Virilio, *War and Cinema: The Logistics of Perception* (New York: Verso, 1989); Rey Chow, *The Age of the World Target: Self-Referentiality in War, Theory, and Comparative Work* (Durham, N.C.: Duke University Press, 2006); James Der Derian, *Virtuous War: Mapping the Military-Industrial-Media-Entertainment-Network* (New York: Routledge, 2009); and Caren Kaplan, *Aerial Aftermaths.*

31. Judith Butler, *Frames of War: When Is Life Grievable?* (New York: Verso, 2009), and Virilio, *War and Cinema.*

32. Rey Chow, *Age of the World Target,* 30–31. This brief discussion on vision and war is drawn from my previously published work on the performance art of Wafaa Bilal in Kapadia, "Up in the Air and On the Skin."

33. Anne McClintock, "Paranoid Empire: Specters from Guantánamo and Abu Ghraib," *small axe* 28 (March 2009): 91.

34. Daniel HoSang, Oneka LaBennett, and Laura Pulido, eds., *Racial Formation in the Twenty-First Century* (Berkeley: University of California Press, 2012); Lisa Cacho, *Social Death: Racialized Rightlessness and the Criminalization of the Unprotected* (New York: New York University Press, 2012).

35. Jerome Taylor, "Outrage at CIA's Double Tap Drone Attacks," *The Guardian,* September 25, 2012.

36. James Cavallaro, Stephan Sonnenberg, and Sarah Knuckey, *Living under Drones: Death, Injury, and Trauma to Civilians from US Drone Practices in Pakistan* (Stanford, Calif.: International Human Rights and Conflict Resolution Clinic, Stanford Law School, 2012), 74. See also Columbia Law School Human Rights Clinic and Sana'a Center for Strategic Studies, *Out of the Shadows: Recommendations to Advance Transparency in the Use of Lethal Force,* June 2017, and Derek Gregory, "From a View to a Kill."

37. Shaw and Akhter, "Dronification of State Violence."

38. Cavallaro et al., *Living under Drones.* For up-to-date analysis of drone civilian casualties, see *The Intercept*'s "The Drone Papers," a cache of secret documents provided by a whistle-blower detailing the U.S. military's assassination program in Afghanistan, Yemen, and Somalia: https://theintercept.com/drone-papers/. See also Ryan Devereaux, "Manhunting in the Hindu Kush: Civilian Casualties and Strategic Failures in America's Longest War," *The Intercept,* October 15, 2015, https://theintercept.com/drone-papers/manhunting-in-the-hindu-kush/.

39. Feldman, "Empire's Verticality," 338.

40. Shaw, *Predator Empire.*

41. Sepoy Mutiny, "Waziristan, U.S.," *Chapati Mystery,* April 16, 2014.

42. Cavallaro et al., *Living under Drones,* 76.

43. Ibid., 93.

44. Ibid., 98.

45. Ibid., 99.

46. Hussain, "Counterinsurgency's Comeback," ibid., 80–81.

47. Cavallaro et al., *Living under Drones,* 99.

48. Alex Pasternack, "The Story of Drones, as Told by the People Who Live under Them," *Motherboard,* October 25, 2013. See also Madiha R. Tahir, "Wounds of Waziristan," http://woundsofwaziristan.com/.

49. Jasbir Kaur Puar, *The Right to Maim: Debility, Capacity, Disability* (Durham, N.C.: Duke University Press, 2017).

50. Cavallaro et al., *Living under Drones,* 90.

51. Priya Kandaswamy, "Stop Urban Shield, Stop Violence against Our Communities," *SAMAR Magazine,* September 25, 2014. We see these linkages between global War on Terror tactics and the militarization of urban U.S. policing on a

number of fronts that are implicated in the world of drones. First, U.S. law enforcement has greatly expanded its use of domestic drones for surveillance. Second, drone manufacturers are also considering offering police the option of arming remote-controlled aircraft with weapons like rubber bullets, Tasers, and tear gas. Third, the U.S. Customs and Border Patrol are using Predator drones along the borders with Mexico and Canada. See ACLU Fact Sheet on "United States Department of Defense's Unmanned Systems Integrated Roadmap FY 2013–2038."

52. Joy James, ed., *Imprisoned Intellectuals: America's Political Prisoners Write on Life, Liberation, and Rebellion* (New York: Rowman and Littlefield, 2003).

53. Jordan T. Camp, *Incarcerating the Crisis: Freedom Struggles and the Rise of the Neoliberal State* (Berkeley: University of California Press, 2016).

54. Randall Williams, *The Divided World: Human Rights and Its Violence* (Minneapolis: University of Minnesota Press, 2010), xxxii.

55. Patrick Deer, "The Ends of War," *Social Text* 91 (2007): 1.

56. Key works in this growing field include Evelyn Alsultany, *Arabs and Muslims in the Media: Race and Representation after 9/11* (New York: New York University Press, 2012); Sohail Daulatzai, *Black Star, Crescent Moon: The Muslim International and Black Freedom beyond America* (Minneapolis: University of Minnesota Press, 2012); Grewal, *Islam Is a Foreign Country*; Sunaina Marr Maira, *Missing: Youth, Citizenship, and Empire after 9/11* (Durham, N.C.: Duke University Press, 2009); Maira, *The 9/11 Generation: Youth, Rights, and Solidarity in the War on Terror* (New York: New York University Press, 2016); Nadine Naber, *Arab America: Gender, Cultural Politics, and Activism* (New York: New York University Press, 2012); Jasbir Kaur Puar, *Terrorist Assemblages: Homonationalism in Queer Times* (Durham, N.C.: Duke University Press, 2007); and Junaid Rana, *Terrifying Muslims: Race and Labor in the South Asian Diaspora* (Durham, N.C.: Duke University Press, 2011).

57. Rana, *Terrifying Muslims*, 93.

58. Martin, *An Empire of Indifference*, 5.

59. Ibid.

60. See Moustafa Bayoumi, *This Muslim American Life: Dispatches from the War on Terror* (New York: New York University Press, 2015); Deepa Iyer, *We Too Sing America: South Asian, Arab, Muslim, and Sikh Immigrants Shape Our Multiracial Future* (New York: New Press, 2015); Maira, *9/11 Generation*; and Ronak K. Kapadia, *Insurgent Aesthetics of the Forever War: Art and Performance after 9/11* (Durham, N.C.: Duke University Press, forthcoming). See also note 56.

61. Jenna M. Loyd, Matt Mitchelson, and Andrew Burridge, eds., *Beyond Walls and Cages: Prisons, Borders, and Global Crisis* (Atlanta: University of Georgia Press, 2012).

62. Butler, *Frames of War*, xxx.

14

The Cry for Human Rights

Violence, Transition, and the Egyptian Revolution

NADINE NABER AND ATEF SAID

In January 2011, Egypt and, indeed, the world witnessed something immense and unprecedented: millions of people from every sector of society took to the streets to overthrow their dictator. As scholars and activists involved and interested in Egyptian politics, both authors of this chapter were approached to comment on the momentous events and/or speak about them at public forums. Various media outlets sought out Atef Said, an Egyptian human rights lawyer and sociologist living in the area. The questions they asked, however, were disconcerting and followed a similar pattern: "What if Islamists take over? What about the fate of minorities and women?" Nadine Naber had a similar experience. From Facebook conversations to events at the university at which she taught, U.S.-based audiences consistently asked Naber about the potential for an "Islamic takeover" and the consequences for "women's rights."

Since January 2011, the revolution has taken many turns and much has transpired: the formation of new political parties; strikes by doctors, lawyers, and professors; grassroots funeral processions for newly declared martyrs; conflicting efforts to draft a new constitution; continued battles over public space; the formation of new feminist coalitions; the launching of massive campaigns against sexual harassment; the election of a new president; public protests and a military coup ousting that president; and a subsequent backlash against the briefly empowered Muslim Brotherhood—to name just some highlights. Yet despite these dramatic upheavals and ongoing changes, the primary questions we are asked by media or public audiences remain the same: what will happen if/when Islamists take over, and what about women and minorities? Speaking at a policy briefing for the United Nations in 2013, Nadine Naber cautioned audience members against reductive Islamophobic analyses that simply blame "Islam" for attacks against women's rights in Egypt. She urged the international community to take seriously the impact on women's rights of state-based corruption, sexual violence, and economic violence. But still, one audience member insisted on asking, "Do you think it [Islam] is going to spread throughout Africa?"

Our experiences reflect the kinds of analyses emerging from the U.S. media, government, and liberal human rights discourses about the Egyptian revolution and its aftermath. Specifically, they reflect analyses that frame the struggles of the revolution through a liberal–Orientalist cry for human rights that envisions a unidirectional flow of concern and assistance from "here" (the United States) to "there" (Egypt). In this framing, "women" and "minorities" are the primary victims, while Islam is the perpetrator, the specter whose expanded rule would endanger the former.[1] The problems with this framing are twofold. First, it identifies Islam as the primary obstacle to the success of the revolution and the realization of democracy in Egypt; and second, it relies on abstract concepts of individual and political rights under the law to evaluate revolutionary success.

Focusing on examples of this trend within public discussions regarding (1) the process of transition following the Egyptian revolution and (2) violence—specifically, gendered sexual violence and torture in Egypt—this essay interrogates the liberal–Orientalist "cry for human rights." We are particularly concerned with how this framing of human rights both relies on and reinforces global neoliberalism and its attendant forms of violence. We argue that such analyses fail to account for the complex historical and political contexts in which violence and transition take place and the multiple, interconnected structures of power that impact revolutionary change. Far from questioning the value of protecting women's rights or human rights, we seek to examine the limitations inherent to liberal–Orientalist epistemological frameworks and to highlight the connections among interpersonal violence, Egyptian state violence, and U.S.-led imperial practices in Egypt.

The application of distorting Orientalist lenses to Egypt and the Middle East in general is hardly new. More than thirty years ago, Edward Said wrote that Orientalism configures the "East" through ahistorical attributes such as religiosity, tyranny, and oppression, which are then contrasted with the "West's" rationality and modernity. Since the War on Terror, numerous scholars have noted how new versions of Orientalism restage this clash of civilizations thesis: we have freedom and democracy, they have violence and terrorism. According to this thesis, Islam and Arab culture are part of an unchanging tradition fundamentally incompatible with civilization and existing essentially outside history.[2]

Parallel to this literature on new and enduring forms of Orientalism, other scholars have traced the emergence of a particular liberal, abstract conception of human rights, along with a transnational but still Western-dominated institutional apparatus for monitoring and (ostensibly) safeguarding such rights.[3] Overall, this literature contends that liberal human rights approaches developed out of Eurocentric contexts of neoliberal expansion and operate through the epistemological structures of individualism and universality and the material structures of capitalism.[4] Deploying ethnocentric concepts of human rights (freedom, liberty, etc.), these universalist approaches tend to blame oppression in the Global South on abstract concepts of "culture" or "tradition" and have reified colonialist notions of a liberated, developed north and a victimized, underdeveloped Global South that needs to be saved by Western heroes.[5] Such Orientalist approaches to human rights have been particularly prominent in advocacy related to gender and women's rights in Arab and Muslim countries.[6]

Here we focus on human rights discourses that operate through this convergence of liberalism and Orientalism and argue that liberal–Orientalist human rights not only obscure political and historical conditions but also provide an imperialist vocabulary for neoliberal expansion and military domination. The essay is divided into three parts. We begin first by reviewing the primary events of the revolution itself and the transition period up to the ousting of President Mohamed Morsi in 2013. Our point is not to provide a complete summary but to begin challenging some of the narratives of transition (or failed transition) that have circulated in Western-based coverage of events since the revolution. In the second section, we provide a comparison of reports and analyses of violence—with a particular focus on gender-based sexual violence—under, respectively, the Hosni Mubarak regime, the Supreme Council of Armed Forces (SCAF), and Morsi and the Muslim Brotherhood. We examine patterns in how and when discussions of violence alternately connected (or failed to connect) interpersonal violence and state violence, used Orientalist logics to conflate and explain both forms of violence, and obscured from view the broader geopolitical contexts that shape the phenomenon of violence. In the third section, we focus on examples of U.S.-based discussions of torture in Egypt during the same period that ignored the various factors that extended the widespread use of torture by the Egyptian state—factors such as the adoption of harsh neoliberal economic policies and the transfer of governance to a militarized police state. We also analyze human rights reporting after the revolution that focused only on how violations could be traced to the rise of Islamists in power.

BACKGROUND: REVOLUTION AND TRANSITION, 2011–2013

This essay focuses on the "early" transitional period following the Egyptian Revolution of 2011, from the period of military rule under the SCAF to the election of Mohamed Morsi as president and the subsequent Muslim Brotherhood–led government. While the events immediately leading up to and following the July 2013 ousting of President Morsi will be touched on in our discussion, we wrote the majority of this essay before this period. As a result, our discussion is limited to the transitional period preceding those events.

The simplest narrative of events in Egypt from 2011 to 2013 could go something like this. Egyptians took to the streets in huge public protests on January 25, 2011. Pictures that circulated around the world showed millions of people rallying, demanding the end of the Mubarak regime. After eighteen days of protest in Cairo's famous Tahrir Square, Egyptians successfully ousted Mubarak from office. The SCAF, the leadership body of the Egyptian military, succeeded Mubarak in ruling Egypt. This situation lasted for almost a year and a half; in June 2012, Egyptians democratically elected a new president, Mohamed Morsi. Morsi, the leader of the Muslim Brotherhood–backed Freedom and Justice Party, took office on June 30, 2012.[7] But by the end of June 2013, Egyptians took to the streets once again to oust the new president. Using the opportunity of the protest, the Egyptian military staged a coup and removed the president from office on July 3, 2013.

The problem, of course, is not so much with the basic contents of the preceding narrative but with the often sweeping and definitive analyses of causes, effects, intentions, and implications that have followed. Often told and read as revealing simple truths about who is democratic and who is not, whether an entire people is "ready" for democracy or not, who is to blame for the success or failure of the revolution, and so on, the events in Egypt often function like a screen onto which various commentators can project their assumptions and through which they attempt to exorcise various demons.[8]

We briefly review here two ways in which liberal–Orientalist, Western-based coverage obscures the complexity of the transitional period. The first of these concerns the immediate transition of power from Mubarak to the

SCAF.[9] We know that on February 11, 2011, the SCAF took charge of ruling Egypt. The move was framed from the beginning as a transitional one that would be in effect only until a democratically elected civilian government could take charge. What few, if any, Western-based reports noted, however, was how this very development obstructed the revolutionary changes for which Egyptian protesters had been calling. Constitutionally and legally, the SCAF was not chosen by the people to deal with the transition. Rather, Mubarak ceded power to the SCAF—a far less radical move when one takes into account that the council's nineteen army generals oversaw a significant component of Mubarak's political apparatus and were thus *part* of the ruling regime that the revolution aimed to replace. Put simply, the SCAF was hardly a neutral body to govern during the transitional period.

The council's actions soon reflected this. Instead of writing a new constitution to reflect the hopes and aspirations of the people who had called for the end of Mubarak's dictatorship, the SCAF worked with a handful of elites to make only limited amendments to Egypt's Constitution of 1971. The public was invited to vote in a referendum on the amendments only when they had already been drafted. In short, there was no room for wider, public discussions about what to do next; the people in the streets who provided the much-lauded, international "face" of the revolution were not included in deciding the fate of Egypt after Mubarak. Yet despite all of this, Western analysts were quick to celebrate Egypt's "orderly transition"—a phrase coined by then secretary of state Hillary Clinton that captured the tidy way in which U.S. commentators sought to characterize the SCAF transition *and* obscure the complicated history of U.S. partnership with Egyptian military leaders. Egyptian activists and writers soon realized that "orderly transition" meant a tightly controlled transition to a narrow version of democracy that would disrupt neither the economic status quo in Egypt nor U.S. interests. As the scholar Adam Hanieh put it in May 2011,

> the plethora of aid and investment initiatives advanced by the leading powers in recent days represents a conscious attempt to consolidate and reinforce the power of Egypt's dominant class in the face of the ongoing popular mobilizations. They are part of, in other words, a sustained effort to restrain the revolution within the bounds of an "orderly transition."[10]

Importantly, such a controlled process had no room for young revolutionaries, who were viewed as "scattered" and "unpredictable"—in short, the opposite of "orderly."

Also obscured within this narrative of "orderly transition" is the fact that serious abuses of human rights continued under the SCAF. Military forces attacked labor strikes with tanks and stormed peaceful protests in Tahrir many times, resulting in the deaths of many protesters. In October 2011, thousands of Egyptian Christians and Muslim supporters were peacefully protesting sectarian violence and attacks on an Egyptian church in southern Egypt's province, Aswan, when military and police forces attacked the rally, killing about thirty protesters and injuring more than two hundred. Proper investigations were not conducted, and the SCAF resisted taking any serious measures to reform the deadly police apparatus that was responsible for killing and torturing Egyptians in the revolution and previous decades. This resistance was telling and, in fact, marks one of the major continuities linking both SCAF rule and the Morsi government, and the second aspect of this period that has been obscured in Western discussions.

To outside observers, there was a major shift in June 2012: Egyptians held their first democratic elections and voted Mohamed Morsi into power. One of Morsi's first actions was to diminish the authority of the military by discharging two top leaders from the SCAF, a move the *New York Times* described as "stunning" and an "upheaval" within Egypt's ruling apparatus.[11] A constitutional assembly was elected—not directly by the people but by the members of the parliament dominated by the Muslim Brotherhood and Islamic parties. Then Morsi decided to put the draft of Egypt's constitution to a referendum, despite public critiques, and without building a national consensus. In December 2012, the constitution was approved by 63.9 percent of the voters, but only 33 percent of registered voters had participated. Domestic and international human rights groups criticized the constitution as being sectarian and constraining freedom of religion in Egypt, allowing only specific religions (Judaism, Christianity, and Islam) the right to build places of worship. The constitution also established a sort of religious authority over Egyptian politics and legislation, expanding the meaning of shari'a to outlaw Bahaism and Shi'ism in Egypt.

Perhaps the most paradoxical development, however, was Morsi's constitutional decree on November 14, 2012, to limit judicial supervision of decisions. Ostensibly, this was a response to the fact that most of the police officers who were responsible for killing protesters during the revolution were declared innocent and released. The irony, however, was that while Morsi claimed to have expanded his powers to achieve justice for the protesters killed, he continued to resist police reform. Instead, he ignored initiatives for police reform by Egyptian civil society–based organizations and continued to defend the police publicly while blaming protesters for the violence. He also authorized two fact-finding commissions to collect evidence about those responsible for killing protesters since the revolution began (under Mubarak, the SCAF, and Morsi). But when the commission concluded that military and police personnel were involved in these killings, Morsi ignored their reports. In fact, many human rights abuses continued under Morsi, including torture and the killing of protesters.

To be sure, even this summary of events presents an oversimplified picture, and it bears emphasizing that our point is neither that nothing has actually changed in Egypt nor that the SCAF or Morsi ruined everything. The problem is that the complex dynamics of transition—the shifts *and* continuities—have been lost in liberal Western accounts that reduce the Egyptian revolution to a political–democratic revolution *only,* thus reductively equating democracy to a ballot box.[12] Not surprisingly, a common conclusion has emerged among critical scholars in the Middle East and, in some cases, among Western commentators themselves that "the West is getting it wrong." "It" here refers variously to the Muslim Brotherhood, the Egyptian Revolution, and/or the country's liberal and leftist youth.[13] Documenting all the various ways in which Western accounts have, indeed, "got it wrong" is beyond the scope of this essay. But we contribute to this accounting of misrepresentation by focusing on two specific issues that have been decontextualized and distorted in mainstream discussions: violence (particularly gendered sexual violence) and torture. Furthermore, we examine how liberal–Orientalist human rights discourse in particular has contributed to this problem.

GENDERED SEXUAL VIOLENCE

In this section, we argue that human rights discourses based in the Global North have tended to address gendered sexual violence in Egypt before and after the revolution in one of three ways: (1) focusing only on sexual violence in the streets under Mubarak; (2) focusing only on sexualized state violence under Mubarak; or (3) highlighting the interconnections between street and state violence, but only after the Muslim Brotherhood took power. We contend that these strategies have similar effects. In the first instance, dominant human rights discourses isolate sexual violence in the streets from state violence and, in doing so, reinforce Orientalism and culture blaming. In the second instance, attention focuses on Mubarak and the SCAF's sexualized state violence but obscures U.S. complicity in the practice of torture and sexual violence before and after the revolution. And in

Figure 14.1. Photograph of a tear gas container, on which is written "Made in the USA," which was circulated widely in social media in Egypt in 2011 during the revolution. American tear gas shipments persisted throughout the revolution and the transnational period, a fact largely unmarked by the media and even some human rights nongovernmental organizations. Photograph by Gigi Ibhraim. Published with permission.

the third instance, human rights discourses finally connect state and interpersonal sexual violence, but through the specific lens of Islamophobia and concepts such as "conservative Islam." Despite their differences, all three approaches obscure the geopolitical contexts in which sexual violence emerges and reify the cry for human rights from "here" to "there." In contrast, we suggest an alternate framework that situates sexualized violence in the context of local and global power relations and accounts for the historical and material conditions through which such violence is produced.

It was not uncommon for U.S.-based reporting and human rights advocacy related to women in Egypt during the Mubarak era to focus on interpersonal instances of gender violence, such as sexual harassment in the streets.[14] While some international human rights approaches criticized

Egyptian state violence, most avoided drawing any connections between state violence and street violence, and they certainly ignored the United States' role in supporting sexualized state violence in Egypt. By focusing on interpersonal instances of violence, these analyses singled out individual men (particularly poor Egyptian men) as perpetrators and explained sexual harassment as a social and cultural problem. Discussions of sexual violence during the revolution itself adhered to this pattern. U.S. media reporting on the case of Lara Logan (the white South African reporter sexually attacked in Tahrir during celebrations over the fall of Mubarak) exemplified the convergence of liberal–Orientalist approaches during this period. Coverage reified the Orientalist notion of a violent and misogynous Arab Muslim masculinity that is particularly savage toward white European women.[15] To the extent that the story also served to raise questions about Egyptian women's safety, corporate media and dominant human rights agencies focused on whether and to what extent Egyptian women are protected by rights under the law.

More often, however, the coverage accorded to Lara Logan served to obscure the many attacks on Egyptian women in Tahrir Square by Mubarak-sponsored thugs during the same time period. Similarly, there was no mention of the many other forms of gender violence taking place in Tahrir. The clear message seemed to be that Lara Logan's body counts; in stark contrast, the bodies of women such as the Egyptian feminist activist professor Noha Radwan, attacked and severely beaten by plain-clothed Mubarak thugs, or Liza Mohamed Hasan, hit by a police car, do not. Many other Egyptian women could be named here, but the point is that their stories do not align with a liberal–Orientalist framework that sensationalizes gender violence in the Arab Muslim region only when it can be explained as a result of either individual male perpetrators or Arab culture (read Islam). State actors, especially the United States and states supported by the United States (including Egypt), are not held accountable for violence against women. Turning to discussions by Western-based media and human rights groups of state sexual violence, a similar pattern of omission emerges. The Mubarak regime used sexualized torture as a systematic practice, with military police forcing detainees to rape their own spouses in front of them, officers raping men in front of their spouses, or detainees being forced to sexually harass one another.[16] But while Human Rights Watch and Amnesty International documented the use of rape, torture, and sexual assault to threaten and intimidate female activists who criticized the regime, these reports followed a similar pattern as the dominant human rights discourse.[17] They framed state violence and street violence as distinct issues and failed to address the connections between the two. As a result, gender violence was framed as either a domestic problem of authoritarianism (i.e., the state will use gender violence to attack dissidents) or a sociocultural problem (Egyptian culture and/or religion [Islam] condones sexual violence in the streets). More broadly, such approaches also failed to acknowledge a crucial grievance mobilizing Egyptians' demonstrations leading up to the 2011 revolution. For longer than a decade before the revolution, Egyptian activists had been arguing that sexual violence in Egypt was not only perpetuated by U.S. support for Egypt but also directly imported to Egypt via the CIA's extraordinary rendition program. This illegal program, according to the United Nations Convention against Torture, sends people suspected by the United States of terrorism (extremely broadly defined) to countries, such as Egypt, that are known for torture, sexual assault, and threats of rape of prisoners.[18] Through extraordinary rendition, both the U.S. and Egyptian governments have endorsed the use of sexual violence in the War on Terror. Abu Omar, for example, was kidnapped by the CIA in Milan, Italy; sent to Egypt by the United States; and tortured, sexually assaulted, and raped at the hands of Egypt's security forces.[19] In 2005, when women journalists protested Mubarak's domestic policies and the U.S.–Mubarak alliance in Egyptian and regional Arab politics, they were arrested and sexually assaulted by Egyptian military police.[20] In response to this and similar cases, Egyptian feminists fighting against sexualized state violence in Egypt challenged the United States' thirty-year unanswered support and complicity in Mubarak's policies, including President Barack Obama's leadership in the U.S. extraordinary rendition program.[21] The extent of U.S. complicity in sexual violence and torture in Egypt was only reaffirmed after Mubarak stepped down and President Obama promoted Omar Suleiman—the coordinator of the extraordinary rendition program—as a potential new leader of Egypt.

By the time the SCAF took power and the eyes of the world were on Egypt, reports and news articles focusing on state violence against Egyptian women did increase to a certain extent, but continued to follow particular patterns. First, U.S. complicity in state sexualized violence remained completely obscured, as usual. Second, though organizations like Amnesty International and Women under Siege documented security forces calling women protesters whores and using virginity tests to instill fear and suppress women's participation, such stories were still dwarfed by coverage of the Lara Logan incident.[22] And finally, to the extent that coverage of state violence against Egyptian women did increase, it did so in ways that mapped onto long-standing Western Orientalist representations of Egypt, the Arab region, and Muslim-majority societies. Virginity tests or Egyptian men referring to Egyptian women as whores, for example, hardly challenged Orientalist stereotypes.

Likewise, what came to be known as the "blue bra" incident—in which SCAF forces stripped and dragged an Egyptian woman protester through the streets, wearing, by that point, only pants and a blue bra—revealed the readiness of Western media and political figures to react hysterically to images that played on Orientalist fears and fetishes.[23] As the Egyptian feminist scholar and activist Hala Kamal put it, "what was most disturbing to me about the bra incident is the focus on this one woman being dragged by the military. The whole incident was being reduced to this one thing." The "whole incident" to which Hala Kamal referred was a larger set of clashes in December 2011 in Mohamed Mahmoud Street, in which SCAF forces used extreme force, killing more than forty people and maiming many others. As Kamal wearily pointed out, the reduction of these bloody clashes to the single image of an Arab woman in a blue bra offered little critique of state

Figure 14.2. Egyptian women rally in Tahrir Square on April 20, 2012, against SCAF rule and against systematic abuse of women under SCAF rule. Photograph by Gigi Ibrahim. Published with permission.

violence as such but spoke volumes about the Western obsession with the naked, unveiled Arab Muslim woman's body.

Orientalist representations emanating from the Global North became increasingly apparent after the Muslim Brotherhood took power. It was as if the corporate media and liberal human rights advocates finally had license to say what they had been thinking all along: the problem in Egypt is a patriarchal–misogynist culture and the culprit is Islam. Let us be clear: this period *has* witnessed a rise in reports of sexual violence and rape (including gang rapes against women protesters) and increased exclusion of women from political participation.[24] But when dominant discourse focuses only on Islam, as if Islam exists outside history, it fails to account for the broader context in which there are multiple factors at play—not least, a corrupt new neoliberal regime in control, obsessed with power and little concerned about human rights or social justice. Dominant human rights discourses also focus significantly on the need for equal rights for women under the law and women's equal political participation. Yet the problems of sexual violence or equal participation for women in Egypt are not simply about Islam, women's equal representation in the existing government, or even what ends up in the constitution or elections.

Not surprisingly, it is Egyptian women themselves who offer the most compelling perspective on the various (but depressingly similar) ways in which sexual violence has been used as a political tool of oppression both before and after the Egyptian revolution. This excerpt from a statement written by the coalition of Egyptian feminists and their allies illustrates a conceptualization of sexual violence under the Muslim Brotherhood that notes its connection to past practices, but without reifying Islamophobia and Orientalism:

> In an attempt to stop Egyptian women from continuing their struggle towards fulfilling the goals of the January Revolution—Dignity, Freedom and Social Justice—organized groups have begun using weapons of sexual violence, ranging from obscenity and sexual harassment to rape, mass rape, sexual mutilation and attempted murder, against women. . . . Those responsible for these abhorrent acts bargain . . . on the complicity of law enforcement agencies and that they will not fulfill their role of protecting the protestors. The spate of mass sexual assaults against women has not stopped since the Mubarak regime started using sexual violence against women demonstrators in May 2005. . . . As we exposed the Mubarak regime and pursued them nationally and internationally, we will fight the current regime and the institutions that

are responsible for or complicit in these crimes and we will pursue them legally nationally and internationally.[25]

Here the authors indicate that state-led sexual violence was set in place during the Mubarak regime and has continued to be used since as a political tool. They emphasize that women's struggles are connected to a larger revolutionary struggle and that Egyptian women are not victims who need to be saved by Western outsiders but agents who can craft and determine their own destiny.

Indeed, one of the most powerful ways Egyptian women attempt to shape their own destiny is by refusing to allow sexualized violence or even "women's equality," narrowly defined, to monopolize their focus. In ethnographic research conducted with twenty women activists from leading women's organizations, Naber repeatedly heard the women say that the analysis cannot begin or end with women or portray women as the disproportionate victims of the new regime when the country still lacks a functioning democracy. They insisted that the question we need to ask is not simply, "Are women included in or excluded from the new parliament?" Rather, we might ask whether the women of the revolution even *want* to be included in a corrupt government. Focusing only on "women's equality" ignores the reasons why many women are not interested in or do not trust formal politics, especially in the wake of sexual terrorism and excessive violence against them.

TORTURE IN THE CONTEXT OF NEOLIBERALISM AND MILITARISM

Like gender violence, torture and other forms of bodily harm reinforced by the ruling regime should not be abstracted from the historical realities of global economic neoliberalism. In this section, however, we demonstrate and criticize the trend among international human rights groups to ignore the entangled local and global contexts out of which torture in Egypt emerged. Specifically, we argue that we cannot understand the systematic nature of the practice of torture in Egypt without explaining the neoliberal conditions that made and continue to make this practice widespread. To this end, we review the recent history of neoliberal policies in Egypt and note their imbrication with Mubarak's repressive state apparatus. Then we explore the tendency among international human rights reports to ignore the political and societal contexts of torture in favor of approaches that isolate human rights abuses from historical and material realities. We show

how this tendency has the potential to reify what we call "the cry for human rights"—a cry that frames the problem as a local lack of human rights that will be fixed once advocates from the Global North intervene and help to establish these rights. This "cry for human rights" is not Orientalist per se but resembles Orientalism by isolating the problems in Egypt from global conditions, such as U.S. foreign policy in Egypt, and then implying the need to help or even save Egyptians from their corrupt regime and its practices.

Under Mubarak, the Egyptian state initiated a wholesale embrace of neoliberal economic and social policies, especially in the decade directly leading up to the revolution. Mubarak officially began applying structural adjustment programs in 1991. While both the International Monetary Fund and the World Bank praised Egypt for its economic reforms, the country actually became more dependent in terms of food sustainability, and rates of unemployment and poverty increased. In 2009, more than 40 percent of the population lived below the poverty line.[26] Privatization and decreases in state funding steadily eroded public education and health care. Egypt's population suffered falling wages relative to inflation, and official unemployment was estimated at approximately 9.4 percent in 2010 (and much higher for the youth who spearheaded the January 25 Revolution).

Mubarak's Egypt was also a fertile site for corruption, increasingly described in recent accounts as a crony capitalist state, in which narrower and narrower segments of businessmen and elites controlled the economy, especially Mubarak's family and its networks. In addition, it is estimated that the Egyptian military controls at least 30 percent of the Egyptian economy, via industries that are not subjected to any civilian oversight. In June 2010, a group of fifteen local Egyptian human rights organizations submitted a report to the Human Rights Council on the status of economic and social rights in Egypt. The report highlighted how the failed economic and social policies of the neoliberal state in Egypt were becoming the most important challenge to any decent enjoyment of social and economic rights by the majority of Egyptians.[27]

Dominant liberal human rights discourses tend to ignore this context when discussing what they often describe as Mubarak's police state. And yet, as Samer Soliman explains in *The Autumn of Dictatorship*, the rise of the police state in Egypt was crucial to and fused with Mubarak's crony capitalism and neoliberal policies.[28] These policies and the state's constant budget deficiency created a crisis of legitimacy for the regime. It needed to increase taxation but risked sparking public unrest among the already impoverished population. The solution was to rely on a steadily expanding repressive machinery. Under Mubarak, the Central Security Forces, a specific branch of police that works as an antiriot police force, reached almost half a million soldiers, while the total police force reached more than one million personnel. Far from being limited to riots, these forces were used to attack protests and assemblies of all sorts. Central Security Forces were essentially a parallel army run by the Ministry of Interior. In 2009, the annual costs of this army were estimated to be around 900 million Egyptian pounds, which at the time was about $150 million a year.[29] In the last year before the revolution, the budget for national security and police reached almost 20 percent of Egypt's total budget, while the high rates of poverty and unemployment continued.[30]

Closer analyses of torture in Egypt show that its use has not been limited to political prisoners. Torture requires no criminal accusations, nor is it necessarily employed to secure information or confessions. It has been used to punish not only political activists but also workers who tried to strike against harsh neoliberal policies and peasants who resisted land reforms.[31] Such practices have continued after Mubarak: Egyptian human rights groups affirm that revolutionaries who criticized the SCAF and then the Muslim Brotherhood have similarly been targeted for torture, along with workers and peasants.[32] This brings us to two prime examples of the ways human rights reporting from the Global North about torture in Egypt lacks the context noted here: in its overemphasis on the *numbers* of torture cases, on one hand, and the establishment of crude comparisons between torture under Mubarak and his successors (the SCAF and then Morsi), on the other. Neither provides sufficient attention to the conditions and context of the torture itself.

First, although quantitative indicators and descriptive reporting are useful, they are not adequate, especially after a revolution.[33] Relying on numbers to indicate how widespread or common the practice of police torture is in Egypt is deeply problematic, especially given how systematic the practice has become. With years of practice, many officers (especially those who worked with state security intelligence) have become extremely skilled at leaving no marks on victims' bodies and knowing how long to detain them for most marks to disappear. And cases of mental torture, of course, leave no visible evidence. In some cases, victims fear retaliation and further torture and thus do not go to lawyers or human rights organizations to seek justice. The Forensic Medicine Agency is the main body that is responsible by law to inspect torture cases, including cases in which torture led to death. But the agency lacks independence as it is supervised by the minister of justice and is subjected to pressure by state security intelligence. There are therefore good reasons to question even the accuracy of quantitative reports.

Nonetheless, the larger problem here is that torture cannot be discussed outside the context of police reform or the socioeconomic context in which the necessary reforms have failed to materialize. Critical anthropologists who study human rights abuses have noted that relying on quantitative indicators and statistical measures hides not only the theoretical assumptions of such indicators but also the deeper causes of human rights violations.[34] As Sally Engle Merry states, "the deployment of statistical measures tends to replace political debate with technical expertise. The growing reliance on indicators provides an example of the dissemination of the corporate form of thinking and governance into broader social spheres."[35] There is nothing wrong with numbers per se, but when presented without contextual details, such as the role of the Forensic Medicine Agency in covering up torture, such measures do not tell us enough about the reality of torture in the country.

The tendency to draw crude comparisons between human rights problems under Mubarak and his successors is another example whereby international reporting of torture in Egypt can lack critical context.[36] This problem builds, in large part, on the first, for such comparisons are primarily based on the number of torture cases before and after Mubarak. But while it is important to note continuities in state practice over time, it is also important to examine the shifting contextual issues that shape and enable human rights violations. Consider, for example, the role of laws that narrowly define torture or that limit the rights of citizens to sue public officers. To compare only human rights abuses under Mubarak and his successors tells us little about how or why things got better or worse. Rather, we need in-depth, qualitative comparisons that examine how Mubarak and his successors dealt with the policing apparatus, and we need research that looks at what changes have been made to the despotic legislative structure. Similarly, we need comparisons that gauge how people's awareness of torture and their anger about these issues have shifted over time and whether, for example, this has made them more likely to report and demand responses to abuses. Conversely, we need also to consider whether Egyptians felt any pressure to suppress accounts of torture under Morsi, given their desire to present a success story of the country's first democratically elected president.

On a fundamental level, the framing of the problem in terms of whether more or less torture is happening in Egypt misses the point. The more important questions concern who is being targeted for torture and why; how structural conditions in the police apparatus, the legislature, and the economy have enabled the continuation of such practices; and what impact the revolution has had on people's mind-set.

As discussed earlier, under Mubarak, systematic torture was used against not only accused criminals and political dissidents but also the economically marginalized. The most important cases here are incidents of collective punishment for peasants who resisted new land reform laws and workers who organized or attempted to organize strikes. In some cases, security forces and armored vehicles blatantly attacked factories and killed workers; the most famous instance of this was the storming of the state-owned Helwan Steel Factory in 1989 to end a workers' strike by force, in which a worker was killed. To what extent, then, have the economic conditions that underpinned such practices shifted since the ousting of Mubarak?

During the transitional period under the SCAF and then Morsi, Egypt has been undergoing a serious economic crisis.[37] For example, the last budget under Morsi (2013–14) revealed astonishing numbers. This was the budget being discussed in the upper house (Shoura Council) when this essay was first being drafted. According to these numbers, new investments are expected to be no more than 15 percent, compared to 22 percent in 2008. The growth rate declined 2 percent to its lowest point in years. Government representatives stated their hope to raise this to 7 percent by 2022. In the meantime, the unemployment rate is approximately 13 percent of the workforce. Poverty affects about 50 percent of the population in some areas of the countryside. The poorest 20 percent in Egypt are getting only about 10 percent of Egypt's national gross domestic product (GDP), while the richest 20 percent control nearly 40 percent of the GDP. The deficit in Egypt's budget was projected to reach almost $32 billion in 2013–14 alone.[38]

Yet both the SCAF and Morsi continued to seek international loans and pursue neoliberal adjustments, without questioning their effect on the rising numbers of poor or on the development of democratic institutions. Furthermore, both regimes resisted proposals for police reform, and indeed, Morsi decided to raise the salaries of police officers.[39] The state security apparatus has been renamed the National Security Agency, but the change appears to be entirely superficial. Police and military have continued to storm factories and use force against workers in different parts of Egypt to end labor strikes, and torture has continued in Egyptian police stations.[40] Indeed, systematic violence and police assaults have increased radically against protesters in the streets. But the key is not just to point to the rise in statistical rates of torture from one regime to another but to provide a contextual comparison of the impact of neoliberal conditions and the resistance of the state repressive apparatus to reform, regardless of who has been in power.

The specific forms of human rights abuse and torture that emerged during the Muslim Brotherhood's year in power, for example, warrant study. Alaa al-Aswany, a prominent Egyptian novelist and writer, has suggested that the undemocratic nature of the Muslim Brotherhood explains the specific forms of abuse under Morsi's rule.[41] Other Egyptian critics have proposed that we need a new framework to understand how the Muslim Brotherhood has been transformed from a historically victimized group under Mubarak to an authoritarian group that justifies torture of its opposition. In spring 2013, a conservative prosecutor ordered that a detainee, arrested while drunk, be whipped, in keeping with shari'a law.[42] The vagueness of the new constitution provided room for this interpretation. One can thus argue that human rights abuses in Egypt took a new twist when the Islamists came to power. But as we have argued, this is still only a small part of the story of human rights abuses in Egypt, both before and after the revolution.

Notably, the reporting on torture has the potential to reify colonialist savior discourses that manifest here in terms of the cry for human rights from here (the Global North) to there (Egypt). For instance, nearly all of the international human rights reports we studied define torture as a problem internal to the Egyptian domestic state while ignoring the ways the United States and Egypt collaborate in the torture that takes place within Egypt. This omission has the effect of reducing the culprits to excessively repressive Arab regimes and thus reinforcing the existing conceptualization in the Global North of Arab societies as excessively violent and in need of Western democracy, human rights, and intervention.

Consider, for example, Human Rights Watch's and Amnesty International's reporting on torture in Egypt. On one hand, it is important to recognize that both organizations seek to reveal grievous practices around the world that tend to affect the most marginalized populations. Both organizations also produce high-quality, rigorous research that is, in many cases, conducted with the assistance of human rights colleagues and local representatives in the countries in question. What they also share in common, however, is a tendency to focus on civil and political rights to the detriment of social and economic rights.[43] Amnesty International's reports accord some attention to international geopolitics, such as the United States' constant support of consecutive regimes in Egypt since the revolution, but Human Rights Watch reports tend to frame the human rights situation in Egypt as a purely domestic problem between repressive regime(s) and a suffering or struggling population.[44] Overall, both organizations fail to provide a more in-depth discussion of the broader political and economic contexts in which human rights abuses occur.

In this sense, both approaches reify the liberal–Orientalist discourses that have emerged repeatedly in the U.S. corporate news media. A report published in the *New York Times* during the period of Morsi's rule exemplifies these discourses.[45] Providing examples of torture that took place under Morsi, including violence by his supporters against revolutionary youth and the opposition, the report explains the torture through an analysis of primarily sectarian and religious differences that characterized all of these cases. Despite the usefulness of the report and the fact that the cases were, indeed, well documented by Egyptian human rights nongovernmental organizations, the discussion of sectarianism and religion is simplistic. The dominant narrative—that Islamists are torturers and that they torture their opposition out of sectarian and religious motives—fails to comment on the broader political context, including the fact that both the SCAF and the Muslim Brotherhood relied on sectarian policies as a strategy for maintaining political power in the context of an ongoing revolution. In other words, they did not practice torture simply because they are Islamists; they practiced torture because it was politically efficacious to do so.

Conclusion

Human rights are a crucial indicator for the evaluation of democratic processes. After all, the revolution itself was triggered by incidents of police brutality, and the famous Facebook page "We Are All Khaled Said" that mobilized so many people for the revolution was named after a blogger who died as a result of police brutality. Egyptians revolted against Mubarak's despotism and corruption, specifically against election fraud, police brutality, and attacks on freedom of assembly and association, among other things. But as many Egyptians and outside critics have emphasized, the Egyptian revolution was *against* the neoliberal state as much as it was *for* democracy.[46] The main slogans of the revolution reflected this: protesters called for bread, liberty, and economic and social justice at the same time. The decontextualized liberal–Orientalist "cry for human rights" fails to grasp this about the revolution and, thus, fails to recognize the full range of aspirations that have yet to be realized.

What, then, does it mean to contextualize the problems of gendered sexual violence and torture within the local and global conditions that both led to the revolution and face Egyptians today? An analysis that focuses primarily on interpersonal violence perpetrated by Egyptian men on Egyptian women cannot comprehensively explain problems such as sexual harassment in the Egyptian streets. As we have seen, the various Egyptian governing powers (Mubarak, the SCAF, and the Muslim Brotherhood) practiced gendered sexual violence directly (by targeting women protesters, for instance) and indirectly (by legitimizing it through their actions or failing to hold perpetrators accountable). U.S. imperial practices have also contributed to sexual violence in Egypt as programs such as extraordinary rendition support, enable, and reinforce the acceptability of such violence as a form of domination and control. Similarly, problems such as women's exclusion from official politics cannot be solved solely through methods that seek to achieve equality between individual men and women (such as quota systems). These issues require larger structural changes, among them ending the violence against women activists that can dissuade women from political participation and creating a democratic regime that is not corrupt.

A comprehensive analysis of torture similarly requires an examination of the neoliberal conditions through which torture and other forms of violence have developed and expanded in Egypt. It requires stepping back from the misleading allure of statistics and the search for easy answers rooted in assumptions about the inherent violence and repression of certain regimes or religions. It requires recognizing the ways that broader neoliberal economic strategies continue to create the conditions of torture and repression. It also requires more rigorous analysis about how torture targets both political opposition and economically marginalized groups—something that was happening before the revolution and continued in the transition.

Locating violence in Egypt within these transnational contexts can inform the ways scholars and activists seek to build solidarity with Egyptian people and the Egyptian revolution. For instance, feminists committed to supporting Egyptian women's struggles might consider working for change in relation to multiple, simultaneous structures of gender violence, including U.S.-led militarism and war as well as Egyptian state corruption. We might imagine what it could look like if more scholars and activists in the

United States were to focus on the accountability of the U.S. state in contributing to various forms of violence that Egyptian women and men face (such as poverty, torture, and gender violence) rather than pointing their finger at abstract notions of Egyptian culture, gender, sexuality, or rights. Efforts to reimagine transnational solidarity with a critique of the U.S. empire at the center is one strategy for transcending liberal–Orientalist approaches to human rights and their colonial underpinnings. Ultimately, this essay is a call to develop forms of transnational scholarship that analyze political transitions, human rights, and diverse forms of violence, while taking into account the role of international geopolitics and imperialism as well as the neoliberal conditions of misery that characterize the Middle East, Africa, and so many developing nations. Such scholarship should be based on international solidarity, not cultural homogenizations and Orientalist epistemologies and methodologies. And perhaps most important, such scholarship should be less concerned with "saving" certain populations and more concerned with recognizing and representing the full breadth of their experiences and aspirations.

Notes

First and foremost, we acknowledge every Egyptian martyr, each person who has stood on the front lines in Egypt, and everyone who has participated in our research. We are also immensely grateful to Amal Fadlalla, Omolade Adunbi, Kim Greenwell, Jesse Carr, and the external reviewers for their invaluable feedback and editorial assistance. We also would like to thank Gigi Ibrahim for permission to use her photographs in this essay.

1. See a good analysis on the *Salon* website about *Fox News* coverage during the first few days of the Egyptian revolution in 2011, when most of Fox's discussion centered on Islam and Islamists. "The Egyptian Revolution as Told by Fox News," *Salon*, February 1, 2011.

2. Edward W. Said, *Orientalism* (New York: Vintage, 1979). See also Nadine Naber, *Arab America* (New York: New York University Press, 2012); Minoo Moallem, *Between Warrior Brother and Veiled Sister: Islamic Fundamentalism and the Politics of Patriarchy in Iran* (Berkeley: University of California Press, 2005); Melani McAlister, *Epic Encounters: Culture, Media, and U.S. Interests in the Middle East, 1945–2000* (Berkeley: University of California Press, 2001); and Evelyn Alsultany *Arabs and Muslims in the Media: Race and Representation after 9/11* (New York: New York University Press, 2012).

3. Lila Abu-Lughod, *Do Muslim Women Need Saving?* (Cambridge, Mass.: Harvard University Press, 2013); Miriam Ticktin, *Casualties of Care: Immigration and the Politics of Humanitarianism in France* (Berkeley: University of California Press, 2011).

4. Sally Engle Merry, "Transnational Human Rights and Local Activism: Mapping the Middle," *American Anthropologist* 108, no. 1 (2006): 38–51.

5. Leti Volpp, "Feminism versus Multiculturalism," *Columbia Law Review* 101, no. 5 (2001): 1181–218.

6. Lila Abu-Lughod, "Seductions of the 'Honor Crime,'" *differences: A Journal of Feminist Cultural Studies* 22, no. 1 (2011): 17–63; Sherene Razack, *Casting Out: The Eviction of Muslims from Western Law and Politics* (Toronto: University of Toronto Press, 2007).

7. The difference between the Muslim Brotherhood and the Freedom and Justice Party confuses many observers, particularly given the former's increasing politicization over time. Briefly, the Muslim Brotherhood was illegal under Mubarak but continued to survive and grow. After the revolution, its leaders established the Freedom and Justice Party as an explicitly political party. But not all members of the Muslim Brotherhood are members of the Freedom and Justice Party, and indeed, the relationship between the two entities is often unclear and ambivalent, even to those within the organizations.

8. Ali Younis, "Egypt: The First Nation Ever to Revolt against Democracy?," *Foreign Policy in Focus*, November 8, 2013. See also Ray Hanania, "Egypt Proves Western Democracy Doesn't Work in Arab World," *Creators*, June 2013; Michael Hirsh, "When Democracy Doesn't Work," *National Journal*, January 15, 2014.

9. We refer to this as the "early" or "first" transitional period, given that yet another transition is now taking place following the ousting of Morsi in July 2013.

10. Adam Hanieh, "Egypt's 'Orderly Transition'? International Aid and Rush to Structural Adjustments," *Jadaliyya*, May 29, 2011.

11. Kareem Fahim, "In Upheaval for Egypt, Morsi Forces Out Military Chiefs," *New York Times*, August 12, 2012.

12. Atef Said, "Imperialist Liberalism and the Egyptian Revolution," *Jadaliyya*, April 13, 2013. Also see Dina el-Khawaga, "Democracy Is Not Just a Ballot Box," *Egypt Independent*, January 4, 2013.

13. See, e.g., Hassan Hassan, "Even as the Sands Shift, the Brotherhood Stays the Same," *The National*, February 4, 2014; Cynthia Schneider, "U.S. Gets It Wrong with Egypt," Brookings Institution, January 25, 2013, http://www.brookings.edu/research/opinions/2013/01/25–egypt-schneider; Khaled Shaalan, "Why the Western Media Is Getting the Muslim Brotherhood Wrong," *Jadaliyya*, July 3, 2013; and Michael Totten, "Getting the Muslim Brotherhood Wrong," *World Affairs Journal*, July 11, 2013.

14. Amnesty International, "Egypt: Human Rights in the Arab Republic of Egypt," http://www.amnesty.org/en/region/egypt; see esp. annual reports 2007–11.

15. Alexandra Petri, "What Happened to Lara Logan Was Unacceptable," *Washington Post*, February 15, 2011, and "Lara Logan Breaks Silence on Cairo Assault," CBS News, May 1, 2011, http://www.cbsnews.com/news/lara-logan-breaks-silence-on-cairo-assault/.

16. Atef Said, "The Paradox of Transition to 'Democracy' under Military Rule," *Social Research: An International Quarterly* 79, no. 2 (2012): 397–434. El Nadim Center for Rehabilitation of Victims of Violence, "Once Again, Women Speak Out: Results of a Field Research on Violence against Women in Egypt," April 5, 2009, https://alnadeem.org/en/node/384; Paul Amar, "Turning the Gendered Politics of the Security State Inside Out?," *International Feminist Journal of Politics* 13, no. 3

(2011): 299–328. In 2005, Mubarak's military attacked and sexually assaulted women journalists, as reported by the Committee to Protect Journalists and the Egyptian Organization for Human Rights. Although this case led to a constitutional referendum in 2005, it received virtually no attention from the international community. See Committee to Protect Journalists, "Egypt: Documents, 2005," http://cpj.org/mideast/egypt/2005/, and "New Law Still Threatens Press Freedoms," July 12, 2006, http://cpj.org/2006/12/new-law-still-threatens -press-freedoms.php.

17. See, e.g., Human Rights Watch Staff, "Egypt: Prosecute Sexual Assaults on Protesters: Punish Military and Police Attackers," *Human Rights Watch,* December 22, 2011; Human Rights Watch Staff, "Egypt: Military Impunity for Violence against Women," *Human Rights Watch,* April 7, 2012; Amnesty International, *Egypt: Checklist to Combat Sexual and Gender-Based Violence* (London: Amnesty International Publications, 2013); Amnesty International, *Egypt: Gender-Based Violence against Women around Tahrir Square* (London: Amnesty International Publications, 2013).

18. Peter Bergen, "I Was Kidnapped by the CIA," *Mother Jones,* March/April 2008.

19. Ibid.

20. El Nadim Center for Rehabilitation of Victims of Violence, "Testimonies," https://alnadeem.org/en; Jasbir Puar, *Terrorist Assemblages: Homonationalism in Queer Times* (Durham, N.C.: Duke University Press, 2007); Sherene Razack, "How Is White Supremacy Embodied? Sexualized Racial Violence at Abu Ghraib," *Canadian Journal of Women and the Law* 17, no. 2 (2005): 341–63; Amar, "Turning the Gendered Politics of the Security State Inside Out?"; Committee to Protect Journalists, "Attacks on the Press, 2005: Egypt," http://cpj.org/2006/02/attacks-on-the -press-2005–egypt.php.

21. Ken Coates, *Extraordinary Rendition* (Nottingham, U.K.: Spokesman Books, 2006).

22. See, e.g., Amnesty International, "Egyptian Women Protesters Forced to Take 'Virginity Tests,'" March 23, 2011, http://www.amnesty.org.uk/ news_details .asp?NewsID 19340; "Egypt Court Ends Virginity Tests," BBC, December 27, 2011, http://www.bbc.co.uk/news/world-middle-east-16339398.

23. See, e.g., Sally Quinn, "The Blue Bra Revolution," *Washington Post,* December 30, 2011; "Blue Bra Beating Spurs Rallies from 'the Girls of Egypt,'" *National Post,* December 20, 2011, http://nationalpost.com/news/the-girls-of-egypt-rally-after-blue -bra-beating.

24. Nazra for Feminist Studies, "Position Paper on Sexual Violence," February 3, 2013, http://nazra.org/en/2013/02/position-paper-sexual-violence-against-women -and-increasing-frequency-gang-rape-tahrir; Dina Samir, "Egyptian Women Still Struggling for Rights Two Years after Revolution," *Ahram Online,* February 12, 2013.

25. "Sexual Violence and Sexual Torture against Women Will Not Thwart Their Struggle to Fulfill the Goals of the Revolution,"   , http://nwrcegypt .org/?p 8257.

26. In September 2009, the World Bank named Egypt one of "the world's 10 most active reformers" for the fourth time. In February 2010, just days prior to the revolutionary uprising, the IMF issued a glowing report on the Egyptian economy, declaring that "economic performance was better than expected" and praising the

government's "careful fiscal management." Stephen Maher, "The Political Economy of the Egyptian Uprising," *Monthly Review* 63, no. 6 (2011), http://monthlyreview.org/2011/11/01/the-political-economy-of-the -egyptian-uprising/.

27. Groups of Civil Society Organizations, "Egypt: Universal Periodic Review, Midterm Evaluation Report," http://www.upr-info.org/followup/assessments/session20/ egypt/Egypt-Joint.pdf.

28. Samer Soliman, *The Autumn of Dictatorship: Fiscal Crisis and Political Change in Egypt under Mubarak* (Stanford, Calif.: Stanford University Press, 2011).

29. Abdel Khaleq Farouq, *Roots of Administrative Corruption in Egypt* (Cairo: Shorouk Press, 2008).

30. Mohamed Abdel Hakam Diab, "Egypt between Mummifying Mubarak and the Succession Catastrophe," *Egypt Window*, July, 4, 2009.

31. Atef Said, *Torture in Egypt Is a Crime against Humanity* (Cairo: Hisham Mubarak Law Center, 2008).

32. Omar Ashraf, "100 days of Morsi Rule: 100 Days of Detentions, Torture, Violent Crash on Protests and Killing Outside the Law," El Nadim Center for Rehabilitation of Victims of Violence, https://alnadeem.org/en/node/421.

33. By "descriptive reporting," we mean reports that emphasize describing incidents or tallying numbers only, without making connections to previous incidents or discussing torture's commonality context more broadly.

34. Lughod, "Seductions of the 'Honor Crime'"; Sally Engle Merry, "Measuring the World: Indicators, Human Rights and Global Governance," *Current Anthropology* 52, suppl. 3 (April 2011): 583–95.

35. Merry, "Measuring the World," 584.

36. Osman El Sharnoubi, "Is Torture on the Rise under President Mohamed Morsi?," *Ahram Online*, February 21, 2013.

37. Shana Marshall and Joshua Stacher, "Egypt's Generals and Transnational Capital," *Middle East Research and Information Project* 42, no. 262 (2013), http://www.merip.org/mer/mer262/egypts-generals-transnational-capital; Rachel Shabi, "Egyptians Are Being Held Back by Neoliberalism, Not Religion," *Guardian*, December 20, 2012.

38. Al-Masry al-Youm, "State Budget Submitted to Shura Council for Discussion," *Egypt Independent*, April 23, 2013.

39. Sally Roshdy and Wessal Montasser, "Restructuring the Egyptian Police Sector: A Genuine Attempt towards Reform, or an Insincere Effort?," One World Foundation, September 2012, http://www.owf-eg.org/Gallery/10_31_2012_11_15_20_AM.pdf.

40. "Egypt Orders $2.5mln Worth of Teargas from US Despite Plunging Economy," *RT Question More*, February 23, 2013.

41. Alaa al-Aswany, "Acts of Torture Reveal True Nature of Egypt's Muslim Brotherhood," *Al-Monitor*, March 2013.

42. Mamdouh Thabet, "Egypt Probes Prosecutor Who Ordered Drunk Flogged," *ABC News*, April 22, 2013.

43. This conclusion is based on a quick survey of all the titles and tables of contents of reports produced by the two organizations from 2011 to mid-2013. The titles and reports are available on the Egypt page of each organization's website.

44. See, e.g., Amnesty International, "USA Repeatedly Shipped Arms Supplies to Egyptian Security Forces," https://www.amnesty.org/en/news/usa-repeatedly -shipped-arms-supplies-egyptian-security-forces-2011-12-06; Human Rights Watch, "Egypt: Rash of Deaths in Custody," https://www.hrw.org/news/2015/01/21/egypt -rash-deaths-custody.

45. Robert Mackey, "Evidence of Torture by Egyptian Islamists," *New York Times*, December 11, 2012, http://thelede.blogs.nytimes.com/2012/12/11/evidence-of-tor ture-by-egyptian-islamists/.

46. Walter Armbrust, "Egypt: A Revolution against Neoliberalism?," *Al-Jazeera*, February 24, 2011, http://www.aljazeera.com/indepth/opinion/2011/02/201122414 315249621.html; Jane Kinninmont, "'Bread, Dignity, and Social Justice': The Politi- cal Economy of Egypt's Transition," Chatham House Briefing Paper, April, 2012; Maher, "Political Economy of the Egyptian Uprising."

15

Learning in the Shadow of the War on Terror

Toward a Pedagogy of Muslim Indignation

ARSHAD IMTIAZ ALI

> The government says that I was obsessed with violence, obsessed with "killing Americans." But, as a Muslim living in these times, I can think of a lie no more ironic.
>
> —TAREK MEHANNA, *United States v. Mehanna*

On April 12, 2012, Tarek Mehanna, a twenty-nine-year-old American-born pharmacist, was sentenced to seventeen and a half years in prison for conspiring to provide material support to terrorists, conspiring to kill in a foreign country, and providing false evidence to the FBI. Mehanna's convictions were based on two primary activities: (1) U.S. attorneys alleged that in 2004, he spent an entire week in Yemen purportedly to seek out an al-Qaeda training camp—although none were known to exist in Yemen at the time—and (2) he provided "material support" for al-Qaeda and other jihadist groups through his online activity, although the government conceded that he was not coordinating his writing with any organization. A few of the "criminal" activities named in Mehanna's indictment were that he "watched jihadi videos," explored the "religious justification" for suicide bombings, and "created and/or translated, accepted credit for authoring and distributed text, videos and other media to inspire others to engage in violent jihad." The consumption of media and participation in online discussions were themselves the crimes he committed.

When Mehanna was convicted for speaking and writing publicly about the right to defend one's homeland in opposition to U.S. empire, he made a compelling statement at his sentencing hearing:

> So, this trial was not about my position on Muslims killing American civilians. It was about my position on Americans killing Muslim civilians, which

is that Muslims should defend their lands from foreign invaders—Soviets, Americans, or Martians. This is what I believe. It's what I've always believed, and what I will always believe.

. . . When that home is a Muslim land, and that invader is the US military, for some reason the standards suddenly change. Common sense is renamed "terrorism" and the people defending themselves against those who come to kill them from across the ocean become "the terrorists" who are "killing Americans."[1]

Regardless if one believes or opposes Mehanna's positions, his words and beliefs—rather than particular actions—were the basis of his conviction. I begin this chapter about Muslim students on college campuses because the ideologies that fueled Mehanna's conviction insidiously guide the surveillance and policing of Muslim students, both on and off campus. Such a theory, of Muslim radicalization, not only informs the direct legal targets of prosecution like Mehanna but also creates a context for cultural suspicion and violence against Muslim bodies. Like Mehanna, Muslim students are treated as suspects on their college campuses. Policing agencies (local and the FBI) have spied on Muslim college students throughout the country and have noted that college campuses are specific "sites of radicalization" without any evidence. The former spokesperson for the New York Police Department (NYPD) specifically stated that college campuses were sites of al-Qaeda recruitment.[2] There is no evidence of this. All Muslim students are suspects because of the bodies they occupy. As Sohail Daultazai and Junaid Rana remind us, "terror is the new race talk—the 'terrorist' (or the 'militant' or the 'radical') is the twenty-first century way of saying 'savage.'"[3] This chapter examines how a context of suspicion of Muslim bodies and politics in private and public spaces limits dissent, controls political subjectivity, and hampers the development of a left Muslim politic and community in the United States, particularly on college campuses. Like in the case of Mehanna, Muslim student speech and thought are what policing agencies target.

The domestic strategy of the U.S. War on Terror is guided by a loose theory of radicalization that assumes a linear trajectory of political critique to violence.[4] Within a framework of radicalization theory, increased religiosity and community participation contribute to a process in which "good Muslims" transform into terrorists.[5] Accordingly, all Muslims are susceptible to "radicalized" violence through this process of religious engagement and political grievance.[6]

U.S. law enforcement agencies have operationalized the notion of radicalization through simplistic, narrow, and reductionist understandings of human consciousness. Together, law enforcement and the FBI have conceived of a "religious conveyor belt" model in which an individual moves along a linear path, beginning with political grievance and culminating in terrorism.[7] This is depicted in *Radicalization in the West*, the 2007 FBI document that outlines a stepwise process in which an individual "becomes radicalized," spanning grievance, personal crisis, religiosity, adoption of radical beliefs, and, ultimately, terrorism.[8] Many of the FBI-identified markers are common spiritual and communal activities in Muslim communities, including regular mosque attendance, religious conversion, and growing a beard or wearing a kufi for men.[9] Islamic practice is a precursor to terrorism within this framework. Succinctly, this translates to the more a Muslim engages an Islamic tradition, the higher the level of suspicion grows. As Arun Kundani notes, the claims made to support "radicalization theory" in publications such as the NYPD document are based on poorly designed research, a lack of evidence, and inconsistent logic.[10]

In Mehanna's case, the government argued that his writings, studies, and conversations were indisputable proof that he would eventually engage in violence against civilians in the United States. The Mehanna trial, moreover, provides an important case study to situate the lives and experiences of Muslim college students, particularly in the New York Tri-State area, as young Muslims were well aware of his case and the evidence used in his conviction. Tarek Mehanna is not simply context; his case was a practical lesson for Muslim youth activists in the region. Beyond the cultural racism embedded in radicalization theory, this theory presupposes the notion that to act violently with a political objective is only legitimate when done by the U.S. empire. Thus the surveillance of Muslim communities throughout the United States should not be understood as isolated from what is happening on college campuses; rather, the campus should be seen as an extension of the national landscape. For example, the USA PATRIOT Act (2001/2011) gives the FBI the ability to collect e-mails, academic records, rosters, or "any tangible thing" that it deems relevant to an investigation.[11] With the FBI's wide reach, Muslim students are taught that participation in any form of political critique may be read as a step toward "radicalization" by the state security apparatus.[12] Muslim students and professors at institutions of higher education are particularly vulnerable to government surveillance and other attacks upon their First Amendment rights.[13] In this context, NYPD spokesperson Paul Browne asserted, "Some of the most dangerous

Western Al Qaeda–linked/inspired terrorists since 9/11 were radicalized and/or recruited at universities in MSAs [Muslim student associations]."[14]
As Piya Chatterjee and Sunaina Maira remind us,

> while the FBI has interviewed unknown numbers of Muslim and Arab American college students and infiltrated and monitored Muslim student organizations since 9/11, counterterrorism experts have generated models of "radicalization" of Muslim youth, especially males, invoking cultural pathologies of "hate" and alienation.[15]

Such formulations reflect the basest forms of cultural racism—they structure the way programs and policies observe and police Muslim communities nationally. As Muslim organizations increasingly partner with law enforcement to establish the "counterradicalization programs," they adopt the logic of empire to monitor their own communities, thus creating a society in which, as Jeremy Bentham described more than 225 years ago, "each comrade becomes an overseer."[16] The surveillance regime pushes Muslim communities to adopt a logic of suspicion toward each other; this suspicion is operationalized through viewing anti-imperialist politics as a precursor to non–state sanctioned violence, or terrorism. Beyond the state, we must ask, What does the treatment of entire Muslim communities as potential terrorists mean for young Muslim women and men? What does the criminalization of the opposition to state terrorism teach Muslim students? What does the surveillance regime teach Muslim youth activists about their role within the United States? In this context, when Muslim youth and communities are criminalized and targeted by the police state, Muslims are also subject to increasing threats of violence and discrimination.[17] Schools are where this happens most often.[18]

In this chapter, I draw on data from an eighteen-month-long research project working with Muslim student activists in New York City. The project gauged young Muslims' experiences of one of the domestic strategies of the U.S. War on Terror—the silencing of political discourse. I examined how university and college students understand what they are "allowed" to discuss in public spaces and how they construct their roles and identities within the U.S. body politic. These young people have grown up in a world in which the domestic War on Terror limits their ability to express dissent and manages their political subjectivity.[19] I argue that the silencing of their political voices creates fear, suspicion, and localized terror within communities and serves to further U.S. imperial objectives globally.

MUSLIM STUDENT ACTIVISTS IN NEW YORK CITY

In August 2011, the Associated Press reported details of the NYPD's surveillance of Muslims throughout the northwestern United States.[20] One of the initial reports documented surveillance of Muslim students on college campuses among a much broader surveillance net that targeted mosques, community centers, cafés, restaurants, and parks. The *Weekly MSA Report* named dozens of campuses that were surveilled each week through reading e-mails, attending events, and noting organizers and speakers as well as the topics of discussion, activities, and events.[21] Although the information in this report was seemingly benign, the sheer idea that Muslim students on college campuses were seen as threats deeply troubled many students.

In light of this information, a small group of political activists engaged in youth work—including myself—convened at the New York Muslim Students Coalition (NYMSC) to engage Muslim students and help them develop community organization skills in order to challenge the NYPD surveillance program. Through this project, I conducted a participatory action ethnographic study of Muslim student politics and political organizing in New York City. In my role as a cofacilitator of the NYMSC, I conducted informal and formal interviews with students, recorded selected meetings and focus groups, and took ethnographic field notes at NYMSC meetings and community events.[22]

STAY OUT OF THE CROSS HAIRS

Radicalization theories provide the ideological foundation for spying on Muslim communities and create the political context in which "anti-American viewpoints" are criminalized. These are but two ways the United States disciplines Muslim bodies in the domestic wing of the War on Terror. The young people with whom I worked in New York City were ever cognizant that their very lives—being young, Muslim, and politically engaged—constituted suspicious activity. They consistently censored their speech and conversations in public places because of these fears. In community centers, political organizing meetings, or even informally while eating at restaurants, students regularly confided, "I don't want to talk about that here." Politically active Muslim youth feared that the NYPD was listening to their conversations and potentially targeting them. Young people saw a decade of spurious convictions and believed they could just as easily become the next target.

Amal, for example, was a youth leader and volunteer at the Brooklyn community center where I did much of my fieldwork. She participated in a youth activism training program that I cofacilitated. Amal spoke extensively with her friends, members of the center's staff, and me about her personal and familial experiences of being tracked by the U.S. surveillance regime. In spring 2012, as part of a youth activist training program, youth leaders hosted a focus group and discussion addressing NYPD surveillance. In that meeting, Amal actively resisted talking about her experiences, even when asked about them directly. In the following days, I asked Amal about why she clammed up in our meetings—I knew she wasn't shy about speaking in public. She said that although she knew and trusted the people in the room individually, she didn't know if the center was a safe space to speak— she didn't know if the building itself was bugged. She didn't feel safe speaking openly about her political concerns inside of the building.

Through this exchange, Amal made clear that not only was she aware of an abstracted surveillance regime but she understood that surveillance was a reality in her specific community—at the mosque she attended and quite possibly at the center she went to after school. In this context, Amal obfuscated the question of who to trust by concerning herself with "where to trust." But in this regard, Amal was not discussing issues that policing agencies might consider "radicalized," as she was not talking about U.S. imperialism; rather, she was simply discussing the realities of the surveillance regime in her personal life. The material manifestations of police surveillance of Muslim bodies make naming the surveillance off-limits for young Muslims—Amal was concerned that in simply naming her reality, she might become a target of policing agencies. Thus a physical place youth spent hours each week after school was not considered a "safe space" to share the experiences of government repression.

We don't know if the building was bugged, and that is not particularly important. Rather, what is important is that Amal was consciously fearful that it *might* be, and that fear disciplined a particular speech act from occurring. It is through small acts of self-discipline, like this one, that the surveillance regime steals the ability of young people to build active, politically engaged, and radical communities. They are afraid to share their perspectives and struggles, which are at the heart of building political solidarity and radical movements.

Not only did fear of the surveillance regime exist in community spaces but young people were also concerned about who was listening to their words in public. In summer 2012, during a meal with a group of Muslim student activists in New York City, the topic of U.S. militarism in the Middle East came up. Before the conversation took shape, Ishmael, a recent college graduate and community organizer, stated, "Let's not talk about that here" and quickly changed the conversation to the upcoming NBA season. Many of these young people, including Layla and Ishmael, whose voices I share later in this chapter, discussed anti-imperialist critiques of the United States, debated forms of resistance to U.S. Middle Eastern policy, and explored forms of direct action political organizing in the United States in private homes. In addition, Ishmael was not shy about sharing his political perspectives, but it was clear that he was uncomfortable engaging the topic of U.S. military intervention in the Middle East. Later that evening, in a more private exchange, he stated to me that he "didn't want to talk about that stuff in public . . . you don't know who's listening, you know? Or whose ears open up."

Ishmael's desire not to talk about Middle Eastern politics in a restaurant reveals that Muslim youth recognize a stark difference between what James Scott has referred to as the public and private transcripts of communication. Scott's work teaches us that subordinated groups "sanitize" their public speech to "engage in the rituals that will keep them from harm."[23] The young men and women are conscious that "everyday Americans" look at them with suspicious glances and that the surveillance state may always be listening. For many of these young people, a clear strategy to stay out of the cross hairs is to talk sports instead of politics.

I asked Layla how she understood that break in the conversation, to which she replied,

> That was good. He wasn't being too cautious. We shouldn't talk like that. . . .
> We [Muslims] have to think about what we say in public. . . . I mean it's like
> you know you shouldn't even talk about certain things . . . like Israel or resis-
> tance or even the U.S. in critical ways. . . . It's not that we shouldn't, but we
> can't. Come on, [we] know what happened to [Mehanna].

Layla's comment points to the fact that these young Muslims believed discussing global politics raised red flags for the surveillance regime. Knowing about the numerous cases of young Muslims being imprisoned on fallacious charges, these youth cannot forget the reality in which they live. Through working with Muslim student activists in New York City, it became clear to me that young Muslims believed some conversational topics were simply off-limits in public. They feared having such conversations in places where others might be listening or with individuals they did not know well. Their self-censorship grew out of the FBI's and NYPD's ideological policing of Muslims. The students were keenly aware that the NYPD was employing agent provocateurs—spies—and hiring community members as informants to report on what was being said and done within community spaces. Thus they regularly worried about who they could and could not trust.

In this anxious atmosphere of suspicion and self-censorship, politically significant conversations are pushed into private spaces. In a context in which people fear being labeled a radical because they critique U.S. imperialism, and in which they worry that their words over a meal might be reported to the state security apparatus, young people not only censor what they say in public but will inevitably alter what they think in private. This process limits dissent, controls political subjectivity, and stunts the development of a politically engaged community of young Muslims.

The University Is Not a Safe Space for Muslim Student Associations

Proponents of the liberal university imagine classrooms as spaces of curiosity, freedom, and intellectual exploration, although American universities have been tied to the building and maintenance of U.S. empire for decades.[24] Muslim students on college campuses know better than to believe in this liberal ideal. Even though Muslim student organizations were targeted by the NYPD and named as "sites of radicalization" by the FBI, many student activists found the Muslim organizations on their campuses to be apolitical or politically liberal. Layla was engaged with multiple community-based organizations off campus. She was also involved in a campus political organization but steered clear of the Muslim student organization because "they don't care about anything happening in the world; it's just talks about intentions." Likewise, Ibrahim, a sophomore at a Brooklyn college, did not want to participate in his campus Muslim student organization, yet he was a leader in his mosque and local community and served as a coordinator for a community organization engaged in political education and service work. Ibrahim and Layla were just two of the many students who did not feel that their campus Muslim student organizations were places for political activism, organizing, or education.

The students with whom I worked considered their campus Muslim organizations to be politically benign and unengaged. The NYPD's surveillance of Muslim student organizations—alongside mosques, cafés, and other locations—which were, in their experience, the least politically charged or effective venues, provided further evidence to the students that Muslims as a whole are being targeted. Muslim student organizations have become increasingly depoliticized in the twenty-first century. As discussed earlier, Muslim students and student organizations are closely monitored by state surveillance agencies, and often by campus officials as well. In this political context, it is easy to understand why young people in college might veer away from discussing politics—they fear they might be increasingly targeted if they do.

As student groups avoid politically "dangerous" topics, the opportunities to discuss shared perspectives, histories, or experiences are muted. In "Muslim spaces," Muslim students cannot discuss radical politics or even their experiences of surveillance.

Beyond participation in the Muslim student organization, students believed that their classrooms were not safe spaces to share their perspectives either. Meena, a junior humanities major, said that in her Middle Eastern studies courses, she was cautious of what she said in discussions. She stated, "You don't know who is listening or really who anyone is. I don't want to say anything that might be read the wrong way." Likewise, Malik, a senior Middle Eastern studies major, explained, "Of course, it's not just that some people disagree with what I say—whatever. It's the police spying and the fact that what I say could be 'un-American' or something." Students regularly expressed that they were concerned that their words and perspectives would be "read the wrong way." This fear reminds us that the Muslim occupies the role of the "savage" in contemporary American political discourse.[25] The Muslim, even the upwardly mobile college student, has the potential to "go extremist."

Students knew that the NYPD was present on college campuses, as the secret documents released by the Associated Press revealed. Numerous students from throughout the city reported that they had heard of someone who was approached by the NYPD because of what the person had said in a class. This knowledge cultivated an intellectual and cultural space in which Muslim students believed that speaking publicly against U.S. empire—even in a classroom—would put them in the cross hairs of the surveillance regime. As Amal succinctly stated, "of course, just because it's a classroom doesn't make it safe."

This did not mean that all students stopped engaging in classroom discourse and debate. Rather, students had to make active choices about when to potentially draw increased scrutiny. For example, Layla believed she could not shield herself from being watched. She said, "The NYPD is already surveilling us in our communities and the mosque, so why should

I not say what I think when I am in a classroom?" Likewise, many of the students saw this as a catch-22. They believed the surveillance regime would hone in on them if they were outspoken but also knew their communities were generally being monitored. As one of the young women said, "you are damned if you do, or if you don't, so why not?" Such comments evidence the students' awareness that the NYPD tactics serve to police speech acts and thoughts rather than to serve and protect residents of New York like themselves.

All of the students with whom I spoke thought deeply about what they said on their college campuses, whether in student group meetings, in classrooms, or socially among peers. Although they did not have homogenous opinions on how to engage, or what to share, it is clear that all Muslim students carefully thought about how and what perspectives and opinions they would express publicly. Thus the college campus did not provide a "safe space" for students to feel they were free from surveillance; rather, some students were willing to speak openly while knowing policing agencies may be listening. The campus was simply another space for political disciplinary action for Muslim students, not a space for free or democratic discourse.

As the surveillance regime became increasingly normalized within U.S. culture, young Muslims from throughout New York City learned to negotiate and navigate this political context. In making choices of what beliefs to state and where, their opportunities for communal discussion narrowed. In losing opportunities simply to talk about their opposition to U.S. empire, they may have also internalized the view that such conversations are inherently unacceptable or wrong.

Within the apprehensive atmosphere provoked by the surveillance regime, young people monitored their words and asked themselves, Am I someone who should be watched? Should I not be who I am or think what I think? They recognized that simply being a Muslim critical of empire was enough to be labeled a Muslim radical.

Don't Trust Your Leaders

Muslim community leadership provided little support or direction for students who wanted to develop a more critical political agenda. Although students cited a few community leaders and imams who encouraged their activism, they saw the "Muslim establishment" as compliant with the state security apparatus, particularly in regard to NYPD surveillance. Although many Friday khutbahs denounced the NYPD's actions, few sermons offered structural critique of American empire or imperialism or even linked NYPD surveillance of Muslim communities to a larger project of the NYPD targeting Black and Brown communities for decades in New York City. The youth saw few community leaders as allies in developing a critical or radical position toward policing. Furthermore, several students said that their campus chaplains advised them that there was "nothing we could do about it [the NYPD], so we should just focus on being a good student," as Meena stated. At a February 2012 community meeting at a New York City campus, students were advised that they should not try to organize a response to the NYPD "on their own" but rather work with the "leadership" advocating on their behalf. The students were skeptical of guidance that encouraged political passivity. Many of the students pointed to the close relationship Muslim community leaders, particularly in New York City, had with the NYPD specifically and with city hall in general. Students were not simply critical of any leader who met with the political establishment in the city but were skeptical of those who had formal ties or who would not criticize or critique police and politicians.

Ultimately, student activists' skepticism of the direction they received from "responsible adults" in Muslim communities produced opportunities for students to ask questions about positionality, power, and political agendas. As Malik stated, "I'm sure campus administration knew when the NYPD was spying on their campus. Obviously, they don't want that getting out, so yeah, I bet they were pressing chaplains to slow us." Although students did not know if their chaplains, imams, or community leaders were working in collusion with the NYPD or FBI, the specter of fear and uncertainty created a social and political context in which students did not know who they could trust and who was actually working on their behalf. Students differed from one another about whether they believed their leaders were working in collaboration with the state, but they wholly disagreed with the guidance being offered. Furthermore, it allowed them to recognize that not all people who have power in their communities should be representing their interests. As Ibrahim stated, "when they aren't eating at Gracie Mansion [the New York City mayor's residence], maybe I'll take what they have to say seriously." As community leadership encouraged students to take a more passive political role or, at least, not actively organize themselves, the surveillance regime was reinforced. This was simply another way in which young Muslims were—and still are—tacitly told to keep their political critiques to themselves, or eliminate them altogether. Students were not able to find support for political activism and felt some parts of the Muslim community leadership concerned themselves more with their personal political objectives than with the needs of the community.

Make It Plain

Young Muslims are living in the shadow of the War on Terror. Their knowledge of NYPD surveillance and the reactions of Muslim community leadership created a crucible in which young people developed material understandings of the relationship between local policing and global politics. They experienced policing domestically as a way to quell dissent toward U.S. militarism overseas.

Although the students with whom I worked read about how the past decade had altered the social, political, and cultural landscape, and specifically the lives of Muslims in the United States, they cannot attest to this change firsthand. They have experienced a world in which a Muslim body is always looked at with suspicion and being Muslim is itself a threat to the state. They do not know a moment other than this. They do not know a "pre-9 11 world." Through their experiences, the United States has treated and continues to treat Muslims as domestic targets of an international war. Deportations, disappearances, domestic wiretapping, and the targeting of Muslim communities compose the domestic manifestations of the global War on Terror.[26] It is ever present in the dubious legal convocations and allegations of terrorism. In this moment, Muslim communities have an opportunity to develop a holistic understanding of policing, state violence, and power that connects the struggles of Muslim communities domestically and abroad with a broader militarization of U.S. society through security cameras, sentencing laws, stop-and-frisk policies, and anti-immigrant policing and legislation. The Muslim undergraduates I have worked with are often aware of these policies but have not fully connected them with the project of empire. Furthermore, these youth do not see these policies as a shift or aberration—it is simply what life has looked like in the United States. While they have seen the U.S. government torture, imprison individuals indiscriminately *and* racially, search young people as they walk the streets, spy on individuals and entire communities, and justify all of these actions publicly and legally, these youth do not yet have the tools to connect these seemingly disparate concerns. As Muslims continue to bear the brunt of the state's coercive militarism, community leaders, activists, and advocates must help make these relationships legible. In supporting Muslim students as they develop their political voice and critique, we can find a place of hope through their expressions of anger and dissent.

NOTES

1. Transcript of disposition, United States v. Mehanna, No. 09-cr-10017-GAO (D. Mass. 2012), April 12, 2012, PACER No. 439.

2. Al Baker and Kate Taylor, "Bloomberg Defends Police's Monitoring of Muslim Students on the Web," *New York Times,* February 21, 2012, http://www.nytimes .com/2012/02/22/nyregion/bloomberg-defends-polices-monitoring-of-muslim-stu dent-web-sites.html.

3. Sohail Daulatzai and Junaid Rana, "Left," *Critical Ethnic Studies* 1, no. 1 (2015): 39–42.

4. Randy Borum, "Radicalization into Violent Extremism I: A Review of Social Science Theories," *Journal of Strategic Security* 4, no. 4 (2011): 7–36.

5. "Q&A: The Myth of 'Radicalization,'" ACLU, https://www.aclu.org/other/ qa-myth-radicalization?redirect=free-speech-national-security-religion-belief/qa -myth-radicalization.

6. FBI Counterterrorism Division, *The Radicalization Process: From Conversion to Jihad* (Washington, D.C.: FBI, May 10, 2006), https://cryptome.org/fbi-jihad.pdf.

7. Akbar Amna, "Policing 'Radicalization,'" *UC Irvine Law Review* 3, no. 4 (2013): 809–33.

8. Mitchell D. Silber and Arvin Bhatt, *Radicalization in the West: The Home-grown Threat* (New York: NYPD Intelligence Division, 2007), https://www.bren nancenter.org/sites/default/files/legacy/Justice/20070816.NYPD.Radicalization .in.the.West.pdf.

9. "Q&A: The Myth of 'Radicalization.'"

10. Arun Kundnani, *The Muslims Are Coming! Islamophobia, Extremism, and the Domestic War on Terror* (London: Verso Books, 2014).

11. ACLU, *Unpatriotic Acts: The FBI's Power to Rifle through Your Records and Personal Belongings without Telling You* (New York: ACLU, 2003), http://www.aclu .org/files/FilesPDFs/spies_report.pdf.

12. Arshad Ali, "Citizens under Suspicion: Responsive Research with Community under Surveillance," *Anthropology and Education Quarterly* 47, no. 1 (2016): 78–95.

13. Shafiqa Ahmadi, "The Erosion of Civil Rights: Exploring the Effects of the Patriot Act on Muslims in American Higher Education," *Rutgers Race and the Law Review* 12, no. 1 (2011): 1–56.

14. Baker and Taylor, "Bloomberg Defends Police's Monitoring."

15. Piya Chatterjee and Sunaina Maira, *The Imperial University: Academic Repression and Scholarly Dissent* (Minneapolis: University of Minnesota Press, 2014), 27–28.

16. Jeremy Bentham, *An Introduction to the Principles of Morals and Legislation* (1789; repr., Mineola, N.Y.: Dover, 2012).

17. Council on American-Islamic Relations, *The Status of Muslim Civil Rights in the United States* (Washington, D.C.: Council on American-Islamic Relations, 2007), https://www.cair.com/images/pdf/CAIR-2007-Civil-Rights-Report.pdf.

18. Engy Abdelkader, *When Islamophobia Turns Violent: The 2016 U.S. Presidential Elections* (Washington, D.C.: The Bridge Initiative: A Georgetown University Research Project, 2016), http://bridge.georgetown.edu/wp-content/uploads/2016/ 05/When-Islamophobia-Turns-Violent.pdf.

19. Arshad Ali, "Quelling Dissent: Disciplining Liberalism on Muslim College Students' Speech and Action," *Critical Education* 5, no. 18 (2014): 1–18; Sangita Shresthova, Henry Jenkins, Liana Gamber-Thompson, Neta Kligler-Vilenchik, Arely M. Zimmerman, and Elisabeth Soep, "Between Storytelling and Surveillance: The Precarious Public of American Muslim Youth," in *By Any Media Necessary: The New Youth Activism,* 149–85 (New York: New York University Press, 2016).

20. Matt Apuzzo and Adam Goldman, "With CIA Help, NYPD Moved Covertly in Muslim Areas," Associated Press, August 23, 2011.

21. New York Police Department, *Weekly MSA Report,* November 22, 2006, http://hosted.ap.org/specials/interactives/documents/nypd-msa-report.pdf.

22. Through the course of the study, I collected more than ninety hours of video and audio recordings, along with field notes from community meetings and at spaces where recording was not possible. In addition, I conducted one-on-one interviews with twenty-five undergraduates who were involved in the NYMSC or Muslim student politics in New York City. Some participants were interviewed multiple times during the eighteen months, whereas others were interviewed only once. I facilitated five focus groups exploring issues of community, politics, and identity. Throughout this chapter, I use pseudonyms to protect the identities of my research participants.

As a South Asian Muslim male, I was actively involved in community politics and organizing, beyond the scope of a particular study. My relationships within the city and with community organizers allowed me the opportunity to work on this project and granted me some level of access within a community besieged by NYPD monitoring. Although on the surface, my relationships and background as an engaged member of Muslim communities gave me space to engage this project, my university affiliation and research focusing on youth politics raised suspicion among some community members that I could be working with, or for, the surveillance regime.

23. James Scott, *Domination and the Arts of Resistance* (New Haven, Conn.: Yale University Press, 1990), 24.

24. Noam Chomsky et al., *The Cold War and the University: Toward an Intellectual History of the Postwar Years* (New York: New Press, 1997).

25. Daulatzai and Rana, "Left."

26. Trevor Aaronson, *The Terror Factory* (New York: IG, 2013).

16 How Stereotypes Persist despite Innovations in Media Representations

EVELYN ALSULTANY

Examining representations of Arabs and Muslims on television and film after September 11, 2001, a few things become apparent.[1] Story lines and characters have become more complex. The "good guys" have bad qualities: they torture and murder people, sometimes indiscriminately. Conversely, the "bad guys" now have good qualities: they articulate reasonable justifications for their murderous actions. Many of the terrorists represented in story lines about the War on Terror are white men, Arabs and Muslims are sometimes portrayed as patriotic Americans, and the U.S. government is often portrayed as abusing its power. At first glance, it looks like the representational landscape has significantly changed from the days of simple binaries of good and evil and that stereotyping is on the decline. However, upon closer examination, it is important to analyze the ways in which racialized meanings can be produced through even the most innovative or complex story lines.

In my book *Arabs and Muslims in the Media: Race and Representation after 9/11*, I discuss my surprise at finding an increase in "positive" portrayals of Arabs and Muslims after 9/11.[2] What I found in my research was a new mode of representation that I term *simplified complex representations*. These are strategies used by television producers, writers, and directors that give the *impression* of complex, multifaceted representations, yet continue to present Arabs and Muslims in a simplified way. It is an approach that seeks to balance a "negative" representation with a "positive" one in order to circumvent stereotyping. For example, if a television show or movie is focused on terrorism perpetrated by Arabs or Muslims, then to counteract the stereotype associating these groups with terrorism, the production team will also typically include a "positive" representation of an Arab or

Muslim, usually as a patriotic U.S. citizen or an innocent victim of a hate crime. While such strategies are certainly an improvement over past depictions of one-dimensional villains, they remain far from ideal. The "positive" images often seem gratuitous, thrown in simply to appease Arab and Muslim American[3] civil rights groups like the Council on American-Islamic Relations and the American-Arab Anti-Discrimination Committee. Furthermore, even though intended to defuse stereotypes, such strategies are themselves counteracted by broader story lines that simultaneously rely upon and reinscribe those same stereotypes. My point here is not to diminish the efforts by various writers and producers to create more nuanced stories and characters but rather to highlight the meanings produced about Arabs and Muslims in the post-9/11 era. I place the terms "positive," "negative," "good," and "bad" in quotation marks when discussing this increase in representations of Arabs and Muslims in roles other than terrorists, rich oil sheikhs, and oppressed veiled women to highlight that asking whether an image is positive or negative leads to a simplistic and limiting binary framework (e.g., "yes, it's positive" or "no, its negative"). To shed light on how representations produce meanings about identities, it is vital to examine story lines and narratives alongside visual images. Such an approach exposes the ideological work of representations and its implications in constructing meaning about Arab and Muslim identities.[4]

In this essay, I examine one film, *Argo* (2012);[5] one TV drama, *Tyrant* (FX, 2014–16); and one reality television show, *All-American Muslim* (TLC, 2011–12) to illustrate how simplified complex representational strategies operate in contemporary popular culture, particularly in making characters and story lines more complex, while reinscribing limited or stereotypical portrayals of Arabs, Iranians, and Muslims. Focusing on the ideological work articulated by these productions reveals the limits of the innovations in simplified complex representations and ultimately the limits to inclusion in liberal multiculturalism. I argue that despite an increase in complex characters and story lines, the meanings produced about Muslims remain that they are violent, irrational, threatening, incompatible with democracy, opposed to liberal principles, and thus the opposite of everything defined as "American." When Islam is incidental or irrelevant to a Muslim person or character, then Muslims can be included in conceptions of U.S. liberal multiculturalism. However, when Islam is central to one's identity and religious practice, those Muslim persons or characters must prove their loyalty and patriotism to the United States to gain access to belonging.

Argo's COMPLEX BACKSTORY

The film *Argo*, about the 1979 Iran Hostage Crisis, has been met with critical acclaim, winning an Academy Award for Best Picture. The film utilizes simplified complex representations or efforts to diffuse the potential stereotype of Iranians and Muslims as violent and fanatical. Unfortunately, each time an effort is made to make the story more complex, it is quickly undone by overpowering stereotypes.

The most important gesture made by *Argo* toward complexity is the opening of the film, which serves essentially as a preface—a two-minute visual montage partly animated with narration that provides context to the Iran Hostage Crisis. This context explains that in 1953, the United States and England got rid of Iran's democratically elected leader, Mohamad Mossadegh, because he did not serve their oil interests and replaced him with Reza Pahlavi, who focused on Westernizing Iran at the expense of the Iranian people. The narration explains, "In 1979, the people of Iran overthrew the shah. The exiled cleric, Ayatollah Khomeini, returned to rule Iran. It descended into score settling, death squads, and chaos. Dying of cancer, the shah was given asylum in the U.S. The Iranian people took to the streets outside the U.S. Embassy demanding that the shah be returned, tried, and hanged." And seconds later, the words "Based on a true story" appear on the screen.

This incredibly brief context is followed by an opening scene that undoes it with its emotional force. Thousands of Iranians are protesting outside the U.S. Embassy: an American flag is set on fire, a man is shown stabbing something that looks like a pillow with an image on it, and they are shouting something in Farsi. A few men begin scaling the wall of the American Embassy, while a man manages to cut the lock to the gate, unleashing this Iranian mob into the embassy while the American government workers try to burn confidential documents. The Iranians are relentless, violent, and unreasonable. The Americans fear for their safety. One American says he is going outside to reason with them, and he becomes the first hostage taken. He is immediately blindfolded with a gun pressed against his neck. The Iranians storm the building and start taking hostages—blindfolding them and threatening them with guns—while six of them manage to escape and find refuge at the home of the Canadian ambassador. It is a chilling scene, undoing the historical preface and what little impact it may have had.

The context of U.S. intervention in Iranian internal affairs does not offer any insight into what drove the Iranian hostage takers to such extreme action. Any moment that acknowledges the point of view of the Iranian hostage takers is fleeting and quickly undone through repeated portrayals of Iranians as threatening and unreasonable. There is the one exception, the housekeeper at the Canadian diplomat's house, who functions exactly for this purpose, to be able to say that not *all* of them were depicted stereotypically. We do not get to know her in any way. We are suspicious of her throughout the film, and what makes her "good" is that she is willing to betray her nation to protect Americans. This is the most common technique of simplified complex representations: the insertion of a "good" Muslim who is defined as good because of her allegiance to the United States.

Critics and viewers have debated the extent to which *Argo* is unusually complex for a Hollywood film because of this opening sequence and its narrative. Middle East scholar and blogger Juan Cole wrote, "Although the film begins with an info-dump that explains that the U.S. screwed over Iran by having the CIA overthrow the elected government in 1953 and then helped impose a royal dictatorship in the form of the restored shah, that part of the film is emotionally flat. It tells, it doesn't show. It is tacked on. It does not intersect with the subsequent film in any significant way. It therefore has no emotional weight and does little to contextualize the Iranian characters (none of whose names I think we even learn)."[6]

At the same time, however, many disagree with the perspective that the film's opening accomplishes little, if anything. One Internet poster responding to an article in *The Guardian* about the film insisted, "The opening to Argo does a great job in explaining the source of Iranian ire towards the U.S., with a wonderful animated history of 20th Century Iran including the U.S. overthrow of Mossadegh's democratically elected government in 1953. If that doesn't question U.S. foreign policy, then I don't know what else Affleck can do to satisfy anti-American viewers."[7] This commenter simultaneously labels those criticizing the film as "anti-American," revealing an unproductive "us versus them" logic that, ironically, reveals the film's failure to promote complexity over polarizing discourse.

More complex characters and story lines, contrary to popular belief, often tend to reinscribe stereotypes, revealing a paradox: attempts to defuse stereotypes can covertly or inadvertently perpetuate them, thereby making racist meanings more difficult to detect. Despite the unusual complexity offered by the opening context, Iranians are nonetheless portrayed as violent, irrational, and threatening as a people. They are portrayed as incompatible with democracy and not deserving of the tolerance that liberal principles promote.[8] The inclusion of a two-minute preface does little if anything to mitigate this negative, one-dimensional portrayal. The fact that the film won an Academy Award shows how comfortable we still are with some stereotypes and how far we have yet to go. What makes this stereotyping all the more dangerous is the claim to truth the film makes. Creative liberties or not, that *Argo* is based on a true story makes Iranians *truly* appear insane. *Argo* seems like an updated version of the last stereotypical popular Hollywood film based on a true story in Iran, *Not without My Daughter*. *Argo* might as well be retitled *Not without My Daughter 2*.

What might a more complex film look like? Such a film might have allowed the viewer to get to know some Iranian hostage takers and gain insight into their reasoning and internal debates. Juan Cole says that the film could have included "a moment when Americans come to terms with their Cold War role as villains in places like Iran. It could have been a film about what intelligence analysts call 'blowback,' when a covert operation goes awry."[9]

Would the film have been better off without gestures toward complexity? Well, not exactly. *Zero Dark Thirty* would have benefited from an opening contextual moment that explained that in an effort to win the Cold War, the United States engaged in proxy wars that included assembling a militia group in Afghanistan and recruiting Osama bin Laden to be its leader, with President Reagan referring to them as "freedom fighters." *Zero Dark Thirty* would have benefited from beginning the story during the Cold War rather than on September 11, 2001. The point is that how we tell stories matters. Where we begin the story matters. Whose point of view we allow audiences to identify with matters. Simplified complex representations tend not to challenge stereotypes; they tend to affirm them in the guise of complexity.

Tyrant's COMPLEX ARAB BROTHERS

The TV drama *Tyrant* offers another case study of this paradoxical process through which writers and producers attempt to defuse stereotyping but end up reproducing it. *Tyrant* premiered on the FX network in 2014 and lasted three seasons. The show centers on the relationship between two Arab brothers, the sons of the dictator of a fictional Arab Muslim country, Abuddin. It has become increasingly common for the country of the terrorist characters in television dramas to go unnamed. This simplified complex representational strategy rests on the assumption that leaving the nationality of the villain blank eliminates potential offensiveness; if no particular country or ethnicity is named, then there is less reason for any particular group to be offended by the portrayal.

Jamal al-Fayeed, brilliantly played by Ashraf Barhom, may have been the only Arab actor playing an Arab in a leading role on U.S. prime-time television (until his character was killed during season 3); he is a complex character who is also a brutal dictator. His brother, Bassam, aka Barry, played by Adam Rayner, returns to Abuddin with his American wife and two teen-aged children after living in the United States for twenty years. Barry, now a successful pediatrician, has been in self-imposed exile from his country of origin. He is reluctant to return to Abuddin and plans a very brief trip only to attend his nephew's wedding. During the visit, however, his father passes away, his brother becomes the new president/dictator of the country amid a growing popular revolution, and Barry feels compelled to stay to help his brother through this crisis. *Tyrant*'s brothers predictably clash over how to rule the fictional Abuddin. Americanized Barry wants to introduce democracy to his estranged homeland. He tries to reason with the Arab Jamal to consider a new way of governing, to listen to the opposition and address the desires of the people. But Jamal seems incapable of anything but ruthless repression, dealing with problems through violence, killing the opposition and any dissenting voices.

Many post-9/11 TV shows with Arab or Muslim characters have been directly or indirectly about the War on Terror. *Tyrant* diverges by picking up on other global events, in particular the Arab Spring. Its focus is not on the U.S. government combating terrorism but rather on an Arab dictatorship facing demonstrations by people demanding democracy. Its premise provides room for multiple Arab characters and perspectives and thus holds more potential for representational complexity than other TV dramas focused on terrorism. And, indeed, at first glance, the show presents a seemingly diverse array of Arab characters. There is Fauzi Nadal (played by Fares Fares), Barry's childhood friend, now a reporter and supporter of the revolution against the al-Fayeed dictatorship. Fauzi is a rare combination: an Arab character played by an Arab actor and portrayed as having integrity and believing in democracy. Other Arab characters include a young gay man (closeted, of course), a brutal military general, and the innocent victims of the al-Fayeed regime. The development of such characters *could* explore complex themes, but this potential is overshadowed by the show's central relationship and narrative: the relationship between the two brothers.

Here, too, there are multiple opportunities for character development, but each time an effort is made to explore this potential, depressingly familiar binaries between Americanness and Arabness are reasserted instead.

The brothers have not seen each other for twenty years, and the show highlights the dynamics between them, playing up the fact that they were raised in the same family but with drastically different outcomes. As the eldest son, Jamal has been burdened with the expectation and responsibility of succeeding to his father's rule. Flashbacks to their childhood reveal a traumatic incident in which a young Jamal is handed a gun by his father and instructed to kill a man as part of his training. When Jamal is too scared to do it, Bassam/Barry does it for him. The flashback provides a glimpse of Jamal as young and vulnerable, giving the audience an opportunity to develop a more layered understanding of the character and the events that made him who he is today. He was innocent once; being a violent dictator is not inherent or in his blood. On one hand, the show makes a point that Jamal was raised to be violent and therefore it is not inherent, but on the other, it suggests that it *is* presumably part of the cultural expectations in which he was raised. This is a device typical of simplified complex representations in which a stereotype is challenged and then inadvertently reinscribed.

But whatever depth is added with these childhood flashbacks is offset by the binaristic relationship contrasting the two brothers as essentially Arab versus American. Barry returns to Abuddin with no hint of an Arab accent. His speech is American, while Jamal speaks English with a distinctly Arab accent. Furthermore, Barry is played by a British actor (Adam Rayner) who is not of Arab descent, while, as noted earlier, the Arab actor Ashraf Barhom plays Jamal. In the show, Barry's non-Arab appearance is attributed to their white British mother. We are to assume that one mixed-race brother turned out lighter than the other; that one can pass as a white American or British while the other cannot. Ultimately, Barry doesn't even register as an Arab or Arab American; his self-presentation conveys to the audience that he is a white American.

The Arab–American binary is only reinforced by the brothers' respective relationships with women. Barry's white American wife, Molly (Jennifer Finnigan), is also a doctor, and their relationship is portrayed as an egalitarian one in which they operate as best friends and faithful partners. In contrast, Jamal and his Arab wife, Leila (Moran Atias), are united in ruling Abuddin by force to maintain their powerful status, but theirs is not a marriage of love or faithfulness. Jamal is a philandering rapist. He rapes women and sexually assaults his daughter-in-law on the day of her wedding. He pays an American prostitute to be available to him and has a loving relationship with her until he shares his most vulnerable feelings with her and then decides that he must kill her to prevent anyone else from knowing. The message is clear: Arab men are incapable of egalitarian relationships with women; American men are capable of them.

At the same time, however, Barry exists in a liminal space as both Arab and American, so there are moments when he, too, reveals his "essential" Arab nature and becomes more tyrannical with his wife and children. This depiction of internally dueling Arab and American identities is a familiar one. In the 1921 film *The Sheik*, Rudy Valentino's character exhibits a similar capacity for both rational thought as a European and brutishness as a Westerner "gone Arab." If we fast-forward to the 1991 film *Not without My Daughter*, we are introduced to an Iranian American doctor who is a kind husband and father in Michigan but then transforms upon arrival in Iran into an abusive husband, as if regressing and revealing his "true" roots. The longer Barry stays in Abuddin, the more he becomes a dictator. During season 3, he becomes the interim president. While he purports to support democracy, he imprisons anyone who opposes his rule. The struggles of such characters make for compelling drama, but when dealing with the Middle East, they also reinscribe long-standing binaries between East and West.

Thus, despite occasional glimpses and a potential for complexity, *Tyrant* devolves into clichéd binaries about Arab and American identities: Arab men are violent narcissists, incapable of egalitarian relationships with women or any others over whom they rule, while American(ized) men are reasonable and believe in freedom, democracy, and equality, both in their intimate relationships and in the public and political spheres. Representations of Arabs and Muslims in *Tyrant* are consistent with wider trends on television post-9/11, characterized by unusually complex characters and story lines that nonetheless reinscribe stereotypes. The ideological work of the show echoes common Western discourses that Arabs and Muslims are incompatible with liberal principles like equality and freedom of speech, that Arab culture and the religion of Islam are incompatible with democracy.[10] *Tyrant* holds the potential to challenge the notion that Arabs and Muslims are incompatible with democracy and liberal principles. However, Arabs and Muslims are portrayed as incapable of embracing democracy despite their best revolutionary efforts. The Americanized Barry turns into a dictator. The leaders of the revolution are ruthless and bloodthirsty. If they were to win, the country would resemble rule-by-ISIS. As for the common people demonstrating for democracy, they don't have a chance, given that there are these larger forces and given that there is no character development, proving that they are inconsequential to the story.

All-American Muslim's Patriotic Antidote

Premiering on the TLC network in November 2011, *All-American Muslim (AAM)* chronicled the everyday lives of five Muslim families in Dearborn, Michigan. The show was unprecedented in its representation of Muslims on U.S. television, particularly in the ways it attempted to expand the representation of Muslim identities. For one, it offered the possibility of moving away from representing all Arab and Muslim characters in contexts exclusively focused on terrorism. Second, it portrayed Arabs and Muslims in leading roles rather than in their more frequent supporting or inconsequential roles. Third, it included diverse Muslim identities that ranged from more to less conservative: two people had tattoos, one was scantily clad while another decided to don the hijab, and one was marrying an Irish Catholic American.

Almost as soon as it aired, *AAM* kindled unexpected controversy. Many Muslims had criticisms of the show. Some claimed that the cast was not composed of "real Muslims" because some had tattoos. Others claimed the show portrayed one Muslim community (Lebanese Shi'a) as representative of all Muslims in the United States, overlooking other Arab Americans who are Muslim and, more importantly, overlooking those who compose the largest segment of Muslims in the United States: African Americans and South Asian Americans. One Muslim commenter on the entertainment website IMDB.com stated that the show "is a joke and utter insult to the diversity that is Islam" and should be renamed "All-Lebanese American Shia Muslim."[11] Such critiques served to highlight the impossible pressure on a single show to undo more than a century of stereotypes.[12]

Less surprising were the negative responses from other kinds of viewers. It was precisely the show's effort to offer a more nuanced and positive picture of Muslims in America that drew the ire of some, most notably the Florida Family Association (FFA) run by David Caton, a right-wing activist normally known more for his antigay agenda. In December 2011, the FFA organized an e-mail campaign protesting the show's "deceptive" portrayal of Muslims and calling on advertisers to withdraw their sponsorship. The FFA's outrage was sparked because *AAM* dared to portray Muslims outside of the context of terrorism. Because there are no terrorists on the show and Muslims are depicted as ordinary people, Caton charged that it was propaganda "attempting to manipulate Americans into ignoring the threat of jihad."[13] Soon after the FFA's campaign, the retailer Lowe's Home Improvement and the travel website Kayak.com pulled their commercials.

Apparently, even this modest expansion in representing Muslims disturbed those who saw the show as denying the essential incompatibility of Islam and the United States. Even the *Wall Street Journal* faced the wrath of this audience when an article on the controversy described the show as reflecting the reality that "Islam in America today is a story of rapid assimilation and even secularization, not growing radicalism."[14] Online reader responses to the article included the following:

> I will happily sing the praises of middle class American Muslims as soon as middle class American Muslims denounce the jihad their brethren are leading against the rest of us. Until then, they are suspect.[15]

> The Koran is not a book compatible with American middle-class values. Nor is the life of Mohammed.[16]

> I wonder if the media will ever stop trying to brainwash us. Now, the drumbeat telling us Muslims are just nice American people trying to live normal lives. And we are being unfair. . . . Sorry, but they are not ordinary Americans. They are engaged in a global religious war against us. . . . We must be vigilant to not allow them to spread their violent religion and Sharia law in this our great and free nation.[17]

Such responses reveal the existence of an audience for whom *any* representational strategy that does not condemn all Muslims as inherently anti-American is unacceptable. It is important to note, however, that this controversy also generated a sizeable backlash that critiqued Lowe's and Kayak.com for their decision to withdraw sponsorship. A National Lowe's Boycott Campaign was launched, and hip-hop mogul Russell Simmons offered to purchase any remaining advertising space.[18]

For all its effort to provide a more nuanced portrayal of Muslims, *AAM* relied in other ways on narrow representational strategies—simplified complex representations—that have become standard fare in TV representations since 9/11, namely, the focus on Muslims as patriots and/or as innocent victims of post-9/11 hate.[19] Among the people featured on *AAM* are a police officer, a football coach, a county clerk, and a federal agent, mirroring the now standard inclusion of "patriotic" Muslim American characters on fictional television shows. These portrayals, although certainly "positive," reflect the ongoing demand for Muslims Americans to continually prove their patriotism. Victims also appear on *AAM*, but to a much lesser extent than does the trope of patriotism. We witness discrimination and harassment when one of the married couples leaves Dearborn to visit a neighboring town, only to be ignored at a restaurant while other customers are offered seating,[20] and when high school students recount being called "camel jockeys" by students at other schools.[21] The emphasis here is on the innocence of Muslim Americans, thus assuring viewers that not all Muslims are guilty or threatening.

These representations of "patriots" and "victims" are undoubtedly improvements over past images of Muslims and Arabs as terrorists, oil sheiks, belly dancers, and oppressed, veiled women. Nonetheless, these "improvements" reveal an equally narrow and one-dimensional script of representation. By attempting to make Islam seem less frightening and more familiar through association with occupations and leisure activities that emphasize U.S. citizenship, *AAM* uses a narrow conception of patriotism as an antidote to portrayals of Muslims as terrorists. *AAM* adopts a strategy of normalization through patriotism that distinguishes it from the other portrayals of alternative lifestyles and atypical families on the TLC network, such as the reality show *Sister Wives* (TLC, 2010–), about a polygamous Mormon family.

In *Sister Wives*, the Brown family members are portrayed as unjust victims of prejudice given the stigmatization of their lifestyle in mainstream society. They cannot legally marry because polygamy is illegal, and they must hide their identity as a polygamous Mormon family from the general public and from the community in which they live. But while the Brown family is burdened to prove that they are simply living a nonnormative lifestyle and are not perverted religious fanatics, their religious difference does not demand that they *also* prove their patriotism or citizenship. In contrast, *AAM*'s focus on its cast members' patriotism marks the show as distinct and reveals that Muslim identity, unlike Mormon identity, necessitates a framework that proves its protagonists are not just unfairly stigmatized but also really and truly *American*.

To this end, *AAM* features "normal" people living a "normal" middle-class life with very little conflict. The ironic result: the show was widely perceived as boring. The "difference" of being Muslim is featured—we see, for example, a twelve-year-old girl putting on the hijab for the first time, an Irish American Catholic converting to Islam for marriage, conflict over having a dog as a domestic animal, and special accommodations at the high school for football training during Ramadan—but these instances of difference are normalized and seemingly neutralized by their familiar, domestic contexts and patriotic vocations. Discussing the show online, viewers seemed unanimous: where were the exciting scenes of drunk people and screaming fights that characterized other reality shows? On the *Hollywood Reporter* website,[22] for example, viewers commented, "Watched it once and was bored to death" and "It shows everyday people doing what . . . people do everyday. I don't watch TV for that."

As the show's title and its portrayal of the protagonists' religious beliefs and practices demonstrated, the inclusion of Muslim Americans that the producers were promoting sought a delicate balancing act that embraced religious difference—specifically, Islam—as normal. While the term "All-American" showcased the producers' efforts to evoke the framework of patriotism, the term "Muslim" dared to foreground, rather than downplay, religious identity. This was a risky representational strategy that inadvertently revealed the limits of liberal multiculturalism—an idealized form of inclusion that remains ambivalent at best, especially when it comes to Islam. Raka Shome points out that parts of one's identity that do not conform to the logic of multiculturalism, or shared notions of Americanness, are bracketed out in public discourse, "thus disallowing their interruptive political possibilities to emerge."[23] The show raises troubling questions about the place of Islam in U.S. liberal multiculturalism and the space afforded, if any, to specific forms of religious diversity within that vision. It seems that Muslims can be included in liberal multiculturalism only when and if Islam is, at minimum, not that important to their identity and, ideally, completely irrelevant. When Islam is relevant, it must be portrayed through a narrow conception of patriotism, placing Muslim Americans in a position in which challenging the terrorist stereotype involves a limited alternative: narrow displays of patriotism as the antidote.

The Logic of "Post-race" Racism and the Limits to Liberal Multiculturalism

Simplified complex representations are consistent with the larger phenomenon of "post-race" racism. Within this new racial formation that Jodi Melamed calls "neoliberal multiculturalism" and that Eduardo Bonilla-Silva calls "color-blind racism," "racism constantly appears as disappearing according to conventional race categories, even as it takes on new forms that can signify as nonracial or even antiracist."[24] In other words, representational progress reflects the logic of post-race racism, a paradox in which efforts to circumvent stereotyping and racism inadvertently reproduce logics that legitimize exclusion. Analyzing media representations of Arabs and Muslims in the Obama era reveals the interrelationship between liberal multiculturalism and post-race racism. Representational innovations that include an increase in "positive" representations of Muslims do not necessarily challenge stereotypes. Rather, they produce the illusion of doing so while perpetuating logics that legitimize the exclusion of Muslims from liberal multiculturalism and thus reveal the limits of the liberal multicultural project. Both *Argo* and *Tyrant* portray Iranians, Muslims, and Arabs/"Abuddinians" as incompatible with democracy and liberal principles. The exceptions are those who have been Americanized or who prove their compatibility through their allegiance to the United States. In the case of *All-American Muslims*, Muslims can be included when Islam is incidental to one's identity, but when it is more central, loyalty and patriotism are essential to inclusion.

For all their apparent innovations, such complex story lines and characters have minimal impact on viewers' perceptions of Iranians, Arabs, and Muslims and can perpetuate a simplistic vision of good and evil. Given that characters and story lines are becoming more complex, we still need to consider the production of racial meanings and be vigilant about the power of media to shape our perceptions on who is and is not deserving of rights and humanity. These three cases remind us that we must think beyond whether an image is "good" or "bad" to consider how images produce meanings and logics that justify exclusion or provide narrow alternative possibilities, and how true complexity requires more than two minutes of backstory, stark contrasts between binary oppositions, and proving U.S. patriotism.

NOTES

1. Parts of this essay were previously published. The section on *All-American Muslims* was originally published in "The Cultural Politics of Islam in U.S. Reality Television," *Communication, Culture, and Critique*, August 2015. The section on *Argo* was originally published in "Argo Tries but Fails to Diffuse Stereotypes," *The Islamic Monthly* 29, no. 1 (2013): 104–7. The section on *Tyrant* was published in "*Tyrant*: Ou Comment Lutter Contre les Stereotypes," *Afkar/Ideas*, no. 46 (Summer 2015): 75–77.

2. Evelyn Alsultany, *Arabs and Muslims in the Media: Race and Representation after 9/11* (New York: New York University Press, 2012).

3. In my work, I often use the term *Arab and Muslim Americans* because in looking at representations, that is how the group is portrayed by the media—as monolithic, as conflated. If I am not talking about media representations, then I try to be more specific: *Muslim American, Arab American, Iraqi American,* and so on. While some scholars prefer the term *American Muslim,* I tend to use *Muslim American* because in ethnic studies, it is customary when discussing hyphenated identities to place American last: *Arab American, Asian American, African American.* Yes, being Muslim is a religious designation and not a racial or ethnic one; however, it has been racialized. Thus it is in line with how racialized communities have identified in the United States and acknowledges the ways in which Islam has been racialized.

4. My use of "ideological work" comes from Louis Althusser, "Ideology and Ideological State Apparatuses," in *Lenin and Philosophy and Other Essays*, 85–126 (New York: Monthly Review Press, 2001).

5. Chris Terrio and Tony Mendez, *Argo*, dir. Ben Affleck (United States: GK Films/Smokehouse Pictures, 2012), DVD.

6. Juan Cole, "'Argo' as Orientalism and Why It Upsets Iranians," *Informed Comment*, February 26, 2013, http://www.juancole.com/.

7. Saeed Kamali Dehghan, "Why Argo Is Hard for Iranians to Watch," *The Guardian*, reader comments, Londonzak, November 13, 2012, http://www.guardian.co.uk/.

8. For more on the limits to discourses on tolerance, see Wendy Brown, *Regulating Aversion: Tolerance in the Age of Identity and Empire* (Princeton, N.J.: Princeton University Press, 2008).

9. Cole, "Argo."

10. For an in-depth analysis of the ways in which Islam has been constructed in relation to liberalism, see Joseph A. Massad, *Islam in Liberalism* (Chicago: University of Chicago Press, 2015).

11. Ztlfire, "The Most Inaccurate Portrayal EVER All American Muslim Is RIDICULOUS," forum comment, December 12, 2011, http://www.imdb.com/.

12. Jack G. Shaheen, *Reel Bad Arabs: How Hollywood Vilifies a People* (Northampton, Mass.: Olive Branch Press, 2001).

13. Brian Tashman, "Religious Right Groups Launch Fight against TLC Reality Show," *Right Wing Watch*, November 28, 2011, http://www.rightwingwatch.org/.

14. Naomi Schaefer Riley, "Defining the 'All-American Muslim,'" *Wall Street Journal*, March 22, 2012, http://online.wsj.com/.

15. Ibid.

16. Ibid.

17. Ibid.

18. Alan Duke, "'All-American Muslim' Sells Out, Despite Lowe's Withdrawal," CNN, December 13, 2011, http://edition.cnn.com/.

19. Alsultany, *Arabs and Muslims in the Media*.

20. "The Fast and the Furious," *All-American Muslim*, season 1, episode 2 (November 20, 2011).

21. "How to Marry a Muslim," *All-American Muslim*, season 1, episode 1 (November 13, 2011).

22. Michael O'Connell, "TLC's 'All-American Muslim': Controversy Does Not Equal Ratings," *Hollywood Reporter*, December 14, 2011, http://www.hollywoodreporter.com/.

23. Raka Shome, "Mapping the Limits of Multiculturalism in the Context of Globalization," *International Journal of Communication* 6 (2012): 156.

24. Jodi Melamed, "The Spirit of Neoliberalism: From Racial Liberalism to Neoliberal Multiculturalism," *Social Text* 23, no. 4 (2006): 1–24. Also see Eduardo Bonilla-Silva, *Racism without Racists: Color-Blind Racism and the Persistence of Racial Inequality in the United States*, 2nd ed. (New York: Rowman and Littlefield, 2006). Also see Tim Wise, *Colorblind: The Rise of Post-Racial Politics and the Retreat from Racial Equity* (San Francisco: City Lights Books, 2010).

17

"Grounded on the Battlefront"

An Interview with Hamid Khan on the Police State in the War on Terror

SOHAIL DAULATZAI

SOHAIL DAULATZAI (SD): Over the last several years, a lot was made, for good reason, of the NYPD [New York Police Department] surveillance program that revealed the monitoring of the Muslim community on the East Coast, including grocery stores, hookah cafes, and college students on campuses. But I think what has often gone under the radar is the ways in which Los Angeles has been a laboratory or a model of national policing that is imbricated with the national security state. We can go back further, but of course, SWAT [Special Weapons and Tactics], the paramilitary wing of the LAPD [Los Angeles Police Department], was specifically developed to crush the Black Panthers here in Los Angeles. Can you talk about how Los Angeles has been a crucible for thinking about policing on a national level?

HAMID KHAN (HK): Absolutely, Los Angeles has been a laboratory for many reasons. We actually have a timeline on our website of LAPD surveillance going back to 1923 and, very methodically, how things are broken down. But first, I would point back to the Port of Los Angeles, which is one of the biggest hubs of commerce in the United States, which generates close to about half a trillion dollars in revenues in the United States. When you think about the Red Squads of the Los Angeles Police Department, they came out of the 1886 Haymarket Strike in Chicago. So that by 1888, Chicago was the first local police department that had created its own covert, intelligence-gathering section. And there's this documentation of Chicago's police chief saying, "We've entered a new age of ideological warfare." So with labor strikes and mobilizations [at the Port of Los Angeles], that's one part of what infiltration and surveillance would look like. But of course, the issue of race still remains at the heart of it, with the role of police going from slave catchers to slave patrols.

272

So tracing back to the LAPD Red Squads, in the early 1920s, what we have found out is that the Red Squads were based out of the Chamber of Commerce; over 80 percent of their budget was being shelled out by the Retailers and Manufacturers Association in Los Angeles. So I think that is one piece. The other piece was COINTELPRO, Counter Intelligence Program, and all that in partnership with the FBI with the rise of the Panthers. So with worker organizing and Black folks now getting more actively militant as well, picking up guns and arms as well, the LA chapter of the Panthers was very, very active. But of course, Oakland is just up the coastline as well. So California, and given the scale and sheer size of Los Angeles, it was a huge place to experiment and to build these tactics as well. So that's why when we talk about the SWAT, the introduction of the helicopters very early on, and creating a fleet of helicopters, that's referred to as the "ghetto bird" to surveil the ghetto. Also Operation Hammer, and the battering ram, and various other things. It was just a natural extension and a setting of the tone. To the extent, then, that when finally the Public Disorder Intelligence Division, or the Red Squads, was busted, people found out that over two hundred nonprofits had been infiltrated, a lot of labor unions were infiltrated. Every city council member's office was infiltrated by the LAPD. Mayor Tom Bradley's office was infiltrated by the LAPD, to the extent that as Tom Bradley was having conversations with the United Farm Workers, all that conversation was being pulled by the LAPD and shipped to the Western Goals Society, which is based out of San Francisco and an extension of the John Birch Society [a far right wing conservative think tank].

SD: We've seen and continue to see here in the city a deep overlap between the military and the police and a sharing of tactical training and technology up to and including today. It reminds me of a quote by Malcolm X, who said, "What the police do locally the military does internationally." Former chief William Bratton had lobbied, and in many ways succeeded, in making the LAPD the epicenter for the relationship between domestic policing and the Department of Homeland Security. He testified in Congress that the federal government "needs to get pre-occupied with the internal war on terrorism as well," and has suggested that gang activity is "homeland terrorism." Also, LAPD officers have gone to Iraq and Afghanistan, and U.S. military personnel have been here in Los Angeles receiving training from local police. Not to mention through JINSA [the Jewish Institute for National Security of America], the LAPD and other high-ranking police officials went to Israel for "antiterrorism cooperation." I

know that Stop LAPD Spying has devoted considerable time and energy
into exploring this nexus, particularly through the Suspicious Activity
Reports [SARs] that the LAPD is using. These are essentially reports filed
by police based on a call or "tip" that someone is engaged in "suspicious"
behaviors, and these reports are then uploaded into these fusion centers
where these individuals arc brought into a broad panorama of surveillance technology. Can you talk about SARs and how they are central to a
new strategy of policing?

HK: One of the things that started emerging which really has now helped a
lot of the work at the Stop LAPD Spying Coalition was that it is not just
about the police, it is about *policing of the body*. And how does this really
work? Because vocabulary sometimes gets the better of us, because in a
way, when we speak of surveillance, otherness, infiltration, we do so in
silence. The national security police state is the most intersectional body
that you would think of. We talk about intersectional movement building, but they are the most intersectional. So for us, it was about examining what is this intersectionality and how are these practices and rules
replicated and applied in the larger public and private sectors? That has
really been one of the key works of the Stop LAPD Spying Coalition.

So when I first came across the Suspicious Activity Reporting program, which was basically on the heels of the *9/11 Commission Report,*
and just after Congress passed the Intelligence Reform and Terrorism
Prevention Act of 2004, that was the first time that, post-9/11, we became
more aware of how information is going to move, because that man-
dated the president to create the information-sharing environment. They
had attempted that in the past, but it had not worked very well, because
of the turf wars among the FBI, local law enforcement, the ATF [Bureau
of Alcohol, Tobacco, and Firearms], the DEA [Drug Enforcement Agency],
et cetera. But this was the first time that the fusion of information was
happening and where it could move seamlessly both horizontally and
vertically. And these main conduits of information gathering and ware-
housing would be called "fusion centers," these central spy centers, if
you will. And through the workings of the LAPD, it was informing these
things as well.

So suspicious activity reporting was the first time, or at least where I
would say post–civil rights, that while we were hearing about "driving
while Black," at the same time to then legitimize your protected actions as
being suspicious, where they became codified. Which then opened up a lot
of opportunities for law enforcement to then legitimize their speculative

and hunch-based policing. So that's, I mean, if we were to look at a template and a foundation for where we are, I would say SAR is one of the earliest. That's where they then define, for the director of national intelligence, "observed behavior," "reasonably indicative," or "preoperational planning." So the codification of this practice was happening as well.

SD: And you're saying this emerges after 9/11 as well?

HK: This was after 9/11, yes.

SD: And so how does that work? Obviously, my understanding of SAR comes out of DNI [director of national intelligence], the *9/11 Commission Report,* and that the premise or the precondition for it is "antiterrorism." And what is now called "See Something, Say Something." So it has a kind of public buy-in already because of 9/11 and the fear of threat. But while it does target what we might call immigrant Muslim communities, how have you seen the SARs being used in the city of Los Angeles, which targets non-Muslim communities? How has it worked to further criminalize already criminalized Black and Brown communities?

HK: Of course, it has been built on this narrative of the other, the "Muslim terrorist," and "we've got to protect ourselves." But when we got the inspector general of the LAPD to do the audit, I mean three audits have come out, and the initial first two audits clearly showed an overwhelmingly disparate impact on the Black community. To the extent that the audit that was released in January of 2015 showed that over 30 percent of these—and these files are all secret—over 30 percent of these files that were sent to these spy centers by the LAPD identified individuals as Black. So, in a community, in a city that has 9.6 percent Black population, you have over 30 percent of these files. And then, wherever gender was identified in these files, 50 percent were identified as Black women. And then overall, 82 percent were identified as nonwhite. So that's one piece. The other piece that SAR created was to further build on speculative and hunch-based policing and to formalize what has now come to be known as "predictive policing." And then, let's also remind ourselves that all of these things are grounded on the battlefront. So war abroad is war at home, it's war on the people. The War on Terror needs to be seen in that whole context of the War on Drugs, the War on Gangs, the War on Crime. Because ultimately the recipients of state violence are overwhelmingly the same communities.

But when we talk about "predictive policing," its origin comes out of Afghanistan, where previous data were used and run through data processing and algorithms to predict acts of insurgency. That was the whole idea. It's very interesting that the model that they use is based on earthquake reading, as to what are the aftershocks and all that. This was designed by an anthropologist, who is a professor at UCLA, Jeffrey Brantingham. So the predicting of battlefront insurgencies was brought to the United States.

SAR went from a national security technique to an "all-crimes" strategy; it is part and parcel of local policing, which gives them a lot of power to place people in files so they can continue to monitor and follow. "Predictive policing," which as I said comes from the battlefront in Afghanistan, has taken on this shape of location-based and person-based predictive policing. So where a community may be calling in, or any crime data for burglary or car theft or these kinds of things, then all those data go in through algorithms and processing, it spits out hot zones. And these hot spots are in the same communities where there has already been heavy policing. So now, these are becoming proxies for racism, which now legitimizes an interaction for more stop-and-frisk and lays a siege in that community, and the potential for things to escalate is always very high.

The record shows that over 80 percent of these SARs were coming through the "See Something, Say Something" program. So this is a license for people to engage in their racism. This is a license for racial profiling, this is a license for bigotry, this is a license for you know, I mean, basically people calling people of color out. We have to see how this is a continuation of, and a more fancy way to pathologize and criminalize the community. That's what stop-and-frisk is also based on. So I think it's a pathologization of young men of color that "you men are up to no good, because that's who you are." So predictive policing basically is a model. But it's taken on another shape, which is person-based predictive policing, which means that the model then releases, if they identify people, there are these criteria they've created as a potential "threat." We are in the process of researching and getting more information from them, like what are these predetermined criteria, because if you've had any history of gun violence, if you're on parole or probation, mostly it's young Black and Brown men, you are given points, and through data processing, your history is put out with patrol cars with your face, and your photo, and everything, and they call them "chronic offender bulletins." So these are like "most wanted" posters.

These chronic offender bulletins, with the use of StingRay technology— which by the way is developed by the U.S. Navy and Marine Corps—the cell phone catchers, the use of license plate readers, and closed-circuit television, are used to monitor the movements of these individuals as well. The last few police killings in Los Angeles that we have seen, we are probing them to see if they are an extension of chronic offender bulletins. Because you follow them, you stop them, you search them. Escalation happens, and next thing you know, somebody gets shot. Richard Risher was killed by the police. Ezell Ford, how did Ezell Ford die? The officer said Ezell Ford was engaging in some sort of suspicious activity. "We thought he had a baggie of marijuana." So with suspicious activity reporting, was there a hot zone created, a hot spot created as a result of predictive policing? Was Ezell Ford in a gang database or something? We have to look at these national security programs in the larger context of how policing is working, so there's a reason that we call it the national security police state and not just a police state, because national security prerogatives have now been incorporated and codified. "Counterterrorism" and counterinsurgency tactics and programs are increasingly being incorporated and codified into domestic policing, which gives them an immense amount of power, extrajudicial power I would say, because they execute and murder people and assassinate them.

SD: The context you provide is great. And I think that is a big part of why you and I cowrote that December 2014 letter "The War at Home: Bowing Down to White Supremacy" (included after this interview) that gives more context to SARs and the Muslim Mapping Program. We wrote that letter to the Muslim Public Affairs Council [MPAC] because they were awarding LAPD deputy chief Michael Downing their Community Partnership Award, which, as we discussed in the letter, was happening during a heightened moment of national protest around the police killing of several Black people. We ended up putting the letter up online and receiving the support of thousands who were also appalled that MPAC would be awarding the LAPD at this time, especially considering the history of the department. Can you talk about MPAC and their long-standing relationship to law enforcement?

HK: So I started working toward understanding how the national security police state, with the FBI visits after 9/11, their process of interview, the unleashing of the USA PATRIOT Act, that was also recognizing and understanding the failure and the complicity of the leadership within the Muslim community as well. Because the very first meeting, as soon as the USA PATRIOT Act came out, was organized by the Muslim Public Affairs Council at the FBI building. And they [MPAC] were already in partnership with them. So I remember going there with some of our comrades, and there was the FBI selling us the USA PATRIOT Act. So we immediately questioned that. And then MPAC playing this mediator role like, "Well, let's listen to them and what would community outreach look like?" So I think that was in the early sort of memory, or going back to the understanding that, you know, it's not just, who are the mediators of that? Who are the gatekeepers of that? Who are complicit and who are going to help them, you know, just mark the community and go after the community? There was a whole lot of community outreach that was set up by the FBI. You would hear about them going to mosques, having these community meetings, community gatherings, which was also their own surveillance and infiltration. And find out, knowing now, but sometimes back, how they would go to the mosques, they would ask for the architectural blueprint, where their communication thing was, going into various communities. So it was a clear, very organized infiltration and mapping out of the community that was going on. Which led to the LAPD then starting this project, the Muslim Mapping Project in LA, which was finally scrapped, but they've used various other conduits to continue it.

So MPAC has always been on the front lines of mediators and building relationship. And I think that the argument that I've heard from them is that look, this is upon us. So how do we mediate the impact on our community, how do we build a relationship with them, and how do we protect ourselves? So for them, it's more like a harm reduction strategy. I think what is missing in that, which is really, really insidious, is that instead of a harm reduction strategy, this is really a harm expansion impact. And that's what we are looking at. Because what it does is it legitimizes the role of law enforcement, and legitimizes all the programs, and legitimizes everything that is going on through the relationship with MPAC of not just LAPD but the Sheriff's Department, the Department of Homeland Security, with various other organizations.

SD: Obviously, the public premise for these police practices is through the lens of security, and under the War on Terror, there is considerable public support for this. Can you talk about how it is then that within a diverse Muslim community, particular organizations, like MPAC, have been used to give sanction to a policy that in some ways is more disproportionally affecting non-Muslim Black and Brown communities? And what do you think that kind of complicity suggests?

HK: I mean, the immediate answer is that it reflects on and shows a profound complicity with white supremacy that enacts a deep anti-Black racism which has always been the most convenient tool of criminalization. Related to that is the orientation, which is very common and deeply rooted as people who were colonized, is this assumption of whiteness and the honorary Caucasian as well. So I think that also plays out very deeply as well, in terms of who are we going to build solidarity with? So coming to the United States, the solidarity, and it's in practice as well, people who get a bit affluent, and you know, everybody is like, "We don't go to neighborhoods where there are Blacks and Mexicans." So it is a part of our vocabulary, it is a part of our lived experiences. So that gravitation is toward the white picket fence, where both race and class play out very effectively as well.

SD: And there is also this urgent need to define what's a "good immigrant" and what's a "bad immigrant." What's a "good Muslim" and what's a "bad Muslim." Who is the "modern liberal subject" and who is someone stuck in time. Whether here or abroad, these kinds of politics have at their core a deep desire for honorary whiteness that when given positions of relative power and authority to the national security apparatus, end up sanctioning and legitimizing the control and even killing of Black and Brown bodies worldwide, including ironically, Muslims.

HK: Exactly, absolutely. The internalized self-hate and the sense of inferiority as well, where you are constantly in this role where you submit. And when you intersect this with self-hate and this desire to think white, it becomes a very lethal combination.

SD: Can you talk about some of the strategies and programs that Stop LAPD Spying has initiated as a means of organizing against these new models of policing?

HK: So it's a multilevel strategy, of course, of mass community education and outreach. I think one of the things that we are trying to do is to mainstream and popularize the language about surveillance and infiltration. Because typically people always associate it with the FBI and COINTELPRO and federal agencies. But we want to really bring it home, on a very local level, that this is happening by law enforcement agencies constantly. The second piece is to really kind of then build and draw parallels on how they're replicated and applied in the public and private sectors. So really looking at how data move. For example, when we think of surveillance, we need to demystify that thing and talk about it in the context of information gathering, information storing, and information sharing. So you can be traced, and tracked, and monitored.

Also, how does it intersect with public services, such as Section 8 vouchers? How does it work in the housing projects? Because in essence, Broken Windows policing is surveillance policing. So how is it impacting people's daily lives? Like, right here, we are in the community of one of the largest, most densely unhoused communities ever. So how is the community, and how are their data, moving through various systems as well? What would that look like? So kind of just understanding that, and organizing that, and realizing that while it's the Muslim community being targeted, it's not just them. So through research, through numbers, through facts, showing who is really being impacted. Right now, this is the face of that community. For example, one of the programs in the Muslim community that has picked up a lot is the Countering Violent Extremism [CVE]. Which we have basically rolled it around that, while yes, there are a lot of Muslim groups working on that, what we are bringing in, through the teacher's union and looking at it through the larger impact on Black youth and Brown youth as well. That what would countering and preventing violent extremism look like where there is already a history of gang databases, there's already a template of gang injunctions, there's already a praxis of random searches, there's already a practice of wanding that is going on of students in schools. So here now, how is this building?

In a sense, the strategy really is one, to demystify this. Number two, in the long run, for the Muslim community not to be operating in isolation and be a voice in the wilderness. Through this practice, saying like, look, there's a much larger community that is ultimately impacted. And three, for the community itself, the Black and Brown community, to come to a clearer understanding that man, it's not just the Muslim community, ultimately, *we* are the primary targets of all of this. So it's a very sort of layered approach, but through actual work. So for example, one of the things we have been able to do is to have the UTLA [United Teachers of Los Angeles] pass a very strong motion against Preventing Violent Extremism [PVE] and CVE. Their house of representatives has passed a motion against that. So now our goal is to get the LAUSD to come out publicly against CVE and PVE. So that sends it's own message as well to the City of Los Angeles. And that also creates a point of entry to engage in middle schools. Now we are being invited into middle schools and high schools, to go to talk to youth about surveillance and the architecture of surveillance. Like, what would predictive policing mean to them, because chronic offender bulletins are like gang databases on steroids. So in essence, when we talk about mass incarceration, we are looking outside the structures of incarceration and asking, "What is the carceral state?" and "How is it being created?"

But this is nothing new; it's been built. It's not a moment in time but a continuation of history. Our strategies really are grounded, and guided, and driven by communities who have always been impacted.

THE WAR AT HOME: BOWING DOWN TO WHITE SUPREMACY

Sohail Daulatzai and Hamid Khan wrote this letter to the Muslim Public Affairs Council in December 2014. The letter was signed by over 450 students, activists, professors, and organizations.

The streets are on fire. The most widespread social upheaval in at least a generation has engulfed the United States, as the questions and concerns around policing and its brutality have taken center stage. In this volatile and urgent time, we find it deeply troubling and offensive to those who are protesting, to the families who have lost loved ones and to those who have lost their lives, that the Muslim Public Affairs Council (MPAC) would choose to honor Los Angeles Police Department's (LAPD) Deputy Chief Michael Downing for the "Community Partnership Award" at its annual banquet on December 13, 2014.[1]

The relatively recent murders of Sean Bell, Oscar Grant, Rekia Boyd, Trayvon Martin, Michael Brown, Ezell Ford, and Eric Garner, to name a few, reveal a deeply rooted racial animus at the heart of the United States, as the shooting and murder of Black peoples has become routine. According to the Malcolm X Grassroots Movement, every 28 hours a Black person is killed by an official of the State.[2] And just recently, in the wake of the non-indictment of Darren Wilson, the United Nations Committee on Torture issued a report that criticized the United States for the "frequent and recurrent police shootings or fatal pursuits of unarmed black individuals."[3] Here in Los Angeles, the Youth Justice Coalition issued a report in August 2014 which revealed that law enforcement in Los Angeles killed 589 people since 2000.[4]

Embedded within this matrix of murder are deeply rooted issues of racial profiling, the militarization of policing, and the role of police as a form of domestic counter-insurgency within Black and Brown communities that has included everything from "Stop and Frisk" policies, to gang injunctions, as well as the increasing collusion between local police and the U.S. military. And the LAPD is no stranger to these policies—in fact it has been at the forefront of many of these developments, and Deputy Chief Michael Downing has been a central figure.

Michael Downing has been the Commanding Officer of LAPD's Counter-Terrorism Special Operations Bureau (CTSOB) since 2006. Under his leadership the LAPD has created one of the largest architectures of surveillance, profiling, spying and infiltration of any police department in the United States.[5] Contrary to MPAC's claims that Downing has spoken out against Islamophobia, the very programs Downing leads are creating a culture of fear and suspicion that gives further rise to anti-Muslim racism and the continued profiling of Black and Brown communities.[6] Here are some examples:

In November 2007 the LAPD Counter-Terrorism Bureau under Michael Downing launched the Muslim Mapping program.[7] At an October 2007 U.S. Senate hearing, Downing said the intent of the program was "to take a deeper look at their history, demographics, language, culture, ethnic breakdown, socio-economic status, and social interactions."[8] In an interview with the *Los Angeles Times* Downing stated that MPAC "had embraced the vaguely defined program 'in concept.'"[9] The program was ultimately scrapped due to a strong backlash by the larger Muslim community and their allies.

In March 2008 the LAPD-CTSOB spearheaded the National Suspicious Activity Reporting (SAR) program by issuing Special Order 11—changed to Special Order (SO) 1 in January 2012.[10] Defining suspicious activity as "observed behavior reasonably indicative of pre-operational planning of criminal and/or terrorist activity," SO 1 requires LAPD officers to open a secret file (SAR) on such activities as taking pictures, using video cameras, drawing diagrams and several other benign behaviors. Many of the files are transmitted to Fusion Centers, where they may be uploaded into national databases to be shared with thousands of law enforcement agencies, private contractors, and other government agencies and entities.[11] Michael Downing is one of the strongest proponents of this program. A March 2013 LAPD Inspector General audit of the SAR program revealed that in a four-month sample of race data, 82% of these secret files—SARs—were opened on individuals identified as non-white and the largest number was Black people, proving the inherent racial profiling embedded in such programs.[12]

In June 2011 Michael Downing testified at the U.S. House of Representatives on "The Threat of Muslim-American Radicalization in U.S. Prisons" where he raised the specter of "inmate meetings and gatherings taking place using religion as a ruse for other activities" and for jail staff to monitor such activities and use video and audio equipment for these purposes.[13] Given that young Black men are disproportionately the overwhelming majority of incarcerated folks in the United States, many converting to Islam, it is not surprising that Michael Downing would be so concerned as to "take our [LAPD'S] model and counter-terrorism strategy for Los Angeles and as much as possible apply these principles to prisons."[14] This practice of policing prisoners reflects a deeper fear of the politicization of inmates, in the tradition of Malcolm X, George Jackson and others—the rise of Black liberation movements and the demand for social justice is too high a price for state actors like Michael Downing to allow to flourish.

The racism of the LAPD and of every other police department in the country is a racism that permeates the social and political fabric of American life. As people of conscience, we cannot continue to support repressive policies in the name of political expediency and what amounts to rank opportunism, particularly when it's at the expense of the very Black and Brown communities that many of us come from. Let's stand in solidarity with our brothers and sisters who are protesting and raising their voices, and let us abandon our desires for "honorary whiteness"—for there is no truth to this lie. The sooner we realize this, the closer we will get to real political engagement. Wake up, MPAC, you are on the wrong side of history.

Notes

1. http://www.lapdonline.org/lapd_command_staff/comm_bio_view/7598.

2. https://mxgm.org/wp-content/uploads/2013/05/we-charge-genocide-FINAL.pdf.

3. http://tbinternet.ohchr.org/Treaties/CAT/SharedDocuments/USA/INT_CAT_COC_USA_18893_E.pdf.

4. http://www.youth4justice.org/new-release-of-data-from-yjc-on-law-enforcement-use-of-force-resulting-in-a-homicide.

5. http://www.laweekly.com/2014-02-27/news/forget-the-nsa-la-cops-spy-on-millions-of-innocent-folks/; http://stoplapdspying.org/resources/architecture/; http://www.cityofsound.com/blog/2010/01/michael-downing.html.

6. https://www.youtube.com/watch?v=Yl-_pedrJUQ&feature=youtu.be; http://stoplapdspying.org/wp-content/uploads/2013/04/PEOPLES-AUDIT-UPDATED-APRIL-2-2013-A.pdf.

7. http://articles.latimes.com/2007/nov/09/local/me-lapd9.

8. http://www.lapdonline.org/assets/pdf/MichaelDowningTestimonyfortheU.S.Senate-Final.PDF; http://www.npr.org/player/v2/mediaPlayer.html?action=1&t=1&islist=false&id=16162012&m=16161963.

9. http://articles.latimes.com/2007/nov/09/local/me-lapd9.

10. http://stoplapdspying.org/wp-content/uploads/2013/04/PEOPLES-AUDIT -UPDATED-APRIL-2-2013-A.pdf.

11. https://www.documentcloud.org/documents/446073-10-2-12-psi-staff-re port-re-fusion-centers.html.

12. http://stoplapdspying.org/wp-content/uploads/2013/03/IG-audit.pdf.

13. http://homeland.house.gov/sites/homeland.house.gov/files/TestimonyDown ing.pdf.

14. http://www.theislamicmonthly.com/locking-people-in-cages/.

IV

POSSIBLE FUTURES

Dissent and the Protest Tradition

18 To Be a (Young) Black Muslim Woman Intellectual

Su'ad Abdul Khabeer

So much love . . . sometimes it makes me hostile
—AMIR SULAIMAN, "The Meccan Openings"

ALL THE MEN ARE MUSLIM

The first time I heard this verse by Amir Sulaiman, it was as if, for a moment, the world shifted into alignment. It seemed to explain what I had begun to experience too many times to count: my deep love for and unwavering commitment to my community recast as inappropriate aggression. In this verse, I believe Sulaiman describes how love can make the lover unrelenting—in her desire and pursuit for what is best for the beloved. This is a powerful sentiment that made me reflect on my own experiences and observations as a U.S. American Muslim engaged in intellectual work in a raced and gendered body. Like Sulaiman, I am indeed unrelenting in my commitments and love, but what I experience as a result of this passion is not my own hostility but the *mis*-recognition of others. From the 'hood to the boardroom, Black women encounter the world as "a crooked room . . . bombarded with warped images of their humanity."[1] Among the stereotypes or myths that circulate around this crooked room is that Black women are uniquely, irrationally, and unnaturally angry, aggressive, and independent. Unique, irrational, and unnatural are the key terms here, because anger, aggression, and independence are typically seen as falling well within what is considered the range of human expressions and are even at times lauded. Yet when Black women express these sentiments, they immediately leave the realm of normal human activity and become Black female pathology. My experience and the experiences of the Black Muslim woman intellectuals who precede me and are my contemporaries speak to the reality that this mythology does not meet its death at the masjid door but is in fact "live and in full effect" inside the walls of U.S. American Islam.[2]

Exhibit A

Some time ago, I attended a religious lecture at a local Muslim community center. The speaker was a young and promising Black U.S. American Muslim scholar, whom I consider a colleague and friend. During his talk, he made what I thought was a somewhat outlandish claim, something to the effect of "most young people no longer actually want to be good people." During the Q&A session, the topic of youth came up, and I turned to the youth worker in the room to ask him what he thought of that statement—I completely disagreed with it. He did not directly answer but deferred to me. What then ensued was a back and forth between the scholar, who wanted to defend his claim, and me, who critiqued it. The scholar passionately defended his position, but I remained unconvinced. The room got restless, as the audience, multiracial, Muslim and Christian, wanted to move on. I too was ready to move on and was also grateful when the speaker began to take new questions. Immediately after the session was over, the scholar approached me, and we came to a mutual agreement that what he had said was a gross generalization, yet it came from a place of love and frustration with many young people he had recently come in contact with. What is notable about this moment is *not* how the scholar and I engaged each other. Rather, what is notable is that for almost a week after the lecture, at each Muslim event I attended, there was at least one person (sadly, mostly Muslim women of color) who greeted me with "you really went in on [scholar]" or feigned some kind of fear of me in reference to that interaction. I was even approached this way from people who were not at the talk! Why? Had I really "gone in on him"? Doubtful. What I did, however, was to have the audacity to be Black and woman with a voice and opinion, and that was read as a challenge to male authority.

Racist myths about Black women are able to sustain life within U.S. American Muslim communities because patriarchal ideologies structure much of our collective life. U.S. American Muslim communities are entrapped by misguided notions of piety that reify particularized notions of who men and woman could and should be. While these specific gender roles aspire to a model social order through an idealized male authority, they actually result in the infantilization, emasculation, and dehumanization of Muslim men, illustrating the reality that patriarchy damages men as well as women. Men are incapacitated by patriarchal regimes that establish a singular frame through which they are allowed to imagine and interact with women, children, other men, and themselves. This is a frame of power and dominance, which is diametrically opposed to the prophetic framework of compassion, mutual cooperation, and support.[3] Thus, rather than seeing men as fully capable of managing, for example, their heterosexual desire in the model of the Prophet Muhammad, our communities make women responsible for managing male desire. Women must aspire to be neither seen nor heard lest they stoke the fire of the male libido. In this configuration, men are made to be childlike, unable to practice self-restraint, while ironically anointed as the rational authority over women.

Feminist scholars have long noted the many damaging effects of patriarchy for women.[4] Here I want to briefly focus on its effects for the Black Muslim woman scholar. It is by way of patriarchy that the kinds of qualities of intellect, insight, and passion that are lauded in non-Muslim U.S. American professional settings become liabilities for the Muslim woman who seeks to be an active part of the collective. The moment she/I steps into a U.S. American Muslim community space, these qualities become liabilities. Her/my intellect and insight are immodest and unfeminine. Her passion is irrational and unnatural. Racism and patriarchy intersect to construct the crooked room of the U.S. American Muslim community—a room that is the product of caricature of angry Black womanhood and also reproduces this myth. Identified as Black, woman, and pathological, she/I is ostracized through open hostility, rumors, and/or benign neglect of the expertise she/I seeks to put to the service of her/my community. Critically, she/I is held with such little esteem by men as well as women. Thus the Black Muslim woman intellectual finds herself devalued not only at the hands of men but at those of women as well, women who, either with seditious intent or out of habit, act in complicity with patriarchy. Importantly, these qualities, such as the ability to articulate powerfully and passionately, to critically analyze complex ideas, and to imagine new possibilities, are at a certain level dangerous for any U.S. American woman to embody. The Black Muslim woman intellectual too lives with this danger. She takes on this danger when she challenges those who benefit from race, class, gender, and religious privilege. With her voice, her words, her art, her activism, her mind, her spirit, and her body, she engages individuals, communities, and institutions by pushing them to acknowledge their privileges and participate in dismantling the systems of inequality from which privilege is born, systems under which her Muslim community, male and female, suffers. This is hard work. It is alienating and isolating work. And to have that compounded by her community is heartbreaking.

Heartbreak and deep frustration are what come with living in a context of such psychic and spiritual exclusion. For the Black Muslim woman, intellectual racism and spiritual patriarchy intersect in deeply perverse ways and on a deeply personal level. Yet the "personal is political," and thus the experience of the Black Muslim woman intellectual reflects realities of even broader concern.

All the Americans Are White

Exhibit B

Officially, the reality TV show *All-American Muslim* was not "renewed for a second season" because of its relatively low ratings. Many US Muslims were skeptical about this cancellation. The major hardware store chain Lowe's had just pulled its ads from the *All-American Muslim* time slot. The company had succumbed to pressure from the well-orchestrated campaign of a far right group that claimed the show was a farce. The show, this group argued, failed to show who Muslims really are, namely, a group of brown-skinned fanatics looking to take your women, replace Jesus with Allah, and steal the freedom you won by pulling on your bootstraps. So soon after the Lowe's fiasco, it left many wondering if anti-Muslim racism won—but over what exactly? See, even without this controversy, the show was not without its critics. Some U.S. Muslims were critical because they believed the show "aired our collective dirty laundry," so to speak. This was because not all of the show's characters were religious observant, or they were observant in nontraditional ways. Others, like myself, thought the show should have really been called "Lebanese, American, and Muslim in the D," since it was hardly representative of the U.S. American Muslim community yet marketed itself as such. Some claimed the demographic was because of location, but word on my Twitter and Facebook news feeds was that the next-door neighbors of one of the show's families were Black U.S. American Muslims . . . but I get why they would not make the cut. Black, U.S. American, and Muslim really undercuts the Muslim-equals-foreigner story told by Islamophobes and bleeding-heart liberals alike.

The same logics that seek to marginalize and exclude the Black Muslim woman intellectual in the classroom, the public square, and the masjid alike motivate the marginalization and exclusion of Muslims *as U.S. Americans* on the national scene and *as fully human* on the global one. As theorized by acclaimed feminist author bell hooks, white supremacy and patriarchy align with capitalism and imperialism to form "the interlocking political systems that are the foundation of our nation's politics."[5] By grouping these terms, hooks's theory underscores their relatedness as systems of oppression. They interlock because one can be multiply excluded, based on gender, class, race, nationality, and other markers of identity. They are systems because their effects do not solely or even primarily occur on the person-to-person basis, although this is a potent site of discrimination. Rather, as *systemic,* their effects are reproduced *within and across* our major institutions of influence and power, such as the government and the media. In the specific case of U.S. American Muslims, this can be seen in government rhetoric, both when it is hostile and when it is multiculturalist; in law à la the USA PATRIOT Act; and in the media, such as on *Fox News* and TV serials like *Homeland,* which systematize what I like to call the "facts of Muslimness."

Using Frantz Fanon's "facts of blackness" as a model, I use the phrase "facts of Muslimness" to identify the core assumptions about Muslims that have dominated the Euro-American conversation on Islam in the past century.[6] The term *Muslim* conjures the image of someone who is "Middle Eastern looking," has an accent, and is irrationally obsessed with violence because of his uniquely fanatical attachment to religion and tradition. Thus, when a white non-Muslim child shouts out, "Look, Mom! A Muslim!" she or he is rehearsing these "facts": the Muslim is Brown, the Muslim is foreign, the Muslim is backward, the Muslim is pathological, the Muslim is dangerous. These assumptions are replayed over and over, reinforcing not only who Muslims supposedly *are* but who they are *not*: white, native, progressive, and peace-loving, that is, U.S. Americans. These "facts" are the products of processes of racial formation that construct and reproduce the normative assumptions of "Muslim as other" and "American as white."[7] As a result, if Muslims are *always* and *already* "other," then it becomes fairly commonsensical to presume they are outside the nation. Yet if Muslims are *always* and *already* a "dangerous other," it also becomes common sense to seek to exclude Muslims from the nation for the sake of its preservation.

It goes without saying that this process that positions whiteness, specifically heterosexual male Christian white identity, and U.S. American identity as equivalents has been a basic and violent reality for people of color in the United States. This discourse of white normativity persists despite the country's long and increasing racial, ethnic, and cultural diversity. In fact, it persists alongside the multiculturalist rhetoric deployed by the state. The face of U.S.-style multiculturalism embraces "diversity." Native American "nobility," Black U.S. American "struggle," and Asian U.S. American and Latinx "success" are endorsed as proof of the United

States's exceptionalism in the league of nations. Furthermore, U.S.-style multiculturalism positively asserts bonds between different kinds of U.S. Americans. Yet these bonds are "appropriately hierarchal."[8] Nonwhite Americans are incorporated into the nation, yet only according to terms that do not destabilize the status quo, that is, the basic assumption that privileges whiteness in the United States and around the globe. Thus inclusion is always incomplete. Accordingly, every time a violent public act takes place, U.S. America's Muslims hold their collective breath and pray the alleged perpetrator is anything *but* Muslim. In stark contrast, even in the face of the most recent spate of mass shootings by white men, white men carry no such burden—another violent act by a white male will not result in ramifications for white men either as individuals or as a group.

This normative landscape that marks U.S. Muslims as "other" in relation to the nation is paralleled in the global discourse on Islam, and how we talk and think about Islam and Muslims today is historically rooted in the Western European quest for empire. The labor of Black and Brown peoples played a central role in the empire building of the British, the French, and other European colonial powers. Were it not for slave labor, the triangular trade, the extraction of the natural resources, and violence against local peoples, the world as we know it, including and especially its technological and industrial advancement, would not exist. The hierarchical relationships critical to this kind of domination were also central to the project of modernity, and as such, the growth and development of liberalism and free-market capitalism are also indebted to Black and Brown bodies.

When I use the word *labor,* I include the physical labor of enslaved and colonized Africans, Asians, and indigenous peoples as well as their psychic displacement from subject to object, from human to other. This labor was just as involuntary and just as important. As object and other to be owned and subjugated, they performed conceptual labor in the construction of a "hierarchy of man" that elevated the European. This link between capital, industry, domination, and white supremacy sustains itself today. Our current world system of power and commodities from gold and petroleum to iPads and coffee also would fail to exist were it not for Black and Brown bodies from California to China. Furthermore, capitalism generates false desires—to extract profit from new markets, there must be new "needs." What is critical to underscore is that many of these desires and needs are directly tied to white supremacist and patriarchal notions of what is beautiful, what is good, what is true, what is normal, and what is necessary. This is also part and parcel of U.S. dominance as a world power.

Thus how we talk and think about Islam and Muslims today are also tightly bound to U.S. imperial pursuits. While talk of biological hierarchies between the "races" has fallen out of favor (at least publicly and, at least, for now), *culture,* whether identified as practices (i.e., bikinis or burqas) or worldviews (i.e., secular or religious), is now the determinant factor that distinguishes "inferior" and "superior" human societies. Cultural difference, or rather, to be culturally distinct from the global white normative standard, is deficiency. Within the discourse of the War on Terror, we find well-worn ideologies of racial and cultural superiority and inferiority now cloaked in "culture-talk."[9] The world is divided: the Middle East/Orient/"the Rest" is identified as the home of violent, dangerous, antidemocratic, and brown-skinned peoples with the United States/the "West" as home to a peace-loving, powerful, fair, and democratic civilization, in which whiteness is privileged but not everyone is white skinned. Accordingly, Muslims are deficient and in need of a pater to monitor, supervise, and dominate them.

My use of pater, or "father," here is not incidental. Scholars have identified the ways the patriarchal motif plays itself out beyond the ideal of male-headed households. Patriarchy is an epistemological framework, which means it makes a certain set of claims about the nature of human relationships. Patriarchy constructs a relationship between people based on dominance, authoritarianism, submission, coercion, and violence.[10] This epistemology operates systemically, within and across powerful institutions, and normalizes hierarchical relationships not only between men and women but between whites and nonwhites and the "West" and Islam.

Fundamentally, contemporary Muslims, in the United States and abroad, find themselves confronted with ideologies and systems in which what makes them different is recast as deficiency. This is not only a geopolitical reality but an ethical and spiritual one as well. In an online lecture, Islamic studies scholar Sherman Jackson articulated the possibility that white supremacy could be considered a modern form of shirk (idolatry).[11] He argued that white supremacy traffics in notions of white normativity and racial hierarchies in which the loyalty and fidelity that belong only to God are misplaced onto the human beings and human systems that are raced white. This is for the Muslim the ultimate transgression, because it denies God's oneness and incomparability. For the Muslim, this also transgresses God's decree. In the Qur'an, God speaks about difference. God states, "We have created you [humanity] all out of a male and a female, and have made you into nations and tribes, so that you might come to know one another. Indeed the most noble of you in the sight of God is the one who is most deeply conscious of him" (49:13). Thus in difference, in distinction, is not deficiency but a divine decree and purpose. Humanity was created to be different, and the purpose of that difference is knowledge. Thus there is an ethical imperative here, because it is impossible to know what you despise, debase, and destroy. There is also a spiritual imperative here, because in the Islamic tradition, knowledge of God's creation is a pathway toward greater knowledge of God.

A similar logic regarding patriarchy has also been articulated by the Qur'anic scholar Amina Wadud,[12] namely, that patriarchy traffics in notions of male normativity and gender hierarchies in which the loyalty and fidelity that belong only to God are misplaced onto human beings and human systems that are gendered male. As with the racial logic of white supremacy, in the logic of patriarchy, what makes women different from men has been recast as deficiency. This argument is probably harder for many to swallow because of their investments in patriarchy. Yet the argument holds: "When a person seeks to place him- or herself 'above' another, it either means the divine presence is removed or ignored or that the person who imagines his or herself above others suffers from the egoism of shirk."[13] The egoism of shirk and its recasting of difference as deficiency are a divergence from the ethical and spiritual imperatives of knowledge.

Difference becomes deficiency and leads to dominance. It is the interplay between imperialism, patriarchy, white supremacy, and capitalism that enabled past colonial and contemporary domination of Muslim peoples under regimes of neoliberalism and wars of democracy. Muslims know intimately imperialist white supremacist capitalist patriarchy. They deeply experience the ways these interlocking systems restrict and limit their movements, possibilities, and opportunities. And as well as they know them, they rightfully seek to dismantle them. Yet when they simultaneously exclude the Black Muslim woman intellectual, they fight against themselves—they reproduce these imperial logics and become complicit not only in her subjugation but in their own.

But Some of Us Are Brave

My subtitles, "All the Men Are Muslim, All the Americans Are White, but Some of Us Are Brave," is meant to enunciate the explicit, which has been obscured by power. This is the reality that the social worlds of the Black Muslim woman intellectual and all American Muslims are defined, in many ways, by two normative assumptions: to be Muslim is to be male and to be American is to be white. I refer to these assumptions as normative not because they are "normal" or "true" but because they have been normalized and thus given the authority and expectation of common sense. Muslims are not only men, yet it is the male experience that is treated as proxy for the experience of all genders (hence the rarity of a "Men in Islam" panel at the local masjid, community center, or yearly national convention). Likewise, all U.S. Americans are not white, but the advantages and the indisputable claim to U.S. American belonging are still tied to white identity, hence the intense and troubling battles we are now witnessing in the United States over immigration, over gun control, over reproductive rights, and over the country's religious or secular character.

My title is also deeply citational; it is a riff off a riff. Islamic studies scholar Aminah McCloud contributed to a recent anthology written in tribute to the career and activism of Wadud. In her reflection, she described the attempts to exclude Wadud from the Islamic studies canon in the following statement: "All the Muslims are men, all the Muslim scholars are men from the Muslim world (Arab first and then a few others) and this is the end of the story. . . . Where did/does Wadud fit?"[14] In McCloud's word play, I hear a riff on the seminal Black women studies text "All the Blacks Are Men, All the Whites Are Women, but Some of Us Are Brave." This pioneering text made a critical intervention in the marginalization of Black women from feminist theory and praxis and from the narrative of the Black American experience and liberation struggle. Through its collection of Black female scholarship, it rejected the assumption that the Black male perspective was *the* Black experience and that white middle-class woman could represent the realities and struggles of all women, particularly women who lived with race and class discrimination as well as gender oppression. In this riff off a riff, I endeavor to function within and extend a tradition of spiritually engaged intellectual work that challenges hegemony by increasing our collective body of knowledge about the history and lifeways of humanity, especially of those whose lives and ideas have been hidden yet who were brave enough to exist, to speak, to fight, and to thrive despite this. Like them, we must be brave.

EXHIBIT C

On the Saturday evening of New Year's weekend, the beloved community leader and activist Sister[15] Aliyah Abdul Karim (May God be pleased with her) would open her home for what in some circles might be called a cipher or, in others, a salon. I began attending these gatherings as a child with my mother and through my late teens continued to look forward to it. I recall tables filled with a potluck of delicious food and desserts, but it was the energy of the conversation that has left its greatest impression on me. My whole community was there and everybody could speak. The elders in the room would speak from their knowledge and experience, but Sister Aliyah was also very intentional about inviting the younger people to speak and share their own perspectives and wisdom. The men would contribute to the conversation, and so would the women. And the topics were serious—racism, structural inequalities, polygamy, parenting, the arts, war. In this all-Muslim crowd that hailed from all parts of the Black diaspora, we would identify our collective struggles, dissect and debate their causes, and envision solutions. In retrospect, this gathering itself was a solution. Everybody had a seat, everybody had a share, everybody gave something, everybody was welcome, and everybody was valued.

U.S. America's Muslims spend a lot of time hemming and hawing over their outside status. Scratching at the doors of power, they plead to be let in—they see a crooked room and tilt their heads. This is unfortunate, but not inevitable. Rather, this community could take its cues from the bravery of the many Sister Aliyahs that were and are still among us, who look at the crooked room and go about setting it aright. Hence bravery becomes a key sensibility to inculcate in this community in these times. What does it mean to be brave? It means to resist and thrive. It means to resist being marginalized and excluded but also to resist complicity in the marginalization and exclusion of others. Yet to do so, bravery also requires knowledge. We have to study the past, our collective histories. We do this to encourage our appreciation and application of the spiritual and ethical imperatives that come from differences within humankind and the natural world. We do this to fine-tune our ability to decipher domination and its effects, which includes our oppression and our privilege. It is critically important that we do not deny the privileges that we may be privy to because of race, gender, and nationality. Rather, we must acknowledge these privileges so that we may use all the resources at our disposal to push forward to build a more equitable world.

Yet bravery comes at a high cost. Bravery is to speak when everyone else has been rendered silent, to speak against the chorus of nays. Sometimes bravery is quiet in its valiance; it can consist of just being there, claiming the space you were given despite all efforts to eliminate your presence.

Bravery can be frightening—but if we do it together, there is security in our solidarity and true success in sight.

NOTES

1. Melissa Harris-Perry, *Sister Citizen: Shame, Stereotypes, and Black Women in America* (New Haven, Conn.: Yale University Press, 2011), 29.

2. I placed the modifier "young" in parentheses in this chapter title as a reflexive move that acknowledges my status as a new or emerging Muslim intellectual and how that shapes my perspective. I also did so to question if there are in fact significant qualitative differences in the Black Muslim woman intellectual experience over time. If there are indeed any qualitative differences, it is that senior scholars such as Amina Wadud and Aminah McCloud, and others, are mentoring junior academics like me.

3. bell hooks, *The Will to Change: Men, Masculinity, and Love* (New York: Washington Square Press, 2004).

4. Michelle Rosaldo and Louise Lamphere, eds., *Woman, Culture, and Society* (Stanford, Calif.: Stanford University Press, 1974); Combahee River Collective, *The Combahee River Collective Statement: Black Feminist Organizing in the Seventies and Eighties* (Albany, N.Y.: Kitchen Table: Women of Color Press, 1986); Patricia Hill Collins, *Black Feminist Thought: Knowledge, Consciousness, and the Politics of Empowerment* (New York: Routledge, 2008); bell hooks, *Feminism Is for Everybody: Passionate Politics* (New York: Routledge, 2014).

5. hooks, *Will to Change*, 17.

6. Frantz Fanon, *Black Skins, White Masks* (New York: Grove Press, 1967).

7. Michael Omi and Howard Winant, *Racial Formation in the United States: From the 1960s to the 1990s* (New York: Routledge, 1994).

8. Melanie McAlister, *Epic Encounters: Culture, Media, and U.S. Interests in the Middle East since 1945,* updated ed. (Berkeley: University of California Press, 2005), 259.

9. Mahmood Mamdani, *Good Muslim, Bad Muslim: America, the Cold War, and the Roots of Terror* (New York: Harmony, 2005).

10. hooks, *Will to Change*.

11. Sherman Jackson, "White Supremacy: The Beginning of Modern Day Shirk?," *Lamppost*, March 1, 2017, http://www.lamppostproductions.com/white-supremacy-the-modern-day-shirk/.

12. Amina Wadud, *Inside the Gender Jihad: Women's Reform in Islam* (Oxford: Oneworld, 2006).

13. Ibid., 32.

14. Aminah Beverly McCloud, "Amina Wadud: Scattered Thoughts and Reflections," in *A Jihad for Justice: Honoring the Work and Life of Amina Wadud,* ed. Kecia Ali, Julianne Hammer, and Laury Silvers (2012), 235, http://www.bu.edu/religion/files/2010/03/A-Jihad-for-Justice-for-Amina-Wadud-2012-1.pdf.

15. *Sister* here is used as an honorific, as is commonly done among African American Muslims.

19

Letter from a West Bank Refugee Camp

ROBIN D. G. KELLEY

Dear Members of the Vanguard Leadership Group (and African American "leaders" everywhere),

While visiting the Aida Refugee Camp in the occupied West Bank, I came across your recent statements defending Israel against charges that it is an "apartheid" state. You accuse Students for Justice in Palestine (SJP) of spreading "misinformation" and invoking an "illegitimate analogy" that anyone familiar with "the truth about the Israeli's record on human rights" would find "patently false." The evidence? Unlike Black South Africans, the "Arab minority in Israel enjoys full citizenship with voting rights and representation in the government."[1]

As I reflect on your words, I take in the landscape from the rooftop of a deteriorating housing complex inside the refugee camp. On this extraordinarily clear, crisp day, the illegal "apartheid wall" dominates the terrain, abutting the camp and snaking in both directions as far as the eye can see. Rising above the twenty-foot wall is the notorious Bethlehem checkpoint, where Palestinians entering Jerusalem are subject to frequent interrogation, harassment, and delay. Beyond the wall atop a low-sloping rise sits the illegal Jewish settlement of Gilo. In the valley adjacent to the camp are the remains of what was a Palestinian village—a couple of small dwellings occupied by families who refuse to be driven off by settler violence. We learned that the children attend the camp's United Nations (UN)-run school, but the wall has turned a ten-minute walk into a two-hour ordeal each way.

Your statement reveals a woeful ignorance of Israel's history and a basic understanding of apartheid. First, apartheid did more than strip

Black South Africans of voting and civil rights. The regime dispossessed Africans from their land and, through legislative and military acts, razed entire communities and transferred Africans to government townships and Bantustans. It was a system of racial classification and population control that limited the movement of Africans in towns and cities and denied them social and economic privileges based on race. And it outlawed every organization that challenged the right of an apartheid state to exist, that is, a state based on racial or ethnic hierarchy, and used state violence and detention to suppress opposition.

Israel has been practicing a form of apartheid since its inception. After destroying some 380 Palestinian villages, and ethnically cleansing Palestinian towns and neighborhoods in mixed cities in 1948, confiscating land without compensation—what Palestinians call *al Nakba* (the catastrophe)—Israel passed the Absentees' Property Law (1950), effectively transferring all property owned or used by Palestinian refugees to the state, and then denied their right to return or reclaim their losses. The land grab continued after the 1967 war and military occupation of Gaza, the West Bank, and East Jerusalem—which compose merely 22 percent of Western Palestine to begin with. In violation of the Fourth Geneva Convention, Jewish settlements in the occupied territories have expanded exponentially since 1967. Currently more than five hundred thousand settlers are living in the West Bank, and at least 43 percent of the land has been allocated to settler regional and local councils and therefore is off-limits for Palestinian use. And so are certain roads. Israel has built an elaborate system of paved settler-only roads that cross over crumbling, often blockaded Palestinian roads. Special licenses are required to travel on the settler roads. Unauthorized vehicles could be confiscated and their drivers detained.[2]

Your statement ignores the four million Palestinians living under Israeli occupation and the millions living abroad or in refugee camps in neighboring countries. Instead, you refer only to the alleged citizenship rights of the 1.5 million "Arab Israelis" (roughly 20 percent of the population) living within Israel. Yes, they have voting rights, and yes, a small minority has been elected to office, but Israeli law is very clear: the only "citizens" who enjoy *full* rights and nationality are Jews. Under the Law of Return, Jews from anywhere in the world can obtain automatic citizenship and residency in Israel, whereas the Citizenship Law abolishes the rights of the Palestinian citizens' relatives to return to their homes and land. The "non-Jew," namely, Palestinian citizens of Israel, are legally denied equal access to property, social and welfare services, and material resources administered by the state—including 93 percent of the territory of the pre-1967 borders administered by the Israel Lands Administration. And then there are Palestinian citizens who live in Israel but are bizarrely classified by the Absentees' Property Law as "absent" because they allegedly "abandoned" their property. They have no rights to lands, houses, bank accounts, bank safes, or other property they had owned prior to 1948.

For Palestinian citizens in Israel, however, discrimination defines their daily reality. Most are obliged to live in exclusively "Arab" villages that have been prohibited from expanding, are legally excluded from residing in non-Arab communities based on their "social unsuitability," attend severely underfunded schools, are denied government employment, and are prohibited from living with their spouse if she or he is a Palestinian from the occupied territories. Little wonder that more than half of all Palestinian families in Israel were classified as poor in 2009. And every Palestinian citizen of Israel traveling through Tel-Aviv's Ben-Gurion Airport endures systematic racial profiling, is subject to interrogation and manual bag checks, and is issued a different passport sticker and luggage tags to signal their "Arab" ethnicity and higher "threat level." Palestinian Israelis can expect their check-in process to take about twice as long as that of their fellow Jewish citizens.

What about their precious political rights? Palestinian citizens of Israel, including minors, are routinely arrested for participating in protests critical of the state. Indeed, as I write these words, hundreds of Palestinians— many of whom are students—are being held in Israeli prisons for political activity or for reasons unknown based on "secret evidence." Israel can detain Palestinians for up to six months without charge or trial, with no limits on renewal. Administrative detention, as it is called, is based on three laws: Military Order 1651, which empowers the army to issue orders to detain civilians in the West Bank; the Unlawful Combatants Law, which applies to Gaza residents; and the Emergency Powers Detention Law used against Israeli citizens. These laws violate Article 9 of the International Covenant on Civil and Political Rights, which prohibits arbitrary detention, requires that detainees be told why they are being held, and stipulates that every person has the right of habeas corpus.[3] Political organizations advocating boycott of Israeli products, or calling for a secular state with equal rights for all, are essentially illegal.[4] The Knesset even passed a law forbidding the commemoration of the Nakba or even mentioning it in school textbooks.[5] You praise Israeli democracy and its record on human rights, and yet several Palestinian members of the Knesset have been indicted or had parliamentary privileges revoked for legitimate political activities and speech.[6]

Just these laws and practices alone meet the UN's definition of apartheid, that is, any measures designed to "prevent a racial group or groups from participation in the political, social, economic and cultural life of the country," including "the right to leave and to return to their country, the right to a nationality, the right to freedom of movement and residence, the right to freedom of opinion and expression."[7] Even if you find the UN definition of apartheid "illegitimate," how do you respond to Shulamit Aloni, former minister of education under Yitzhak Rabin, who declared, "The state of Israel practises its own, quite violent form of apartheid with the native Palestinian population"? Or Michael Ben-Yair, Israel's attorney general from 1993 to 1996, who observed, "In effect, we established an apartheid regime in the occupied territories immediately following their capture."[8]

Although your statement deplores the apartheid analogy, it fails to express any concern for the conditions of Palestinians. You say you want "justice, and the hope of peace and reconciliation," but until you've seen Palestinians' homes demolished and their olive trees uprooted by the Israeli Defense Forces; walked through the souk in Hebron, which is littered with bricks and garbage and human feces thrown at Palestinian merchants by messianic settlers; negotiated the narrow, muddy pathways separating overcrowded, multistoried shacks in the refugee camps in Nablus or Jenin or Bethlehem; met mothers who had to give birth on the side of the road or watched their severely ill children die for want of emergency care because they were held up at an Israeli checkpoint; spoken with parents whose boys had been detained, maimed, or even killed for throwing rocks at tanks; or had to explain to a child why her family has to ration water while the Jewish settlement a couple of miles away maintains swimming pools, you will never comprehend what is required for a just peace and genuine reconciliation.

But is a just peace in the Middle East your real objective? Your founders, Darius Jones and Jarrod Jordan, both graduates of Clark Atlanta University, claim that the mission of the Vanguard Leadership Group (VLG) was to nurture a new generation of African American leaders "possessed of a more expansive and inclusive world view." And yet, you've foreclosed an "inclusive world view" for the tunnel vision of your primary financial

backer, the American Israel Public Affairs Committee (AIPAC). For at least
the past four years, VLG members have participated in AIPAC-sponsored
tours of Israel and developed its talking points through its Saban Leadership Training seminars. AIPAC not only honored Jones and Jordan with
its Jonathan Barkan Israel Advocacy Award in 2009 and named the VLG
its AIPAC Advocate of the Year for its attack on SJP but rewarded Jones
with a lucrative gig as its southeast regional outreach director.[9]

Let's be clear. You do not speak for African Americans, nor does
AIPAC speak for most American Jews. And you certainly do not embrace
the principles of social justice and liberation, despite your identification
with Dr. Martin Luther King Jr. You speak for the state of Israel—which
is not the same as speaking for Israelis, many of whom want an end to
the occupation and the apartheid system in their country. And the fact
that you *do* speak for AIPAC reveals a lobby so desperate for Black allies
that it is willing to overlook your own leaders' problematic comments.
Mr. Jordan, for example, compared the SJP's decision to hold its 2011
national conference at Columbia University "to the Ku Klux Klan holding
a conference at Morehouse College in Atlanta, a total affront to Jewish
culture and identity."[10] In other words, as Morehouse is a historically
Black college, Columbia University is a historically *Jewish* institution in a
historically Jewish city! Reeking of Jesse Jackson's "hymietown" slur, it
not only ignores Columbia's anti-Semitic past and paints "Jewish culture
and identity" as a monolith but also equates a student solidarity movement with the Klan—an organization whose anti-Semitism rivaled its
anti-Black racism.

And then there is the curious case of Darius Jones, who, just two years
before his involvement with AIPAC, wrote a blog called *9Ether News* that
reads like a cross between Oswald Spengler, Herbert Spencer, and *Mein
Kampf.* "Our race," Jones wrote on October 4, 2006, "would be wise to
learn from nature. We would be even better served to harmonize with its
evolutionary designs. Clearly, survival of the fittest is the moral of the
story. However, we continually ignore what is patently obvious. . . . Social
dynamics move more in accordance with biological prerogatives than
humanistic ideals."[11] Perhaps Mr. Jones also sees Israel–Palestine in
social Darwinian terms. Israel prevailed because Palestinians could not
compete. Expansion of the fittest?

None of this is surprising. AIPAC, through the American Israel Educational Foundation and Christians United for Israel (CUFI), founded by
the controversial Reverend John Hagee, has been working overtime to

recruit Black students, elected officials, and religious leaders to serve as moral shields for Israel's policies of subjugation, settlement, segregation, and dispossession. CUFI's coordinator of African American outreach, Michael Stevens, invokes the ghost of Dr. Martin Luther King Jr. to the cause, declaring in a recent interview, "King was a strong African-American Zionist."[12] King certainly dissuaded Black militants from criticizing Zionism, and he avoided taking a public stand on the 1967 war, but had he lived long enough to see the crippling effects of the occupation, his unequivocal opposition to violence, colonialism, racism, and militarism would make him an incisive critic of Israel's current policies. He would probably join Bishop Desmond Tutu in his support of the Boycott, Divestment, Sanctions (BDS) campaign. Indeed, I can envision Dr. King in Palestine, waging a nonviolent campaign to bring down the wall, perhaps writing another memorable letter to those who remain silent in the face of such egregious violations of human rights. This time around, he would probably address his letter to Black leaders rather than clergy. Except for the usual suspects among the Black Left—Bill Fletcher, Angela Davis, Gina Dent, Cornel West, Ron Daniels, Barbara Ransby, Danny Glover, Alice Walker, and Reverend Graylan Hagler, among others—mainstream African American leadership has been eerily silent on Palestine and virtually absent from the BDS campaign. Even veterans of the U.S. Free South Africa Movement have been slow to join their South African counterparts in opposing Israeli apartheid.

Ironically, while you, CUFI, and like-minded Black organizations claim Dr. King's legacy, I am witnessing King's vision in practice—his vision of nonviolent resistance, creative tension, love—right here in the Aida Refugee Camp. Aida is home to the Alrowwad Cultural and Theater Society, a genuine community center and youth theater founded by director, poet, playwright, and educator Dr. Abdelfattah Abusrour. For him, theater is a "nonviolent way of saying we are human beings, we are not born with genes of hatred and violence, we do not conform to the stereotype of Palestinians only capable of throwing stones or burning tires." Having grown up in the camp, Abusrour gave up a promising career in science to devote his life to creating a "beautiful theater of resistance" aimed at releasing the creative capacity of young people to turn their stories into transformative experiences. In Abusrour's play *We Are Children of the Camp,* children speak from personal experience about Israeli soldiers invading the camps, shooting parents, and denying them access to hospitals on the other side of the wall. They long for human rights, a clean environment, freedom, a right to return to their land, and the right to know and own their history. They encapsulate this history in the play's title song, in which they sing of being made refugees in their own land, of colonies built and villages demolished.[13]

The children at the Aida Camp remind me that what is most apt about the South African analogy is not the litany of laws and abuses but the struggle—the optimism of the will, the prefiguring of a postapartheid/ post-Zionist society. As one song from Children of the Camp puts it, "Occupation never lasts . . . / The government of injustice, vanishes with revolution." Let us all hope that as more and more young Palestinians create democratic alternatives to settler colonialism and its racist, antidemocratic ideology, and more Israelis come to see how occupation and apartheid distort their own lives and dreams, and more people around the globe join the BDS movement and refuse to invest in Israel's regime of occupation and apartheid, injustice will give way to something beautiful.

Yours for the cause of Peace and Justice,
Robin D. G. Kelley

NOTES

A different version of this chapter was previously published as "Letter from a West Bank Refugee Camp," *Portside*, June 24, 2013, https://portside.org/print/2013-06 -27/letter-west-bank-refugee-camp.

1. See Yaman Salahi, "Truth Matters: The Vanguard Leadership Group Is Wrong," *Mondoweiss* (blog), April 11, 2011, http://mondoweiss.net/2011/04/truth-matters -the-vanguard-leadership-group-is-wrong.html; Gary Rosenblatt, "Black Group Defends Israel against Charge of Apartheid," *The Jewish Week*, October 10, 2011, http:// www.thejewishweek.com/news/new_york/black_group_defends_israel_against_ charge_apartheid; Seth Freed Wessler, "The Israel Lobby Finds a New Face: Black College Students," *Colorlines*, January 18, 2012, http://colorlines.com/archives/2012/ 01/why_the_israel_lobby_looks_to_black_students_for_support.html.

2. Katie Hesketh, with Suhad Bishara, Rina Rosenberg, and Sawsan Zaher, *The Inequality Report: The Palestinian Arab Minority in Israel* (Yaffa: ADALAH: The Legal Center for Arab Minority Rights in Israel, March 2011).

3. "Israeli Military Orders Relevant to the Arrest, Detention and Prosecution of Palestinians," Addameer: Prisoner Support and Human Rights Association, http:// www.addameer.org/israeli_military_judicial_system/military_orders; see also United Nations General Assembly, Human Rights Council, *Human Rights in Palestine and Other Occupied Arab Territories: Report of the United Nations Fact-Finding Mission on the Gaza Conflict*, report A/HRC/12/48 (New York: United Nations, 2009), 308–9, for earlier military orders that set precedent for military detentions that circumvent international law.

4. Harriet Sherwood, "Israel Passes Law Banning Citizens from Calling for Boycotts," *The Guardian*, July 11, 2011, http://www.theguardian.com/world/2011/jul/11/israel-passes-law-boycotts.

5. Shiri Raphaely, "The 'Nakba Law' and Erasing History," *Mondoweiss* (blog), March 31, 2011, http://mondoweiss.net/2011/03/the-nakba-law-and-erasing-history.

6. Stephen Lendman, "Israel Persecuting Palestinian Knesset Member Hanin Zoabi," *Global Research*, March 7, 2013, http://www.globalresearch.ca/israel-perse cuting-palestinian-knesset-member-hanin-zoabi/5325683; Sophie Crowe, "Israel's Political Persecution of Palestinian Parliamentarians," *Palestine Monitor*, February 27, 2012, reposted on http://www.uruknet.info/?p=86077; "Hanin Zoabi Suspended from Knesset for Six Months," *Times of Israel*, July 29, 2014, http://www.timesof israel.com/hanin-zoabi-suspended-from-knesset-for-six-months/; Revita Hovel, "MK Hanin Zoabi Must Report for Questioning," *Haaretz*, August 5, 2014, http://www .haaretz.com/news/national/.premium-1.609077.

7. International Convention on the Suppression and Punishment of the Crime of Apartheid, G.A. res. 3068 (XXVIII), 28 U.N. GAOR Supp. (No. 30) at 75, U.N. Doc. A/9030 (1974), 1015 U.N.T.S. 243, entered into force July 18, 1976, http://www1.umn.edu/humanrts/instree/apartheid-supp.html. For an elaboration on Israeli apartheid, see Uri Davis, *Apartheid Israel: Possibilities for the Struggle Within* (London: Zed Books, 2003). See also Nima Shirazi, "Defending Apartheid: Then in South Africa, Now in Palestine," *Mondoweiss* (blog), September 5, 2014, http://mon doweiss.net/2014/09/defending-apartheid-palestine.html; Musa Keilani, "Apartheid in Israel," *Jordan Times*, January 14, 2012, http://jordantimes.com/apartheid-in -israel; Ben White, *Israeli Apartheid: A Beginner's Guide*, 2nd ed. (London: Pluto Press, 2014); Saree Makdisi, *Palestine Inside Out: An Everyday Occupation*, rev ed. (New York: W. W. Norton, 2010); Ilan Pappe, *The Ethnic Cleansing of Palestine* (Oxford: Oneworld, 2007); Nur Masalha, *The Palestine Nakba: Decolonising History, Narrating the Subaltern, Reclaiming Memory* (London: Zed Books, 2012); Palestine Solidarity Committee, *Declaration by South Africans on Apartheid Israel and the Struggle for Palestine*, Durban, South Africa, August 31, 2001.

8. Murray Dobbins, "Israel's Apartheid," *The Tyee*, March 8, 2010, http://the tyee.ca/Opinion/2010/03/08/MurrayDobbinIsrael/.

9. "Vanguard Leadership Group Recieves Prestigious AIPAC Award," https://vimeo.com/13280175; Darius Jones, https://www.linkedin.com/in/darius-jones-58 676b20.

10. Rosenblatt, "Black Group Defends Israel."

11. Darius Jones, "Compete or Die!," *9Ether News* (blog), October 4, 2006, http://9ethernews.blogspot.com/.

12. Nathan Guttman, "Christian Backers of Israel Reach Out to Blacks," *Forward*, October 19, 2011, http://forward.com/articles/144558/christian-backers-of-is rael-reach-out-to-blacks/; Ira Glunts, "The Pro-Israel Lobby Courts African Americans," *Truthout*, November 6, 2011, http://www.truth-out.org/news/item/4583:the -proisrael-lobby-courts-africanamericans.

13. Abdelfattah Abusrour, "Beautiful Resistance, Revolting Memory," *Ongoing Nakba*, Spring 2006, http://www.badil.org/en/component/k2/item/956-beautiful -resistance-revolting-memory.html.

20

Sami Al-Arian and Silencing Palestine

HATEM BAZIAN

Arabs, Muslims, and Palestinians, as subjects of research and investigation, are a complicated affair these days. On one hand, the groups are an intense site for subhumanness discourses harkening back to eighteenth- and nineteenth-century colonially deployed language, while on the other, a globally sanctioned civilizational rehabilitation project is under way through massive and structured violence intended to produce the new and improved good Arab, Muslim, and Palestinian. We have become accustomed to a daily dosage of extreme reports coming from the frontiers of subhumanness that energize a sizable section of American and European policy makers' circles to call for further interventions and violence. The impacts across the Arab and Muslim worlds are visible, with death and destruction at every turn as well as millions of refugees. Inside the United States, the post-9/11 period has witnessed the systematic targeting of Arabs, Muslims, and, in particular, Palestinians under the rubric of fighting the War on Terror. Domestically, the scares of the War on Terror are made invisible as individuals ensnarled in the wide security dragnet become untouchables after arrest and subject to treatment fitting the assigned subhumanness. As of the writing of this chapter, the total number of legal cases involving Arabs, Muslims, and Palestinians is not known. However, the Muslim Legal Fund of America estimates some 3,746 civil rights– and terrorism-related cases, with a large number of these connected to the intersection of the USA PATRIOT Act, immigration law, and the growing securitization structure that is targeting Arabs and Muslims as an ethnic and religious group.

No case represents the intrusion, criminalization, and otherization of American Muslims better than the systematic and successful government targeting of Professor Sami Al-Arian. The targeting of Al-Arian begins before

September 11 but takes shape and moves into government "legal" action after the terrorist attacks. More importantly, the case represents the intersectionality of the War on Terror and the targeting of pro-Palestine activists and institutions in the United States, which also led to imprisonments of the leadership and the shuttering of the Holy Land Foundation, a critical humanitarian institution dedicated to providing relief for orphans and the poor inside the Palestinian occupied territories. Examining Professor Al-Arian's case will provide a clear idea of how the government utilized the catchall "War on Terror" label to target Arab and Muslim communities as a suspect class. The government's effort, if examined correctly, will provide a clear comparison to the COINTELPRO period whereby Hoover's FBI agents sought to "expose, disrupt, misdirect, discredit, or otherwise neutralize" African American organizations and leaders, which is similar to what is under way in relation to Arab, Muslim, and pro-Palestine activists.

Al-Arian Is Deported: A Success for the War on Terror!

"After 40 years, my time in the U.S. has come to an end," was the opening line of Professor Sami Al-Arian's letter to supporters and the Muslim American community as he was finally deported from the United States on February 5, 2015.[1] Professor Al-Arian's deportation brought to an end a painful and torturous episode in the life of one of the most active Palestinian, Muslim, and Arab civil rights advocates. Sami bade farewell to the United States after admitting in a plea bargain to "one of the charges in exchange for a promise that after a maximum of incarceration of 57 months, he would be allowed to leave the country by April 2007."[2]

The agreement Sami signed with his lawyers in 2007 was not implemented until federal prosecutors, on June 27, 2014, finally "dismissed criminal contempt charges" that kept Al-Arian in legal limbo for years.[3] Al-Arian's case is emblematic of the politically motivated and preemptively constructed approach to law post–September 11, 2001, which utilizes the law to criminalize Arabs and Muslims through unfounded terrorism charges, entrapment schemes, and material support charges. Even before the events of September 11, Arabs and Muslims were subject to systematic targeting and criminalization on the basis of their collective political, religious, and ethnic identities, in one case, the LA 8 arrests, dating all the way back to 1987 and lasting more than twenty years. In thinking about Professor Sami Al-Arian's case, one must take a broader lens and examine more closely how, under the rubric of fighting the War on Terror, the Justice Department and successive U.S. administrations have systematically criminalized Arabs, Muslims, and, in particular, pro-Palestine activists in the United States and targeted them using selective and distorted prosecutions, grand juries, and forced and voluntary deportations.

Before September 11, 2001, Arab, Muslim, and Palestinian activists and community organizers were subject to harassment and a well-designed federal strategy to entangle them in legal proceedings, an effort dating back to the Reagan administration. One of the most famous and long-running cases involved the arrest and prosecution of the LA 8, a group of seven Palestinians and a Kenyon charged at the time with supporting terrorism for no reason other than because they had passed around copies of *al-Hadaf* magazine, the Popular Front for the Liberation of Palestine publication, in community gatherings. The case lasted from 1987 until 2007, a twenty-year ordeal that effectively criminalized advocacy for Palestine in the United States and targeted Arab Americans based on constitutionally protected political activities.[4] Here the targeting of activists working on Palestine predates September 11, 2001, by decades, and cases are documented that go back to the early 1960s, which witnessed the rise of the Palestine Liberation Organization (PLO) around the globe. The history, targeting, and structural defamation of Palestinians and pro-Palestine activists in the United States is an important subject that needs to be undertaken, and this chapter is too limited in scope to be able to give it justice.[5]

Coming back to Professor Al-Arian's case, what is certain is that his troubles began long before the events of September 11 and date back to the early 1990s, when he was targeted by the government under then President Clinton's newly adopted Anti-Terrorism and Effective Death Penalty Act of 1996 (AEDPA) and suspected of supporting Palestinian organizations opposing Israeli occupation.[6] Provisions in the AEDPA permitted law enforcement agencies to use "secret evidence" to arrest, prosecute, and possibly deport individuals without a crime having been committed. It was in the 1996 AEDPA that the machinery was implemented for creating a new legal structure to prosecute individuals on the basis of thought connected to Islam and, in particular, the concept of jihad.

What started in the 1990s during Clinton's era accelerated post–September 11, making it possible for the neoconservatives and pro-Israel advocates inside and close to George W. Bush's administration to utilize the USA PATRIOT Act to go after Palestinian activists and charities providing support for needy families living under occupation and to criminalize groups by linking them to terrorism through fictitious "material support" claims. What developed is a new COINTELPRO strategy directed at Arabs and Muslims and laser focused on Palestine's advocates and supporters, resulting in imprisonment for some, such as in the Holy Land Foundation case; deportation for others, such as Professor Sami Al-Arian; and bogus entrapment instances for many others.

Consequently, since the events of September 11, 2001, the FBI and other security agencies have resorted to the recruitment of Muslim informants by means of enticement and, if necessary, threats of deportation or financial ruin. From the cases that have come to light, it is clear that vast sections of the Arab and Muslim communities and their civic and religious institutions are the intended targets of these new types of FBI and COINTELPRO operations. As a matter of fact, the Bush administration's attorney general Alberto Gonzales stated after the Lodi, California, indictments, "Since the terrorist attacks of Sept. 11, 2001, the number one priority of the [Justice] Department has been to detect, disrupt and prevent terrorist attacks," which means using every tool available, including recruiting and deploying paid informants.[7] For many, this is a legitimate use of national resources to possibly prevent another 9/11, and the Arab and Muslim communities, collectively, should be "ready to cooperate" with the authorities in conducting these much-needed operations. A more direct conclusion drawn from these operations is that the FBI and the Justice Department consider the Arab, Muslim, and Palestinian American communities as incubators of terrorism that must be monitored and, if needed, infiltrated to preemptively catch targets before they plan an attack.

In the same way that COINTELPRO instrumentalized the law as a security tool, the post–September 11 period witnessed the utilization of law and courts as a preemptive instrument to target on a mass basis Arab and Muslim communities. The strategy was to create control structures to effectively silence the voices of Arabs and Muslims as well as intimidate them into supporting U.S. interventions abroad, while pressuring them to distance themselves from supporting Palestinians under occupation. At the intersection of Arab, Muslim, and Palestinian, Sami Al-Arian was a well-known advocate for Palestinians, a professor at the University of South Florida (USF), a community builder, and a major public figure navigating the coercive governmental structures to create political empowerment in Florida and nationally. What brought Al-Arian to government attention was his success in creating a viable local political power base for the community and proactively speaking and organizing for Palestine nationally. Al-Arian's entanglement with the government legal web began on February 20, 2003, with an indictment on terrorism and conspiracy charges, which was followed by an immediate and nationally televised arrest. At the time, the U.S. Justice Department charged Professor Al-Arian with a "conspiracy to commit murder via suicide attacks in Israel and the Palestinian territories."[8] The source of evidence was a foreign intelligence service, which was identified in court proceedings to be Israel, and extensive wiretapping going as far back as the early 1990s.

In a press conference held on the same day, then attorney general John Ashcroft said that "changes in U.S. Law under the USA Patriot Act—anti-terrorism legislation enacted after [the] Sept. 11, 2001, attack—allowed authorities to make a criminal case against Al-Arian." "The new law," adopted in immediate reaction to the attacks, "removed longstanding legal barriers to bringing information gathered in classified national security investigations into criminal courts."[9] In addition to Sami's arrest, both Sameeh Hammoudeh, a USF instructor, and Hatim Naji Fariz were likewise detained in Florida, while Ghassan Zayed Ballut was taken into custody in the state of Illinois. In a 120-page indictment, the Justice Department charged the four of being members of the Palestine Islamic Jihad (PIJ), and the arrests were supposedly made because of the newly permitted classified evidence. In the view of Mathew Levitt, a former FBI counterterrorism analyst and a researcher with the private Washington Institute for Near East Policy, "the new provisions in the USA Patriot Act proved to be the critical factor in putting together this case."[10]

The legal battles fought by Professor Sami Al-Arian, who was accused of being the leader of the PIJ's international *shura* (council), will in the future come to define the post–September 11 period with the introduction of politically motivated and racially selective prosecutions. At the time of his arrest, Professor Al-Arian informed reporters while being led in handcuffs that "it's all about politics," which was an accurate description of what was and still is under way in this country.

The indictment, arrests, and eventual deportation are motivated by a set of political circumstances least of which is the link between the United States and Israel and the attempt to silence a committed and growing opposition to Israeli occupation and failed interventionist policies in the Muslim world. After the first court appearance, Al-Arian's lawyer Nicholas Matassini[11] described the status of his client: "He's a political prisoner right now as we speak," and the government's indictment is a "work of fiction."[12] Al-Arian's case did reach the U.S. Supreme Court, and a precedent-setting decision was made allowing the government a free hand in using secret evidence and introducing into court proceedings foreign intelligence without the possibility of refuting or challenging its validity. Al-Arian's lawyer Jonathan Turley expressed that the case "remains one of the most troubling chapters in this nation's crackdown after 9-11. Despite the jury verdict and the agreement reached to allow Dr. Al-Arian to leave the country, the Justice Department continued to fight for his incarceration and for a trial in his case. It will remain one of the most disturbing cases of my career in terms of the actions taken by our government."[13]

Important to recall is that the Japanese internment during World War II was sanctioned by a U.S. Supreme Court ruling that stands as a moment of shame in the annals of American legal history, and the same conclusion must be reached in Sami Al-Arian's case. In *Korematsu v. United States,* the Supreme Court upheld the order for Mr. Fred Korematsu, "a native-born U.S. citizen," to evacuate his home and report to the internment camps. The court considered the interment justified when "pressing public necessity may sometimes justify the existence of such restrictions."[14] Indeed, the struggles for civil and human rights were not limited to demonstrations in the streets or sitting on lunch counters but also included real, bruising legal battles in the courtroom. The Supreme Court followed the same script from the Japanese internment and granted the government carte blanche to pursue preemptive prosecution and altered for the foreseeable future the rules governing evidence, witnesses, pretrial imprisonment, infiltration and paid informant use, and open-ended surveillance. Just as the LA 8 case was used to create new legal precedent for targeting political activists through the use of immigration laws, Sami Al-Arian's case provided the government with the blueprint for preemptive prosecution and the reshaping of the courtroom to fight the War on Terror without evidence or even a crime having been committed. I am not implying that Al-Arian's and Korematsu's cases are identical or that the internment of the Japanese was the same as what is happening in the current period, because differences do exist, but the larger principle of guilt by association and the failure of the courts to restrain government powers are the points of comparison. Between both the Japanese internment and COINTELPRO comparisons, a major difference is the heavy weight of technology that has allowed levels of tracking, monitoring, and surveillance unprecedented in human history.[15] Likewise, the government's seamless relationship with large corporations and private entities at the hub of the megadata industry allows for both greater ease in hiding actual governmental intrusion while, at the same time, a never-before-seen ability to expose massive amounts of data by a network of computer activists from across the world.

Al-Arian became a government target long before the events of 9/11, dating back to the mid-1990s, when he and his brother-in-law, Dr. Mazen al-Najjar, were arrested under Clinton's newly adopted antiterrorism law and accused of supporting the Palestinian militant organization PIJ. Clinton's antiterrorism bill was adopted after a series of Hamas bombings in Israel, and the president declared a U.S. state of emergency that allowed him to target individuals and organizations. The law made it possible for the Department of State to begin issuing a list of terrorist groups and to prohibit any American from dealing with them directly or extending material support. Immediately after the passage of the bill, the Justice Department moved swiftly and froze the assets of Palestinian businessmen who were accused of having relations with some of the groups on the Department of State list.[16] Following the Department of State designation of most of the Palestinian groups, the U.S. government in 1997 arrested Dr. al-Najjar based on the newly adopted provisions allowing for admittance of secret evidence in court filings. The government kept Mr. al-Najjar in prison for three years based on secret evidence; he was finally released in 2000, after Judge Joan A. Lenard, an immigration and naturalization judge, dismissed the evidence presented by the Department of Justice and ordered the Immigration and Naturalization Service (INS) to decide if Mazen should get bail and be allowed to rejoin his family while he appealed his deportation order. The arrest of al-Najjar was the test case that made it possible for the INS and other law enforcement agencies to see how far they could use the secret evidence provisions to arrest and possibly deport individuals, which, according to House minority whip David E. Bonior, "is one of the most pernicious laws I've seen in my 28-year profession."[17]

What Congressman Bonior described should be considered mild compared to the wide range of powers granted to the Justice Department and law enforcement agencies after 9/11. Timing being of the essence, the events of 9/11 provided the Department of Justice the opportunity to rearrest individuals it deemed a threat to "national security," and sure enough, Dr. al-Najjar was arrested on November 24, 2001, and finally deported to Lebanon in May 2003, which, if anything, provides ample proof that the government lacked any real evidence to keep him in a U.S. jail in the first place. Would the United States let anyone it thinks is a "terrorist" and against whom it has classified secret evidence go free to another country? Al-Najjar's and Sami's cases have more to do with the Palestinian–Israeli conflict and the domestic forces at work targeting pro-Palestine activist at all fronts. It was Palestine that brought Clinton's antiterrorism law into life, which restricted "the opportunity for state and federal prisoners to challenge the constitutionality of their convictions in federal court by filing habeas corpus petitions."[18] In addition, the law permitted the use of Communication Management Units (CMU) for most of the cases involving Arabs and Muslims charged or indicted on terrorism, and many wait years before having their days in court. This CMU phenomenon is not unique and limited to Muslims; rather, African American and Latinx prisoners are well versed and have extensive experience with a prison–industrial complex that works to break down instead of helping to empower and uplift the inmates behind bars. During his stay in jail, Dr. al-Najjar was held in solitary confinement and allowed one hour of exercise each day, while he was strip-searched twice a day.

Professor Al-Arian's case was a little different in the sense that it involved more than the Department of Justice and that his legal battle was brought to bear owing to public pressure on the USF to take action against him in the post-9/11 fervor. At its core, Sami's case is built on an Arabic statement he was reported to have uttered at an anti-Israel rally in 1988, which translates into something like "death to Israel." At the time, the statement was not the center of any debate or major campaign directed at Professor Al-Arian, but it became so some twelve years later. On September 26, 2001, in the aftermath of 9/11, Professor Al-Arian appeared on *The O'Reilly Factor* to talk about the impact of the events on the Muslim community in the United States, but O'Reilly, the host, went after him, asking about the FBI probe and the existence of a link between him and terrorists in the Middle East. On live national television, Mr. O'Reilly brought up the statement "death to Israel," asking Al-Arian to explain his position on it and on Israel in general. On numerous occasions, Professor Al-Arian explained that his statement was a "political rhetoric against Israeli oppression" and came at the time of the Intifada and was not meant as a call to violence.[19] In addition, Mr. Al-Arian said that he was invited to talk about the impacts of 9/11 and to educate the public about the Muslim community, which was far from the focus of *The O'Reilly Factor* during the interview. Here Fox's role in the systematic demonization of Muslim American leaders begins to shape public and government responses, including the eventual arrest and imprisonment of Al-Arian.

Immediately after the interview, USF president Judy Genshaft's office was flooded with complaints directed at Al-Arian and calls to fire him from his tenured academic position. The callers to the university and others who opposed Sami's continued employment began to refer to USF as "Jihad U" and "University of Suicidal Fanatics."[20] In response, President Genshaft, with support from the trustees and then governor Jeb Bush, placed Professor Al-Arian on "paid leave" from his tenured position as a professor of computer engineering because his presence on campus would create security problems for the community.[21] The "paid leave" was initially put in the context of security concerns for the campus community considering the high number of calls the university received after Al-Arian's appearance on Fox. After the initial claim of security, the President's Office cited another reason for placing Professor Al-Arian on "paid leave," which had to do directly with his appearance on *The O'Reilly Factor* and his supposedly speaking without making clear that he did not represent the university. Of all the claims against a professor, this stands to be the flimsiest ever, because any professor employed by a university will always be introduced as a professor there. Needless to say, after Genshaft's decision, Professor Al-Arian was prohibited from entering the campus he loved and from being among his students, who had voted him, on at least two previous occasions, one of the best professors on campus.

Sami's case is not unique in the long history of politically motivated government prosecutions of individuals and groups. Any seriously minded person can appreciate the consistency in approach the government has used against individuals and organizations and whether anything can readily provide us with base knowledge on how to undo these actions. During the days of the House Committee on Un-American Activities (HUAC), from 1945 to 1971, a number of individuals suffered a similar fate to the one Sami has faced in the present period. At the time, the accusation or mere mention of any connection or association with communism or civil rights was sure to land the individual and the organizations to which she belonged in major trouble. The committee's hearings were the main instrument used to identify and target individuals, which often led to job loss, attacks by vigilantes, and local police harassment. In one case, a person who had appeared before the committee sent this letter:

> I am earnestly seeking your help to stop the violence against me that was instigated by Representative Clardy's hearings.
>
> I have been a responsible citizen for forty-three years. . . . I have an unchallenged record as an employee at Chevrolet Manufacturing Company for twenty years. I served conscientiously as a soldier in World War II, and was decorated with the Bronze Star Medal.

Since the hearings I have worked only two weeks. I was severely beaten on returning to work and was placed under a doctor's care for thirty days with broken ribs and contusions. Again last Wednesday I was viciously beaten by a small but well organized gang of hoodlums at the factory gates.[22]

Representative Kit Clardy was informed of this man's situation, to which he responded, "This is the best kind of reaction there could have been to our hearings."[23] The mission of HUAC was to name names and develop a list of possible targets in society. The lists of those mentioned read like a who's who among the most talented America has known, including, after 1947, many Hollywood personalities. The movie industry came under enormous pressure, and a change in emphasis in films away from social content was made to satisfy HUAC.[24] At this time in our history, it is important for us to remember the names of the Hollywood Ten, for they offer a reminder of what uncontrolled power is able to do: Alvah Bessie, Herbert Biberman, Lester Cole, Edward Dmytryk, Ring Lardner Jr., John Howard Lawson, Albert Maltz, Samuel Ornitz, Adrian Scott, and Dalton Trumbo.[25]

So great was the damage to civil liberties that the HUAC period developed its own term, *McCarthyism,* in reference to one of its most famous advocates: Senator Joseph McCarthy. The senator made his political career by attacking communism at every given opportunity, and his hearing on Hollywood stands in a class of its own. One of the least known aspects of the HUAC's and McCarthy's targets is that they included almost every element of society, including the State Department, Voice of America, the International Information Agency, and the U.S. Army—in 1954, McCarthy's accusations of subversion against the U.S. Army led to his political demise.[26] What for many was a legitimate undertaking in its beginnings developed into a full-fledged threat to every element of society, including the military itself.

In this regard, Professor Al-Arian's case has a clear connection to McCarthyism and its most insidious tool—the targeting of individuals to make of them an object lesson to others. The case's comparison with the McCarthy era is an apt one in its concerted effort at demonizing and targeting a class of people, Muslim communities in the United States and abroad, by various layers of governmental and private institutions, while stoking public anger and fear against them so as to justify deploying a securitization structure domestically and undertaking a more militaristic and interventionist foreign policy abroad. The HUAC hearings centered on communism, which at the time was the enemy of choice, considering the Cold War and existing conflicts with the USSR across the world. Certainly the HUAC hearings and the anticommunist witch hunt helped shore up domestic public support for the Cold War as well as rationalized the need for interventions in Latin America, the Middle East, parts of Africa, and Indo-China. Professor Al-Arian was a convenient target who could be used as a poster child to stoke public sentiment and foment an irrational level of fear and anger among society.

Law is born out of social conditions, and the current period has given birth to the USA PATRIOT Act, material support, and preemptive prosecution, with Al-Arian's being a case to test the boundaries of governmental powers in the post-9/11 era. Certainly we must assert and insist on the legal standard that the accused has the right to face his accuser in a court of law with access to all evidence presented and an ability to cross-examine all, including government and foreign experts and witnesses. The USA PATRIOT Act and post-9/11 legal system have shifted the basis of the legal system altogether. Until such a time comes when corrective measures are undertaken, Professor Al-Arian's plea bargain and deportation are only proof of the government's ability to use all its resources against an individual and to drive the person into a corner. In an interview published in the Arab world, Professor Al-Arian points out the painful truth that while "the Constitution . . . guarantee[s] him the right to be considered innocent until proven guilty," nevertheless, "the treatment" Sami "received since the first day of" his "incarceration demonstrates that" the authorities dealt with him as though he "had already been tried and convicted." He adds in the interview that "the prison in which I am being held is considered to be one of the toughest in the world. We remain in solitary confinement for 23 to 24 hours a day, and because the prison is more than 70 miles (that is about 100 km) from the defense team, it is very difficult to prepare a genuine defense, not to mention the fact that the team of lawyers faces severe difficulty in seeing me, meeting with me, or even exchanging papers or documents with me." Here Professor Al-Arian experienced the increasingly inhumane prison system that is set to punish, isolate, and torment prisoners even before they are convicted. The treatment accorded to Al-Arian is the norm for many African American and Latinx inmates in the prison system, which to a large extent explains the high recidivism rate among released prisoners—the system is structured to break down the human spirit to a point of no return. The War on Terror fused the domestic and robust prison–industrial complex with the broader campaign against the Muslim subject, which has been racialized in the process to fit into the preconstructed control epistemic directed at communities of color in the internal colonial structure.

Furthermore, Al-Arian was subject to another level of control involving the denial of or extremely difficult access to pens and was "given only two at a time, not to mention the scarcity of paper." According to Sami, the requests put him at "odds constantly with the prison administration" due to his "requests that they bring . . . a pen and some paper." The War on Terror made it possible to create a renewed Muslim subhumanness that harkened back to the Inquisition, and Sami pointed out that when leaving his "cell to meet the defense team," his "hands are handcuffed behind" his "back, which makes it difficult to carry the papers or files relating to the case; the prison officials refuse to carry them, so" Al-Arian was "obliged to carry them on" his "back by walking hunched over for about 200 meters." Adding to this hardship, Sami painfully pointed further to "the rough, humiliating treatment, such as having to get completely undressed whenever I come out of the cell, and the tight restrictions on the use of the telephone to check up on my family and children." How to transform the human into a subhuman while claiming to do so in defense of civilization, democracy, and rule of law?

The reintroduction of subhumanness by creating and structurally supporting the Muslim terrorist category made it possible to unleash the full power of the U.S. government on its target, which in this case was Professor Al-Arian. Preventing Sami from having access to the telephone for six months was more than a response to a supposed violation but a structural response intended to isolate, punish, and break down the target even before he got his day in court. "Innocent until proven guilty" is the standard, but one has to be able to get to the court, stand in front of the jury, and then argue the case based on evidence and facts. The imprisonment, isolation, and humiliating treatment were intended to force a plea bargain and extract a victory conviction out of thin air so as to prove that the country is fighting a subhuman enemy who does not deserve "our human" and civilized standards. The last part of the interview is very illustrative of the purpose of Al-Arian's imprisonment and the planned treatment for the Muslim, this subhuman subject:

> Since last February 20, I have not been allowed to kiss or hug my children on any visit, since the visits are limited and take place from behind glass barriers. We are also subjected daily to severe psychological pressures. There is noise and disturbance night and day, since they have me in a place where there are

prisoners suffering from severe psychological exhaustion, which causes them to beat on the cell doors and scream nonstop. The prison administration responds by turning on the warning sirens, which are deafeningly loud, for a long time every day. They may turn them on between 5 to 10 times a day. As for leaving the cell, the prison administration is under obligation to bring prisoners out into the prison courtyard one hour a day. However, this does not happen regularly, since the administration has instructed prison guards to let everyone else out before my turn comes up, and there are many times when I never get a turn to come out.

The denial of human contact with family and friends, solitary confinement, and limits on time outside the cell are technologies of dehumanization intended to break down the person. America's prisons are like the hulls of ships that transported the "human cargo" from Africa while assigning it to permanent subhumanness. Indeed, the War on Terror has made it possible to reinvigorate the failed prison–industrial complex, which was facing challenges on the use of isolation, violence, and inhumane treatment behind bars. By positing the internal threat and the extreme danger presented by terrorists, the prison–industrial complex was able to reconsolidate and assert its centrality in dealing with and controlling this new type of subhuman enemy, and all rules must be set aside. Here it should be obvious that the same methods used against terrorists have been utilized against African Americans and other minority prisoners throughout the ages, and the War on Terror removed any recently developed inhibition within this vast enterprise.

During the McCarthy and HUAC era, targets were chosen for maximum impact and to cause fear among the rest of the population engaging in similar fields of work. Through calling individuals to the hearings or charging someone with contempt of Congress, the HUAC committee was able to create a social–political process that led to an intensification of civil rights violations. We should think of Professor Al-Arian's case through the same lens and realize that he is part of a larger security strategy that seeks to criminalize the top strata of the Muslim community leadership and those who have been at the forefront of civil rights and political battles, with particular emphasis on the Palestinian struggle. The target is once again to seek to neutralize, possibly, the most effective members of the Muslim leadership.

Going after Professor Al-Arian was part of an orchestrated campaign directed at Muslim American leadership. A debate is afoot in the community regarding the definition of "mainstream" Muslims—what it is they should support and who or what they should oppose and condemn. It is not enough to condemn al-Qaeda, ISIS, al-Baghdadi, and Osama bin Laden, the critics argue; rather, Muslims who want to belong to the "mainstream" must be ready to distance themselves from all objectionable aspects found in Islam and Muslim societies and embrace a newly crafted imperial secularity. What we have here is a litmus test applied to Muslims as a precondition for their inclusion in American and "civilized" society. At present, Muslim leaders represent, collectively, a singular threat in the eyes of the FBI, the National Security Agency, and the national security apparatus; however, containing the threat from the government's perspective requires diverse tools. It is not what a person does or says that is cause for monitoring or the difficulties encountered from security structures. However, some thought that simply by modifying their own behavior, they could reduce or limit the harm inflicted on them, not realizing that the fact of belonging to a group that has collectively become the enemy of the state is the key issue at hand.

The security structure is looking for access, and the present leadership has not delivered the needed goods, thus the use of the justice system as a way of making the point to everyone else. It seems that Professor Al-Arian's case as well as others did not drive the point home and that more cases are needed to alter the landscape of Muslim national leadership and organizations. The current leadership is seen, by the security structure, as obstructing the fulfillment of the full range of plans to secure America; hence they must be eliminated or their influence reduced in such a way as to make it possible for a more cooperative group to emerge. It is the hope that this new cooperative group will see the world in the same way those in power see it and will be ready to lend a hand to its goals both at home and abroad.

Why is this needed? A community without a strong and experienced leadership is wide-open game for security forces and ill-intentioned segments of American society. Also, neutralizing the leadership sends a very strong message to the rest of the community and to second-tier leaders that such will be your fate if you don't play ball and cooperate in the unfolding security project. Professor Al-Arian is an example for the rest of the Muslim leadership and the Muslim community at large.

Many in the FBI and local police departments have admitted that they lack knowledge of Muslim Americans and as such needed to overcome this handicap by pursuing a dialogue with community members. Immediately after 9/11, however, the FBI was confronted with a lack of contacts with the Muslim community and a high level of suspicion owing to the perceived/

real established links with Israeli security structures. To put it mildly, the FBI for good reason was not considered a protector of Muslim rights; rather, it was seen as being on a witch hunt to find a bin Laden connection in every mosque or school or Muslim home. However, out of fear and in the face of accusations of not being patriotic, members of the Muslim community did cooperate with the FBI with the hope that they would not be considered supporters of terrorism. Since 9/11, almost every large Muslim organization or mosque has felt the need to host a public meeting with the FBI as a way to distance itself from bin Laden's and al-Qaeda's ideas and to calm its membership, who were fearful of what might happen to them. A similar pattern is under way today in relations with ISIS and the federally funded Countering Violent Extremism. On its part, the FBI uses the heightened level of insecurity felt by Muslim communities to push its own agenda to get to know these insular immigrant and convert groups as a way of reducing the level of threat. The FBI sent its agents on a meet-and-greet and to document the experience with the Muslim community to develop an intelligence assessment of the community, with a focus on never again being surprised by another 9/11. The community was approached with an existing perception of terrorist links and the need to "secure the homeland" from this threat. The next stage for the FBI was to seek operatives from within the Muslim community who, after being induced by monetary rewards, deportation threats, or green cards, could act as the eyes and ears of U.S. security agencies inside mosques and Muslim organizations.

What comes out of this is the view that the Muslim community, as a whole, is a suspect class and that it is the duty of the FBI and other security agencies to break into its ranks to catch or entrap targets before threats can be carried out. In this context, Professor Al-Arian was a very useful target, because, on one hand, his arrest provided evidence of the presence of terrorist connections in local Muslim communities and, on the other, was a lesson for those who refuse to cooperate and open their mosque doors to security agencies. In one such community meeting, the FBI person present informed the group of Muslim leaders that the FBI was coming with their help or without it. Even before 9/11, the FBI was already developing a program to infiltrate Muslim organizations and religious institutions for the purpose of gaining greater knowledge about the inner workings of the community and to foster inner division, similar to what was done in the 1960s to the Black Panther Party and the civil rights movement.

As the initial infiltration took hold, the second stage of the program kicked in, and Professor Al-Arian's arrest was one aspect of it. The second stage, based on studying the 1960s COINTELPRO files, involved neutralization of key leadership in the community while creating divisions among existing groups. After Professor Al-Arian's arrest, the number of Muslim leaders who agreed to take on his struggle, as a major civil rights case, was limited, and many were fearful to have any public connection with him. The intent of the second stage was to create such a distance between individual leaders in the process of being neutralized and those who were still active in community organizations. Here one has to spend a minute on the psychology behind such a response from members of the community. The created perception directed at members of the community was that Professor Al-Arian must have done something wrong to be landed in prison. On the other hand, the fearful leaders proclaimed that they had done nothing wrong and were ready to extend a helping hand to the FBI and other security agencies. As such, the leaders had been coerced into believing that it was their cooperation with the FBI and their "good conduct" that prevented them from being treated like Sami. They were surely mistaken, for the leaders are in their present condition because they fit into an overall strategy, which identified them beforehand as possible targets open to coercion so as to produce cooperation, and thus they were pursued with the softer glove of power. However, in the minds of those governed by fear, the relations with the FBI became a stamp of approval and honor and a declaration of innocence from any terrorist wrongdoings.

Now this has been achieved, we arrive at stage 3 of the FBI and security structural strategy toward American Muslims. The FBI would like to develop a well-controlled and nurtured Muslim American voice, which can act as a counterbalance to those who are "problematic" in their approach to Islam and U.S. policies domestically and across the Muslim world. A "good Muslim–bad Muslim" securitization strategy is pursued. The FBI and the security system understand that this must be an internal matter to be taken up by elements within the community itself. Nevertheless, this does not mean that security agencies can't play a role in influencing outcomes in the long run. This area, and this area alone, is the key to the success or failure of the security agencies' strategy to bring about a "good" Muslim American voice that expresses a pro-U.S. stance in the War on Terror that is unfolding across the Muslim world, including the illegal invasion of Iraq and nonstop drone attacks as well as acts to further the expressed goals in partnership. Indeed, American Muslims find themselves recruited in their specific fields of specialization so as to render service to the U.S. government's priorities, even if those run contrary to the Universal Declaration of

Human Rights and community ethical and moral principles. American Muslims are being asked to partner with America's imperial status quo and to mount at home and abroad a defense of the political, economic, military, social, and exceptional worldview that sits at the heart of the American project. This translates to American Muslims calling on segments of the community to refrain from engagement with or critique of America's role abroad and urge a focus on domestic and "our own" problems. Here the call is narrowly focused on refraining from foreign policy issues that may constrain the intended integrationist trajectory, which might face derailment if serious opposition and a different strategy are pursued. One may choose to ignore the "inconvenient truth" of the heavy weight of U.S. power across the globe because centering it in thought and action will complicate American Muslims' ability to "fit in" and be accepted as the jolly next-door neighbor who patriotically flies the biggest and highest flag on the street to protect himself from a security structure organized to systematically target Muslims as a class.

In this FBI-shaped context, the American Muslim community is reduced to a series of engagements initiated by government needs and set in motion according to a predetermined agenda. Rather than being independent, creative, and reflective, American Muslims (with some exception) have accepted their role as problem solvers for persistent U.S. imperial problems that emerge out of intervention abroad, militarism, racism, and obscene capitalism. American Muslims are joining the bandwagon and fitting in perfectly as a functionary of this massive and persistent domestic and global imperial enterprise.

As we begin to understand the extent of present COINTELPRO operations directed at Arabs and Muslims, and intensely so at Palestinians, we must keep in mind the intended outcomes of this campaign. After reading all the existing primary documents from the Church Committee Report related to the 1960s COINTELPRO and looking at some sample cases from the present period, the possible desired outcomes of the current campaign can be summed up in the following five points:

1. prevent the coalition of Arab, Muslim, and Southeast Asian groups
2. prevent the rise of unifying figures
3. prevent the development of independent sources of funding
4. prevent Arab and Muslim leadership from gaining respectability in the "mainstream" of American society
5. prevent the growth of nondomesticated Muslim organizations among youth[27]

The process has not been easy and straightforward, because a far more involved psychological campaign must be undertaken to bring about the needed cooperation from the Muslim community. It would be very naive, on anyone's part, to think that psychological warfare was not part of the tools placed at the disposal of security agencies inside and outside the United States and intensified in the new COINTELPRO-type campaign. Employing the tried and true tool of planted negative coverage and misinformation campaigns brought about leadership as well as, in cases, rank-and-file cooperation, a primary success for security agencies. No one likes to be portrayed negatively; even convicted felons have an adverse reaction to it. As such, the intent of stories and the unending hunt for "terrorists" produce a reaction from some who internalize the message of the campaign and begin to seek ways to change the community, because it has been deemed in public discourse to be at fault. We are not concerned at this time with any actual cases of guilt but with the overall community, which is treated as a guilty party for the mere fact that they share the same faith with the 9/11 hijackers, al-Qaeda, and ISIS. Thinking that they are at fault, leaders and laymen consider ways to prove themselves innocent by cooperating with the security agencies and pointing fingers at those who are deemed "radical" or to hold "extreme views" and who possibly express legitimate opposition to the War on Terror as it has been articulated by successive U.S. administrations. The problem has been identified as being an ideology, that is, a particular understanding of Islam that must be confronted, and to accomplish this task, a cadre from the adherents of this faith must come to the side of the security agencies and cooperate toward eliminating this "cancer," but no one knows when this will be done. The Muslim community is a suspect class and must prove itself innocent of crimes not yet not committed and relating to a legal system that operates on the basis of preemptive prosecution. Preemptive war was globally introduced in the invasion of Iraq and with a preemptive legal system that uses law as a national security tool to silence Muslims. Sami Al-Arian's prosecution and eventual deportation are paradigmatic of the treatment Arabs, Muslims, and Palestinians receive on a regular basis in the current preemptive post-9/11 period, and change is not coming any time soon.

NOTES

1. http://www.counterpunch.org/2015/02/06/on-leaving-the-united-states/.
2. http://jonathanturley.org/2015/02/05/dr-sami-al-arian-leaves-the-united-states/.

3. http://tbo.com/news/crime/prosecutors-move-to-drop-charges-against-sami
-al-arian-20140627/.

4. http://ccrjustice.org/newsroom/press-releases/judge-throws-out-charges-"los
-angeles-eight"-case.

5. See Michael Suleiman's *Arabs in America: Building a New Future* (Philadel-
phia: Temple University Press, 1999) for a longer history of Arabs in America and
the challenges they faced over the generations and Paul Findley's book *They Dare to
Speak Out: People and Institutions Confront Israel's Lobby* (Chicago: Chicago Review
Press, 2003) for an examination of targeting individuals and organizations in the
United States for speaking and taking a public position in support of the Palestine
struggle. See Alfred M. Lilienthal's critical work *The Zionist Connection: What Price
Peace?* (New York: Dodd, Mead, 1978) for an insight into a long history of defama-
tion and erasure of Palestine in America's public and political discourses and Alex
Lubin's chapter "The Black Panthers and the PLO: The Politics of Intercommunal-
ism," in *Geographies of Liberation: The Making of an Afro-Arab Political Imaginary*,
111–41 (Chapel Hill: University of North Carolina Press, 2014).

6. https://www.aclu.org/immigrants-rights/support-secret-evidence-repeal-act.

7. Demian Bulwa, "Lodi Terror Trainee Convicted," *San Francisco Chronicle*,
April 26, 2006.

8. John Mintz, "Fla. Man Indicated as Terrorist Leader," *Washington Post*, February 21, 2003.

9. Ibid.

10. Ibid.

11. In the month of May 2003, Sami Al-Arian fired Nicholas Matassini and
decided to represent himself until such time that enough funds are available to hire
a lawyer of his own.

12. Ibid.

13. http://jonathanturley.org/2014/06/27/federal-court-drops-all-charges-against
-dr-sami-al-arian/.

14. Michael Linfield, *Freedom under Fire: US Civil Liberties in the Times of War*
(Boston: South End Press, 1990), 95.

15. See Hatem Bazian, "Virtual Internment: Arabs, Muslims, Asians, and the
War on Terrorism," *Journal of Islamic Law and Culture* 9, no. 1 (2004): 2–26.

16. Norman Kempster, "U.S. Designates 30 Groups as Terrorists Justice: Label
Triggers Law Freezing Assets, Denying Visas, and Punishing Americans for Financial, Arms Support," *Los Angeles Times*, October 9, 1997. See a detailed account of
Clinton's terrorism law at https://library.cqpress.com/cqalmanac/document.php?id
=cqal96-1092313.

17. Lam Bakri, "Terrorism Law Faces Challenge: Students, Lawmaker Call for
Repeal of Measure They Say Targets Arabs," *Detroit News*, March 21, 2000.

18. https://library.cqpress.com/cqalmanac/document.php?id=cqal96-1092313.

19. Tim Padgett and Rochelle Renford, "Fighting Words," *Time*, February 4,
2002.

20. Ibid.

21. Ibid.

22. Linfield, *Freedom under Fire*, 88.

23. Ibid., 89.

24. Ibid., 90.

25. Ibid., 89.

26. Ibid., 91.

27. For a full discussion, read Hatem Bazian's article "Muslims—Enemies of the State: The New Counter-Intelligence Program (COINTELPRO)," *Islamophobia Studies Journal* 1, no. 1 (2012): 163–206.

21 Raising Muslim Girls

Women-of-Color Legacies in American Islam

Sylvia Chan-Malik

During the 2016 U.S. presidential election, my youngest daughter had nightmares. Aged eight at the time, she would pad down the hall from her room to ours, always around midnight, her face glistening with tears as she opened our door.

Will Trump put us in jail? Will he put all the Muslims in jail?

This is my impudent child, the one who sneaks candy in her shirtsleeves, who never stops moving, who collects bruises all over her knees. She's perfected the "Joisey accent" since we moved to New Jersey from California five years ago, when I began my job at Rutgers teaching American and women's and gender studies. She can deliver the regional patois with a wicked, gap-toothed grin—*how ya doin' daawl-face?, I'm just mahv-e-lous dahl-ing*—before flipping cartwheels across the room. We don't have a television in the house, but Little S (as I'll call her) is an empath and expert eavesdropper who noted the tension in her parents' jaws and heard the harshness in our voices early on in the campaign when speaking Trump's name. From these cues, from the snippets of NPR heard to and from school, the quick glances at the news headlines on the edges of her iPad screen, she became quickly aware of Donald Trump's idea of a Muslim registry.

I dreamed Trump put us in jail. I don't want to go to jail. I don't want you or Daddy, or Nana, or my uncles and aunties, or anyone to go to jail.

I have various reactions to my children's tears. They are not always sympathetic. I do not believe parents should always soothe, that they should act as arbiters between the world and their children's emotional lives. There are some cases that are clear-cut—an injury, for example. But instead of telling them it will be OK, that they shouldn't worry, I prefer to offer an honest assessment of what I believe they're experiencing *(you are hungry, you are tired)* and give practical suggestions *(eat something, go lie down)* for how to alleviate their discomfort or pain.

My assessment here: this child was scared. Her dreams were about what Dylan Rodriguez and others have called "carceral violence"—the "lived surfaces, institutional productions, coercive practices, and global statecraft" of the U.S. prison regime and how it produces the horizons of possibility of our quotidian lives.[1] Little S was scared of going to jail, of her family and loved ones being sent to jail. This fear preceded the 2016 election; it is a fear other small children have. Parents warn them that if they misbehave, the police will come get them. It is a fear many young Black and Brown children have, because people like them go to jail, so they must avert their eyes, speak softly, move carefully, so they might not be captured or, worse, killed. Throughout the course of the 2016 election and afterward, Trump contorted his notion of a Muslim registry from advocacy of Muslim internment[2] to a "complete" ban of Muslims entering the United States to a "partial" ban to an "extreme vetting" and "temporary halt" of immigration and travel from "high-risk" regions notable for terrorism. When the ban was finally implemented in January 2017, it was clear its intended effect was, inexorably, as a "Muslim ban"—a piece of statecraft that would continue to scare Muslim children while asleep or awake. "I think Islam hates us," Trump told CNN's Anderson Cooper during a March 10, 2016, interview. To Trump and his followers, "Islam" is alive, a sentient being that feels hate and acts upon it. Islam infects Muslims, planting hate in our hearts for America, for democracy, for "us."

Will Trump put us in jail?

That night, I put my arms around her.

Is it OK to go to jail for being Muslim? I asked.

No, she replied.

Is it bad to be Muslim?

No, she replied.

Would you let them take me?

No, she replied.

Would I let them take you?

No, she replied.

What should we do if they try?

Fight them.

In my book *Being Muslim: A Cultural History of Women of Color in American Islam*,[3] I introduce the concept of affective insurgency. I define affective insurgency as how women of color in the United States have made Muslimness between Islam as lived religion and racial–religious form during the past century. Lived religion is a concept I borrow from religious studies scholars such as Robert Orsi and Meredith McGuire. Scholars of lived religion consider how religious meanings and actions are enacted and felt through the social environments of their practitioners' daily lives and acknowledge the presence of religion beyond holy texts and organized religious spaces and institutions. To put it another way, lived religion is not what religion is *supposed* to be but what it actually *is* in people's daily lives. So for Muslims, it is not that we should pray five times a day. It is how we plan our lives around prayers, or how we miss our prayers, or how we rationalize missing prayers, or how we call ourselves Muslim but do not pray at all, except sometimes on holidays. It is the bits of Christianity and Buddhism and New Age spirituality that merge with our Islam. It is our diets, our interactions with others, what we wear and why, the daily navigations being Muslim requires. "All religious ideas and impulses," writes Orsi, "are of the moment, invented, taken, borrowed, and improvised at the intersections of life."[4]

Being Muslim in the United States is always circumscribed by Islam's presence as a racial–religious form.[5] By this I mean that Islam's alterity in the United States is articulated and premised upon domestic logics of race and racism as well as long-standing Orientalist conceptions of Islam as a religion inferior to and adversarial to Christianity. Racially, Muslims are culturally imagined as nonwhite, and Islam as antiwhite. These meanings are produced at once through Islam's history as a Black protest religion through groups like the Nation of Islam and figures such as Malcolm X and Muhammad Ali and have come to be bolstered and built upon through the figure of the Islamic terrorist as well as the oppressed Muslim woman, defined as the antithesis of the "free" white woman. Religiously, Muslims are viewed, as Sophia Rose Arjana argues, through the logic of monstrosity, as Islam is viewed in Western eyes as an ideology that interrupts "normative humanity, civilization, and modernity."[6] In other words, Islam is a pathological belief system that exceeds race because of how it renders humans into monsters who follow "Islam" in lockstep, for example, if one Muslim is a terrorist, they all must be terrorists. In the United States, Islam's racial and religious forms collapse into one through the notion that Islam's religious pathologies produce Muslims as a nonwhite "race" that is collapsible and colludes with insurgent movements of Black radicalism and other nationalist movements of self-determination, as well a signifier of invasive racial contagion, as with Asian and Latinx immigrants at various moments in history. In the contemporary United States, Islam's racial–religious form is an amalgamation of who Muslims have been within the nation (e.g., Black, immigrants, "Islamic terrorists") and Orientalist conceptions of Islam as a monstrous religion that infects human souls.

What ties the racial and religious together in Islam's racial–religious forms is the notion of insurgency. In modern parlance, *insurgency* is a term generally employed in the context of warfare, specifically to refer to anti-state actors who rebel against authority through violence yet are not formally recognized as belligerent forces. More straightforwardly, insurgency connotes a revolt or uprising against established power. In regard to both Islam's racial and religious meanings in the United States' cultural imaginary, insurgency ties together Islam's various iterations as Black protest religion, immigrant ideology, and signifier of terrorism. Thus, because Islam and Muslims have continually been viewed and produced by state and cultural discourses as insurgents, being Muslim, I argue, is always insurgent, an act of insurgency. This insurgency occurs not only through acts of interpellation, in which individuals and communities are hailed into existence through, for example, government surveillance programs such as COINTELPRO or Countering Violent Extremism, but in the ways Muslim bodies in the United States position themselves as Muslim in relation to and against such programs and the logics that drive them.

Being Muslim situates insurgency as an affective and constant presence in the lives of U.S. Muslim women of color. I describe how Black Muslim women in the Ahmadiyya Movement in Islam in 1920s Chicago fashioned themselves and their daily lives as Muslims against logics of Black respectability politics and the cultural hegemony of the Black church in the post–Great Migration urban North; how women in the Nation of Islam experienced Islam as a form of liberation through domesticity in the racial and gendered shadows of the Cold War; how Muslim women were framed through exclusionary logics of second-wave feminism at the close of the 1970s; and how South Asian, Arab, Latinx, multiracial, and Black Muslim women have encountered and resisted state and cultural violence in the post-9/11 (and now Trump-era) United States. The contact zone between women's bodies and Islam as racial–religious form is where Muslimness is made. Whether during the War on Terror, the Black Power era, or the Cold War, or in the post–Great Migration North, simply to move through space and time, a Muslim woman is, I argue, and has always been, inescapably insurgent, always an act of rebellion and revolt enacted by women's bodies against Islam's signifying presence as nonwhite, non-Christian, monstrous, deviant.

Yet the insurgency of being Muslim in the United States works in tandem with the fact that to be Muslim connotes a submission to God—a notion that is at times difficult to square with Western feminist notions of empowerment and agency. Scholars such as Carolyn Moxley Rouse and Amina Wadud have continually emphasized women's engagements of Islam as acts of "engaged surrender," in which their surrender and/or submission to Allah is enacted through political actions and a commitment to social change. In the United States, the arena of social change and activism that most closely aligns with the interests and strivings of Muslim women has been the work of women of color, specifically Black and Third World women. Such "surrender" occurs in understanding that insurgency—that is, resistance and rebellion against white supremacy, gender subjugation, dehumanization—is a religious imperative, fashioned through everyday spiritual practices, civic and community engagement, or political protest and activism. Throughout the last century, my work argues that U.S. Muslim women's engagements with Islam constitute a history of affective insurgency, in which Muslimness itself has been iterated and reiterated against its shifting racial and religious alterity in the national imaginary.

Affective insurgency shapes how I raise my daughters as U.S. Muslim women at the intersections of Islamic theology and the legacies of women-of-color feminist activism and politics in the United States, while always teaching and reminding them of the centrality of Blackness and Black people in histories of U.S. American Islam. Their identities are complex: I am a Chinese American convert to Islam, and my husband is a second-generation African American Muslim whose parents converted through the Ahmadiyya Movement in Islam in the mid-1960s, when the vast majority of the movement's members in the United States were Black. My own decision to become Muslim fifteen years ago, while not vehemently opposed by my family, was also not welcomed or understood. As such, while I remain close to them, I have necessarily partitioned our family's religious life as Muslims. As I have recounted elsewhere,[7] my conversion to Islam was the result of my engagements with Muslim communities in the Bay Area following 9/11, which led to a fateful meeting with my future husband. In getting to know him and his upbringing on the north side of Milwaukee, I learned of the deep sectarian tensions within Islam and, in particular, of the persecution of Ahmadiyya communities in Pakistan, which directly impacts the lives of Ahmadi Muslims in the United States, as well as the presence of anti-Muslim bias within Black American communities. Throughout his life, my husband has continually encountered the contempt of Sunni Muslims, who disparage (and have oftentimes threatened) the lives and well-being of Ahmadi Muslims both in the United States and abroad. He has also dealt with misunderstanding and scorn directed at Muslims by some Black Christians as well as constantly confronting a broader climate of anti-Muslim racism that has been exponentially amplified in the last fifteen years.

Thus, as I say, my daughters' identities are complex. My husband and I share an ecumenical approach to Islam, though we honor and acknowledge how his identity is deeply rooted in the Black American contexts in which Ahmadiyya Islam was practiced in the United States. We understand that our racial and ethnic histories shape our individual and our family's collective identities and practices of Islam. We are necessarily vigilant about the very real dangers that confront us because we are Muslim, Ahmadi, Black, and Asian, and strive to honor the specificities of our experiences. For me, this specificity lies not only in my identity as an Asian American but as an Asian American feminist who could only come to an understanding of Islam through the discourses and activism of women of color, specifically Black and Third World feminists. Pursuing my undergraduate studies at the University of California, Berkeley during the early 1990s, "women of color" was a category that emboldened me to pursue activist politics and taught me that praxis was not separable from intellectual work. Though I began in the English department, against the backdrop of the culture wars, the Los Angeles uprisings of 1992, and the first Iraq War, I quickly found my way into the classrooms of great women, such as African American literary scholar Barbara Christian and poet June Jordan and foundational thinkers of Asian American studies such as Elaine Kim and Sau-ling Wong. In their classes, I encountered writers like Audre Lorde and Alice Walker, Gloria Anzaldua and Cherrie Moraga, Louise Erdrich and Leslie Marmon Silko, and Theresa Hak Kyung Cha and Janice Mirikitani. It was because I read these writers that I was impelled to organize around issues of immigrant rights, affirmative action, and sweatshop labor during my time at Berkeley. Because of their expansive voices and trenchant critiques, intersectional analysis was the baseline, and through it, I encountered Islam.

To encounter Islam in the United States through women-of-color politics is to read *The Autobiography of Malcolm X* and note the centrality of women in his life, to acknowledge and honor his legacy while also acknowledging his at times troubling gender politics as well as those of the Nation

of Islam. It is noting the gendered and racial Orientalism that long determined media and cultural representations of Muslim women as well as
how anti-Black racism is part and parcel of the contemporary fear of Islam.
It is both recognizing the strength of women such as Khadijah, Hagar,
Aisha, Maryam, and Fatima in the Islamic tradition and noting the marginalization and dehumanization of women in some Muslim societies and
communities. It is reading Amina Wadud's *Qur'an and Woman,* the first
woman-centered reading of Islam's holy text, written by an African American Muslim woman, and perhaps the most well known Islamic feminist
in the entire world, even while remembering that she herself does not identify as such.[8] It is drawing upon Lorde and Jordan, as well as postcolonial
feminists like Gayatri Spivak and Chandra Talpade Mohanty—alongside
the work of Islamic feminists such as Fatima Mernissi, Riffat Hassan,
and Leila Ahmed—to think through how U.S. Muslim women may challenge the violence that has come to circumscribe their everyday lives. It is
recognizing the racism of Islamophobia, the anti-Blackness of non-Black
Muslims, the imperialism of white feminism, and ubiquitous sexism. It
is supporting and loving queer and transgender Muslims. It is praying in a
side room, the back of the room, side by side, alone, and being aware of
where you are, why, and how this came to be. To encounter Islam through
women-of-color politics, to raise my Muslim daughters as women of color
in the United States, is to teach them to fight—to fight at multiple fronts,
against multiple forces, and with the legacies of Muslim women, of Black
American Islam, and of the women whose voices and activism have shaped
my and so many other women's understandings of Islam—always propel-
ling them and pushing them forward.

You teach your Muslim daughter women-of-color politics so she may
fight against the prisons in her dreams.

My older daughter, age ten, wants to be president. Or rather, she *had* wanted
to be president, when Barack Obama was in office. Big S, as I'll call her,
began stating her intention for the presidency at age four. "Brack Bama,"
she said, looked like Daddy, and the Obamas had daughters, just like us.
The president is the boss of *everything,* she told us, and that would be a good
job for her. She maintained her position, even as I would sometimes
quietly tell her that Obama had ordered attacks that killed people, split
up families through deportations, and refused to stand up for the people of
Palestine. She would not do those things, she assured me, but she still
wanted to be president. Big S is a persistent and unwaveringly determined

child, dogged where her sister is flighty, steady and focused where the younger one is erratic and whimsical. She would be the first Black Muslim female president, and she would change the world. During the 2016 election, Big S did not have bad dreams. Unlike her sister, she was unfazed by then candidate Trump's Muslim ban or his insults to women, the disabled, Mexicans, and so on. He would lose, she was sure, and though she understood her parents' aversion to Hillary Clinton (and our support of Bernie Sanders), she thought it would be cool to have a female president. Thus, following Trump's victory, she was not frightened or intimidated but angry and ready to fight. The presidency was a sham, she told us. How could this hateful man—this man who knew nothing about Islam and Muslims, who incited fear, who constantly lied, become president? We had to *do* something.

In some way, I was glad for her disillusionment. In a poignant piece published in the *Guardian* in February 2016, writer Kiese Laymon speaks of what it means for a Black girl to be president, that to be president of the United States is to evade questions of moral justice, to step into a battlefield of shoulds and should nots where she must "never take any responsibility for her role in domestic death and destruction," while pandering to white voters, rationalizing U.S. military violence, and "deal[ing] with the violent heteropatriarchy and anti-black racism heaped on her back without ever calling it heteropatriarchy or anti-black racism." For a Black Muslim girl to be president, I imagine, would require her to diminish Palestinian lives, to sanction surveillance and detention of her own communities, to narrate the history of American Islam as an immigrant success story, to denigrate Blackness, and to "never take any responsibility" for her actions—to refuse to surrender to imperatives of justice.

Big S is also a voracious reader. Her favorite author is Jacqueline Woodson, and her favorite book *Brown Girl Dreaming*. She adores the One Crazy Summer series by Rita Williams Garcia, which traces the lives of three young African American sisters who travel from Brooklyn to Oakland, California, in 1968 to find the mother who abandoned them and, on the way, encounter the Black Power movement, the Panthers, and all the social tumult of the era. She screamed with joy when I brought her to see Angela Davis at a campus lecture and proudly tells her friends at school that she once met Sonia Sanchez ("a famous poet") at her mom's work. She demanded we take her to see *Hidden Figures*—the film about three Black American women mathematicians who worked for NASA in the 1960s—on the first day it came out, though it was not yet playing in our town and we had to drive an hour to the closest showing. Though she and her sister have been exposed to the same people, books, and stories, for whatever reason, Big S has known she is a woman of color from day one. Somehow, she knows that this is her history, that she is a part of it.

As a parent, my hope for Big S is reflection and self-care, that she may engage Islam as safety and solace from struggle. She storms through life, wanting to battle demons, already knowing she must fight any and all. I want her to encounter women-of-color politics and activism through Islam, to stop and breathe, to laugh and love, and to care for herself and those she loves. Affective insurgency, I teach her, is not only to fight that which diminishes you in the world but to replenish and nourish your soul for the hereafter. It is to know that Muslims begin every prayer with the words "Bismillah al-Rahman al-Rahim," "in the name of Allah the compassionate, the merciful." It is to struggle for compassion and mercy in all of our encounters with injustice, to tend to our souls, even when so many around you incite anger and fear. It is to know that, as Rabi'a Al'Adawiya—an eighth-century Sufi mystic and a female saint of Islam—wrote,

> *I love God: I have no time left*
> *In which to hate the devil.*

On the day following the 2016 election, Big S somberly walked into my office, wide awake, and laid a hand on my shoulder.

Mom, we're in big trouble, she told me.

I know, sweetheart, I replied.

What are we going to do? she asked.

Well, we fight, right?

Yes.

But, what else?

What do you mean, Mom?

What else do we have to do as we're fighting? Because we will have to fight for a long time and sometimes we get tired?

We pray.

We pray.

We pray.

You must teach your burgeoning woman-of-color activist daughter Islam so she may pray and remember God, so that she may rest, knowing the fight will not, ever, end.

Notes

1. Dylan Rodriguez, "'I Would Wish Death on You': Race, Gender, and Immigration in the Globality of the U.S. Prison Regime," *The Scholar and Feminist Online* 6, no. 3 (2008).

2. When running for the Republican nomination for president in November 2015, Trump stated he would "absolutely" implement a Muslim registry. When pressed by a reporter about how this would differ from requiring Jews to register in Nazi Germany, Trump replied, "You tell me."

3. Sylvia Chan-Malik, *Being Muslim: A Cultural History of Women of Color in American Islam* (New York: New York University Press, 2018).

4. Robert Orsi, "Everyday Miracles: The Study of Lived Religions," in *Lived Religions: Toward a History of Practice,* ed. David D. Hall (Princeton, N.J.: Princeton University Press, 1997), 8.

5. My concept of "racial–religious form" builds on the work of Colleen Lye's "racial form" in regard to Asians in the United States. See Lye, *America's Asia: Racial Form and American Literature 1893–1945* (Princeton, N.J.: Princeton University Press, 2004).

6. Sophia Rose Arjana, *Muslims in the Western Imagination* (Oxford: Oxford University Press, 2015), 3.

7. Sylvia Chan-Malik, "Common Cause: On the Black-Immigrant Debate and Constructing the Muslim American," *Journal of Race, Ethnicity, and Religion* 2, no. 8 (2011): 1–39.

8. Wadud has clearly stated that instead of being called a feminist, she is "a pro-faith, pro-feminists Muslim woman." Amina Wadud, *Inside the Gender Jihad: Women's Reform in Islam* (Oxford: OneWorld, 2006), 4.

22

The Audience Is Still Present

Invocations of El-Hajj Malik El-Shabazz by Muslims in the United States

MARYAM KASHANI

i see your human;
flesh,
filth,
breath.
i see your human,
i see you are human
and beloved
to an entire people,
to the Lord who brought you into being.
The Lord made you human, Malcolm.
I feel your human;
your faults are mine.
I'm sorry about that time
when I thought you were other than me.

—ZAINAB SYED, "Poems on Malcolm"

"The Nationalists have claimed Malcolm. The Socialists have claimed Malcolm. Now, it's time for you Muslims to claim Malcolm . . . because he was a believer . . . he was a believer."[1] Imam Zaid Shakir, a Black American Muslim scholar, narrates his account of sitting with Betty Shabazz, the widow of Malcolm X, El-Hajj Malik El-Shabazz, at the "96th Street mosque" in New York. The video cuts to close-ups of the young Muslim audience members (Black, white, Arab, South Asian, and Latinx), creating a multiracial and multiethnic tableau of the American Ummah (community of believers). Their faces are taut, serious, misty, and moved as they are drawn into a genealogy of Muslim struggle through the "claiming of Malcolm," a legacy of blood spilled, a line that tracks to unlikely places, urban and suburban, throughout the United States.

"Where do we go with this . . . strength and fire and energy that Malcolm X's speeches highlight as a potential for us?"[2] Two years later, Black American Muslim artist Nsenga Knight asks this question of her Google Hangout interlocutors, an imam, an activist, an artist, and a scholar, during a performance of *(X) Speaks* (2015). While directed toward Black American Muslims, her question implicates all Muslims who "claim" Malcolm—his words, his spirituality, his praxis. How do we understand Malcolm's "flowing and operating and representing Islam" in both global and American contexts, and how does he serve as a model for "our responsibility to the way that we think, and the way that we move in the world and interact with creation"?[3] Invocations like Shakir's and Knight's are utilized to reframe the present, while suggesting a theology and praxis toward a hoped-for future. The short video *Passing the Baton* (2013) by Mustafa Davis, the related public event *The Life and Legacy of Malcolm X* (2013) held at the Ta'leef Collective in Fremont, California, and the Web- and performance-based social practice project *(X) Speaks* by Nsenga Knight provide examples to consider how particular Muslims in the United States articulate a Muslim legacy of Malcolm X, El-Hajj Malik El-Shabazz, fifty years after his assassination.[4] Following Knight's reminder that Malcolm's speeches are "words we can use" that "give us strength," this chapter considers how invocations of Malcolm enjoin Muslims in the United States to take on the difficult task of reactivating the full force and implications of his words.

Within North American Muslim discourses, Malcolm is often deployed as a rhetorical figure, a metonymic shortcut to communicate ideals of racial and social justice, black masculinity and self-determination, and religious devotion. Invocations of Malcolm work in a register of "Muslim cool," which channels Malcolm's blackness and counterpolitics, while also at times reifying the very logics of white supremacy and multicultural American citizenship that he so vehemently opposed.[5] The U.S. government issued a Malcolm X stamp in 1999 as an attempt to rewrite his narrative, as well as the United States' own racial history, as a morality tale from angry and violent racial separatism to peaceful post-racialist multiculturalism. Recent incidents of police brutality, the increasing incarceration of youth of color, the lack of justice for victims of sexual assault, and ongoing war and occupation in the Middle East and in Muslim parts of Africa remind us that despite civil rights achievements, systems and industries of oppression like racism, sexism, incarceration, and militarism are highly adaptable and persevering. The words of Malcolm X read and spoken again today, more than fifty years after his assassination, do not yield a world unfamiliar or antiquated. His speeches and writings continue to describe circumstances of injustice that resonate as true, not to be assuaged by a multicultural history of American progress. After the *(X) Speaks* performance of "House Negroes and Field Negroes," one interlocutor responds that the "audience is still present . . . some of us have been laboring under the illusion of how much things have changed," not attentive to how we may each still have "a little of the house negro and the field negro within us," in terms of our different levels of complicit maneuvering within the structures of white supremacy and capitalist exploitation.[6] As discussions about race in both American society and the Muslim communities within it continue to wrangle and challenge, it is important to revisit Malcolm's words and life without diluting the ferocity and accuracy of his still-relevant critiques of white supremacy and the racial state, global imperialism and exploitation, and the betrayal of communities by their tokenized leadership. This chapter and the works discussed within it through the metaphors of "passing the baton" and the "X as variable" push against these tendencies, urging Muslims to engage seriously with Malcolm's words and life and to carry on his intellectual, political, and spiritual work, while likewise maintaining a criticality and reflexivity that Malcolm himself practiced toward both his legacy and our interpretation of it.[7]

Passing the Baton was produced by Muslim filmmaker Mustafa Davis in 2013. The short film draws on staged interviews conducted with Zaid Shakir and white American Muslim scholar Umar Faruq Abd-Allah; documentary footage of the public event *The Life and Legacy of Malcolm X*; archival footage of Malcolm X and global postcolonial struggles; and portraits of Muslims in the Bay Area.[8] It was distributed via the Muslim nonprofit Ta'leef Collective, which Davis cofounded with fellow Muslim convert Usama Canon in 2006 in Fremont, California.[9] Ta'leef Collective presents itself as a "third place" for Islam in the United States, where people can learn about Islam, build community, and explore and learn ways of living Islam. The Muslim third space or place is a response to the need for spaces of intentional community that are disaggregated from often highly contested spaces like mosques, schools, and homes that often delimit the types of conversations and activities that can take place as well as the types of bodies that may feel welcome.[10]

Throughout the month of February 2015, artist Nsenga Knight invited "members of the Black American Muslim community to collectively perform or present Malcolm X's final speeches and reflect on his continuing pertinence on the 50th anniversary of his death."[11] By following the pace of the actual speeches, both the embodied temporality of each performed text and the grueling schedule Malcolm X followed in his last month, Knight creates and hails a digital congregation to make "ourselves an audience to Malcolm's words" via Google Hangout, YouTube, Facebook, and Twitter; her website; group chats; and hashtags.[12] Google Hangouts featured Knight and Black imams, academics, students, artists, activists, and Muslim families. Groups of individuals were selected for each of the eight online events, in which they read either the specific text that Malcolm X had delivered on that night fifty years prior or a reportage of it. From "Not Willing to Sit and Wait," originally delivered at the Tuskegee Institute in Alabama on February 3, 1965, to "A Global Rebellion of the Oppressed against the Oppressor," delivered at Barnard College in New York City on February 18, 1965 (he was assassinated a few days later, on February 21), Black American Muslims revisited and reactivated Malcolm's words followed by discussions of what could be learned from them. Employing his texts and life as a kind of exegesis for religious practice and belief, as well as performing an exegesis on the speeches themselves, *(X) Speaks* facilitated a discursive space that incorporated multiple age groups, levels of education, and geographic locations to consider "what Islam is supposed to do for us and for our people."[13]

X as Variable

In the late 1980s and early 1990s, there was a resurgence of interest in and cultural and intellectual production about Malcolm X, what historian Russell Rickford called "Malcolmology," owing to particular conditions of black life, Spike Lee's film based on the *Autobiography,* hip-hop music, and the concomitant commercialization of the X symbol and the man who personified it.[14] Much of this literature on Malcolm X largely discounts the significance of Malcolm's relationship to Islam as an ethical framework that mediates a relationship with God and others. Cultural workers, scholars, and activists have typically focused on particular periods of Malcolm's life, whether Detroit Red, black nationalist, or internationalist, in efforts to marshal his "masculinity, his blackness, and his ghetto grounding."[15] While Muslims likewise invoke Malcolm's masculinity, blackness, and ghetto credentials, they typically focus on the post-Mecca, ex–Nation of Islam Malcolm. While I follow their interpretations here, I urge us not to fall into such fixed periodizations that discount "a totality of lived experiences" that contribute to the man Malcolm was in the last years of his life.[16] Malcolm himself stated that "to understand that of any person, his whole life, from birth, must be reviewed. All of our experiences fuse into our personality. Everything that ever happened to us is an ingredient."[17]

Indeed, one often overlooked aspect of Malcolm's character was his ability to reflect and transform his thinking and practice accordingly, "to engage in introspection without fear."[18] From changes in his language around black nationalism to augmenting and regretting his former statements about the political role of women and whites, Malcolm spoke openly of the processual nature of his philosophic and political development.[19] As Angela Davis writes, "Malcolm did not hesitate to reexamine his ideas and consider the possibility of radical shifts. . . . He was not afraid to explore the likelihood that his ideas could not stand the test of the complexities he encountered in his political travels."[20] Because he died in the midst of a radical rethinking of his organizations and their sociopolitical and religious roles, Malcolm offers us through such unknowns the "X factor," an expansive calculus through which to invoke and interpret his legacy.

MALCOLM AS BELIEVER

Throughout the *Autobiography,* Malcolm reflects upon events in his life, in which "Allah was near." When his sister Ella, who had been saving money to go on hajj, gives Malcolm the funds to go instead, he paraphrases the Qur'an, saying, "Allah always gives you signs, when you are with Him, that He is with you."[21] In other sections of the *Autobiography,* Malcolm reflects on how there is a divine plan of which he is a part: "I've so often thought that Allah was watching over me";[22] "I have thought a thousand times, I guess, about how I so narrowly escaped death twice that day. That's why I believe that everything is written";[23] "I believe, today, that it was written, it was meant, for Reginald to be used for one purpose only: as a bait, as a minnow to reach into the ocean of blackness where I was, to save me";[24] "And there I was, with two Muslim seatmates, one from Egypt, the other from Arabia, all of us bound for Mecca, with me up in the pilots' cabin. Brother, I *knew* Allah was with me."[25]

In Davis's *Passing the Baton,* the camera pans over an image of Malcolm X sitting in a prayer posture in a mosque, then cuts to Shakir speaking, and then back to archival footage of Malcolm speaking intensely in a medium close-up, pointing his finger as he speaks. On the audio track, we hear Shakir discuss Malcolm's struggles with *wudu'* (absolution) and prayer, which are described in the following passage of the *Autobiography:*

Imagine, being a Muslim minister, a leader in Elijah Muhammad's Nation of Islam, and not knowing the prayer ritual. I tried to do what he did. I knew I wasn't doing it right. I could feel the other Muslims' eyes on me. Western ankles won't do what Muslim ankles have done for a lifetime. . . . Watched by the Muslims, I kept practicing prayer posture. I refused to let myself think how ridiculous I must have looked to them. . . . I was angry with myself for not having taken the time to learn more of the orthodox prayer rituals before leaving America. . . . I may not have been mumbling the right thing, but I was mumbling. I don't mean to have any of this sound joking. It was far from a joke with me.[26]

Referencing this autobiographical passage, Shakir states, "He felt bad, like 'I can't worship Allah like I'm supposed to. I'm supposed to be a Muslim.' He felt bad. He was a believer and that faith is what fueled him. Where did that fire come from? The people see the fire, but fire requires fuel. And the fuel is faith . . . people want the fire, but don't want to burn the fuel."

Shakir asserts that faith is what grounded and drove Malcolm. The video footage cuts between the firebombing of the Shabazz home, the four-thousand-plus-page FBI file that was kept on him, and Shakir speaking on Malcolm's hardships and challenges. For Shakir, it was belief in God and divine providence that enabled Malcolm to persevere. Shakir indirectly challenges his audience to reflect upon whether their faith is sincere and can sustain and motivate them. What do they *really* believe in? And are they willing and able to burn the fuel of faith?

Malcolm stated on February 4, 1965, in Tuskegee, Alabama, that while he believes in the will of God, he's "not willing to sit and wait on God to come. If he doesn't come soon, it will be too late. I believe in religion, but a religion that includes political, economic, and social action designed to eliminate some of these things and make a paradise here on earth while we're waiting for the other."[27] This theological pronouncement touches upon a centuries-old debate among Muslim scholars and polities, especially in terms of exercising dissent against political authorities and deference to scholars and other figures of authority. He extends this argument ten days later in Detroit by describing the conditions under which such a stand is given meaning and direction: "I'm not in a society that practices brotherhood. . . . And so, since I could see that America itself is a society where there is no brotherhood and that this society is controlled primarily by racists and segregationists—and it is—who are in Washington, D.C., in positions of power . . . they exercise the same forms of brutal oppression against dark-skinned people in South and North Vietnam, or in the Congo, or in Cuba, or in any other place on this earth where they're trying to exploit and oppress."[28] Malcolm draws attention to the neocolonial role that the United States plays in African and Asian countries—exploitation of natural resources, regime change, "dollarism," and acts of war—demonstrating how the domestic and international are inextricably linked. One *(X) Speaks* participant discusses how Malcolm's analysis would help articulate another vision of the world: "I definitely would love for our community to explore the Bandung conference and the non-aligned movement as a form of challenging some of the hegemonies that were existing. And so now . . . it just seems like we've just resigned ourselves to deal with this world order. . . . We can take some inspiration for what's going on, like what this speech was about, talking about neocolonialism, and how you have this benevolent world order which is just as insidious."[29]

MULTIRACIAL/MULTIETHNIC UMMAH

"This is an honor and a communal obligation," white American Dr. Umar Faruq Abd-Allah begins his introduction to *The Life and Legacy of Malcolm X* event at Ta'leef Collective. "Malcolm is to us a father and he is one of the founders of this great historical phenomenon which is the rebirth of Islam amongst its children in this part of the world." Abd-Allah's designation of this event as being a communal obligation, a *fard kifaya,* speaks to the importance of understanding El-Hajj Malik El-Shabazz as an American ancestor, one who renewed Islam "in this part of the world." The amount of "work" Abd-Allah puts into authenticating Malcolm X, El-Hajj Malik El-Shabazz, as a significant Muslim ancestor (as "father" and "renewer") for *all* Muslims in the United States challenges the dynamics of intra-Muslim racism that determines who leads congregations, who gets marriage proposals, who is seen as religiously authoritative and authentic, and also how Muslims interpolated as non-black situate themselves and are situated within the racial hierarchy of white supremacy and anti-blackness. By articulating the history of Islam in the United States through black bodies, black suffering, and black social movements, an antiracist multiracial formation of Muslimness challenges an anti-blackness that structures racial hierarchies both within the United States and in many Muslim communities. This work of scholars and laypeople is a critical intervention into discourses and practices of racism, while it can also further demarcate people based on pseudo-scientific notions of race as a biological truth. Abd-Allah particularizes Malcolm's "noble lineage" in a way that is reminiscent of the

Islamic tradition of examining the Prophet Muhammad's lineage to show his exceptional prophetic qualities, which, while honoring Malcolm's memory, simultaneously undermines the message of "passing the baton" that much of this discourse is aimed at achieving.

By recognizing El-Hajj Malik El-Shabazz as a global Muslim figure, this remembrance and teaching likewise propose an alternative directionality for and understanding of Islamic knowledge and practice. Islam not only arrives *to* the Americas but emerges *from* it. Abd-Allah's, Shakir's, and Davis's efforts to authenticate and venerate Malcolm, to reclaim the *spiritual* Malcolm, are part of an ongoing effort to locate Malcolm as a common ancestor, thereby drawing lines of spiritual kinship across racial and ethnic lines. This kinship across difference is demanded by Malcolm's post-Mecca legacy; to recall his narrative without working toward the concomitant obligation of ideal brotherhood and sisterhood (both within and beyond the Muslim Ummah) in this world would betray the full implications of his legacy.

PASSING THE BATON

Over archival footage of the Nation of Islam's University of Islam, Abd-Allah discusses how "Malcolm understood instinctively and from his experience, that ideas and charismatic people are not enough. They have to be institutionalized." Throughout this section of the film, Davis uses Nation of Islam footage, suggesting that despite it often being characterized as "not real Islam," the Nation is indeed a critical part of, rather than a precursor to, Muslim history in the United States. Contrary to much of the literature that suggests that Malcolm was more a man of words than action, Muslims draw attention to the significance of his work with young men in the Fruit of Islam, in media with *Muhammad Speaks,* in cities as he proselytized and established temples (now mosques), and in upholding the (black) Muslim family.

Shakir states that institutions "allow us to strengthen the individual to amplify the strengths of the individual. . . . The family is a human institution. The family is a group arrangement that emphasizes and accentuates the strengths of individuals and mitigates and minimizes their weaknesses." The video cuts to archival film of Malcolm X speaking to Nation members—"Get off the welfare, get out of that compensation line. Be a man, earn what you need for your own family, then your family respects you. They are proud to say that's my father; she's proud to say that's my husband. Father means you are taking care of those children." Davis cuts to additional archival footage of a Nation of Islam family praying together around a table. While the audio emphasizes the financial imperative of fatherhood, the images convey a moral responsibility to be present and provide a center for spiritual awakening and companionship. While Malcolm's statements seem to individualize and pathologize the "crisis of the black family" to that of a lost masculinity (which continues to be a narrative with traction in Muslim communities today), it is important to situate them as Davis does within his trenchant critiques of systems of oppression (from the violence of slavery to housing and job discrimination, poor education, biased media, and the psychological effects of racism) that contribute to our sociopolitical circumstances. Malcolm engaged in a process of dual critique, aimed at the agency of his people, whom he loved, and those who benefited from systems that limited the possibilities of black flourishing.

A number of *(X) Speaks* performances and conversations were performed by families in which mothers, fathers, sons, and daughters "passed the baton" of speechifying through the words of Malcolm X and then engaged in intergenerational conversation about the surprises and lessons of the texts. In this way, the project enacted what it means to practice a black Muslim family life that "amplifies strength" and "mitigates weaknesses" of individual members. The *(X) Speaks* collaborators' embodiment of Malcolm's legacy and language demonstrated how "family" is not an overly defined structure of patriarchal hegemony but rather a space of potentiality and criticality, where knowledge and identity are structured and transformed. Children's responses to Malcolm's words on February 15 were sought out and considered in relation to their mothers, fathers, and siblings, shifting everyday relations within the family into a space of mutual exchange. Similarly, lively exchanges on February 14 between the Knight sisters and their father; on February 16 between an elder imam and younger scholars and activists; and on February 11 between a college professor and her students at the HBCU Prairie View A&M University in Texas demonstrated how Malcolm's texts remain relevant and applicable, providing a common ground for critical intergenerational dialogue.[30] While Davis's films and specific events held at the Ta'leef Collective and other Muslim institutions are critical interventions in recontextualizing Malcolm X for a multiracial and multiethnic Muslim Ummah, discursive engagement, exposure, and study as witnessed in *(X) Speaks* demonstrate how Malcolm's political and spiritual imperatives function as *sources* for Islamic knowledge and praxis.

In considering his intellectual trajectory from analysis of the racial status quo to organizing for social change in his last year of life, Audre Lorde asserts that Malcolm would have been confronted with "the question of difference as a creative and necessary force for change."[31] In the final meetings of the Organization of Afro-American Unity (OAAU), Malcolm stated the need to reorganize the organization with clearer roles for women,[32] and in one of his last interviews (with *al-Muslimoon,* an Arabic language monthly out of the Islamic Centre of Switzerland), he discussed the need for Muslim leaders to have a more "well-rounded type of education" and that they "must reevaluate and spell out with clarity the Muslim position on education in general and education for women in particular," because "where the women are encouraged to get education and play a more active role in the all-around affairs of the community and country, the entire people are more active, more enlightened, and more progressive."[33] Betty and her daughters' accounts of their lives with him discuss the respect he had for Betty's opinions (such as requesting her summaries of books he did not have time to read) as well as her resistance to his views on their respective roles in their marriage when she would leave him after each of her first three daughters' births.[34]

Muslim invocations of Malcolm's example often reify patriarchal notions of reclaimed masculinity and specific gender roles, but as images from *Passing the Baton* and *(X) Speaks* demonstrate, they can also be about renewing the Muslim family (within kinships of both blood and faith) as a site of ethical–moral becoming. As articulations of Malcolm's legacy continue to be brought forth, how Muslims interpret the possibilities of family and other institutions will be important in thinking about how Islam as a "kinship by faith" is structured across lines of difference and blood.[35] The idealistic "family" and other social institutions like schools, congregations, communities, or the nation are often contradictory spaces, at times supportive, other times alienating and diminishing. Malcolm recognized that one cannot isolate the dynamics of family from larger structures of white supremacy and racism, sexual violence, the state, and the economy. In narrating his *Autobiography,* he articulates harm suffered and inflicted within his family and larger community; in this way, he draws attention to our participation in the harmful and dehumanizing effects of American society and the need to "wake the people up" to our humanity, worth, and heritage.[36]

In the *Life and Legacy* event at Ta'leef, Zaid Shakir begins with a supplication: "All praises due to Allah who has blessed us with this gathering. He's blessed us with two great blessings, with ample nourishment and with security. . . . 'So let them worship the Lord of this sacred house who has fed them and driven away from them hunger and has made them secure from fear' (106:3–4). So we gather here with no fear by the grace of Allah *subhanahu wa ta'ala.*" Shakir alludes to the differences between the experiences of the community sitting before him and that of Malcolm X, his family, and others. The community seated before him has wealth and "ample" nourishment, and despite attacks on Muslims in the media and through surveillance, they are in relative security. Two days earlier, the body of Malcolm X's grandson, Malcolm Latif Shabazz, was received in Oakland for a funeral at the Islamic Cultural Center of Northern California after his murder in Mexico City.[37] When a call went out to raise $40,000 to transport Shabazz's body back to the United States, money was quickly raised in the Bay Area, with many small gifts of five or ten dollars.[38] After the funeral, his body was sent on to New York, where he was laid to rest with his grandparents, El-Hajj Malik and Betty Shabazz. Shakir uses this account to demonstrate how the Bay Area community (both Muslim and non-Muslim) recognizes the significance and sacrifices of the Shabazz family and likewise how the Bay Area, through a divine design, has produced a number of innovative organizations and institutions that serve the wider American community.

This juxtaposition of security and fear with the two Shabazz deaths draws attention to how this gathering of Muslims is situated within a prejudicial system of who lives and who dies where and for whom. Such ironies of chance and systemic violence are familiar to an immigrant population that crossed waters as refugees of wars in Afghanistan and Yemen and that witnesses relatives in South and West Asia and throughout the Arab world as victims of American drone strikes, proxies, intervention, exploitation, and war. Yet making the connections between such explicit and fleshy forms of violence and the everyday affective and impactful violence of structural and anti-Muslim racism, Islamophobia, targeted incarceration, poverty, and a media structured around white supremacy is harder, though it is a lesson Malcolm clearly articulated and understood. Both Malcolms' lives and deaths exemplify what is at stake in social justice struggles at the intersection of race and religion, as well as the potentialities of an antiracist, multiracial Islam. Much like many other young black and brown youth in the criminal justice system, young Malcolm Latif Shabazz accepted a plea bargain for lesser jail time, pleading guilty to crimes he did not commit rather than taking a chance on a trial in an expensive and racially biased legal system. Once he was released and became politically active and spiritually motivated, speaking to groups around the country as well as abroad, making his hajj, studying Islam, traveling throughout the Middle East, and beginning to write his own autobiography, he may have been targeted by federal agencies, much like his grandfather and other family members. As his grandfather's legacy is much discussed and celebrated, what would it mean to tie in the lessons and legacy of his grandson's? From elder Malcolm to younger Malcolm, could we suture sectarian divisions toward Muslim solidarities and coalitions; take seriously and address the effects of white supremacist racial terror on generations of families, social movements, and neighborhoods; and look toward ways of building strong institutions that recognize and support the vulnerable and besieged among us?

Shakir indirectly reminds, for this is a remembrance, that a baton has been passed, and to drop it—through ignorance, passiveness, denial, or fear—would be a great betrayal to Malcolm's legacy. Black and white archival footage of anticolonial movements and the civil rights movement cut with Shakir speaking and close-ups of women in the audience as Shakir emotionally summons,

> People before us passed us this baton, and in the twentieth century, it was a hard leg of the race. . . . It was difficult to be a Muslim, but despite all those hardships, that baton was put in our hands. Are we going to drop it? Or are we going to pass it on?

Shakir warns his audience against a complicity with or ambivalence to the current political landscape by drawing attention to Malcolm's martyrdom. How do we understand his martyrdom "by blood," within narrow political discourses of "good Muslims" and "violent jihadists"? Just as Malcolm is celebrated as one who put his own life on the line, what does it mean that his strength and zeal also risked his family's security? Islamic notions of responsibility and mutual rights require that Muslims satisfy the claims of others over them before their own needs. How does a community recognize and support those who make sacrifices of or are made to sacrifice their security on our behalf? What is the calculus of living lives of least harm when living (and paying taxes) in a country that consumes and pollutes more than its share of world resources; that calculates the illusion of its citizens' safety and security against global humanitarian crises and mass incarceration; and that wields its influence on the world's politics, economies, and cultures in a multitude of ways? Can we imagine risking our salvation or risking "the security" of employment, education, social standing, property, privacy, aspirational whiteness, or our home, community, and family lives?

The twentieth-century "open war on Muslims" continues into the twenty-first century as anti-Muslim discourses gain traction and drone and proxy wars continue in much of the Middle East.[39] The same weapons used against Palestinians were used against protestors in Ferguson, Missouri, in summer 2014. As *(X) Speaks* participants performed and reflected on Malcolm's words, they were consistently struck by the degree to which his speeches and analyses are still relevant and timely, despite the progress of historical and contemporary social movements. One participant asks, "How long are we going to be 'finally waking up' until we stop nodding back off. . . . The momentum grows but where does it go? Where is that token that is neutralizing our momentum and how has it continued to work fifty years later? Why is this speech still relevant?"[40]

Multiple answers are suggested: state repression of black organizing and resistance; lack of consciousness; tokenization; and the "implacable nature of the enemy that we are up against . . . in a continuum of struggle." Malcolm's ongoing relevance speaks to "the clarity of his own analysis and his own understanding and ability to speak, not in a time frame kind of way, but to speak to the future." While the ongoing nature of such debates is frustrating, *(X) Speaks* participants sought to understand this constancy in spiritual time: "In some sense it's Qur'anic wisdom that struggle is eternal and that vigilance is something that has to be renewed whether that's in communal struggles or societal struggles or whether that's in personal struggles." These collective statements from the multigenerational set of performers articulate the ongoing relevance of Malcolm's words but likewise how to understand a Muslim commitment to social justice as an imperative working in tandem with "the spiritual renewal that gets us up in the morning again." They further articulate Malcolm's "idea that being Muslim and being committed to black liberation are things that go together and that commitment to black liberation is a commitment to human liberation and is a commitment to struggle and this kind of renewed struggle or renewing your intention to struggle . . . that is fully grounded in our tradition, our spiritual tradition as Muslims." As Muslims invoke the figure of Malcolm X as a model for being Muslim in this contemporary moment, what parts of his legacy are they embracing, and what gets left behind?

If Malcolm X were alive today, would he be celebrated as a significant leader or marginalized for his "radical" critiques?[41] Would his singular voice be lost in the cacophony of radio, the Internet, and cable television? Would he be reincarcerated on political grounds?[42] Would he be judged "not Muslim enough," not knowledgeable enough for lack of overseas or "traditional" training? Malcolm's iconicity has increasingly come to stand in for his actual theoretical contributions, "as if theory had no life beyond birth, no interpretive generative property as taken up and reiterated by others."[43] Some contemporary Muslim invocations of Malcolm X, El-Hajj Malik El-Shabazz, reduce his critical analyses and his vision for a unified social movement to platitudes about social justice and faith. To disaggregate his commitment to black life (both Muslim and non-Muslim)—a "complete recognition and respect of Black people as human beings"—and his scathing indictment of white supremacy and the U.S. government from his legacy for Muslims in the United States is a dangerous betrayal of his life's work.[44] As individuals and institutions take up his image or invoke him as an ancestor, how do they negotiate their everyday work in those terms? How are his theories given life, and what do they generate for us in the twenty-first century?

Malcolm's concerns, insights, and errors in the 1960s say a great deal about contemporary debates regarding "real" Islam, "Muslim American" citizenship, minority and majority statuses, and personal and global jihads. More than ever, young Muslims are growing up with a sense of "Muslims as problems" and Islam as something that needs reform and progress. Can a greater sense of Muslim identity, roots, and pride reduce divisiveness and fear within Muslim communities? When identity politics are increasingly criticized and mobilized contradictorily, what kind of Muslim consciousness does one aim for, and toward what end? How do Muslims learn from Malcolm's experiences as a devoted follower and then avowed critic of Elijah Muhammad? He learned to "think with my own mind" after feeling betrayed by someone in whom he had had total faith.[45] How do we produce structures of devotion, discipline, and learning that respect certain notions of authority and hierarchy within the Islamic tradition that do not replicate the kind of blind following to which Malcolm succumbed? Malcolm suggests that rather than changing the minds of leaders, it makes more sense "to go to the people first and let the leaders fall in behind them."[46]

When scholars retain the interpretative authority of who Malcolm was and why he is important, his key insights can be reduced to well-meaning tropes, deactivating their interpretive and prescriptive potential. While their work is an important introductory step in a multiracial and antiracist Muslim recognition of Malcolm X, an annual review on his birthday or during Black History Month does little to further the potential impact and implications of his teachings. Scholars and institutions do not bear the total weight of responsibility; the texts of Malcolm's speeches are widely available. START

A MALCOLM X HALAQA/READING GROUP![47] Malcolm himself stated that "the greatest mistake of the movement . . . has been trying to organize a sleeping people around specific goals. You have to wake the people up first, then you'll get action."[48]

From understanding how blackness or Muslimness is framed by media, to analyzing how militarization, colonization, and neoimperialism are intricately linked to structures of incarceration, racialization, and capitalist exploitation, to having faith in God while seeking justice on earth, the works and life of El-Hajj Malik El-Shabazz provide important lessons and signposts for situating how Muslims should lead lives as brothers, sisters, and citizens. In Knight's project, the "X" symbolizes Malcolm X, the *(X) Speaks* collaborators, a variable, and the unknown. X as variable or unknown is a particularly compelling metaphor for the significance of Malcolm X and how his meaning has been multiply interpreted, mobilized, and transformed. The concept of "passing the baton" likewise enjoins entire communities to take responsibility and act in ways that keep theories moving, transforming, beyond individual lives. Knight's participants consider how Malcolm "always thought of himself and the world bigger than the parameters that were given to him" as a challenge to expand their notions of politics and possibility. By activating Malcolm's texts, memory, and legacy in this way, we could theorize and organize ourselves into a world beyond what we have inherited, a world that actualizes the brotherhood and sisterhood that God and the Messenger decreed.

NOTES

1. Mustafa Davis, *Passing the Baton,* 2013, http://taleefcollective.org/passing-the -baton-short-film/.

2. Nsenga Knight, "Feb 4: 'The House Negro and the Field Negro,'" in *(X) Speaks,* ed. Nsenga Knight (2015).

3. Nsenga Knight, personal interview, April 19, 2015.

4. I have written elsewhere about how Muslims localize and historicize Islam in the United States through invoking Malcolm's life and through visiting his grave in Westchester County, New York. Maryam Kashani, "Seekers of Sacred Knowledge: Zaytuna College and the Education of American Muslims," PhD diss., Department of Anthropology, University of Texas at Austin, 2014.

5. Su'ad Abdul Khabeer, *Muslim Cool: Race, Religion, and Hip Hop in the United States* (New York: New York University Press, 2016).

6. The speaker's "we" referred to Black Americans, but this "we" applies to all people in relations of power largely structured through the injustices of white supremacy and neoliberal capitalism.

7. Throughout this chapter, I mostly refer to El-Hajj Malik El-Shabazz by his more common appellation, Malcolm X, or simply Malcolm. Among Muslims in the United States, the use of "Malcolm" is exceedingly common; however intimate the term, it diminishes neither the esteem he commands nor the lessons his life yields. Malcolm himself stated he would continue to use the name "Malcolm X" despite the fact that his passport used the name Malik El-Shabazz for many years prior to his departure from the Nation of Islam.

8. Mustafa Davis, *The Life and Legacy of Malcolm X: With Dr. Umar Faruq Abd-Allah and Imam Zaid Shakir*, 2015, http://taleefcollective.org/video-and-films.

9. In early 2016, Davis resigned from his roles as media director and board member of the Ta'leef Collective. Both men are of mixed racial heritage.

10. Ta'leef Collective, "Revisiting the Third Place with Usama Canon," http://taleefcollective.org/revisiting-the-third-place-with-usama-canon/.

11. Knight, *(X) Speaks*.

12. Nsenga Knight, "Feb 11th: 'The Oppressed Masses of the World Cry Out for Action against the Common Oppressor,'" ibid.

13. "Interview with Nsenga Knight."

14. Manning Marable, "Rediscovering Malcolm's Life: A Historian's Adventures in Living History," in *Black Routes to Islam*, ed. Manning Marable and Hisham Aidi, 299–315 (New York: Palgrave Macmillan, 2009); Russell Rickford, "The Roots of "Malcolmology," http://www.aaihs.org/the-roots-of-malcolmology/.

15. Michael Eric Dyson, *Making Malcolm: The Myth and Meaning of Malcolm X* (New York: Oxford University Press, 1995), xi. Al-Qaeda's media wing has likewise put Malcolm's critiques to use; in one recent video promoting their English-language magazine *Resurgence*, they mix "graphics, images of George W. Bush and warplanes launching missiles with a speech by Malcolm X, the African-American Muslim leader, in which he said: 'You can't ever reach a man if you don't speak his language. If a man speaks the language of brute force, you can't come to him with peace.'" Rob Crilly, "Al-Qaeda Unveils New Magazine Aimed at Western Jihadis," *Telegraph*, March 10, 2014. Al-Qaeda reifies the image of Malcolm being violent, failing to distinguish that Malcolm defended the use of violence in self-defense. He may have agreed with their assessments of the violence of American imperialism, however.

16. Robin D. G. Kelley, "The Riddle of the Zoot: Malcolm Little and Black Cultural Politics during World War II," in *Malcolm X: In Our Own Image*, ed. Joe Wood (New York: St. Martin's Press, 1992), 175.

17. Malcolm X and Alex Haley, *The Autobiography of Malcolm X*, 1st Ballantine Books ed. (New York: Ballantine Books, 1992), 173.

18. Ron Simmons and Marlon Riggs, "Sexuality, Television, and Death: A Black Gay Dialogue on Malcolm X," in Wood, *Malcolm X*, 141.

19. Malcolm X, *February 1965: The Final Speeches* (1992; repr., New York: Pathfinder, 2012); Malcolm X and George Breitman, *Malcolm X Speaks: Selected Speeches and Statements*, 1st Black Cat ed. (New York: Grove Press, 1965); X and Haley, *Autobiography*.

20. Angela Y. Davis, "Meditations on the Legacy of Malcolm X," in Wood, *Malcolm X*, 40. See also Barbara Ransby and Tracye Matthews, "Black Popular Culture and the Transcendence of Patriarchal Illusions," *Race and Class* 35, no. 1 (1993): 58.

21. X and Haley, *Autobiography*, 237.

22. Ibid., 145.

23. Ibid., 172.

24. Ibid., 217.

25. Ibid., 373.

26. Ibid., 375–78.

27. *X*, February 1965, 22. "Elijah is willing to sit and wait—I'm not." Tuskegee Institute, Tuskegee, Alabama, on February 3, 1965.

28. Ibid., 93. "Educate our people in the science of politics." Ford Auditorium, Detroit, Michigan, on February 14, 1965.

29. Knight, "Feb 11th."

30. The inclusion of Prairie View A&M University as an example of a historically black college or university (HBCU) demonstrates the kind of institution building that Muslim scholars aspire to. Malcolm was at times critical of Black elites at some HBCUs who emulated and aspired to white society, but his overall belief in education and self-determination was aligned with the HBCU project.

31. Audre Lorde, *Sister Outsider: Essays and Speeches* (Trumansburg, N.Y.: Crossing Press, 1984), 135.

32. John Henrik Clarke, A. Peter Bailey, and Earl Grant, *Malcolm X: The Man and His Times* (New York: Macmillan, 1969), 90.

33. *X*, February 1965, 286. "We are fighting for respect and recognition as human beings for all Black Americans." Answers to questions by "al-Muslimoon."

34. Betty Shabazz and Susan L. Taylor, "Loving and Losing Malcolm," *Essence*, February 1992; Ilyasah Shabazz and Kim McLarin, *Growing Up X*, 1st ed. (New York: One World/Ballantine, 2002). See also Maya Angelou, *All God's Children Need Traveling Shoes*, 1st Vintage Books ed. (New York: Vintage Books, 1987). After Malcolm's death, Betty completed her hajj to Mecca. She raised their six daughters and eventually returned to school and earned a doctorate in higher education and curriculum development and was a professor and administrator at Medgar Evans College until her death in 1997.

35. Toshihiko Izutsu, *Ethico-Religious Concepts in the Qur'ān* (Montreal: McGill-Queen's University Press, 2002).

36. Malcolm X and George Breitman, *Malcolm X Speaks: Selected Speeches and Statements*, 1st Grove Weidenfeld Evergreen ed. (New York: Grove Weidenfeld, 1990), 196.

37. Located in downtown Oakland, the ICCNC, a primarily Shiʻa mosque founded by Iranians in 1995, serves the larger Bay Area community as well. (Young) Malcolm Shabazz converted to Shiʻa Islam and believed that his grandfather would have converted to Shiʻa Islam also because of what he considered its social justice imperative. Shabazz had considered moving to the Bay Area because he was inspired by the radical history of the Black Panther Party and was encouraged by activists like Yuri Kochiyama, who had been friends with the elder Malcolm and had written the younger Malcolm letters while he was in prison. Upon his release from prison, he traveled and studied Islam in the Middle East, most significantly for a year in Damascus, Syria.

38. J. R. Valrey, "Malcolm's 29th Birthday Commemorated: An Interview wit' Shaykh Hashim Alauddeen," *San Francisco Bay View* (2013), http://sfbayview.com/2013/09/malcolms-29th-birthday-commemorated-an-interview-wit-shaykh-hashim-alauddeen/.

39. Shakir, in *Passing the Baton.*

40. Nsenga Knight, "Feb 16th: 'Not Just an American Problem, but a World Problem,'" in *(X) Speaks.*

41. Marable, "Rediscovering Malcolm's Life," 314.

42. Consider the incarceration of Jamil Al-Amin (formerly H. Rap Brown) and the 2009 death of Imam Luqman Abdullah of Detroit, Michigan.

43. Patricia J. Williams, "Clarence X, Man of the People," in Wood, *Malcolm X,* 194–95.

44. X, *February 1965,* 187. "Not just an American problem but a world problem." Corn Hill Methodist Church, Rochester, New York.

45. Ibid. "I think with my own mind." Interview with the *New York Times.*

46. Ibid., 276. "We have to learn how to think." Interview with Marlene Nadle for the *Village Voice.*

47. I recommend beginning with the *Autobiography,* then moving on to *X Speaks: Selected Speeches and Statements,* then to *February 1965: The Final Speeches,* and then to Marable's controversial, though detailed, *Malcolm X: A Life of Reinvention* (New York: Viking, 2011). Films include the documentaries *Malcolm X: Make It Plain* (dir. Orlando Bagwell, 1994), *Malcolm X* (dir. Arnold Perl, 1972), and Spike Lee's "joint" *Malcolm X* (1992). Audio and film recordings of his speeches are available online; they provide valuable insight into Malcolm's oratorical skill and how he was received by his audiences. Other recommended texts, videos, and artworks are cited throughout this chapter.

48. X, *February 1965,* 271.

23

"Make a Way Out of No Way"

An Interview with Ustadh Ubaydullah Evans on the Islamic Tradition and Social Justice Activism

JUNAID RANA

JUNAID RANA (JR): In late December 2016, you published an essay titled "Discussing Controversy: Hamza Yusuf at RIS [Reviving the Islamic Spirit] Convention." Tell us about the context that propelled you to write this piece, and give us some details of the intervention.

USTADH UBAYDULLAH EVANS, EXECUTIVE DIRECTOR, AMERICAN LEARN-ING INSTITUTE FOR MUSLIMS (UUE): Seeing as though I did not attend the conference and I'm not on social media, I only heard about Shaykh Hamza's comments at RIS days after the initial controversy had broken. When I was first informed about the situation by a friend, my attention was not only drawn to Shaykh Hamza's regrettable comments but also to the ensuing public conversation about race, power, and privilege within our community. If I am to be totally honest, it was difficult to square the outrage I observed within the community with the applause—from a majority non-Black Muslim audience—I had heard on the recording. In fact, when I first saw the community's scathing repudiations of Shaykh Hamza's comments trending online, my immediate reaction was a half-hearted, "Subhanallah! All these years and I didn't know you actually cared about Black people!"

Indeed, it was difficult to get past the fact that the point of departure for one of the first real conversations about race in the Muslim community was not going to be the social racism, that is, experiences of disrespect and indignity, I and many other Blackamerican Muslims encounter at the hands of our coreligionists of other ethnicities daily. Rather, the issue of race in our community would be introduced while focusing on statements that appeared to uphold the logic of structural anti-Black racism made by an influential white American Muslim scholar. I feared that non-Black Muslims angrily posting or tweeting about Shaykh Hamza's comments (in 140 characters or less!) would create the impression that we were dealing with anti-Blackness and obscure the existence of racism within our community. In offering a short—but hopefully substantive— piece about the situation, part of what I hoped to do was raise the discussion to a place where we could talk candidly about race and anti-Black racism in the context of our understanding of God and our communal mission.

I think 2016 was a year of stark polarities for Black America. The triumphant victory lap of the first Black first family and unprecedented levels of visibility in Hollywood were overshadowed by what some commentators called "the worst year in American race relations since 1968." The heightened media coverage of unarmed Black men and women being brutalized and killed by law enforcement, quality-of-life indices that proved the Obama years had only marginally benefited Black communities, and, finally, the successful presidential campaign of Donald Trump all contributed to a painful year for Black America. For Muslims, if there could be said to be anything resembling a silver lining in the incredible pain we experienced, it might have been the way our community and the nation at large responded to the passing of Muhammad Ali (may God have mercy on him). Referring to the failure of early Muslim immigrants in the 1960s and 1970s to institutionally invest in Blackamerican Muslim religious history and authority, one of my mentors said it was like someone coming onto the set of a movie in which you were the lead actor and demoting you to the status of an extra. The Champ's transition seemed to return the Blackamerican Muslim narrative, with its heroes, distinct history, and unique priorities (Black dignity, economic self-determination, dismantling white supremacy, police accountability, et cetera) back to center stage. In my view, this background served to amplify the impact of the RIS controversy.

When journalist Mehdi Hasan asked Shaykh Hamza Yusuf about standing in solidarity with Black Lives Matter and the latter appeared to create a false equivalency between white American and Blackamerican victims of police violence, it was shocking, to say the least. When Shaykh Hamza continued by mentioning that countering "Black on Black" violence, not police accountability, should be the top priority of the Black community, I was bewildered. Mentioning "Black on Black" violence in the context of police misconduct was like mentioning modesty in the context of rape. Was Shaykh Hamza pathologizing Black communities and saying our wounds were self-inflicted? This trope is employed by those who deny the existence of structural racism, but none of my previous experiences with Shaykh Hamza suggested that he subscribed to such views.

Shaykh Hamza's comments were reprehensible. At base, I wanted to show that one could retain tremendous esteem for a scholar while criticizing the impact of his actions. Clerical infallibility is not a part of Sunni Islam's creed, and critique is not tantamount to disrespect. However, aside from being misdirected and insensitive, was there any merit to Shaykh Hamza's approach? Can an unsparing critique of white supremacy be reconciled with a call to moral responsibility? Does the fear of justifying white supremacy entail abandoning such a call? Could there be liberation in highlighting the capacity of a Living God, who is appealed through righteousness, to redeem Black people? This is where I wanted to attempt an intervention.

JR: How would you describe the challenge of white supremacy and the problem of Black suffering for Muslims? And to take it one step further, in conversation with Dr. Sherman Jackson's eloquently argued *Islam and the Problem of Black Suffering*, why are these issues incumbent on Muslims and anyone interested in justice to consider?

UUE: White supremacy and generational Black suffering have received more attention as sociological and anthropological phenomena provoking academic responses than as theological and spiritual challenges requiring religious ones. Islamic scholars owe a tremendous debt of gratitude to scholars of other disciplines and activists for addressing themselves and their expertise to what, in my view, are the most pressing moral dilemmas of our time. In effect, the virtual absence of Islamic scholarship from the discourse means that scholars seeking to engage must do so without the benefit of a canon. Instinct, creativity, and an active religious imagination are forced to play roles here that are usually reserved for precedent, rigor, and erudition.

In an article titled "Islam and Affirmative Action," Dr. Sherman Jackson identifies white supremacy as a "system of domination, whose daily assaults on black consciousness bludgeon the human spirit and simultaneously undermine and abuse the fact of black humanity."[1] He further elaborates by describing white supremacy as a "process of short-circuiting blacks' efforts to realize their humanity, as a matter of divine fiat as opposed to some honorary recognition granted on the satisfaction of self-serving criteria imposed by the dominant culture." Although these descriptions might be characterized as what I call "luxury" white supremacy by overlooking the more immediate assaults to life, limb, and property and focusing instead on psychological damage, I think they are particularly useful to Muslims.

White supremacy as described earlier, like the Qur'anic concept of *fitnah* [normalized domination], cannot comfortably coexist alongside *īmān,* or faith in God:

> and fight them until there exists no "fitnah" and religion is practiced solely out of devotion to God. (2:193)

Iman entails a recognition that the fundamental value of one's humanity is an indisputable fact; a divine grant not removed under any circumstances—"Verily, We have ennobled the Children of Adam" (17:70)— but singularly enhanced through piety and service. White supremacy, with its complex system of rewards, incentives, privileges, intimidation, incarceration, murder, et cetera, seeks to replace God—as the One who confers value upon human life—with its own self-serving order. On this system, one's humanity is not assigned value unless it is white or civilized: Christian, educated, successful, respectable, decent, liberal, and other vague categories that have been manipulated as euphemisms for white.

In his famed magnum opus *The Souls of Black Folk,* Dr. Du Bois referred to the tragic consequence of pursuing validation within a white supremacist order as "double consciousness." The wounds of double consciousness, opened by the quest to survive and thrive by "being what I can't be," are well documented. However, Blackamerican resistance to white supremacy, which has taken forms martial, cultural, economic, philosophical, and religious, is similarly well documented.

In my own religious imaginary, the Islamic testimony of faith [*shahādah*] provides the basis for an outlook that might mitigate some of the consequences of Du Boisian double consciousness.

Muhammad is the Messenger of God: the Prophetic example [*sunnah*], as documented and recorded in the classical tradition, gives the believer access to a modality of being that is morally inspiring and socially enabling but without the self-effacing "respectability politics" of traditional Black conservatism. Whereas respectability politics assume a normative "white gaze" and seek to thwart the specter of racism and its devaluations by the performance of "decency," *sunnah* seeks to make the believer the object of Divine love: "Say, [O Muhammad], If you love Allah, then follow me, [so] Allah will love you" (3:31). Lest we entertain certain notions of religious passivity in the face of oppression, it is important to note that divine love in Islam is not merely a "feel-good" bromide. It is a means to liberation: "Verily Allah (Glorified and exalted) has said: Whosoever shows enmity to one that I love, then I have declared war against him" (reported by Bukhāri). Lastly, to my mind, the greatest liability of traditional Black conservatism is the near-impossibility of disentangling the values it seeks to impart from ethical systems over which white supremacy still exerts what Gramsci called the "power of definition." Virtue is good; but whose virtue? Islam in general, and *sunnah* in particular, still represents a discursive tradition in which the white supremacist "power of definition" is challenged.

There is nothing worthy of worship besides God: in a sense, the worst possible outcome of playing the game of "respectability politics" and "double consciousness" is winning. For as Jackson writes in the same article, "the feelings of triumph that occur as one approaches redemption habitually obliterate any recognition of the falseness of the exploiter's criterion."[2] A sustained focus on the oneness of God [*tawḥīd*] forces this recognition. When did Black people in America ever lack the God-given human dignity that entails value? Believing that moral excellence is a means to divine love and ultimate redemption (from God) does not mean that citing moral failure as justification for injustice is not racist. This realization, which must be held closest by those who are able to attain some measure of success and recognition within the dominant culture, is reinforced by reflecting upon *tawḥīd*.

In the absence of this kind of religious imaginary, I fear that our ultimatum will be adopting or succumbing to modalities of being that deprive us of the moral excellence of the Sunnah (and, by extension, God's love) in the name of resistance or fall victim to the kind of hollow moralizing and petty "respectability politics" Black Star—quoting the great Toni Morrison—called the "law of the Bluest Eye." Where we would be:

Not strong (only aggressive)

Not free (we only licensed)

Not compassionate, only polite (now who the nicest?)

Not good but well-behaved . . .

JR: What does Islamic liberation theology look like to you? How would you define it, describe it, practice it? How might Muslims find inspiration from Black liberation theology and the Catholic tradition of liberation theology?

UUE: While I personally derive much inspiration from liberation theology and Black liberation theology, I think we have to proceed very cautiously when discussing the prospect of developing an Islamic equivalent.

My sense is that the growing interest in Islamic liberation theology corresponds with the expectation that Islamic teaching engage with revolutionary struggle. This engagement is essential. In fact, one of the most disturbing trends in our community is the widening chasm that separates Islamic scholars and activists. An interpretive approach that addresses the concerns of people fighting oppression would go a long way in bridging this gap. However, I don't think the *usūl* [foundational principles] of theology are the right discursive field in which to plant those seeds. Rather, unleashing the power of the religious imagination and careful creativity, engaging with the established traditions of theology, exegesis, law, et cetera, will yield more fruitful results.

The development of Islamic theology [aqīdah] has struck a remarkable balance between consistency and dynamism. The tendency toward theological reductionism, where every group or issue develops its own theology, has historically been resisted by Muslims. It is quite impressive that Sheikh Ahmadou Bamba, the twentieth-century Senegalese sage who led a pacifist struggle against French colonists in West Africa, and contemporary feminist scholar Amina Wadud both base their vastly different hermeneutic approaches on theologies that could broadly be characterized as Sunni. Sheikh Bamba appearing before the French Conseil d'État [Privy Council] declaring that he could only be ruled by God and Professor Wadud declaring patriarchy a violation of God's oneness are actually articulating creative, highly individualized interpretations of the generic Islamic doctrine of *tawḥīd*.

This kind of postfoundational interpretive creativity can provide a relevance that befits revolutionary struggle but also remain within the boundaries of orthodoxy. To be sure, the boldest example of Islamic liberation theology we've seen in America is that of the Nation of Islam (NOI). By offering a set of theological postulates that spoke directly to the reality of Blackamericans seeking liberation from white racism but which did, in fact, contravene orthodox *usūl*, the NOI assured relevance, but at the expense of continuity. In Sūrah al-Aḥqāf, the Prophet Muhammad (upon him be peace) is commanded, "Say: I am no bringer of new-fangled doctrine among the messengers" (46:9). The Prophet (upon him be peace) being able to declare his mission an iteration of what was given to the messengers before him is a source of continuity and authenticity. Indeed, this gives the Prophet (upon him be peace), or in our case the activist or public truth teller, an aura of confidence that suggests "the core principles of my mission or advocacy have not been crafted merely in response to the oppression of my enemy. My enemy does not occupy that place in my consciousness. Rather, God does. I offer proximate iterations of principles rooted in the very nature of God and the religion of God. This has been attested by women and men of God before me."

In *The Cross and the Lynching Tree,* the pioneering Black liberation theologian Professor James Cone does not offer revisions of Christology, the Eucharist, or the Trinity. Rather, drawing inspiration from these Protestant fundamentals, he shifts the focus of the reader from a Christian understanding of the crucifixion (namely, that Jesus was crucified upon a cross) to the bodies of Black men "twisting in the wind" on the lynching tree. From here, he is able offer a number of social and religious insights that demonstrate why Christians cannot express a deep commitment to their faith while being complicit or silent in the face of white supremacy and racism. It was masterful. To my mind, this represents a solid example of the manner in which Muslims might engage a similar interpretive pursuit.

JR: What do you think are some of the important tools and conceptions that Muslims can bring to antiracist social movements such as Black Lives Matter or, for that matter, solidarity movements for Palestine, Standing Rock, immigrants and refugees, et cetera.

UUE: I really appreciate the way this question is being framed. I used to take for granted that Muslims believed Islam could contribute to the commonweal. However, of late, I've noticed some of our most vocal activists presenting the Muslim faithful with an alternate vision, namely, that being socially responsible hinges on the unqualified acceptance of values, ideas, and strategies whose relationship to Islam has yet to be investigated. In fact, many Muslims appear completely oblivious to the idea that Islamic teaching can offer anything new or unique to issues with which the greater community is also grappling. I deem this a criminal underestimation of our tradition; and while secularism might rightly be identified as an accomplice, the irrelevance and tone-deafness of contemporary Islamic thought are perhaps the real culprits.

One of the core theses of Christopher Lasch's 1991 classic *The True and Only Heaven* is that although modern and postmodern Western Europe—and, by extension, the United States—ostensibly moved away from the public religion that defined Christendom, much of its secular moral and political philosophy is heavily influenced by Christianity. This is hardly a revelation. However, what's surprising is that Lasch brilliantly argues that the idea of "heaven" has actually turned out to be one of the most enduring philosophical attachments of the West. At the risk of summarizing a detailed and nuanced six-hundred-page tour de force in a few sentences, Lasch asserts that rather than completely dispensing with the Christian concept of heaven, that is, a paradisiacal end, a utopia of complete fulfillment and actualization toward which human history is inexorably progressing, many thinkers of the European Enlightenment sought to replace the Christian heaven with earthly utopias. Lasch credits this shift with giving rise to major developments like Smith's capitalism, Marx's communism, the nation-state, et cetera. He also identifies, within the same cultural milieu, the development of more abstract "heavens" like progress, equality, egalitarianism, cosmopolitanism, and meritocracy. To be sure, much of our current human rights and social justice discourse is the direct descendant of this European (and particularly French) utopianism.

Placing the conceptual development of progress, equality, egalitarianism, et cetera, in historical context is thought provoking. On one hand, revolutionaries across a broad spectrum of theaters have effectively taken the dominant culture to task for failing to live up to these ideals. From Toussaint Overture invoking *"liberté, égalité, fraternité"* to the Black Panther Party for Self Defense citing provisions of the U.S. Constitution, effective revolutionary interventions have often deployed this utopian language. On the other hand, pursuit of these earthly utopias and belief in nothing beyond them, if unrealized—and a healthy dose of religious realism suggests that heaven is the only heaven—can be devastating for the oppressed and obscure the tragic–heroic calling of the activist or freedom fighter.

As opposed to a place of complete fulfillment and unrestrained happiness, Islamic teaching ultimately positions the world as a place of faith and work:

I have not created jinn and mankind except to worship Me. (51:56)

It is He who has created death and life to put you to the test and see which of you is most virtuous in your deeds. He is Majestic and All-forgiving. (67:2)

Upon this understanding, the activist is worshiping God and displaying Prophetic virtue by speaking truth to power and striving to establish justice. Because there are no earthly utopias to which to aspire, failure to create utopia is no cause for weakened resolve. The world will remain a place of ineffable joy and unspeakable pain, sensitivity and callousness, justice and oppression, humanity and barbarity, life and death, faith and disbelief; a God-centered activism is content with God as the Disposer of Affairs. Our portion is collective, mutually supportive action in the face of injustice and patience in awaiting the ultimate outcome:

> By the passage of time through the ages (1) Verily men and women are in a perpetual state of loss (2) Except for those that believe, practice righteousness, and join together to uphold Truth and encourage patience (3). (103:1–3)

In a way that perhaps may only be reconciled through faith, Islamic eschatology simultaneously promises the faithful successive regressive epochs of injustice and immorality until the end of time *and* commands them to work to remove these maladies whenever and wherever they find them. The Prophet Muhammad (upon him be peace) is reported to have said, "If the Day of Judgment is announced and one of you is planting a tree, let him continue to plant it." In other words, while there may be both historically and scripturally no reasonable cause for optimism, hope is a religious disposition and refuge for the faithful. We may never witness the triumph of any of our efforts to establish justice in this world, but in so doing, we will have justified our existence and acquitted ourselves as worshippers of God. To my mind, activism requires an embrace of this tragic heroism.

In the midst of competing voices about the disheartening predicament of Black America, I happened upon the story of a young woman from Chicago that I think cuts to the heart of the matter: although many correctly identify the "Savage Inequalities," as Jonathan Kozol famously referred to them, of public education as the true cause of the comparatively diminishing returns among Black students, others cite behavioral and cultural factors. From the now infamous Bill Cosby's "Pound Cake" speech to the perspective one might expect to find from an elderly community member, "there is just something wrong with young Black people. They're not studious, not driven, too influenced by pop culture."

Yet another iteration of the moralist versus structuralist critique that only seems to reside at the center of public discourse about rectifying the condition of the Black community. Indeed, the fact that this binary is so central to our deliberations about Black America is what makes this story instructive.

In summary, a young woman, a public high school student, had finished at the top of her graduating class on Chicago's West Side. She was its valedictorian. Attaining the highest academic standing among a class of 350 students requires dedication, diligence, perseverance, and even a little competiveness, and this young woman had presumably displayed these. During a high school graduation ceremony, the student delivering the valedictory speech is not only assumed to be the most distinguished but also the most promising. High school graduation is an introduction to American meritocracy: the first taste of the payoff for hard work and delayed gratification. The student who preferred achievement to popularity and test preparation to parties is rewarded with matriculation into a top-tier college or university, which will serve as the precursor to a fulfilling career and financial security.

As it turned out, this valedictorian would be attending community college. The well-known bias of standardized testing notwithstanding, after repeated attempts, she was forced to acknowledge that her secondary education had failed to equip her with the requisite math and reading skills to score well enough on the SAT to gain acceptance into a bachelor's program. This was heartbreaking. What did she do wrong? What element of moral character had she failed to display? Activists are dedicated to comprehensive education reform, but what consolation could be offered to this young woman in the present? If she displayed the dedication, diligence, perseverance, and so on, that propelled her to become valedictorian only to enjoy the same prospects as those that barely graduated or completed general education requirements, how do we incentivize her to keep working hard? If one's ZIP code—and not moral code—is the real factor that determines success, why put value into anything besides moving?

I think about this young woman often. I can't imagine "up by your bootstraps" conservatism offering her anything. "*What happens to a dream deferred?*" Similarly, repairing the broken system that betrayed her would not necessarily repair her. This is precisely where I think Islam and faith can intervene. Working to eliminate the structural inequality responsible for this travesty is a religious duty. However, to that young woman, I would offer this: certain of us are called upon to, as Cristal Truscott and Progress Theatre performs in one of their neospirituals, "make a way out of no way." Our striving is an expression of faith, our occasional triumphs are an expression of God's power to will the miraculous, and our continued challenges are opportunities to increase in closeness to Him through patience and prayer. You must continue to work with the same excellence that has always defined your work. None of your striving is in vain. For as the Prophet Yusuf (upon him be peace) said to his brothers after they attempted to leave him for dead; after he was subsequently sold into slavery and made to suffer unwanted attention on account of his physical appearance; after he was accused of a crime he did not commit and jailed despite his innocence; after he gained prominence among the inmates due to his faith, character, and a God-given skill that he possessed; after he was released from prison, granted an opportunity to use his skill, and finally elevated to a place of honor and dignity within the very society in which he had been a slave and a prisoner,

> "I am Yusuf, and this is my brother. God has been gracious unto us. Verily whosoever is reverent and patient—surely God neglects not the reward of the virtuous" (12:90).

NOTES

1. S. A. Jackson, "Islam and Affirmative Action," *Journal of Law and Religion* 14, no. 2 (1999): 410–11.

2. Ibid., 414.

ACKNOWLEDGMENTS

There are many people to thank in what has been a collaborative effort. We have been imagining and planning this book for some time alongside what is a constellation of complementary projects. In doing so, we have shared our ideas with many in the effort to push the envelope and bring together folks who might not be in conversation otherwise. We hope that this book is the first stop in a process of conversation, debate, and taking action. Our thanks first and foremost go to the contributors of this volume, who have offered their time, expertise, and brilliance. When we first envisioned this book, it was the visionary work of Richard Morrison that brought us to the University of Minnesota Press. We have since then been placed in the generous and wonderful hands of our editor, Danielle Kasprzak, and the team at Minnesota.

When we started plotting this volume, we wanted to bring all the folks who, over the years, have been engaging in a wide-ranging conversation with us. In a way, the book's contents represent all our thanks to those who are thinking through the big issues. A range of scholars, activists, and organizers, many of whom are in this volume and others who remain an inspiration, are a part not only of this book but of projects on the horizon.

Acknowledgments are usually where you give shout outs and the mention of debts to others. We would be remiss if we didn't point out our admiration of friends and colleagues with dedication and commitment to what is just in this world. During the crafting of this project, there were always folks who pointed out how it was timely. And now that we are almost done, the book can't be finished quickly enough. These are hard times, and many of our comrades have fought through difficult situations. As scholars, it is not enough that we have to deal with the hypocrisies of the academy;

intellectuals are embattled by a far rightward turn in global politics. Activists and organizers are far from immune from such issues and are in fact often at the forefront of these battles. We are honored to have worked with the folks included in this volume, who are exemplary in how they have represented themselves as intellectuals and activists, acting as beacons through the murk of uncertain times.

Thanks to our loved ones: the Amani and Daulatzai family and the Kashani and Rana family.

JUNAID: Much love to Maryam Kashani for holding it down for the many things we seem to get into. Thanks for the reminder of what we are fighting for.

SOHAIL: To the inner circle (you know who you are!): thanks for keeping me on point. Steel sharpen steel! To the Moon and Star who make all of this worthwhile, and even urgent—one love.

CONTRIBUTORS

RABAB IBRAHIM ABDULHADI is director and senior scholar in the Arab and Muslim Ethnicities and Diasporas Studies Program and associate professor of ethnic studies/race and resistance studies at San Francisco State University. She is lead editor of *Arab and Arab American Feminisms: Gender, Violence, and Belonging*.

ABDULLAH AL-ARIAN is assistant professor of history at Georgetown University's School of Foreign Service in Qatar and author of *Answering the Call: Popular Islamic Activism in Sadat's Egypt*.

ARSHAD IMTIAZ ALI is assistant professor of educational research in the Graduate School of Education and Human Development at the George Washington University.

EVELYN ALSULTANY is Arthur F. Thurnau Professor and associate professor of American culture at the University of Michigan, where she is also the director of Arab and Muslim American studies. She is the author of *Arabs and Muslims in the Media: Race and Representation after 9/11*.

VIVEK BALD is associate professor of writing and digital media at Massachusetts Institute of Technology, author of *Bengali Harlem and the Lost Histories of South Asian America*, and coeditor of *The Sun Never Sets: South Asian Migrants in an Age of U.S. Power*. He is the director of three documentary films: *Taxi-vala/Auto-biography, Mutiny: Asians Storm British Music,* and *In Search of Bengali Harlem*.

ABBAS BARZEGAR is assistant professor of religious studies at Georgia State University and coeditor of *Islamism: Contested Perspectives on Political Islam.*

HATEM BAZIAN is provost, cofounder, and professor of Islamic law and theology at Zaytuna College and author of *Palestine, ". . . It Is Something Colonial."*

SYLVIA CHAN-MALIK is assistant professor of American studies and women's and gender studies at Rutgers University.

SOHAIL DAULATZAI is associate professor of film and media studies, African American studies, and global Middle East studies at the University of California, Irvine. He is author of *Black Star, Crescent Moon: The Muslim International and Black Freedom beyond America* (Minnesota, 2012) and *Fifty Years of* The Battle of Algiers: *Past as Prologue* (Minnesota, 2016); editor and curator of *Return of the Mecca: The Art of Islam and Hip-Hop*; and co-editor of *Born to Use Mics: Reading Nas's Illmatic.*

ARASH DAVARI is assistant professor of politics at Whitman College.

FATIMA EL-TAYEB is professor of literature and ethnic studies at the University of California, San Diego. She is the author of *European Others: Queering Ethnicity in Postnational Europe* (Minnesota, 2011).

HAFSA KANJWAL is assistant professor of South Asian history at Lafayette College.

RONAK K. KAPADIA is assistant professor of gender and women's studies at the University of Illinois at Chicago and author of the forthcoming book *Insurgent Aesthetics of the Forever War: Art and Performance after 9/11.*

MARYAM KASHANI is assistant professor of gender and women's studies and Asian American studies at University of Illinois, Urbana-Champaign.

ROBIN D. G. KELLEY is Distinguished Professor and Gary B. Nash Endowed Chair in U.S. History at University of California, Los Angeles. His books include *Hammer and Hoe: Alabama Communists during the Great Depression; Race Rebels: Culture, Politics, and the Black Working Class; Freedom Dreams: The Black Radical Imagination; Thelonious Monk: The Life and*

Times of an American Original; and *Africa Speaks, America Answers: Modern Jazz in Revolutionary Times*.

SUʿAD ABDUL KHABEER is associate professor of American culture at the University of Michigan and author of *Muslim Cool: Race, Religion, and Hip-Hop in the United States*.

NADINE NABER is associate professor in gender and women's studies and Asian American studies at the University of Illinois, Chicago. She is author of *Arab America: Gender, Cultural Politics, and Activism* and coeditor of *Race and Arab Americans* and *The Color of Violence*.

SELIM NADI is a doctoral student at the Sciences Po History Center in Paris and at the Universität Bielefeld (Germany). He is on the editorial boards of the journals *Période* (revueperiode.net) and *Contretemps* (contre temps.eu) and is a member of the antiracist organization Parti des Indigènes de la République.

JUNAID RANA is associate professor of Asian American studies at the University of Illinois, Urbana-Champaign. He is the author of *Terrifying Muslims: Race and Labor in the South Asian Diaspora*.

SHERENE H. RAZACK is Distinguished Professor and the Penny Kanner Endowed Chair in women's studies in the Department of Gender Studies at the University of California, Los Angeles. She is the author of *Casting Out: The Eviction of Muslims from Western Law and Politics*.

ATEF SAID is visiting assistant professor of sociology at the University of Illinois, Chicago, and author of *Torture as a Crime against Humanity: Study on the Applicability of International Criminal Law on the Practices of Torture in Egypt* and *Torture in Egypt: A Judicial Reality—an Analysis of 1124 Lawsuits of Civil Compensations for Victims of Torture in Egypt*.

STEVEN SALAITA is author of *Inter/Nationalism: Decolonizing Native America and Palestine* (Minnesota, 2016); *Anti-Arab Racism in the USA: Where It Comes from and What It Means for Politics Today*; *The Holy Land in Transit: Colonialism and the Quest for Canaan*; *Arab American Literary Fictions, Cultures, and Politics*; *The Uncultured Wars*; *Modern Arab American Fiction: A Reader's Guide*; *Israel's Dead Soul*; and *Uncivil Rites*.

STEPHEN SHEEHI is the Sultan Qaboos bin Said Chair of Middle East Studies at the College of William and Mary. He is the author of *The Arab Imago: A Social History of Portrait Photography, 1860–1910; Islamophobia: The Ideological Campaign against Muslims;* and *Foundations of Modern Arab Identity.* He is coauthor with Salim Tamari and Issam Nassar of *Camera Palaestina: The Photographic Albums of Wasif Jawharriyeh.*

INDEX